UQ HOLDER!

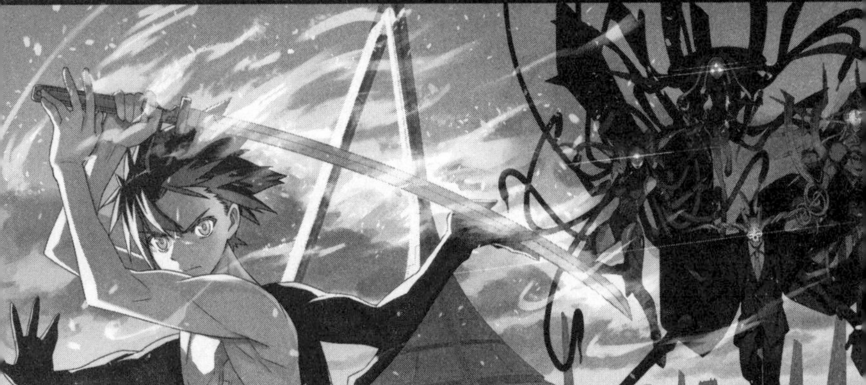

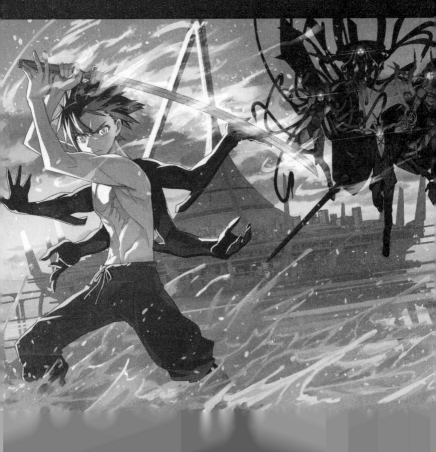

CHARACTERS

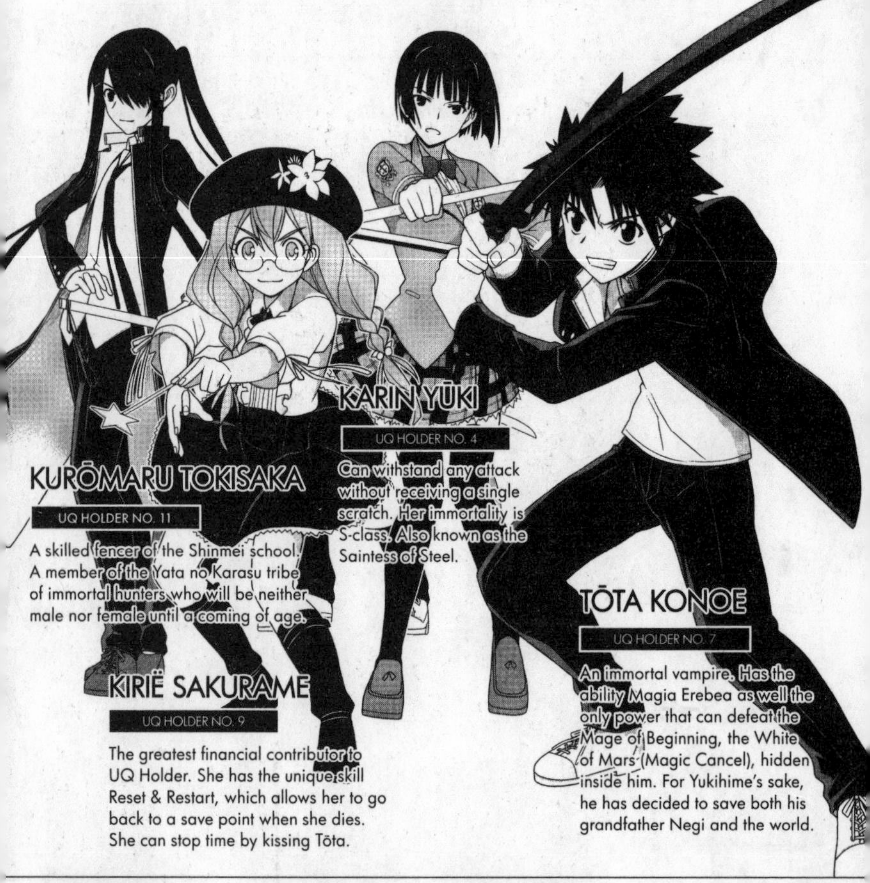

KURŌMARU TOKISAKA

UQ HOLDER NO. 11

A skilled fencer of the Shinmei school. A member of the Yata no Karasu tribe of immortal hunters who will be neither male nor female until a coming of age.

KIRIË SAKURAME

UQ HOLDER NO. 9

The greatest financial contributor to UQ Holder. She has the unique skill Reset & Restart, which allows her to go back to a save point when she dies. She can stop time by kissing Tōta.

KARIN YŪKI

UQ HOLDER NO. 4

Can withstand any attack without receiving a single scratch. Her immortality is S-class. Also known as the Saintess of Steel.

TŌTA KONOE

UQ HOLDER NO. 7

An immortal vampire. Has the ability Magia Erebea as well the only power that can defeat the Mage of Beginning, the White of Mars (Magic Cancel), hidden inside him. For Yukihime's sake, he has decided to save both his grandfather Negi and the world.

UQ HOLDER IMMORTAL NUMBERS

JINBEI SHISHIDO

UQ HOLDER NO. 2

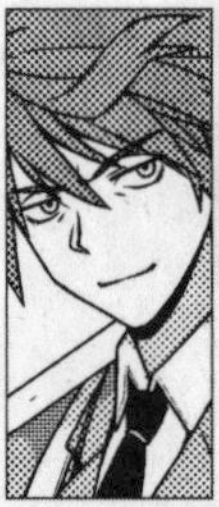

UQ Holder's oldest member. Became an immortal in the middle ages, when he ate mermaid flesh in the Muromachi Period. Has the "Switcheroo" skill that switches the locations of physical objects.

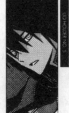

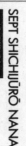

SEPT SHICHIJŪRŌ NANAO

UQ HOLDER NO. 8

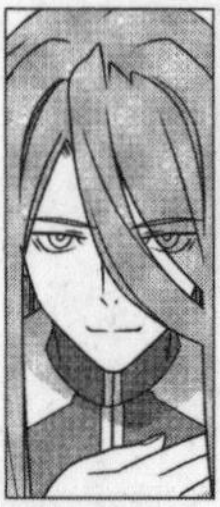

Ba'al's most prized creation. A high-level artificial light spirit.

JŪZŌ SHISHIMI

UQ HOLDER NO. 5

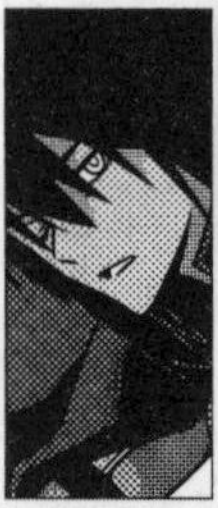

The Numbers' most skilled swordsman. Jinbei freed him from Ba'al's control.

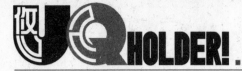

UQ HOLDER!

Ken Akamatsu Presents

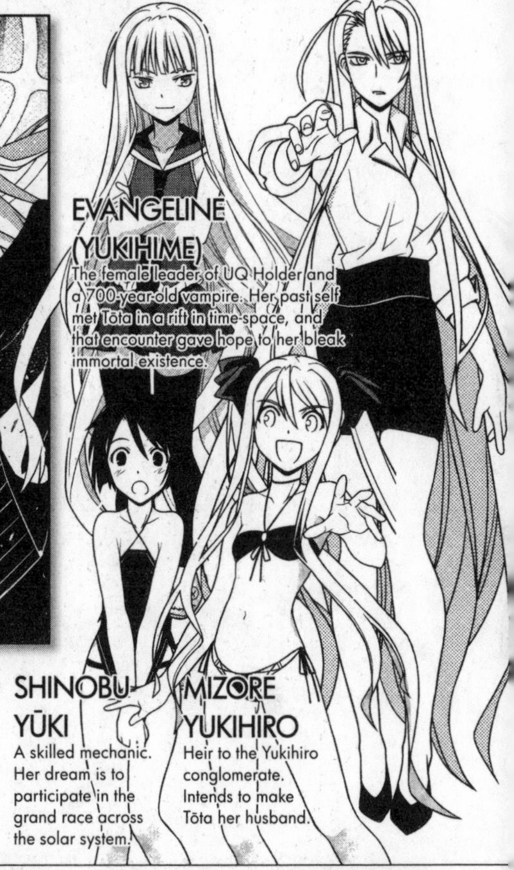
EVANGELINE (YUKIHIME)
The female leader of UQ Holder and a 700-year-old vampire. Her past self met Tōta in a rift in time-space, and that encounter gave hope to her bleak immortal existence.
MIZORE YUKIHIRO
Heir to the Yukihiro conglomerate. Intends to make Tōta her husband.
SHINOBU YŪKI
A skilled mechanic. Her dream is to participate in the grand race across the solar system.

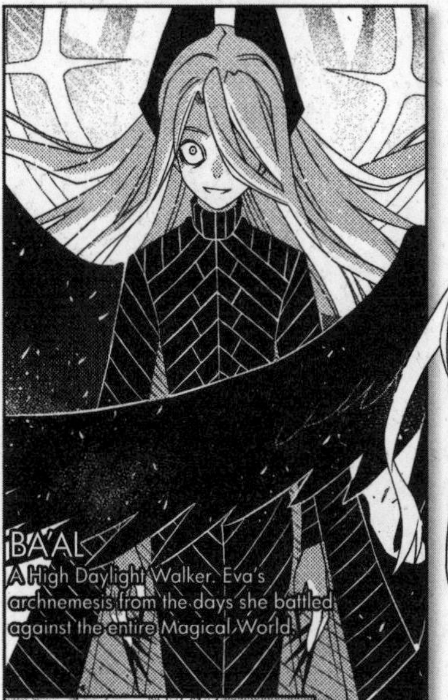
BA'AL
A High Daylight Walker. Eva's archnemesis from the days she battled against the entire Magical World.

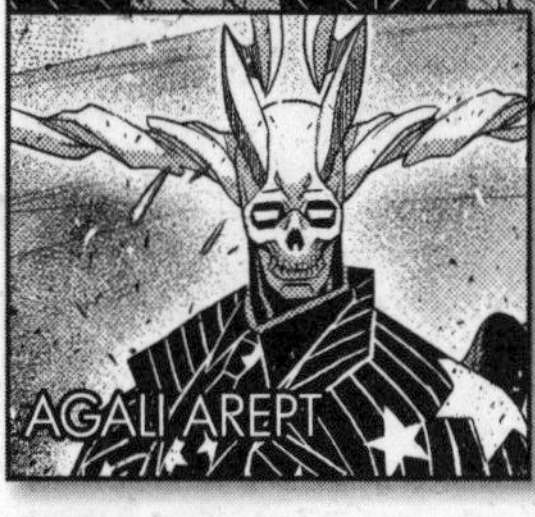
AGALI AREPT

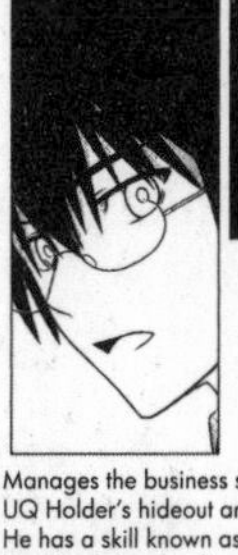

GENGORŌ MAKABE

UQ HOLDER NO. 6

Manages the business side of UQ Holder's hideout and inn. He has a skill known as "multiple lives," so when he dies, another Gengorō appears.

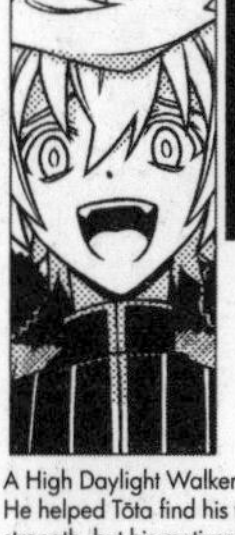

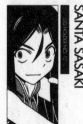

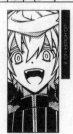

NIKITIS LAPIS

UQ HOLDER NO. 8

A High Daylight Walker. He helped Tōta find his true strength, but his motives remain unclear.

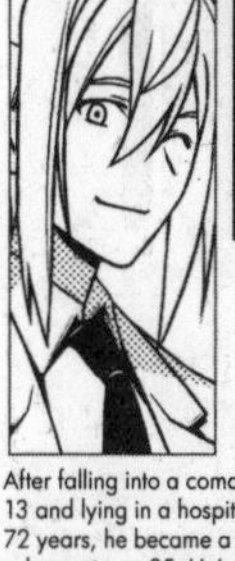

IKKŪ AMEYA

UQ HOLDER NO. 10

After falling into a coma at age 13 and lying in a hospital bed for 72 years, he became a full-body cyborg at age 85. He's very good with his hands. ♡

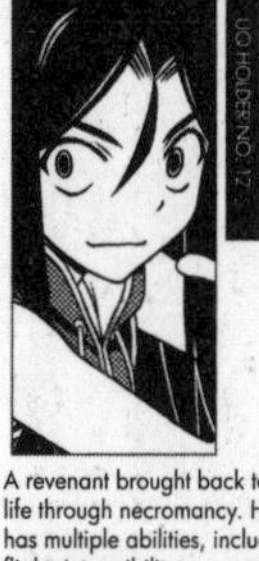

SANTA SASAKI

UQ HOLDER NO. 12

A revenant brought back to life through necromancy. He has multiple abilities, including flight, intangibility, possession, telekinesis, etc.

THE STORY SO FAR

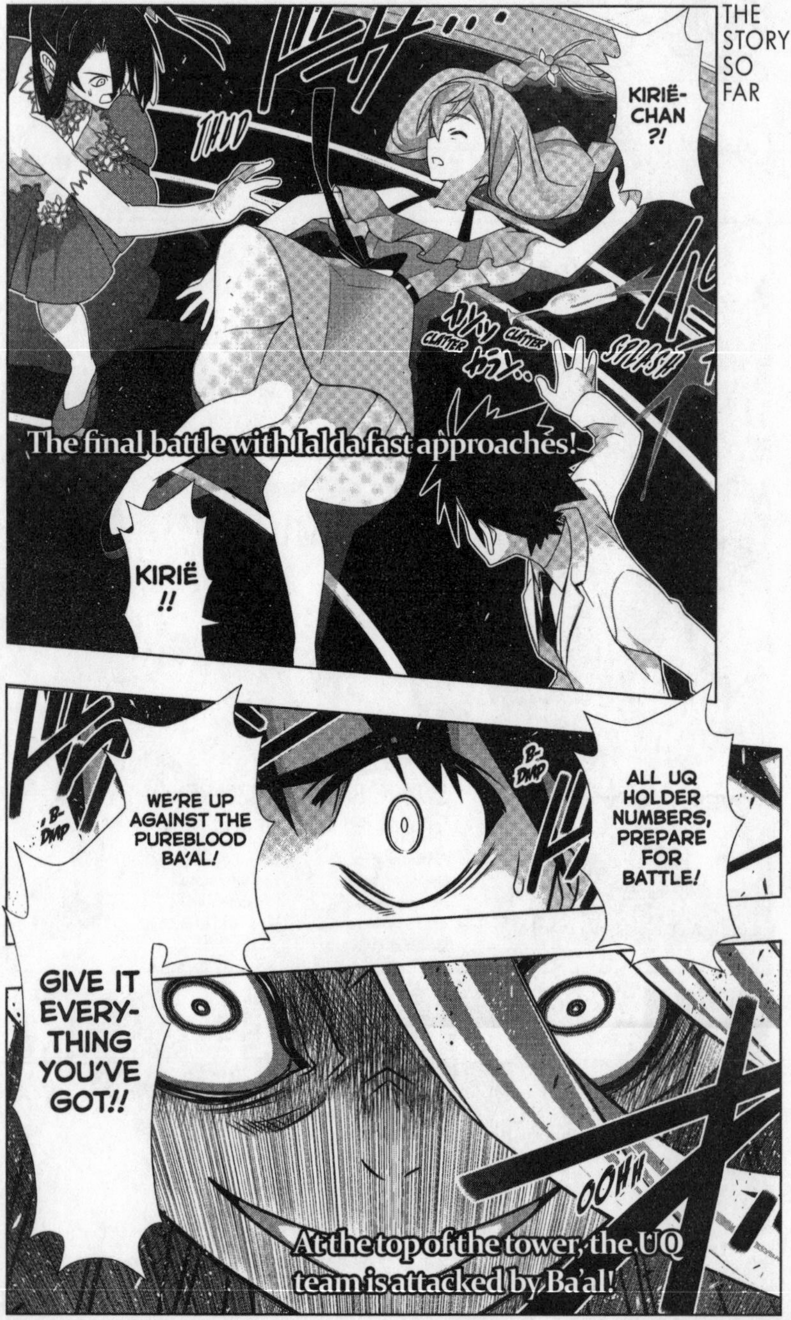
KIRIË-CHAN ?!
THUD
CLATTER
CLATTER
SPLASH!!
KIRIË !!
The final battle with Ialda fast approaches!
ALL UQ HOLDER NUMBERS, PREPARE FOR BATTLE!
B-DMP
WE'RE UP AGAINST THE PUREBLOOD BA'AL!
B-DMP
GIVE IT EVERY-THING YOU'VE GOT!!
OOHH
At the top of the tower, the UQ team is attacked by Ba'al!

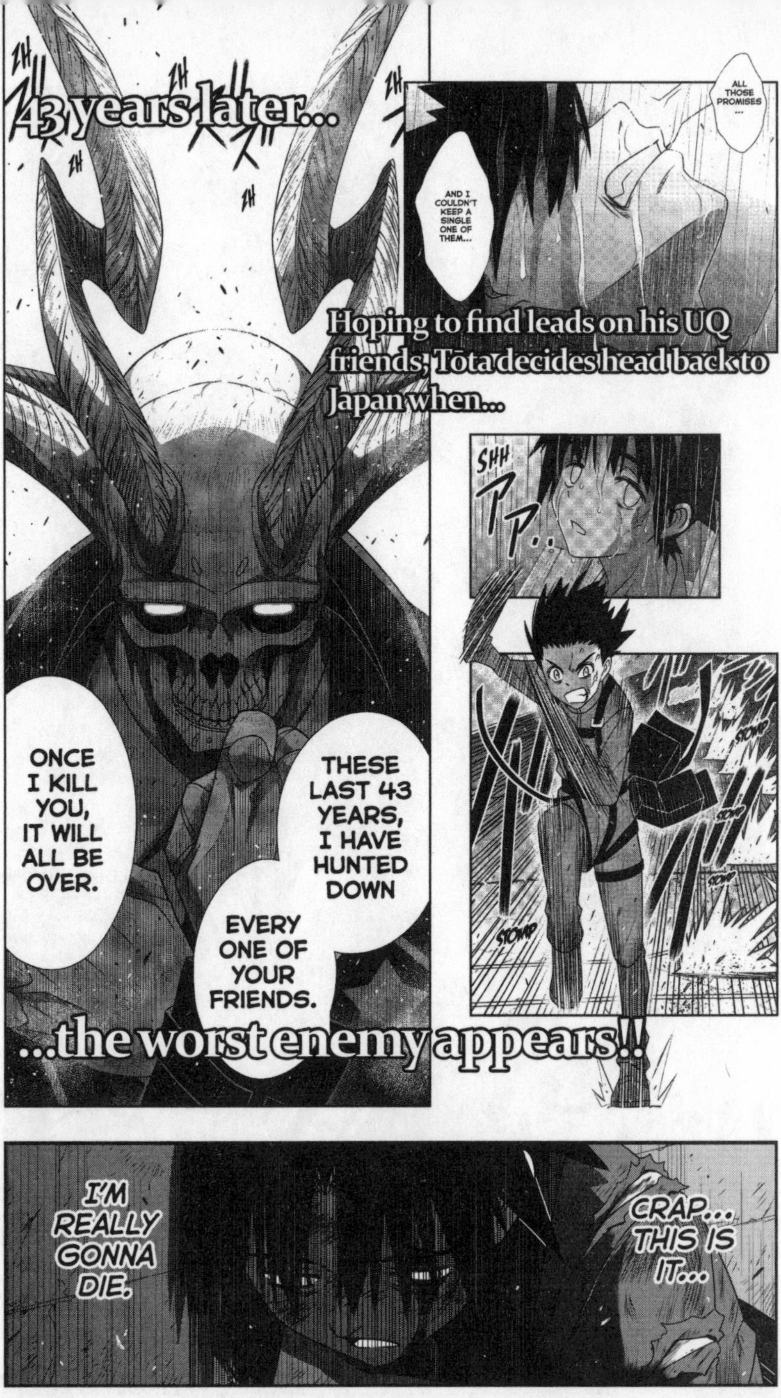

43 years later...
ALL THOSE PROMISES...
AND I COULDN'T KEEP A SINGLE ONE OF THEM...
Hoping to find leads on his UQ friends, Tōta decides head back to Japan when...
SHH
STOMP
STOMP
STOMP
STOMP
ZH
ZH
ZH
ZH
ZH
THESE LAST 43 YEARS, I HAVE HUNTED DOWN
EVERY ONE OF YOUR FRIENDS.
ONCE I KILL YOU, IT WILL ALL BE OVER.
...the worst enemy appears!!
CRAP... THIS IS IT...
I'M REALLY GONNA DIE.

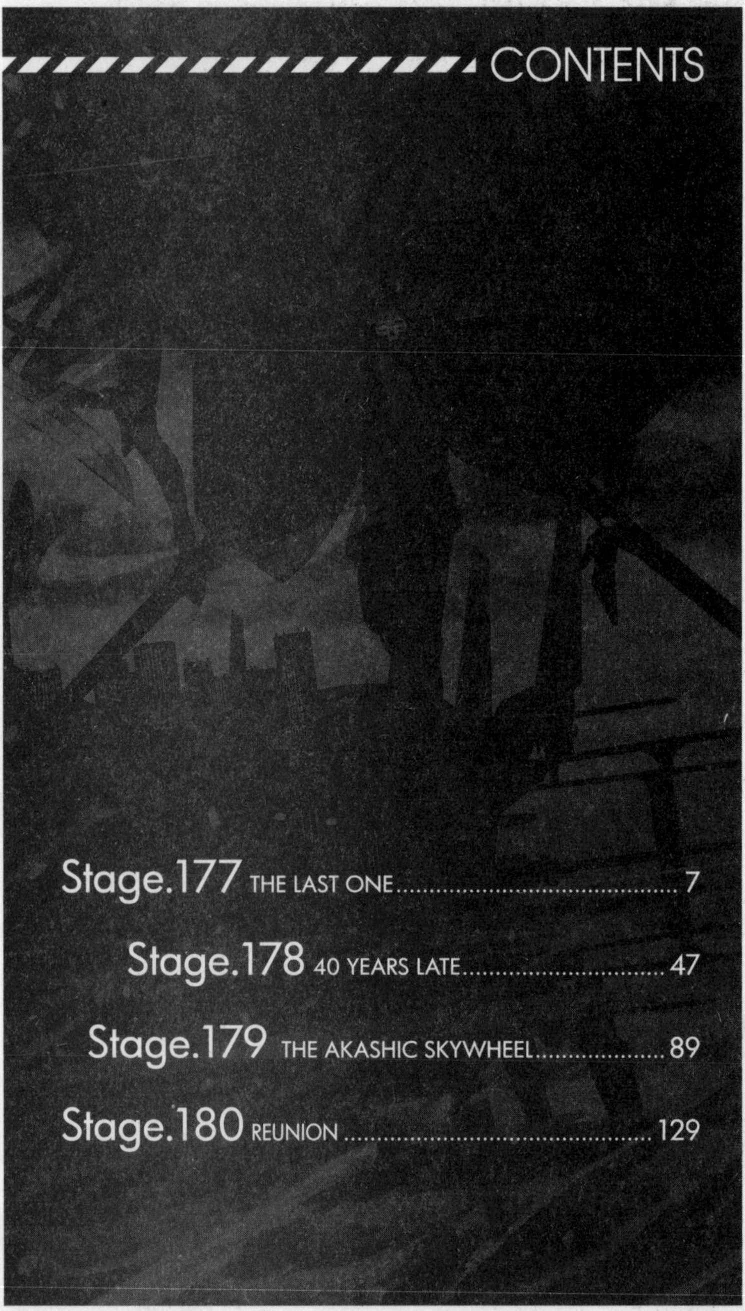

CONTENTS

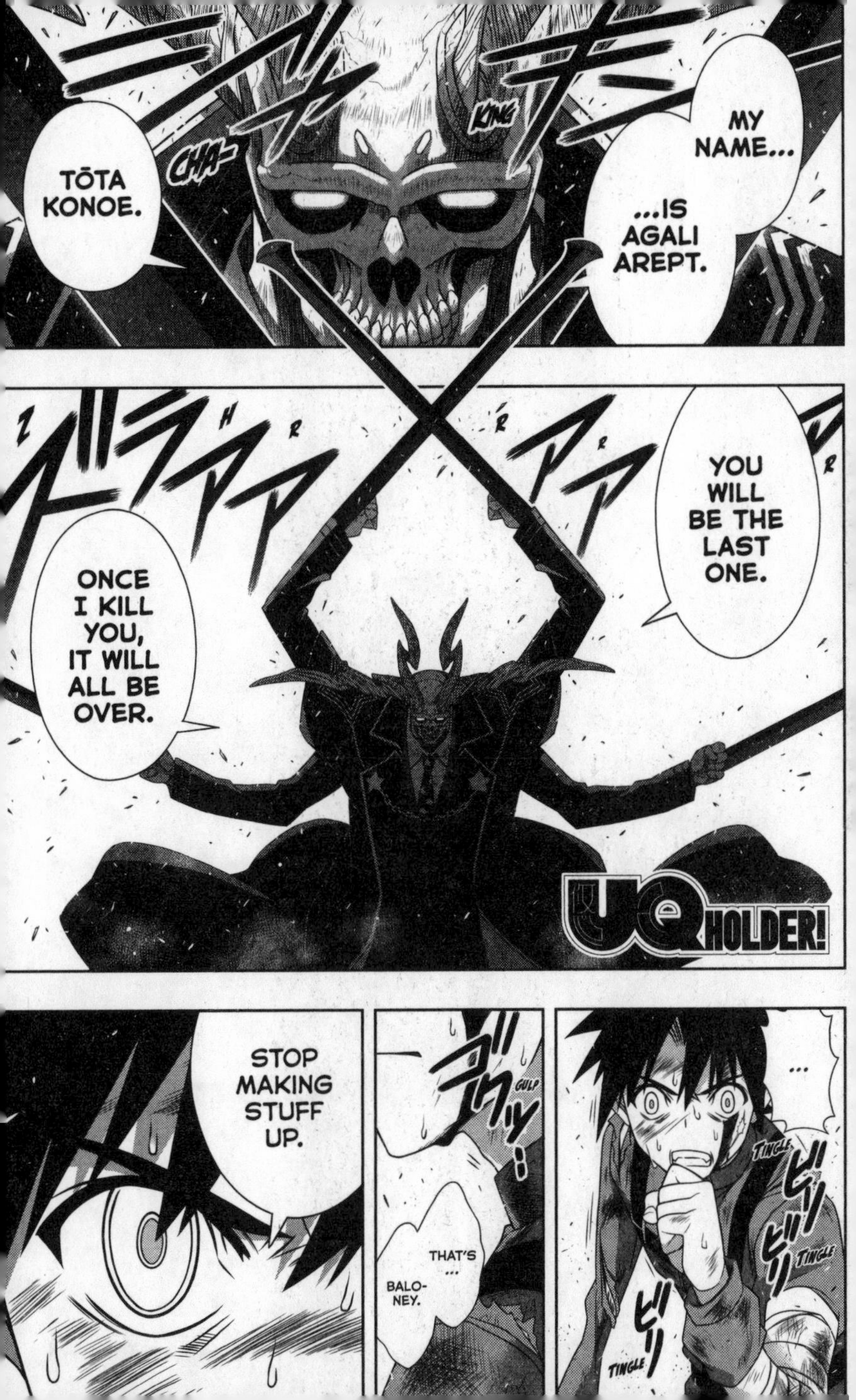

MY NAME...
...IS AGALI AREPT.
KING
CHA-
TŌTA KONOE.
R
YOU WILL BE THE LAST ONE.
R
R
H
Z
ONCE I KILL YOU, IT WILL ALL BE OVER.
UQ HOLDER!
...
TINGLE
TINGLE
TINGLE
GULP
THAT'S... BALONEY.
STOP MAKING STUFF UP.

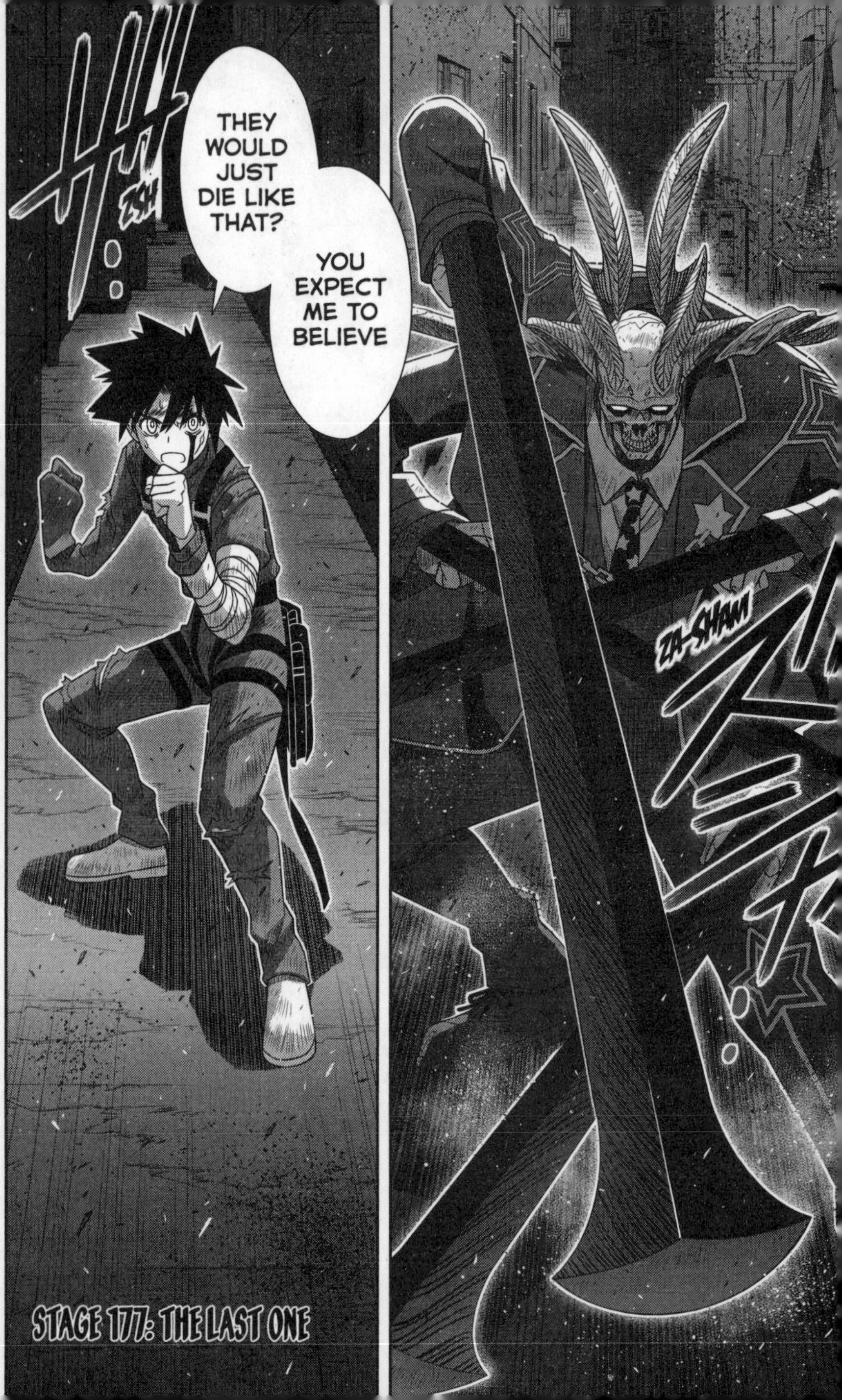
ZA-SHAM
YOU EXPECT ME TO BELIEVE
THEY WOULD JUST DIE LIKE THAT?
ZSH
STAGE 177: THE LAST ONE

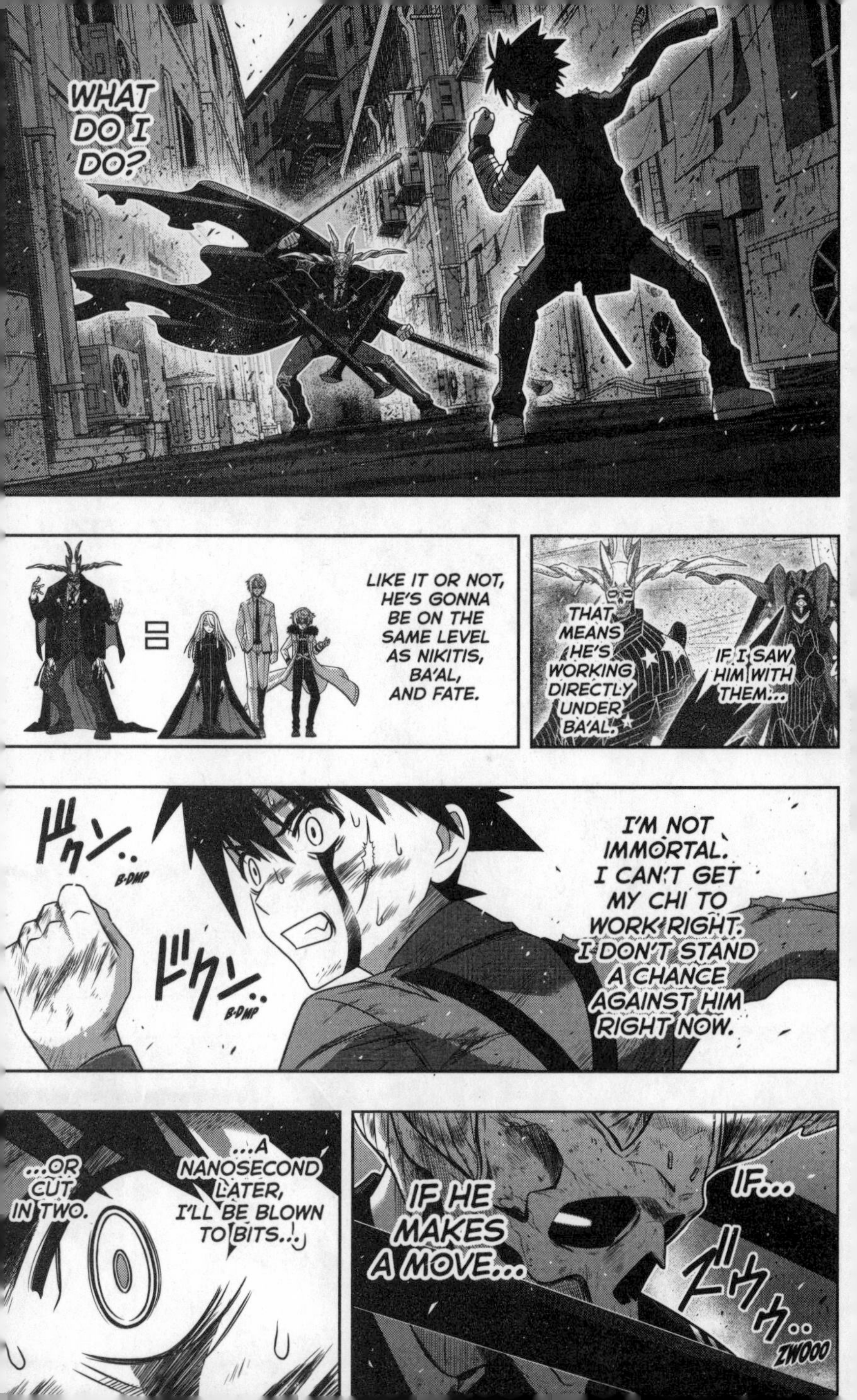

WHAT DO I DO?
IF I SAW HIM WITH THEM...
THAT MEANS HE'S WORKING DIRECTLY UNDER BA'AL.
LIKE IT OR NOT, HE'S GONNA BE ON THE SAME LEVEL AS NIKITIS, BA'AL, AND FATE.
=
I'M NOT IMMORTAL. I CAN'T GET MY CHI TO WORK RIGHT. I DON'T STAND A CHANCE AGAINST HIM RIGHT NOW.
ドクン..
B-DMP
ドクン..
B-DMP
IF...
IF HE MAKES A MOVE...
ズゥゥ..
ZWOOO
...A NANOSECOND LATER, I'LL BE BLOWN TO BITS...!
...OR CUT IN TWO.

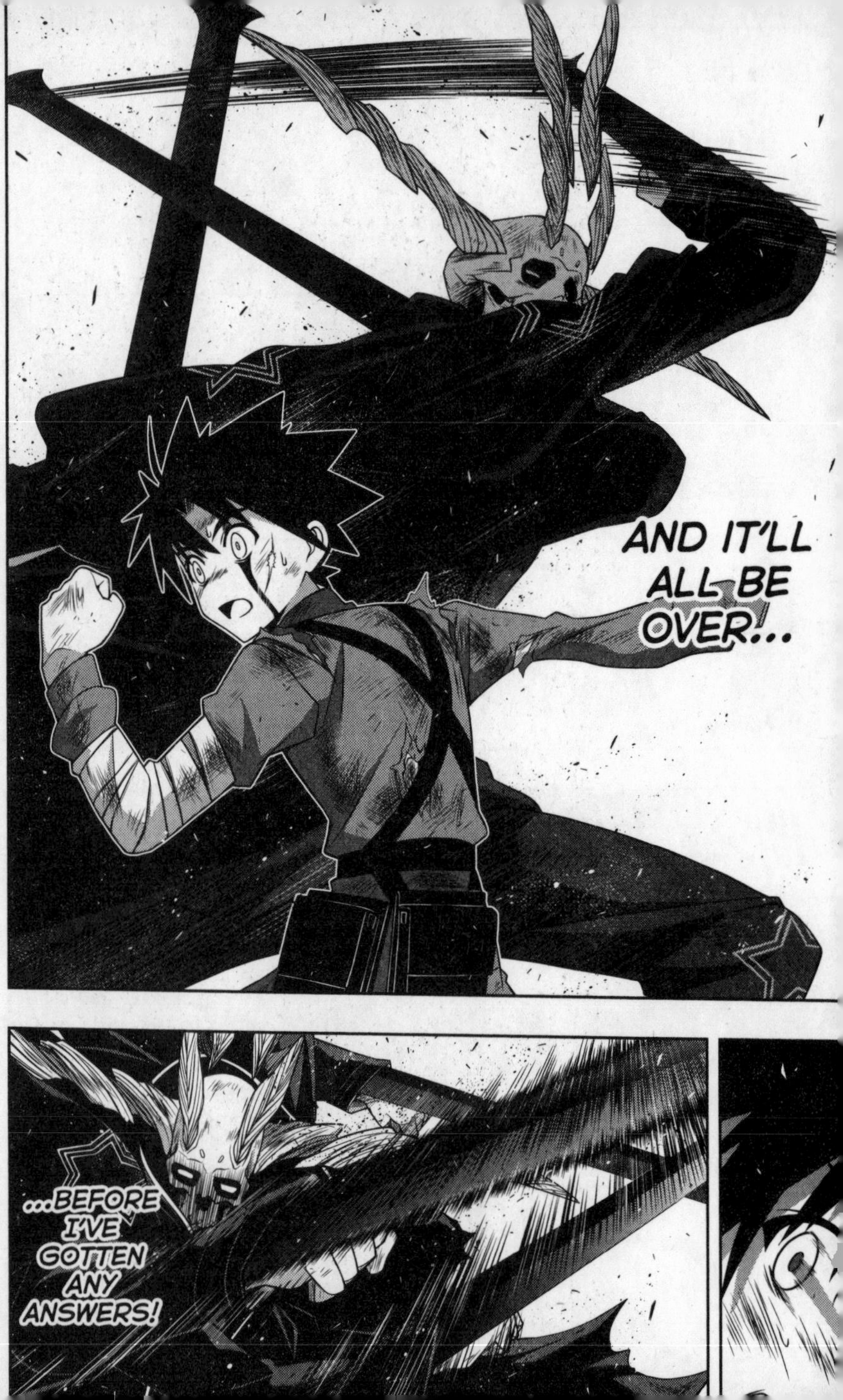
AND IT'LL ALL BE OVER...
...BEFORE I'VE GOTTEN ANY ANSWERS!

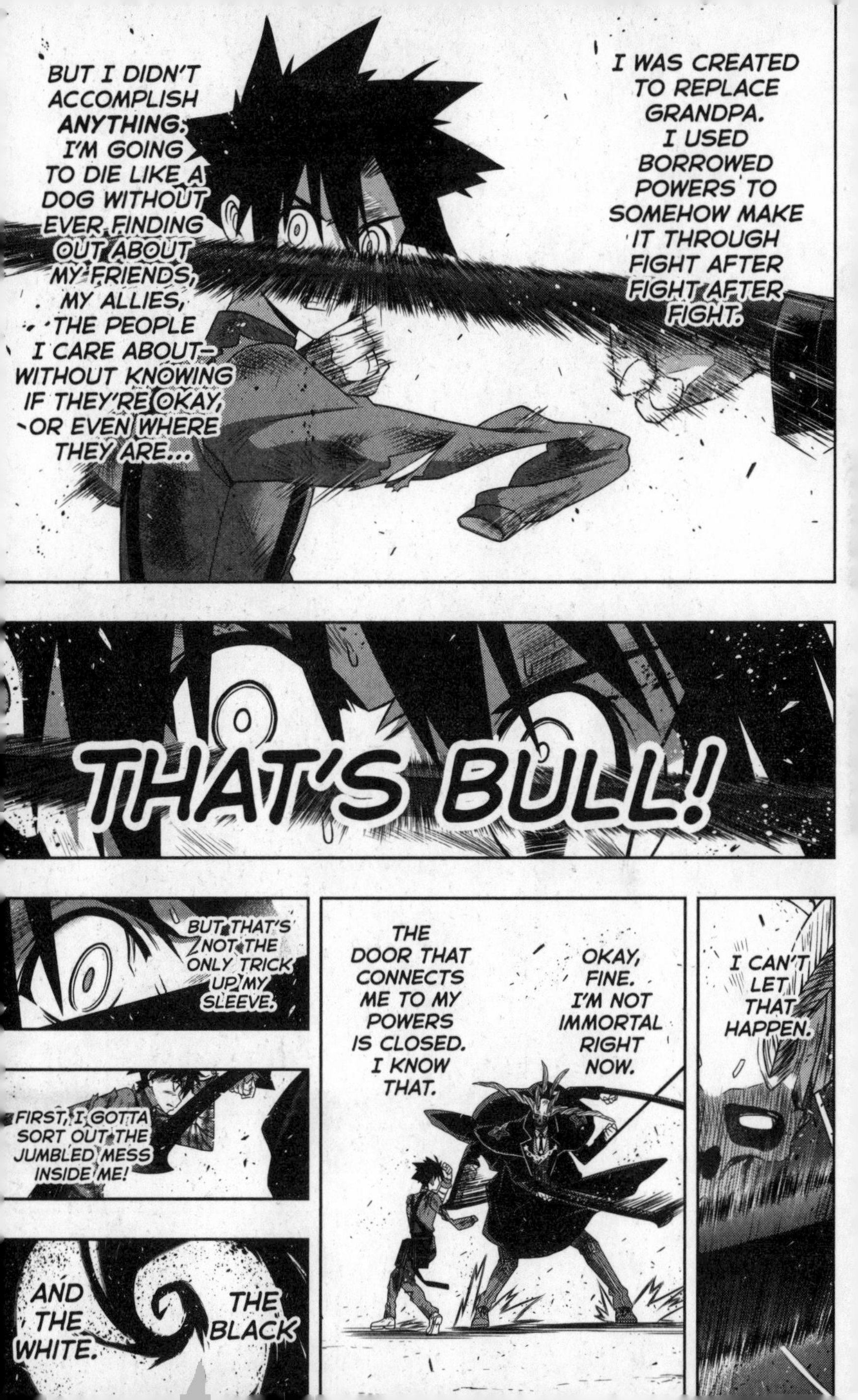
I WAS CREATED TO REPLACE GRANDPA. I USED BORROWED POWERS TO SOMEHOW MAKE IT THROUGH FIGHT AFTER FIGHT AFTER FIGHT.
BUT I DIDN'T ACCOMPLISH ANYTHING. I'M GOING TO DIE LIKE A DOG WITHOUT EVER FINDING OUT ABOUT MY FRIENDS, MY ALLIES, THE PEOPLE I CARE ABOUT—WITHOUT KNOWING IF THEY'RE OKAY, OR EVEN WHERE THEY ARE...
THAT'S BULL!
I CAN'T LET THAT HAPPEN.
OKAY, FINE. I'M NOT IMMORTAL RIGHT NOW.
THE DOOR THAT CONNECTS ME TO MY POWERS IS CLOSED. I KNOW THAT.
BUT THAT'S NOT THE ONLY TRICK UP MY SLEEVE.
FIRST, I GOTTA SORT OUT THE JUMBLED MESS INSIDE ME!
THE BLACK
AND THE WHITE.

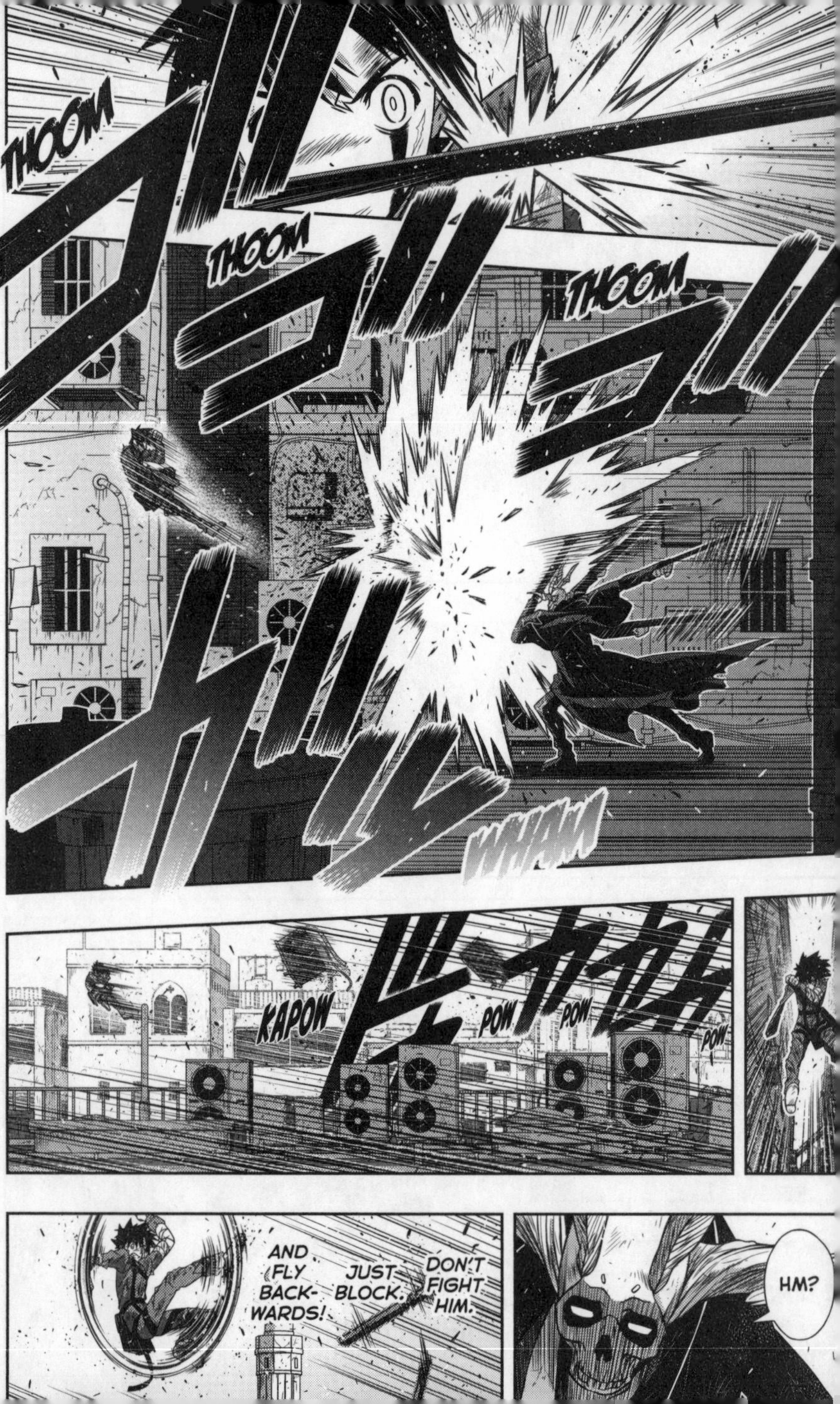
THOOM
THOOM
THOOM
WHAM
POW
POW
POW
KAPOW
HM?
DON'T FIGHT HIM.
JUST BLOCK.
AND FLY BACKWARDS!

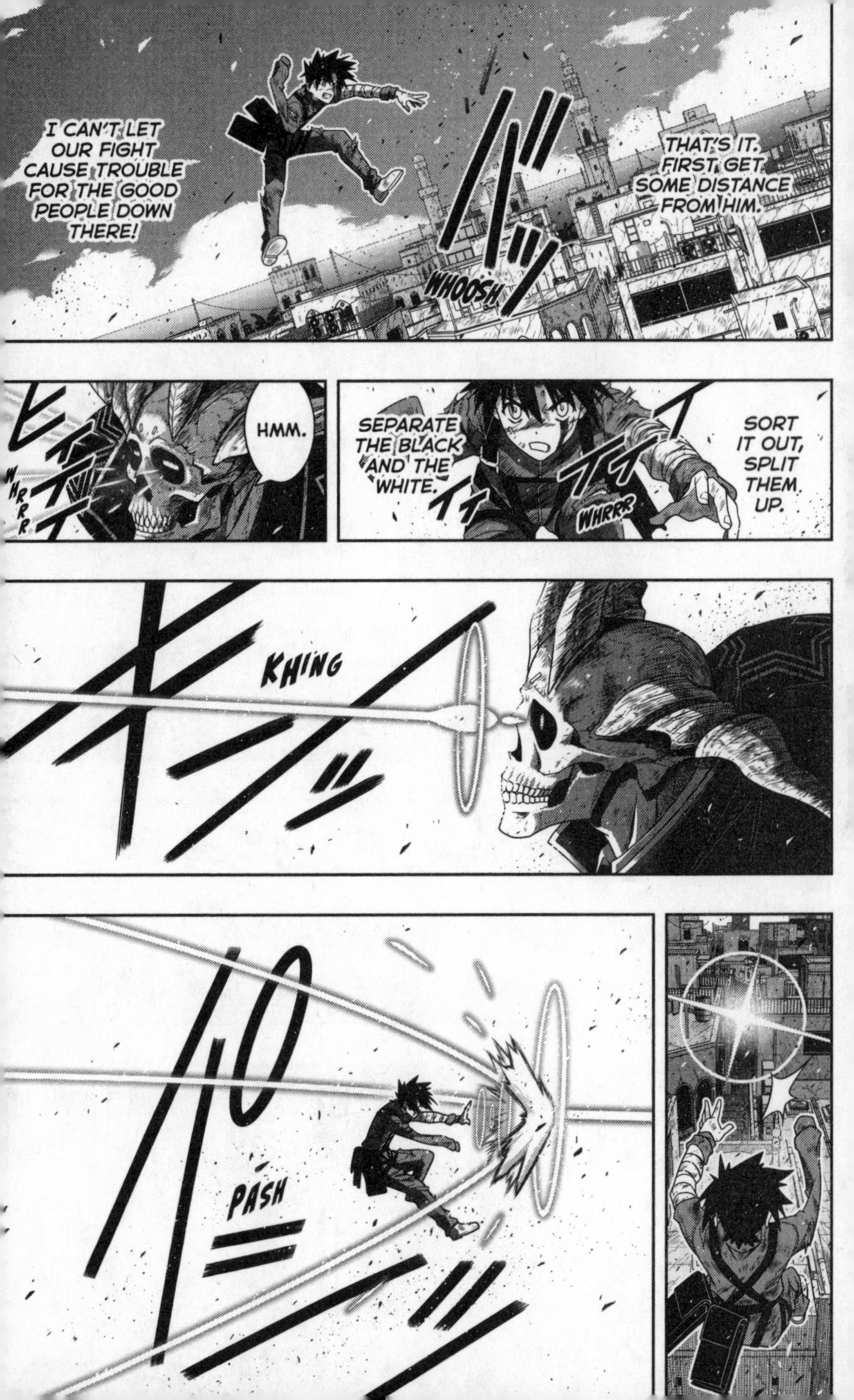
THAT'S IT. FIRST GET SOME DISTANCE FROM HIM.
I CAN'T LET OUR FIGHT CAUSE TROUBLE FOR THE GOOD PEOPLE DOWN THERE!
WHOOSH
SORT IT OUT, SPLIT THEM UP.
SEPARATE THE BLACK AND THE WHITE.
WHRRR
HMM.
WHRRR
KHING
PASH

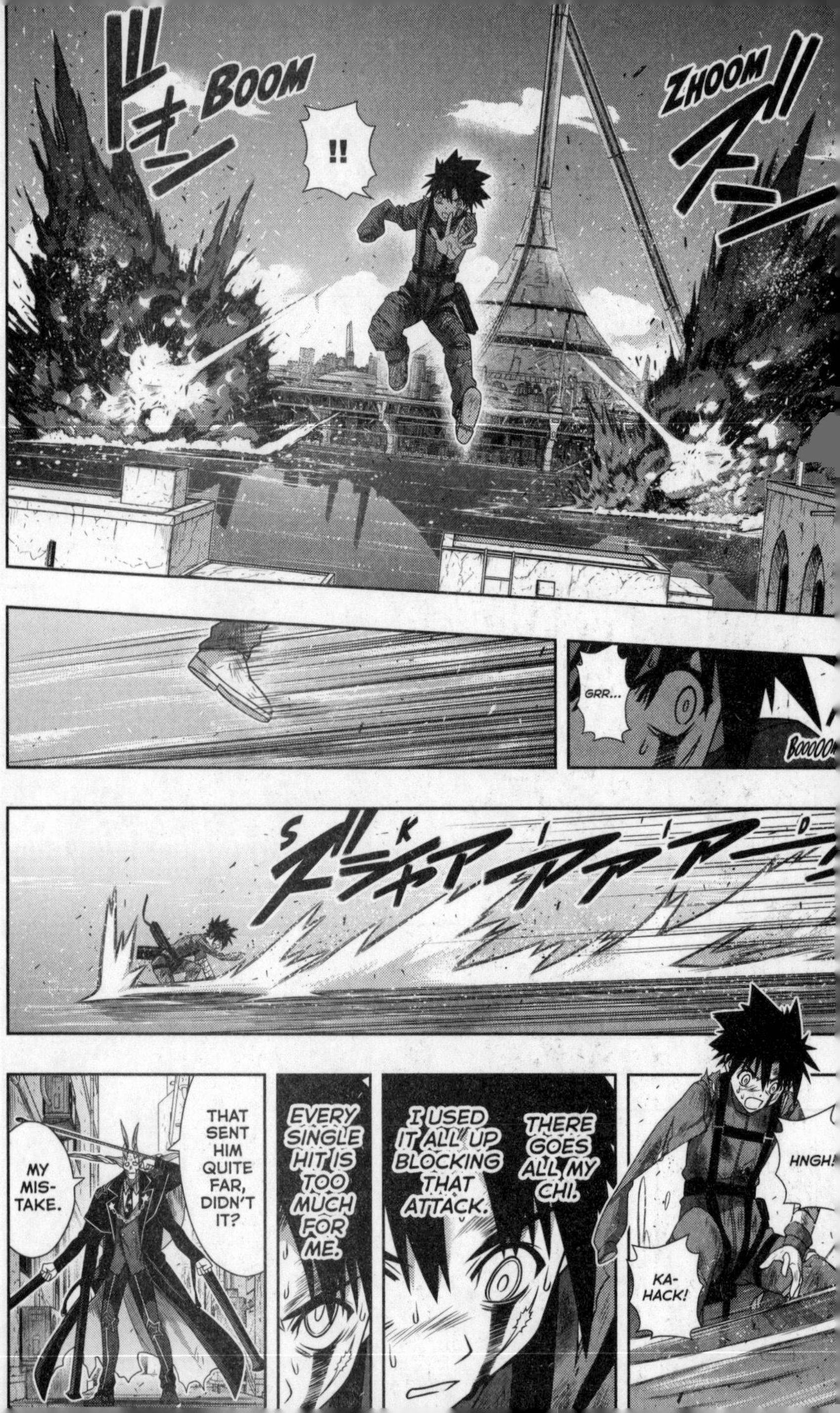
ZHOOM
!!
BOOM
GRR...
BOOOOOM
SKID
HNGH!
KA-HACK!
THERE GOES ALL MY CHI.
I USED IT ALL UP BLOCKING THAT ATTACK.
EVERY SINGLE HIT IS TOO MUCH FOR ME.
THAT SENT HIM QUITE FAR, DIDN'T IT?
MY MISTAKE.

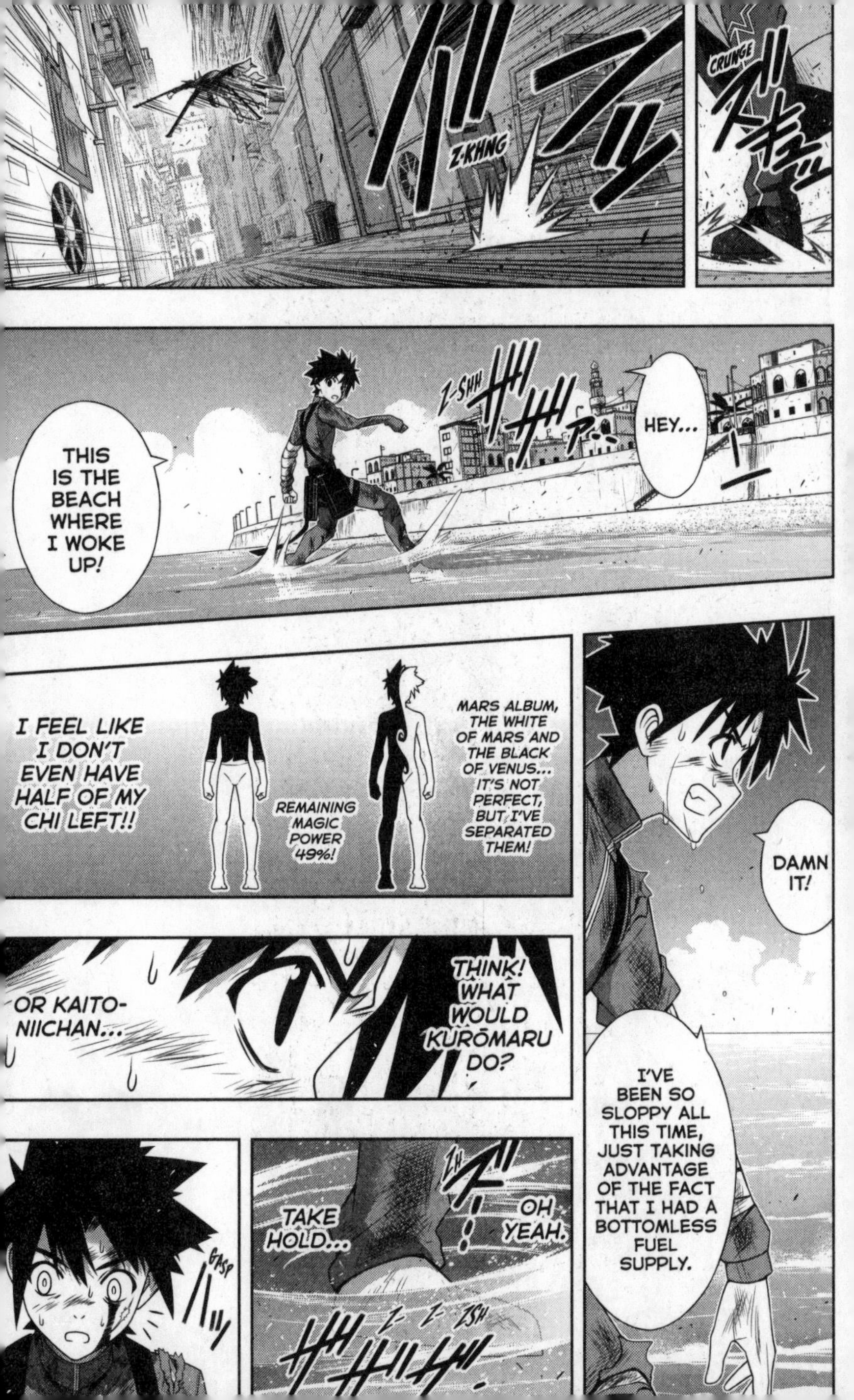
CRUNGE
Z-KHNG
HEY...
Z-SHH
THIS IS THE BEACH WHERE I WOKE UP!
DAMN IT!
I'VE BEEN SO SLOPPY ALL THIS TIME, JUST TAKING ADVANTAGE OF THE FACT THAT I HAD A BOTTOMLESS FUEL SUPPLY.
MARS ALBUM, THE WHITE OF MARS AND THE BLACK OF VENUS... IT'S NOT PERFECT, BUT I'VE SEPARATED THEM!
REMAINING MAGIC POWER 49%!
I FEEL LIKE I DON'T EVEN HAVE HALF OF MY CHI LEFT!!
THINK! WHAT WOULD KURŌMARU DO?
OR KAITO-NIICHAN...
ZH
OH YEAH.
TAKE HOLD...
Z- Z- ZSH
GASP

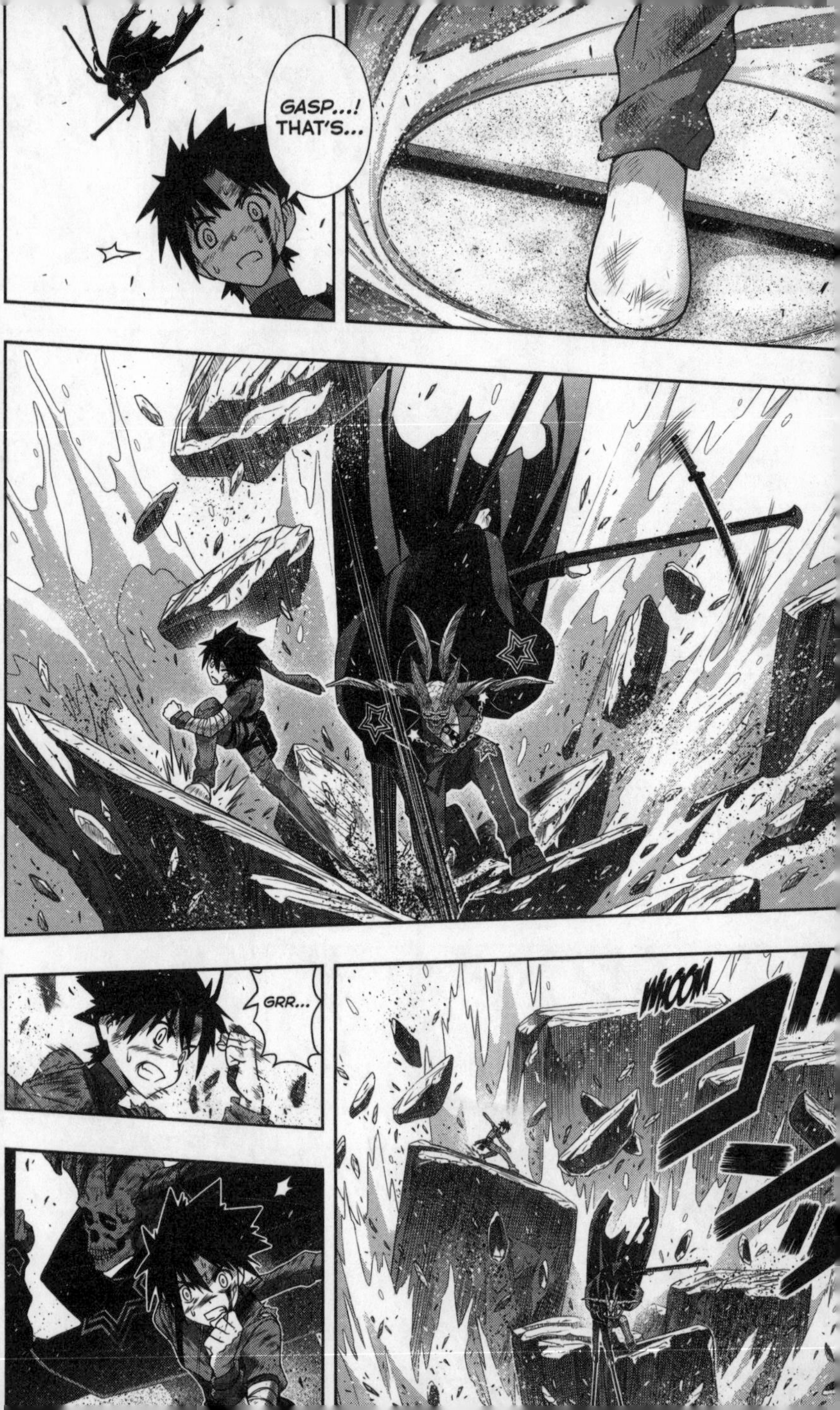
GASP...! THAT'S...
WHOOM
GRR...

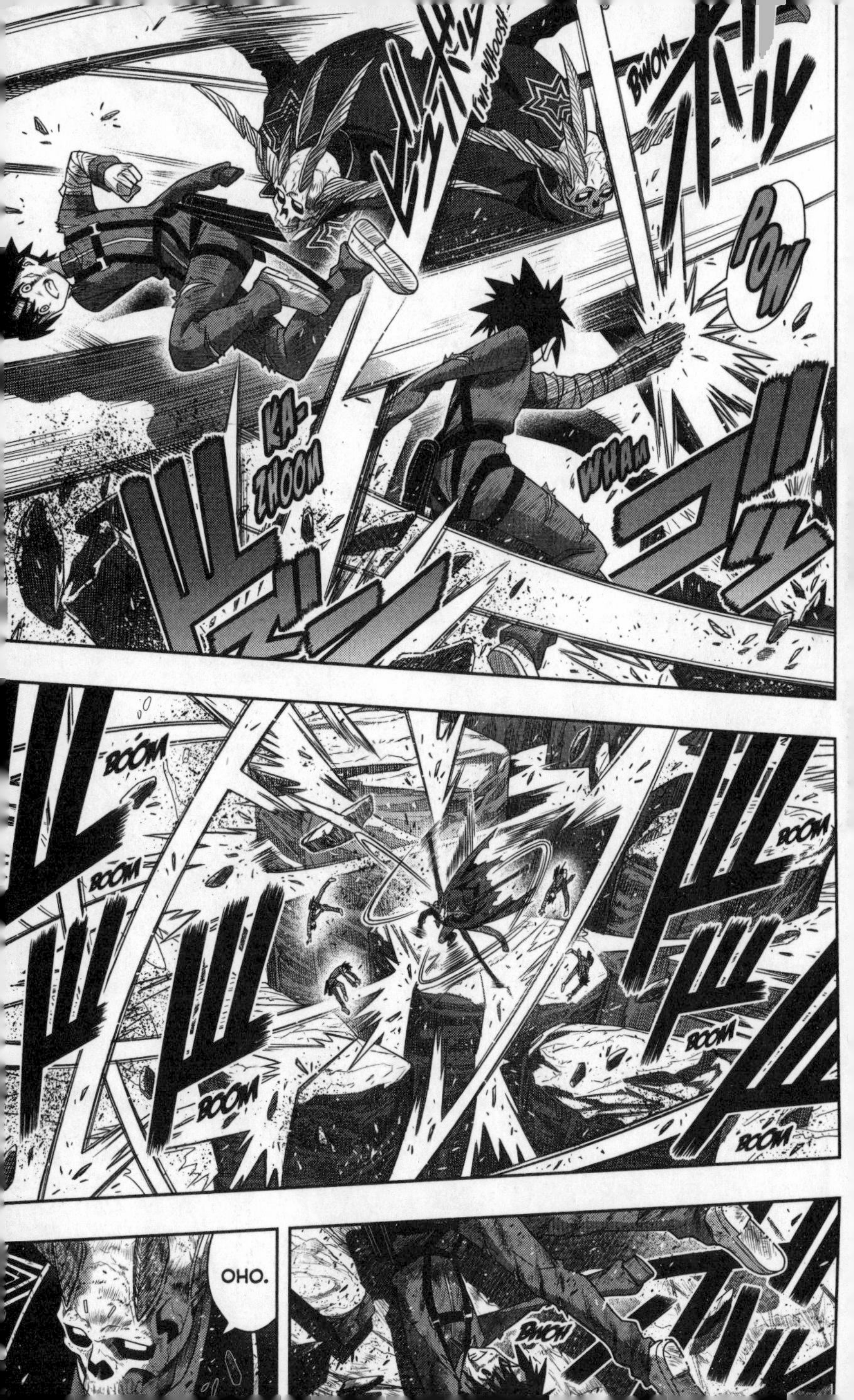
BWOH
FWA-WHOOSH
POW
WHAM
KA-ZHOOM
BOOM
BOOM
BOOM
BOOM
BOOM
BOOM
BWOH
OHO.

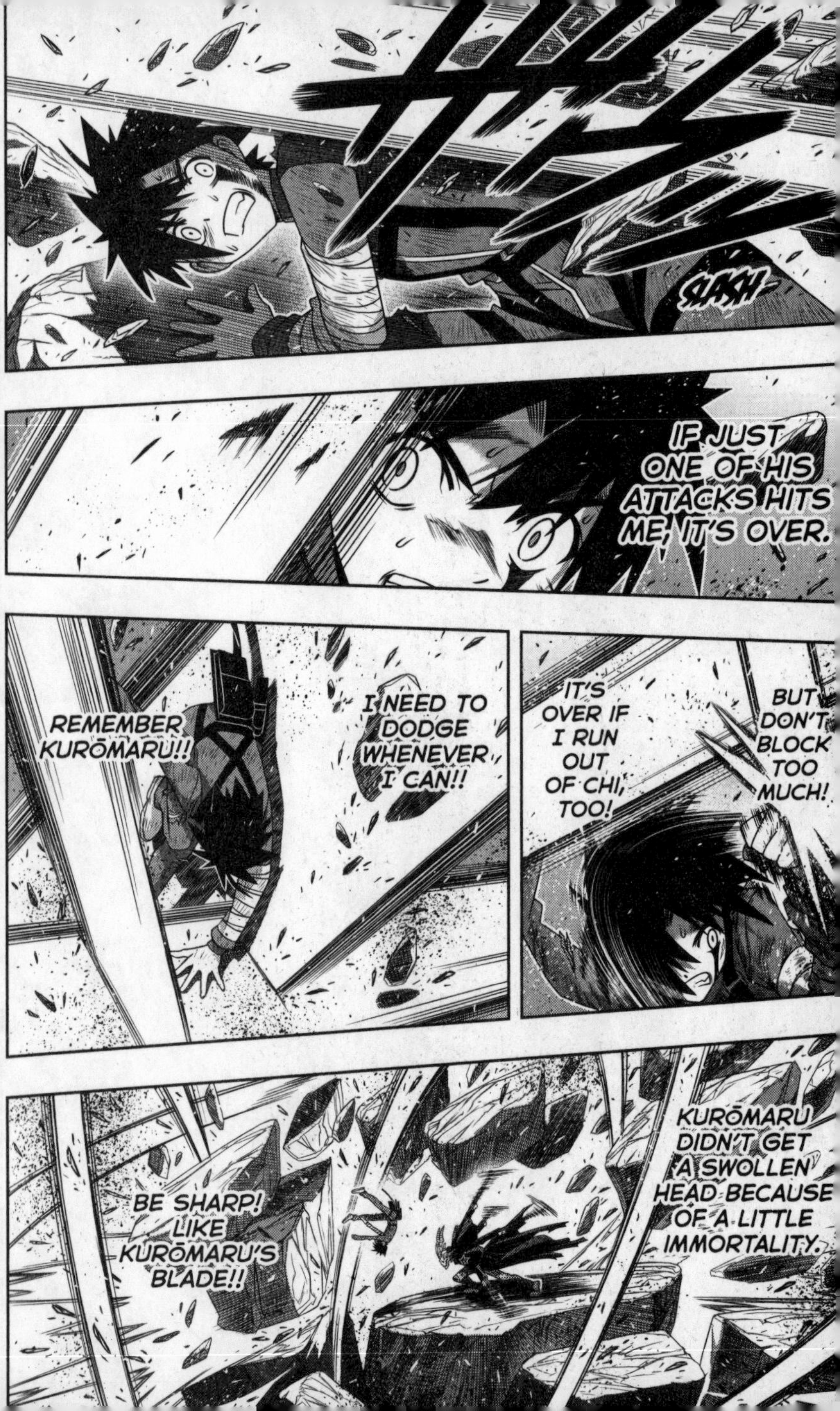
SLASH
IF JUST ONE OF HIS ATTACKS HITS ME, IT'S OVER.
BUT DON'T BLOCK TOO MUCH!
IT'S OVER IF I RUN OUT OF CHI, TOO!
I NEED TO DODGE WHENEVER I CAN!!
REMEMBER KURŌMARU!!
KURŌMARU DIDN'T GET A SWOLLEN HEAD BECAUSE OF A LITTLE IMMORTALITY.
BE SHARP! LIKE KURŌMARU'S BLADE!!

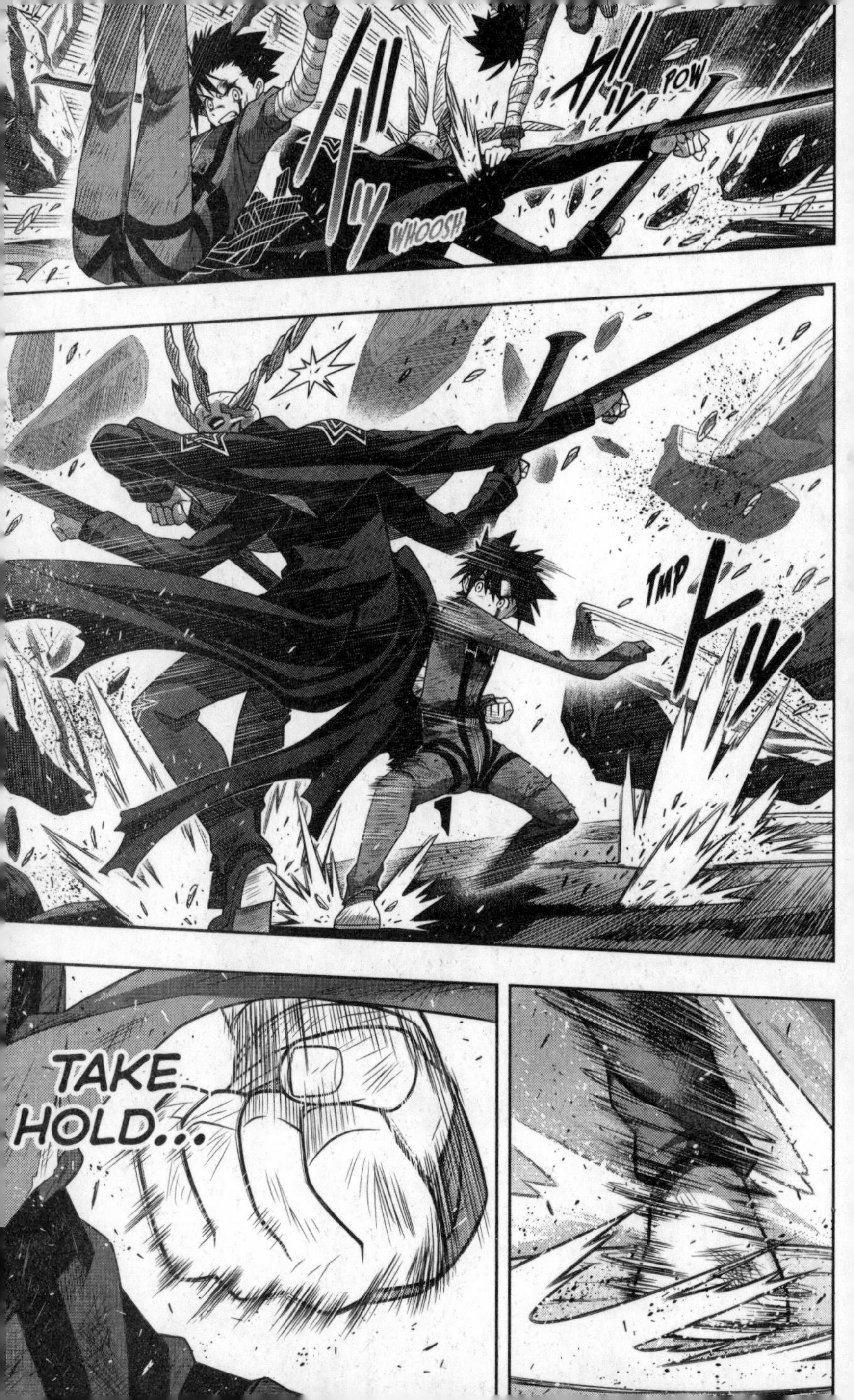
POW
WHOOSH
TMP
TAKE HOLD...

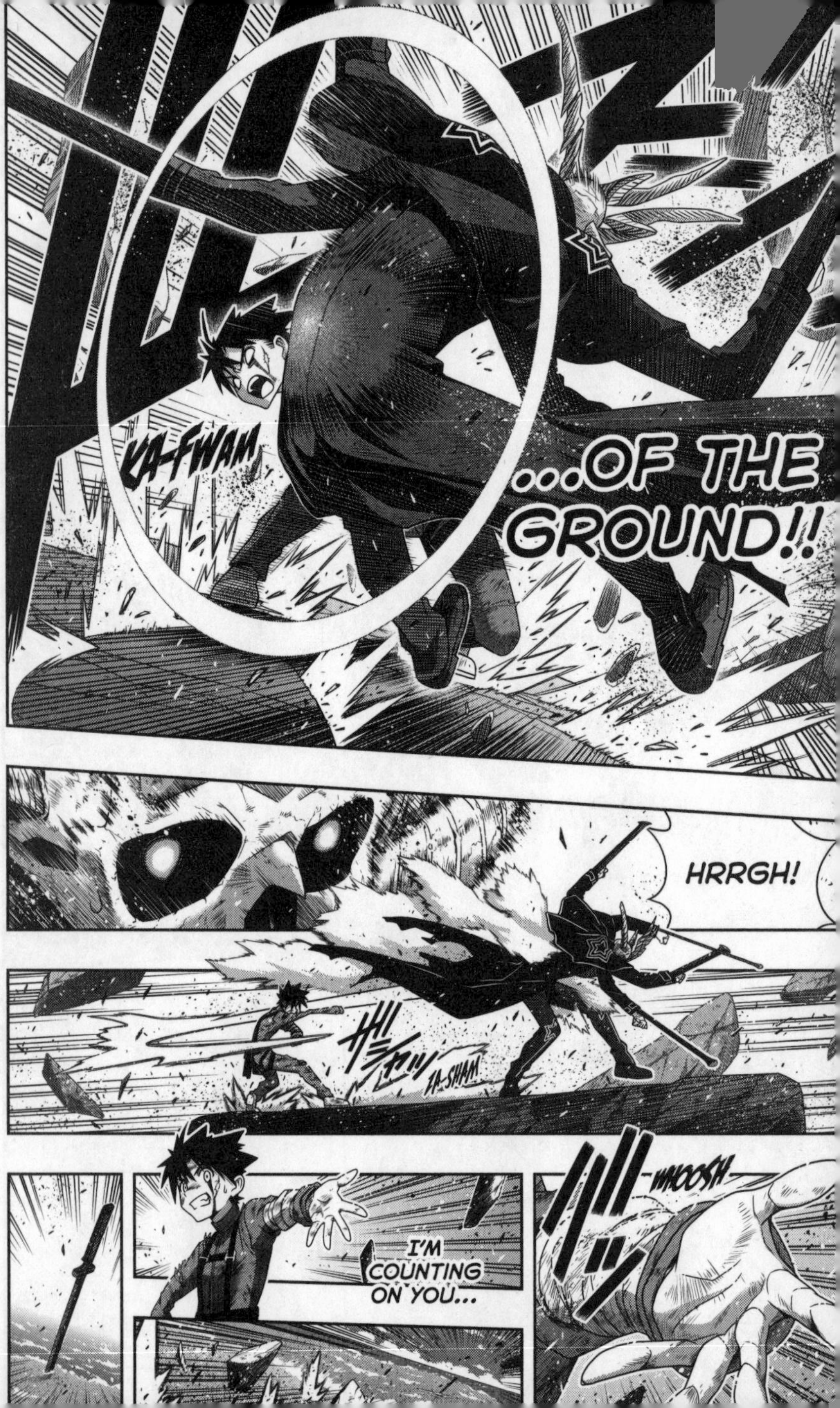
...OF THE GROUND!!
KA-FWAM
HRRGH!
ZA-SHAM
WHOOSH
I'M COUNTING ON YOU...

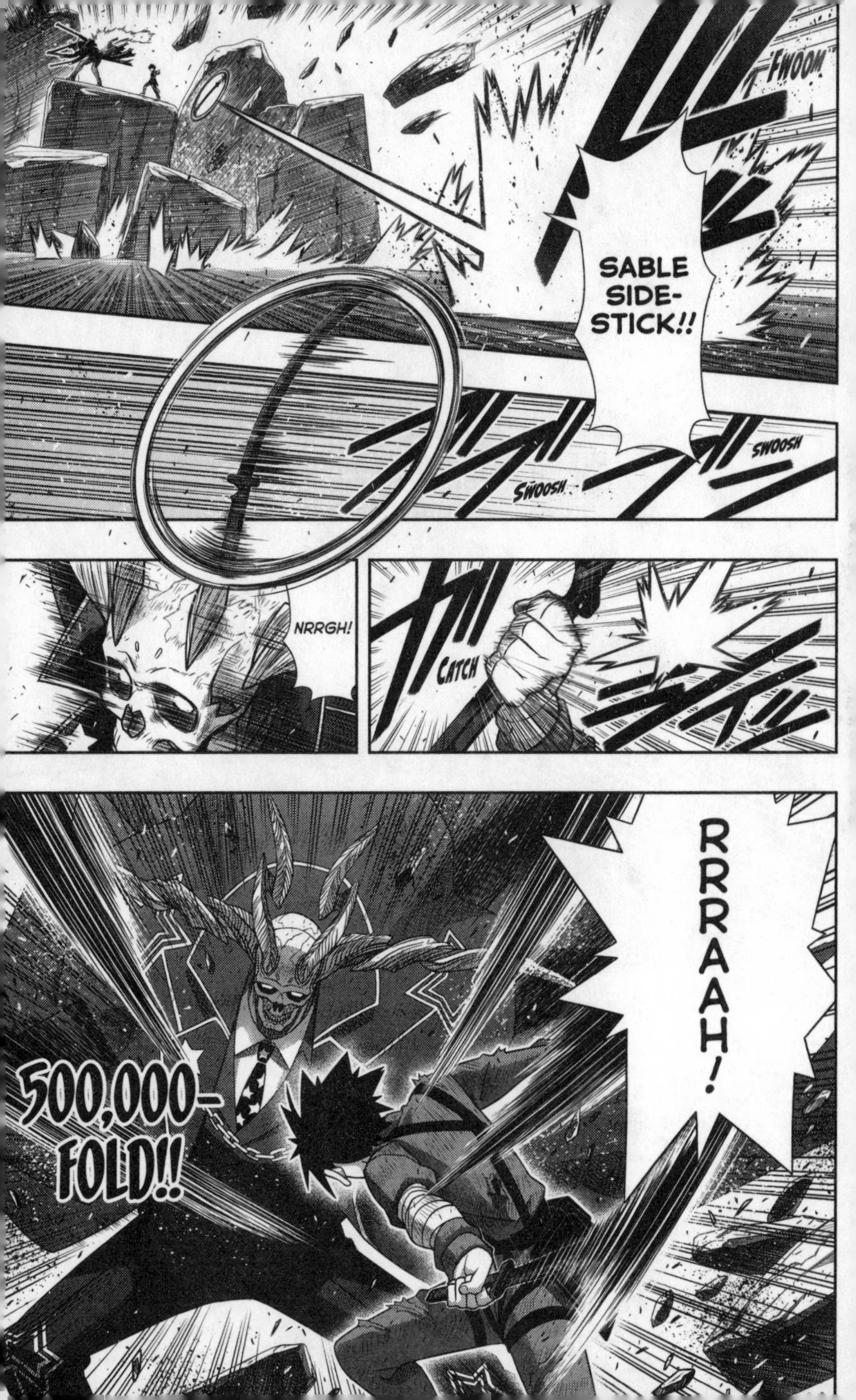
FWOOM
SABLE SIDE-STICK!!
SWOOSH
SWOOSH
CATCH
NRRGH!
RRRAAH!
500,000-FOLD!!

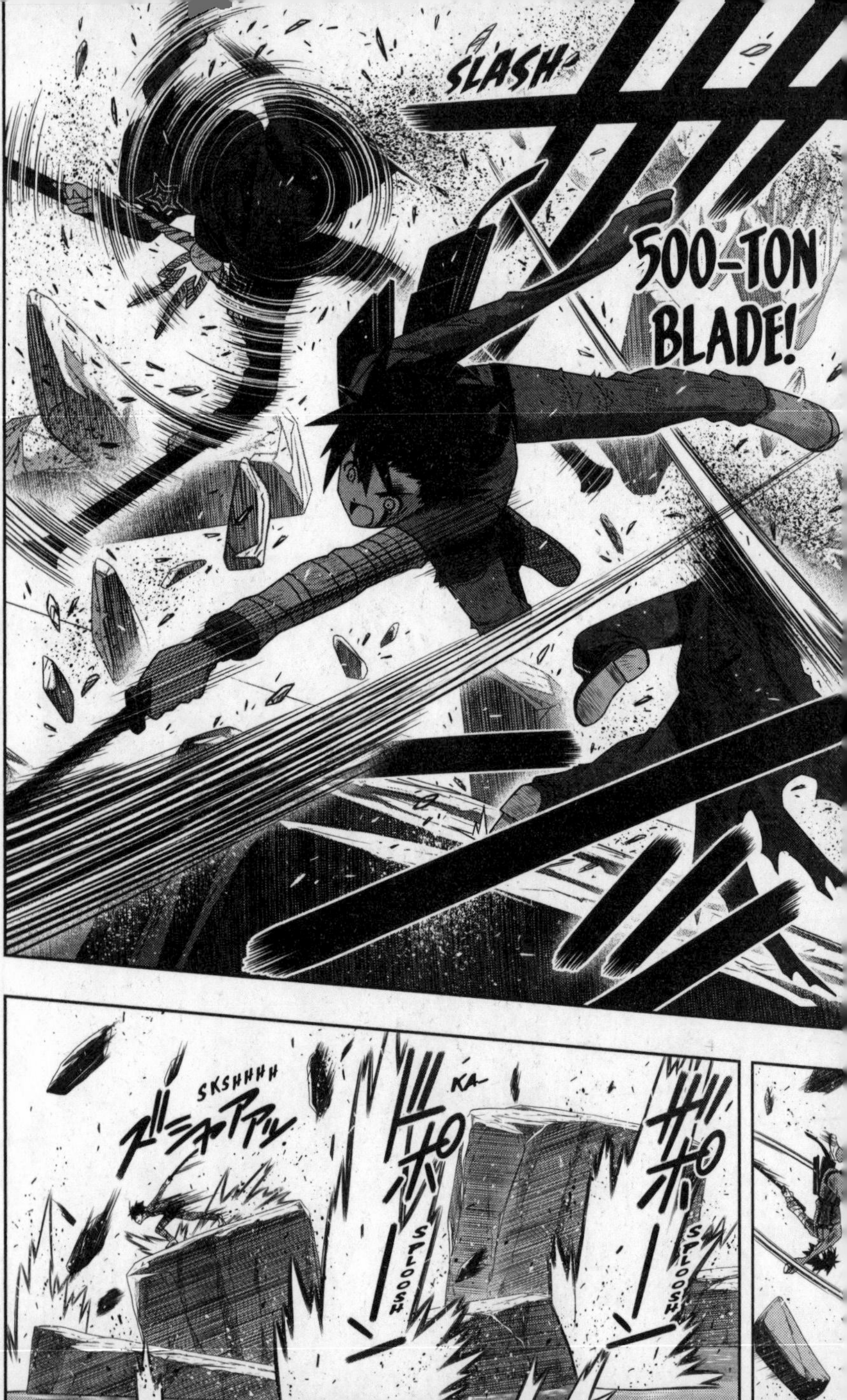
SLASH
500-TON BLADE!
SPLOOSH
KA
SPLOOSH
SKSHHHH

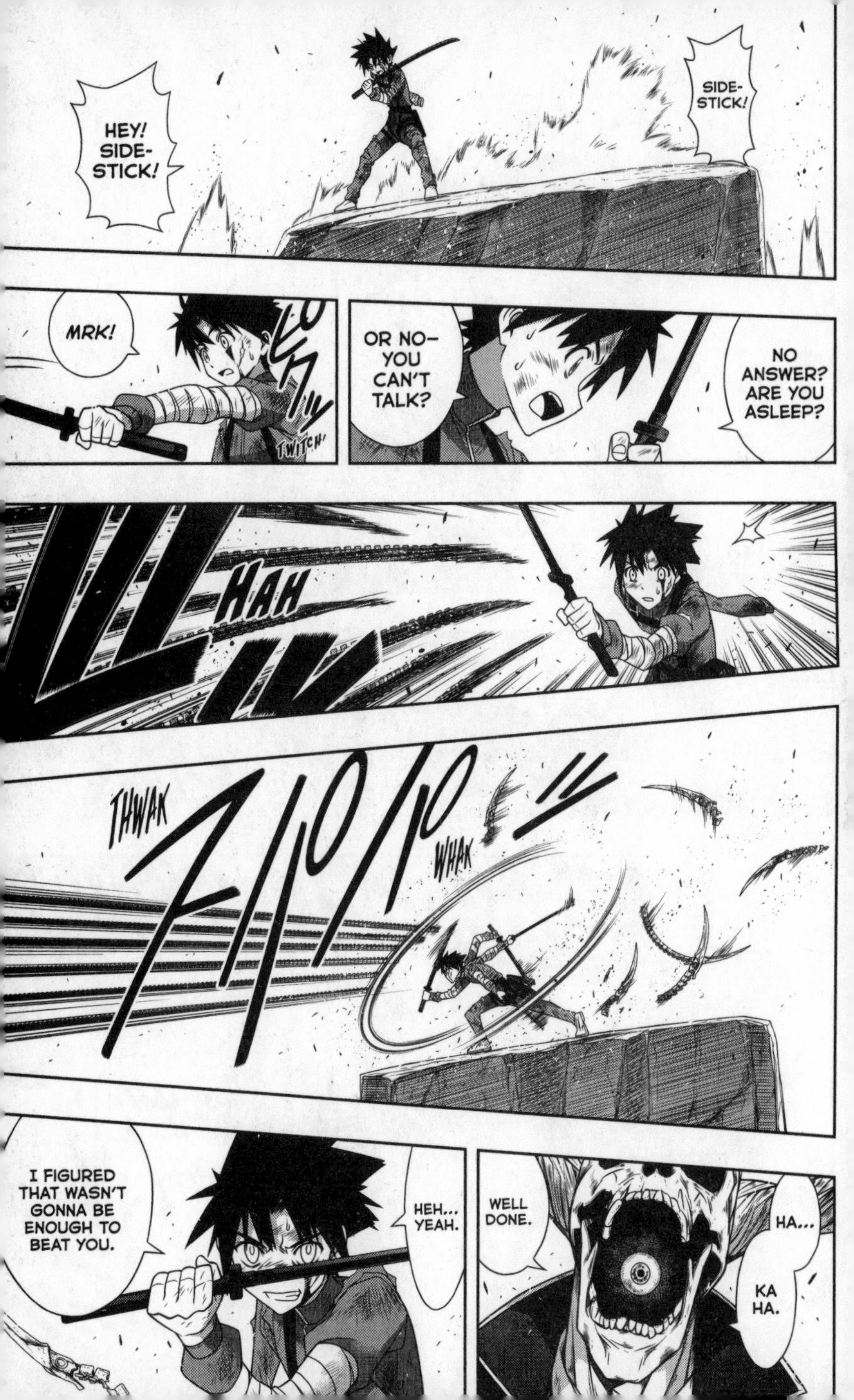
SIDE-STICK!
HEY! SIDE-STICK!
NO ANSWER? ARE YOU ASLEEP?
OR NO— YOU CAN'T TALK?
MRK!
TWITCH
HAH
WHAK
THWAK
HA...
KA HA.
WELL DONE.
HEH... YEAH.
I FIGURED THAT WASN'T GONNA BE ENOUGH TO BEAT YOU.

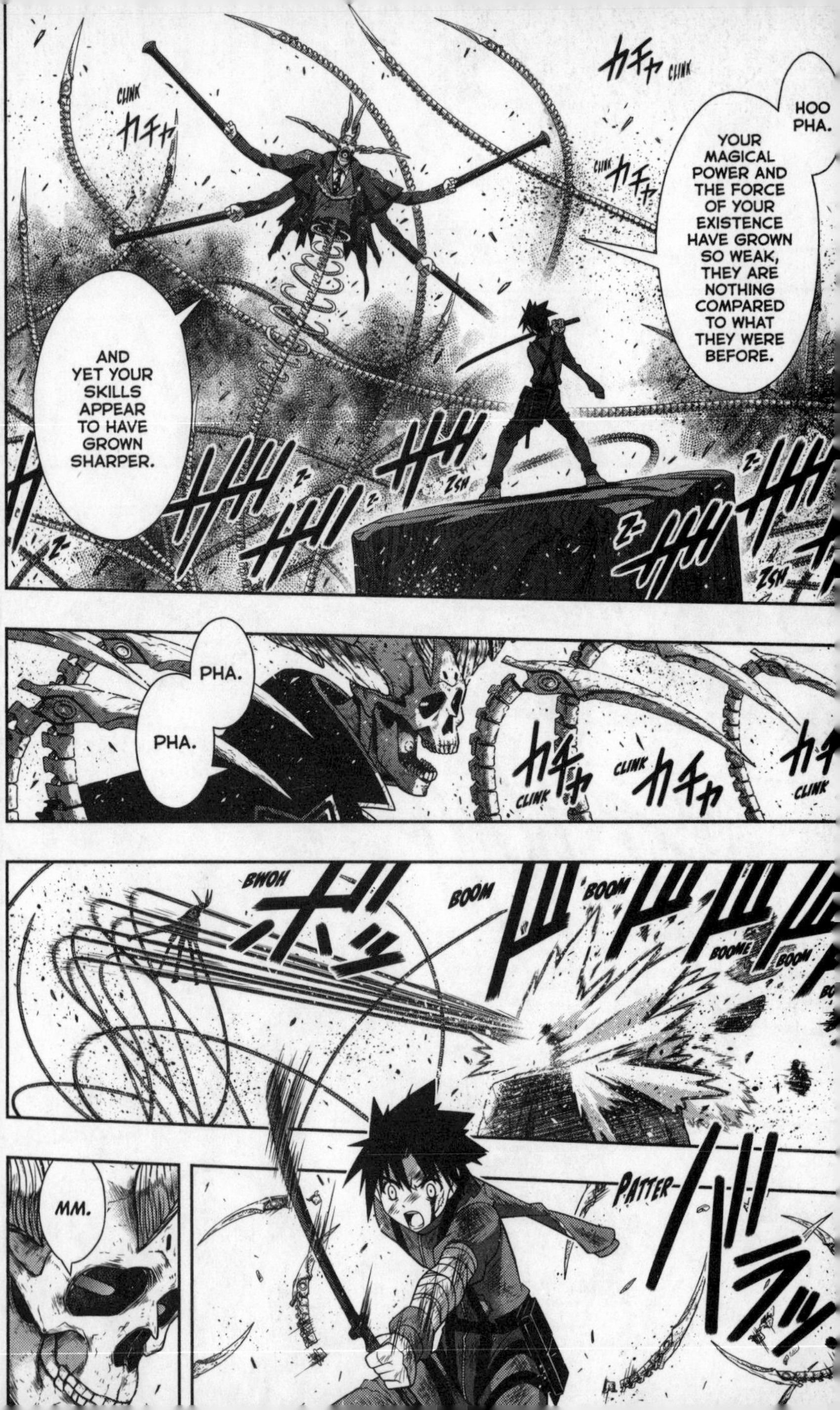
CLINK
HOO PHA.
YOUR MAGICAL POWER AND THE FORCE OF YOUR EXISTENCE HAVE GROWN SO WEAK, THEY ARE NOTHING COMPARED TO WHAT THEY WERE BEFORE.
CLINK
CLINK
ZSH
ZSH
AND YET YOUR SKILLS APPEAR TO HAVE GROWN SHARPER.
CLINK
CLINK
CLINK
PHA.
PHA.
BOOM
BOOM
BOOM
BOOM
BWOH
PATTER
MM.

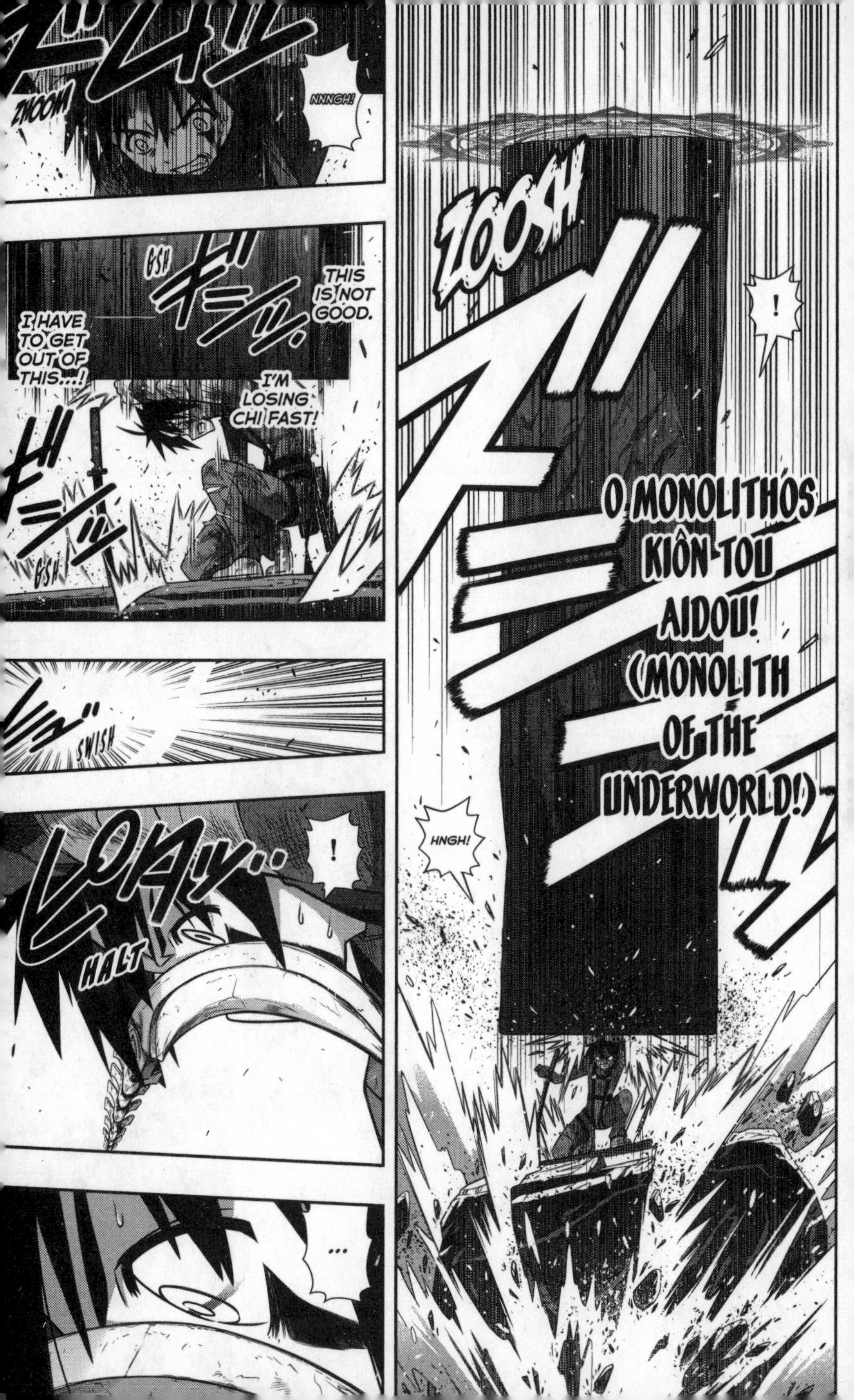
ZOOSH
!
O MONOLITHOS KIÔN TOU AIDOU! (MONOLITH OF THE UNDERWORLD!)
HNGH!
NNNGH!
ZHOOM
THIS IS NOT GOOD.
GSH
I HAVE TO GET OUT OF THIS...!
I'M LOSING CHI FAST!
GSH
SWISH
!
HALT
...

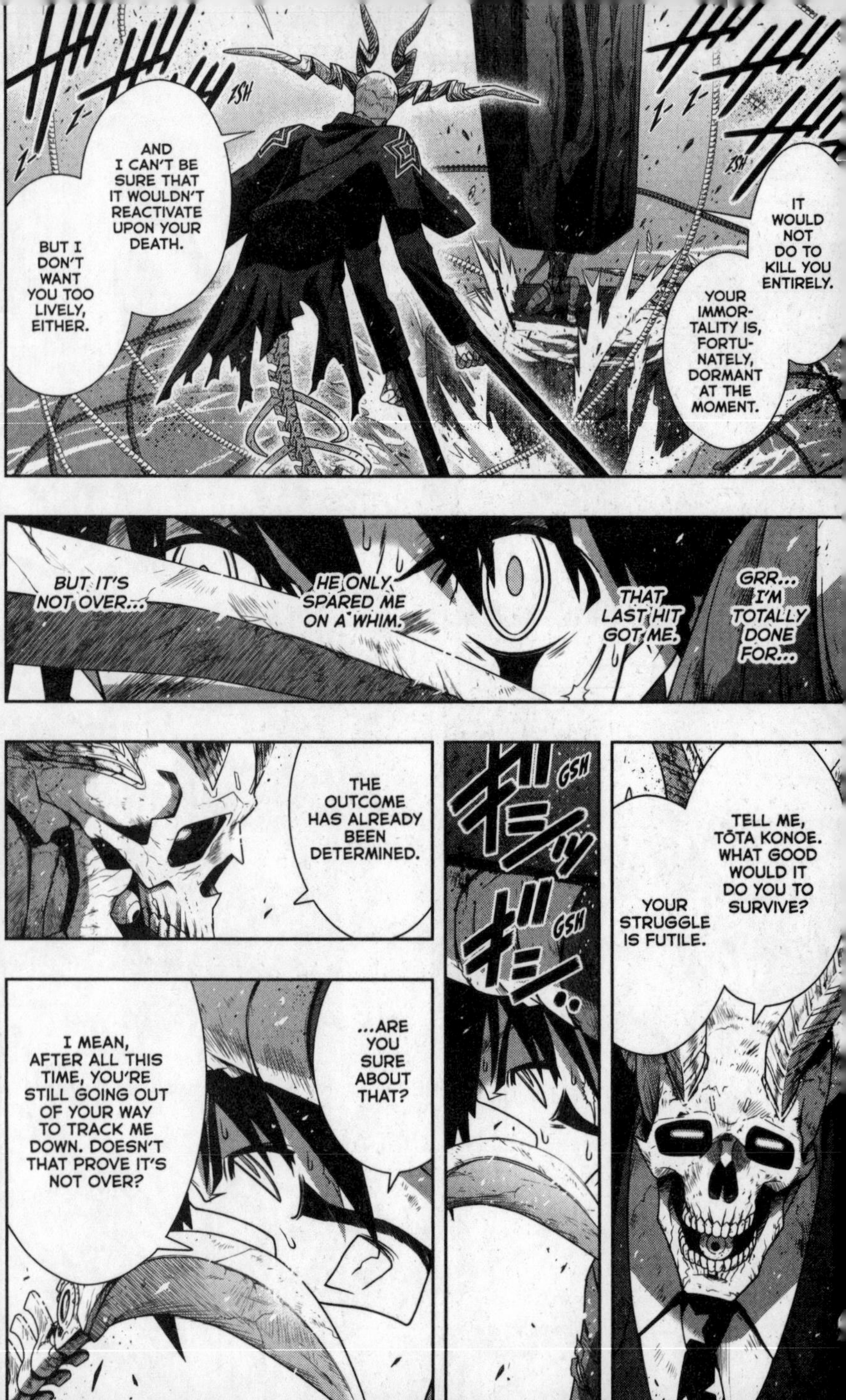
ZSH
IT WOULD NOT DO TO KILL YOU ENTIRELY.
YOUR IMMORTALITY IS, FORTUNATELY, DORMANT AT THE MOMENT.
ZSH
AND I CAN'T BE SURE THAT IT WOULDN'T REACTIVATE UPON YOUR DEATH.
BUT I DON'T WANT YOU TOO LIVELY, EITHER.
GRR... I'M TOTALLY DONE FOR...
THAT LAST HIT GOT ME.
HE ONLY SPARED ME ON A WHIM.
BUT IT'S NOT OVER...
TELL ME, TŌTA KONOE. WHAT GOOD WOULD IT DO YOU TO SURVIVE?
YOUR STRUGGLE IS FUTILE.
GSH
GSH
THE OUTCOME HAS ALREADY BEEN DETERMINED.
...ARE YOU SURE ABOUT THAT?
I MEAN, AFTER ALL THIS TIME, YOU'RE STILL GOING OUT OF YOUR WAY TO TRACK ME DOWN. DOESN'T THAT PROVE IT'S NOT OVER?

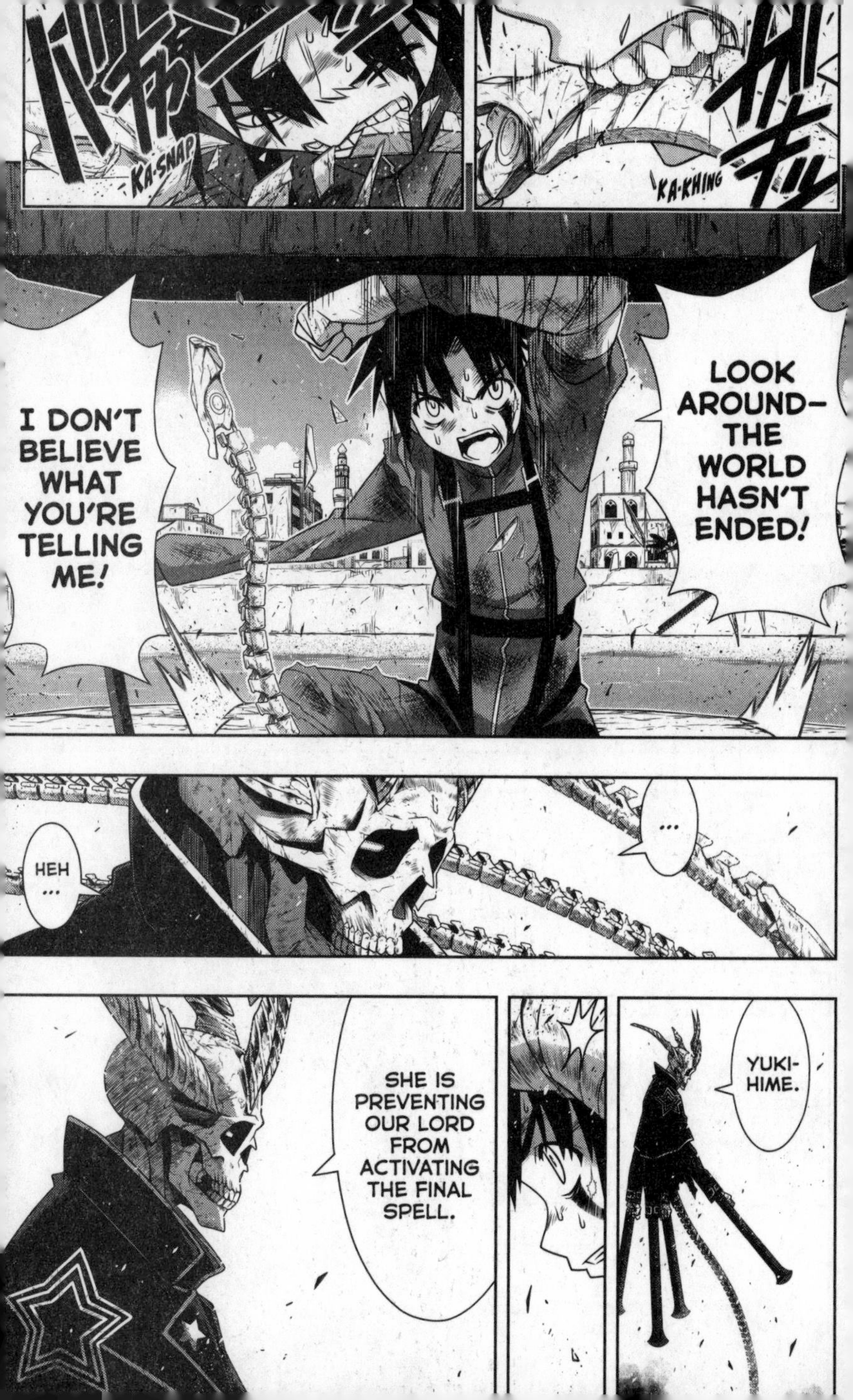
KA-KHING
KA-SNAP
LOOK AROUND— THE WORLD HASN'T ENDED!
I DON'T BELIEVE WHAT YOU'RE TELLING ME!
...
HEH ...
YUKI-HIME.
SHE IS PREVENTING OUR LORD FROM ACTIVATING THE FINAL SPELL.

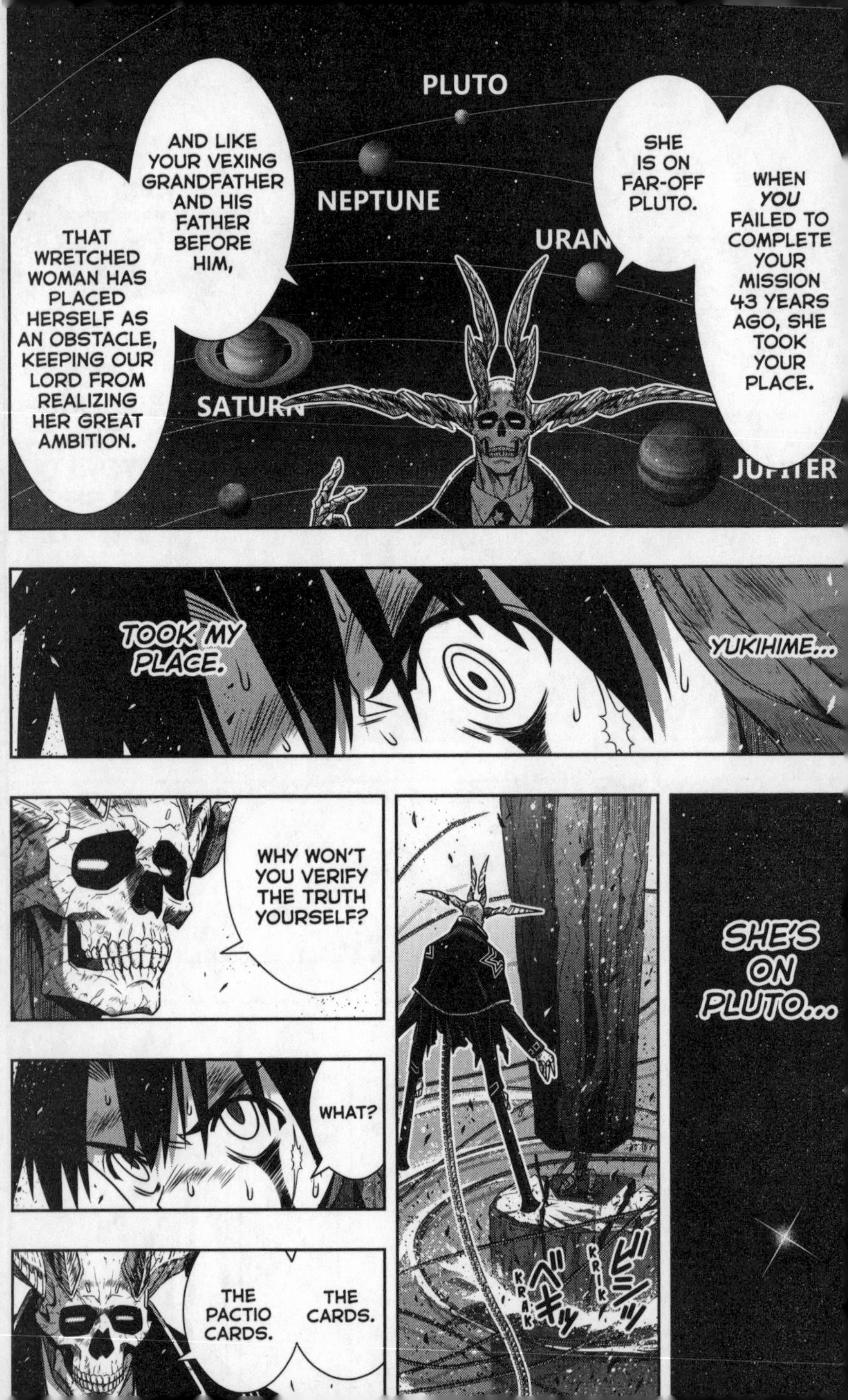
WHEN *YOU* FAILED TO COMPLETE YOUR MISSION 43 YEARS AGO, SHE TOOK YOUR PLACE.
SHE IS ON FAR-OFF PLUTO.
PLUTO
NEPTUNE
URAN
JUPITER
SATURN
AND LIKE YOUR VEXING GRANDFATHER AND HIS FATHER BEFORE HIM,
THAT WRETCHED WOMAN HAS PLACED HERSELF AS AN OBSTACLE, KEEPING OUR LORD FROM REALIZING HER GREAT AMBITION.
YUKIHIME...
TOOK MY PLACE.
SHE'S ON PLUTO...
KRIK
KRAK
WHY WON'T YOU VERIFY THE TRUTH YOURSELF?
WHAT?
THE CARDS.
THE PACTIO CARDS.

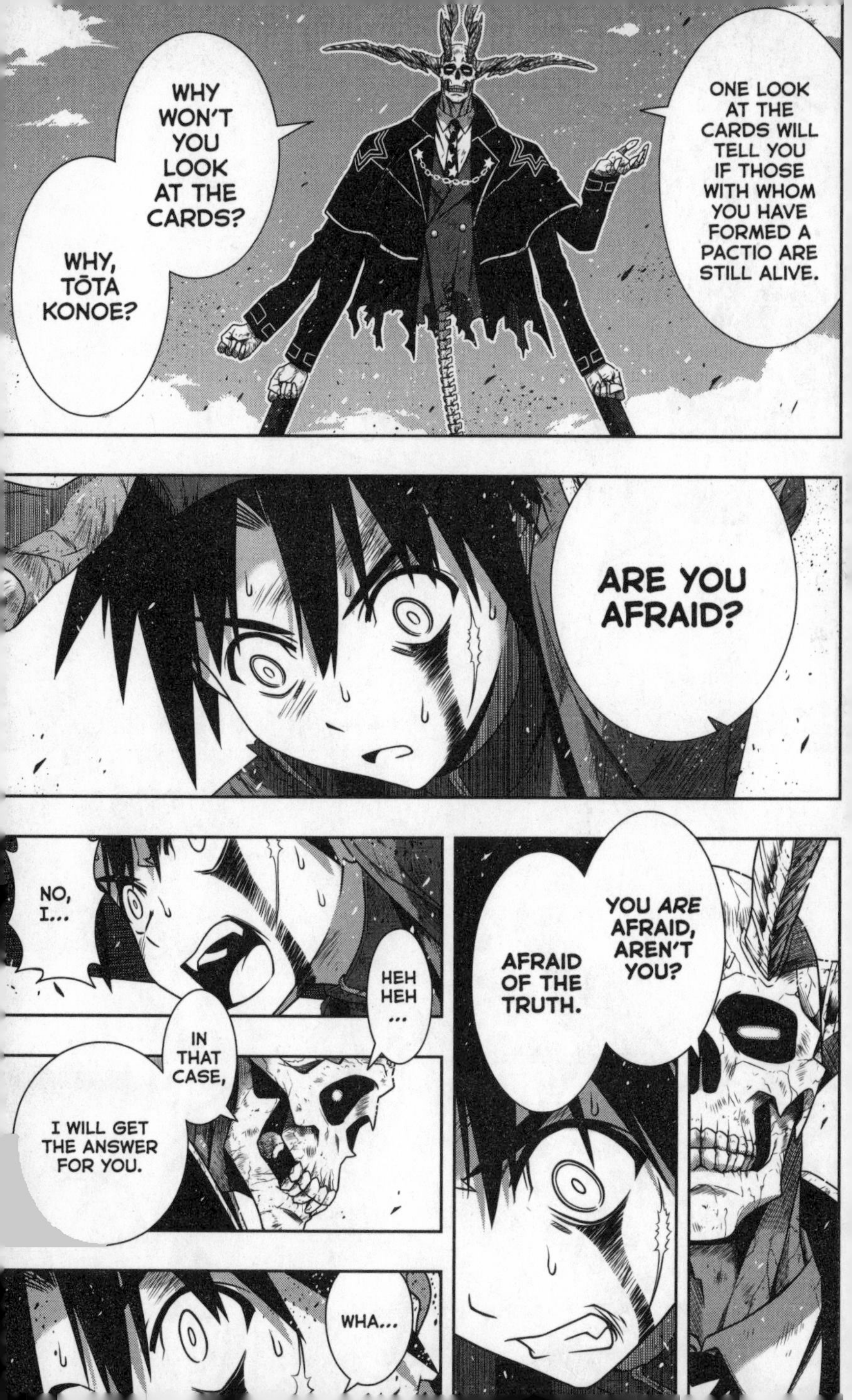
ONE LOOK AT THE CARDS WILL TELL YOU IF THOSE WITH WHOM YOU HAVE FORMED A PACTIO ARE STILL ALIVE.
WHY WON'T YOU LOOK AT THE CARDS?
WHY, TŌTA KONOE?
ARE YOU AFRAID?
YOU *ARE* AFRAID, AREN'T YOU?
AFRAID OF THE TRUTH.
NO, I...
HEH HEH...
IN THAT CASE,
I WILL GET THE ANSWER FOR YOU.
WHA...

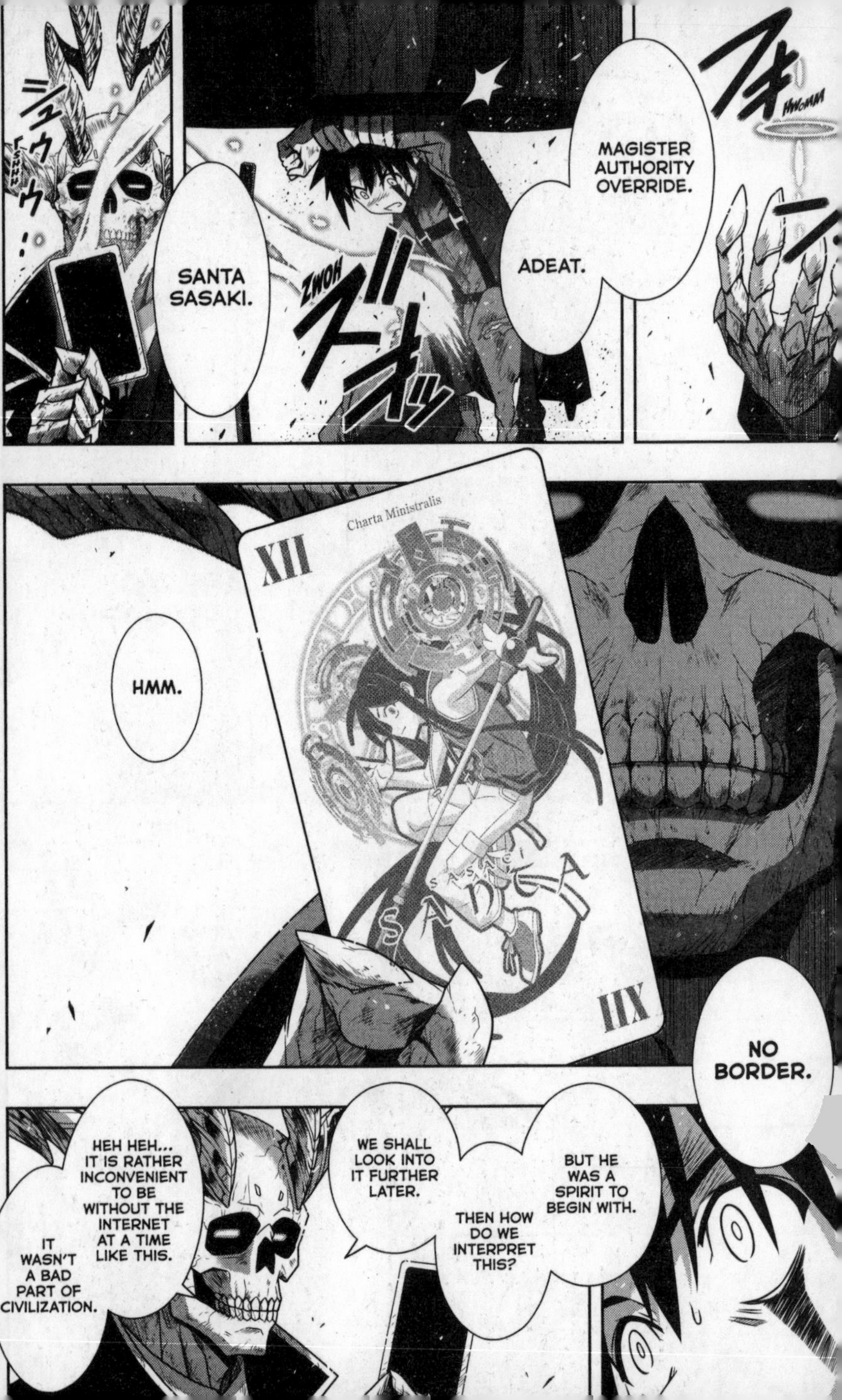
HWOMM
MAGISTER AUTHORITY OVERRIDE.
ADEAT.
ZWOH
SANTA SASAKI.
Charta Ministralis
XII
HMM.
NO BORDER.
BUT HE WAS A SPIRIT TO BEGIN WITH.
THEN HOW DO WE INTERPRET THIS?
WE SHALL LOOK INTO IT FURTHER LATER.
HEH HEH... IT IS RATHER INCONVENIENT TO BE WITHOUT THE INTERNET AT A TIME LIKE THIS.
IT WASN'T A BAD PART OF CIVILIZATION.

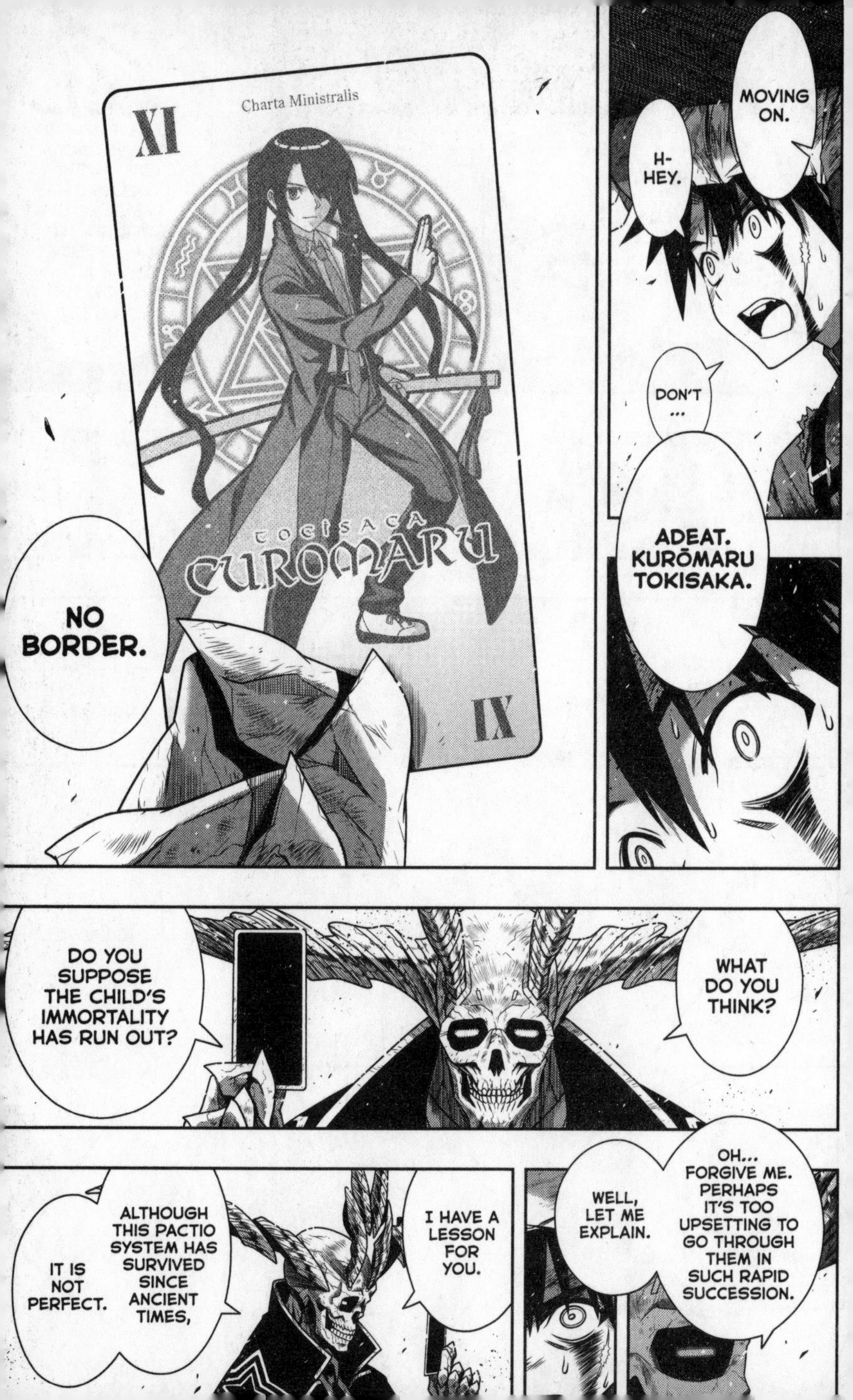
MOVING ON.
H-HEY.
DON'T ...
ADEAT. KURŌMARU TOKISAKA.
Charta Ministralis
XI
TOCISACA CUROMARU
XI
NO BORDER.
WHAT DO YOU THINK?
DO YOU SUPPOSE THE CHILD'S IMMORTALITY HAS RUN OUT?
OH... FORGIVE ME. PERHAPS IT'S TOO UPSETTING TO GO THROUGH THEM IN SUCH RAPID SUCCESSION.
WELL, LET ME EXPLAIN.
I HAVE A LESSON FOR YOU.
ALTHOUGH THIS PACTIO SYSTEM HAS SURVIVED SINCE ANCIENT TIMES,
IT IS NOT PERFECT.

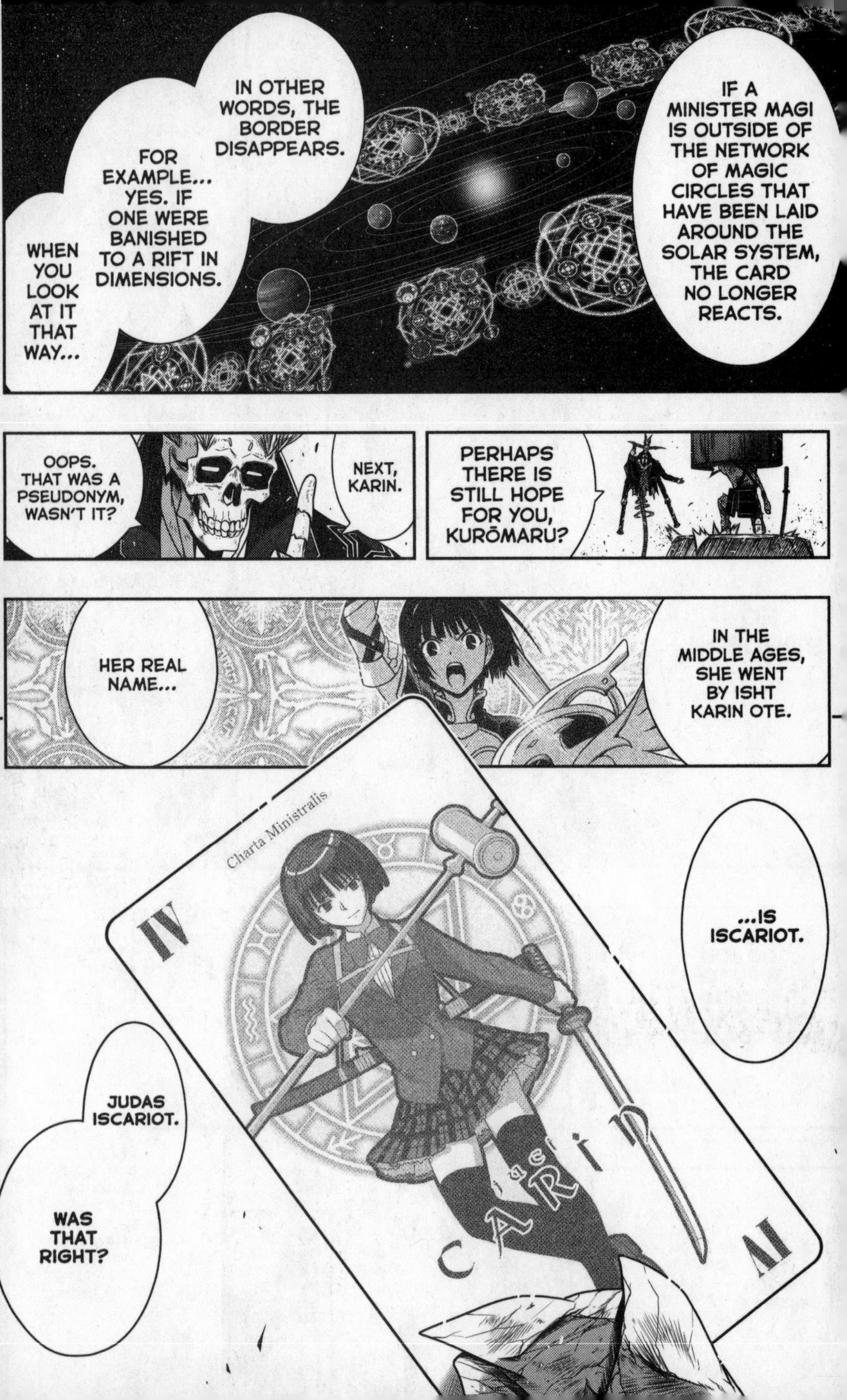
IF A MINISTER MAGI IS OUTSIDE OF THE NETWORK OF MAGIC CIRCLES THAT HAVE BEEN LAID AROUND THE SOLAR SYSTEM, THE CARD NO LONGER REACTS.
IN OTHER WORDS, THE BORDER DISAPPEARS.
FOR EXAMPLE... YES. IF ONE WERE BANISHED TO A RIFT IN DIMENSIONS.
WHEN YOU LOOK AT IT THAT WAY...
PERHAPS THERE IS STILL HOPE FOR YOU, KURŌMARU?
NEXT, KARIN.
OOPS. THAT WAS A PSEUDONYM, WASN'T IT?
IN THE MIDDLE AGES, SHE WENT BY ISHT KARIN OTE.
HER REAL NAME...
...IS ISCARIOT.
Charta Ministralis
IV
JUDAS ISCARIOT.
WAS THAT RIGHT?

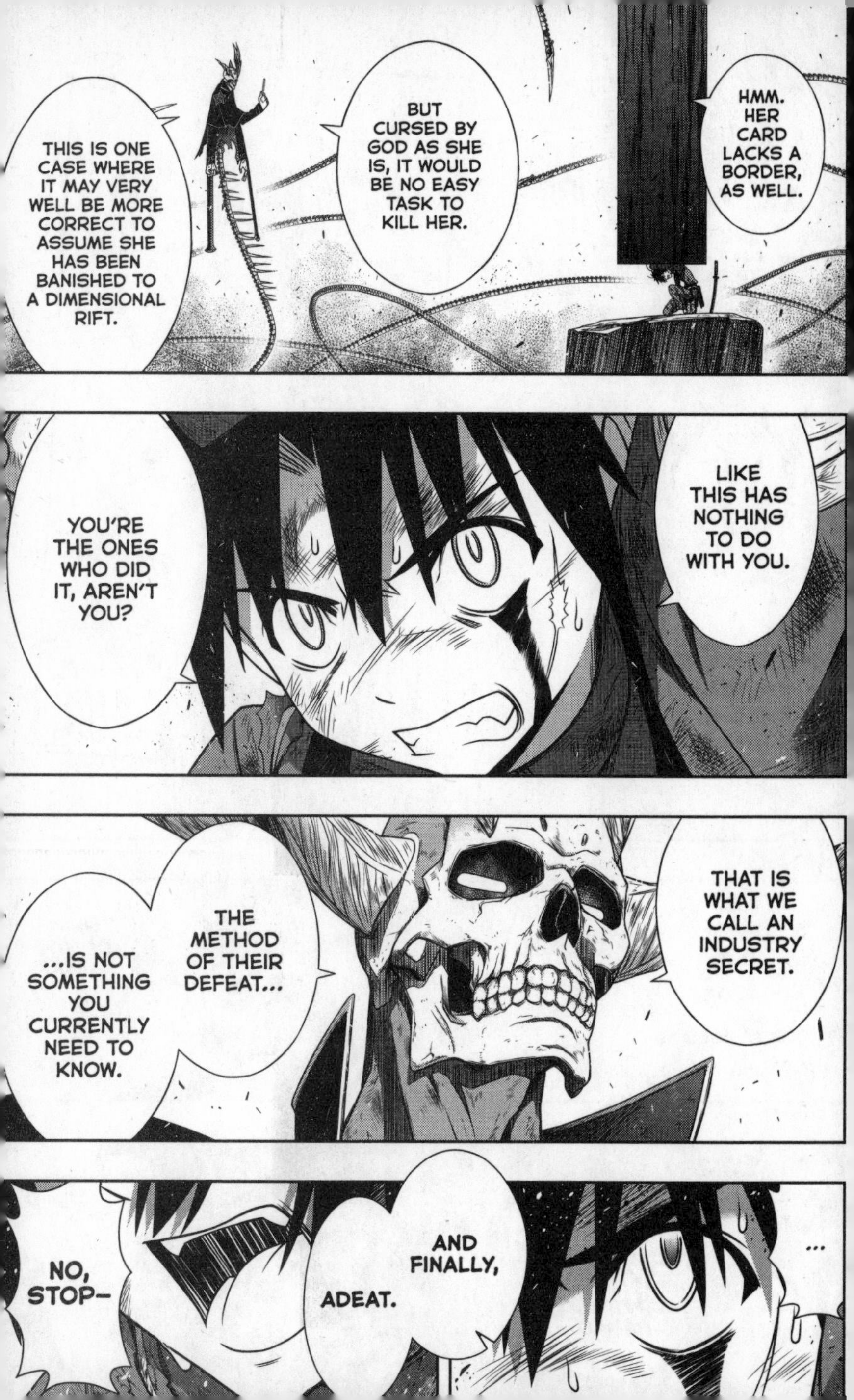
HMM. HER CARD LACKS A BORDER, AS WELL.
BUT CURSED BY GOD AS SHE IS, IT WOULD BE NO EASY TASK TO KILL HER.
THIS IS ONE CASE WHERE IT MAY VERY WELL BE MORE CORRECT TO ASSUME SHE HAS BEEN BANISHED TO A DIMENSIONAL RIFT.
LIKE THIS HAS NOTHING TO DO WITH YOU.
YOU'RE THE ONES WHO DID IT, AREN'T YOU?
THAT IS WHAT WE CALL AN INDUSTRY SECRET.
THE METHOD OF THEIR DEFEAT...
...IS NOT SOMETHING YOU CURRENTLY NEED TO KNOW.
...
AND FINALLY,
ADEAT.
NO, STOP—

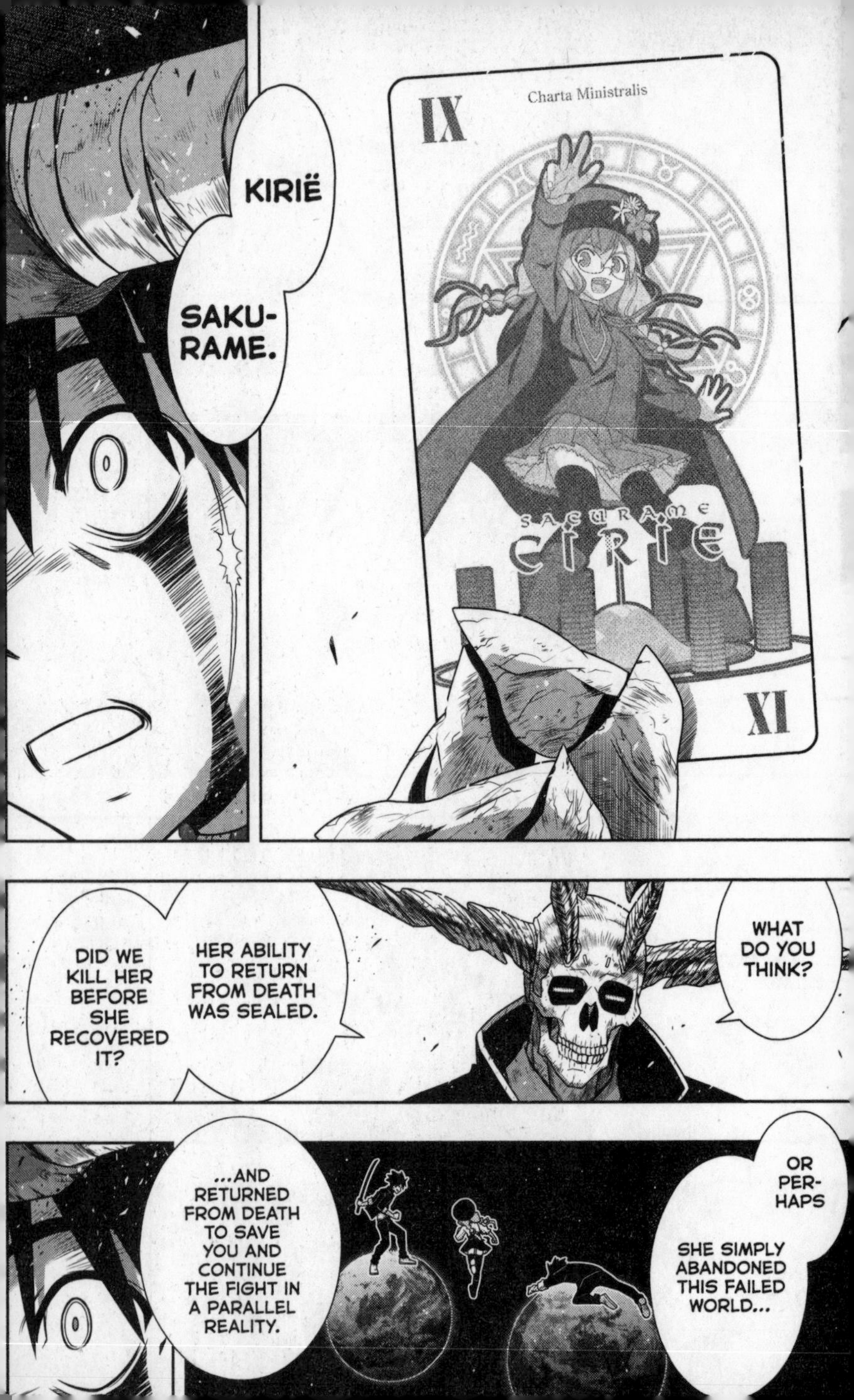
Charta Ministralis
IX
SACURAME
CIRIE
XI
KIRIË
SAKU-RAME.
WHAT DO YOU THINK?
HER ABILITY TO RETURN FROM DEATH WAS SEALED.
DID WE KILL HER BEFORE SHE RECOVERED IT?
OR PER-HAPS
SHE SIMPLY ABANDONED THIS FAILED WORLD...
...AND RETURNED FROM DEATH TO SAVE YOU AND CONTINUE THE FIGHT IN A PARALLEL REALITY.

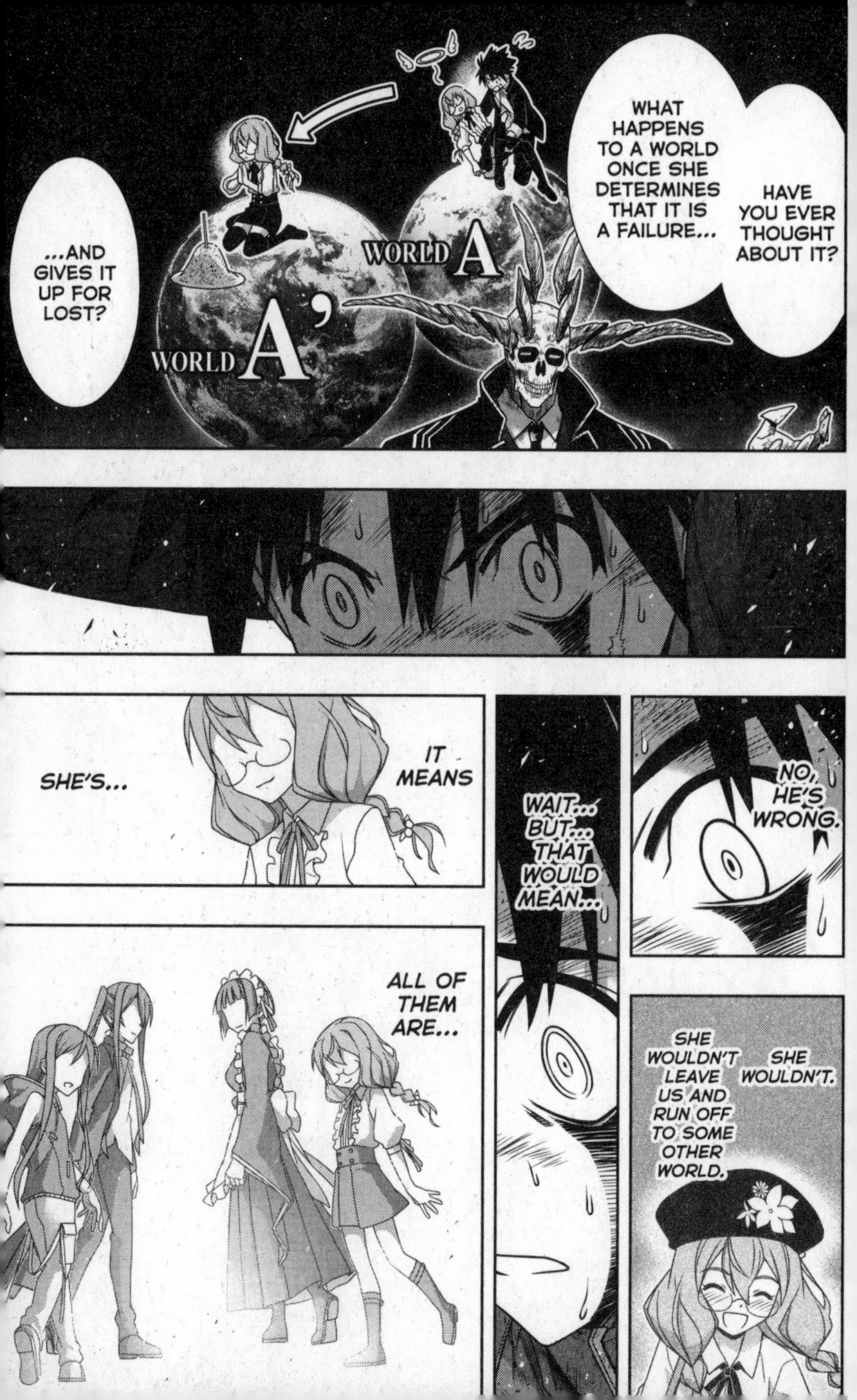

HAVE YOU EVER THOUGHT ABOUT IT?
WHAT HAPPENS TO A WORLD ONCE SHE DETERMINES THAT IT IS A FAILURE...
WORLD A
...AND GIVES IT UP FOR LOST?
WORLD A'
NO, HE'S WRONG.
SHE WOULDN'T.
SHE WOULDN'T LEAVE US AND RUN OFF TO SOME OTHER WORLD.
WAIT... BUT... THAT WOULD MEAN...
IT MEANS
SHE'S...
ALL OF THEM ARE...

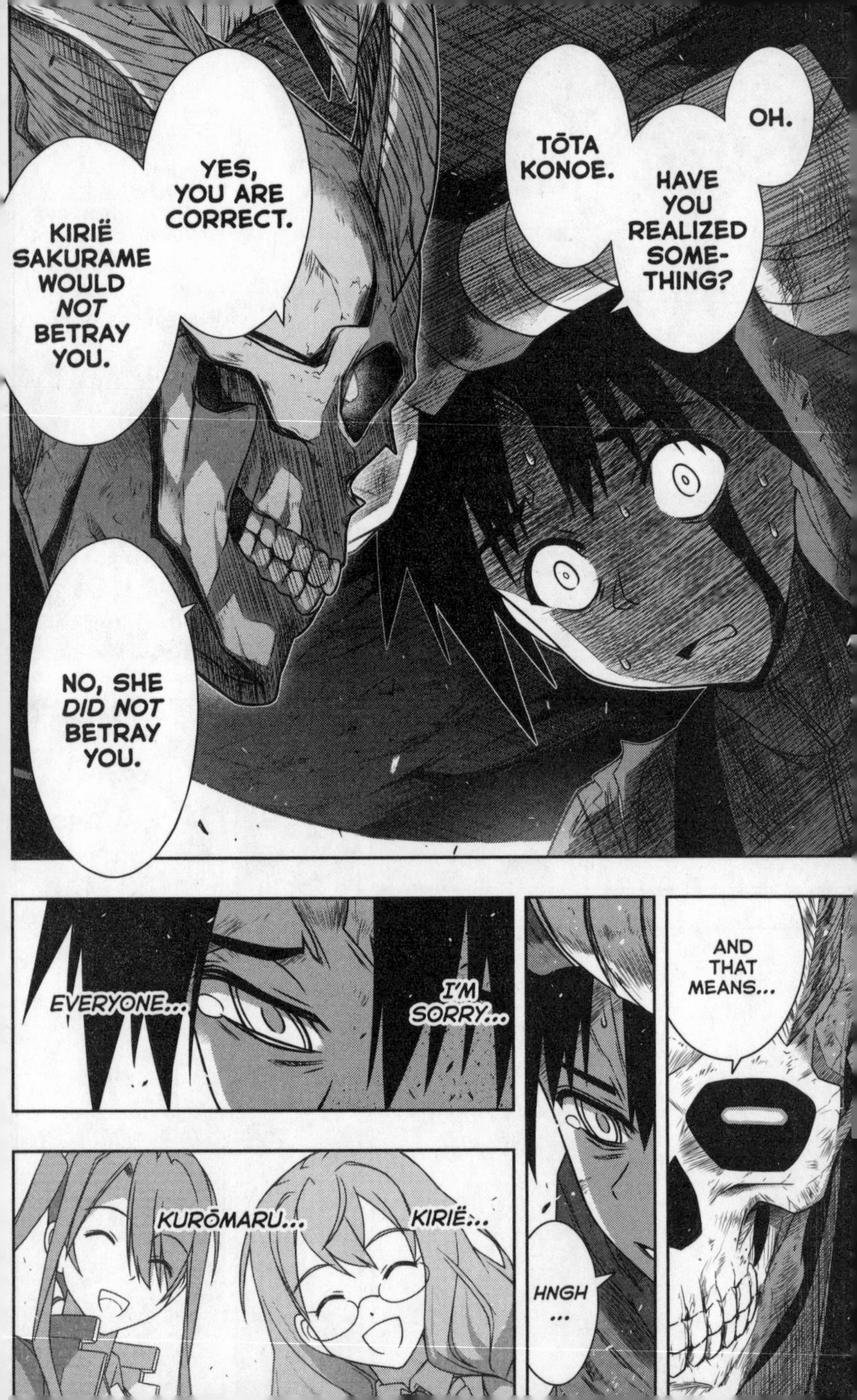
OH.
TŌTA KONOE.
HAVE YOU REALIZED SOME-THING?
YES, YOU ARE CORRECT.
KIRIË SAKURAME WOULD *NOT* BETRAY YOU.
NO, SHE *DID NOT* BETRAY YOU.
AND THAT MEANS...
HNGH ...
I'M SORRY...
EVERYONE...
KIRIË...
KURŌMARU...

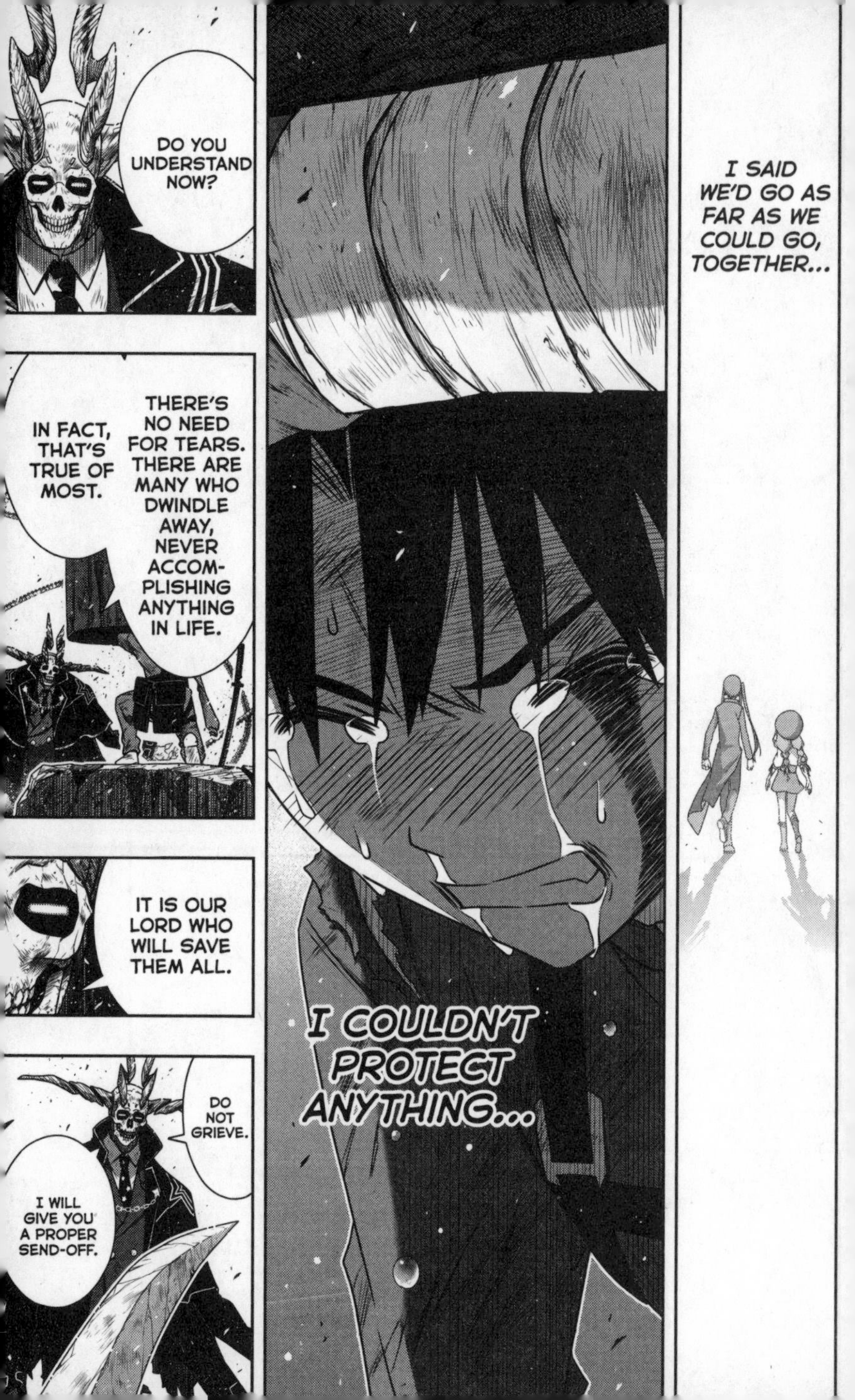
I SAID WE'D GO AS FAR AS WE COULD GO, TOGETHER...
I COULDN'T PROTECT ANYTHING...
DO YOU UNDERSTAND NOW?
THERE'S NO NEED FOR TEARS. THERE ARE MANY WHO DWINDLE AWAY, NEVER ACCOM-PLISHING ANYTHING IN LIFE.
IN FACT, THAT'S TRUE OF MOST.
IT IS OUR LORD WHO WILL SAVE THEM ALL.
DO NOT GRIEVE.
I WILL GIVE YOU A PROPER SEND-OFF.

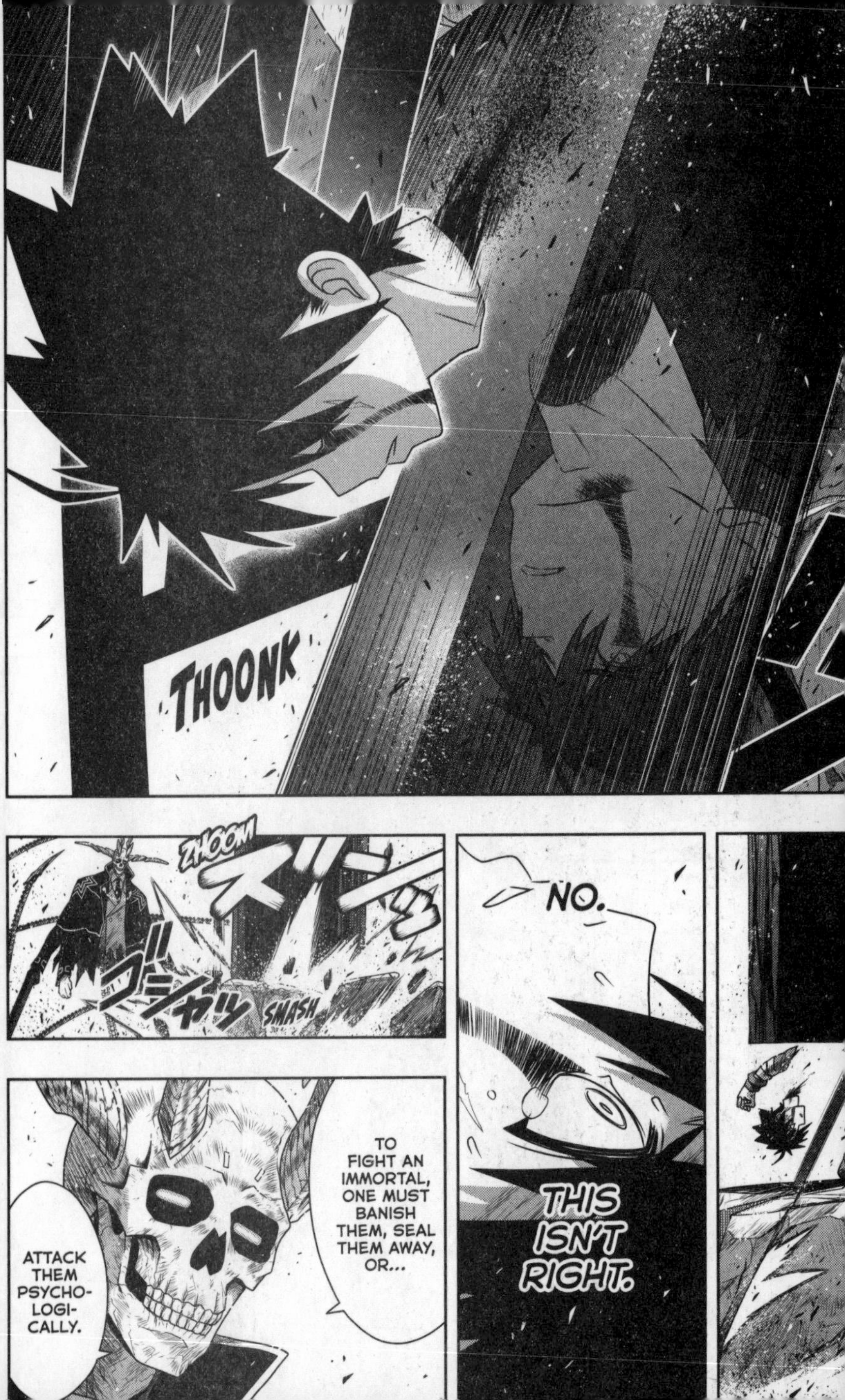
THOONK
NO.
THIS ISN'T RIGHT.
ZHOOM
SMASH
TO FIGHT AN IMMORTAL, ONE MUST BANISH THEM, SEAL THEM AWAY, OR...
ATTACK THEM PSYCHO-LOGI-CALLY.

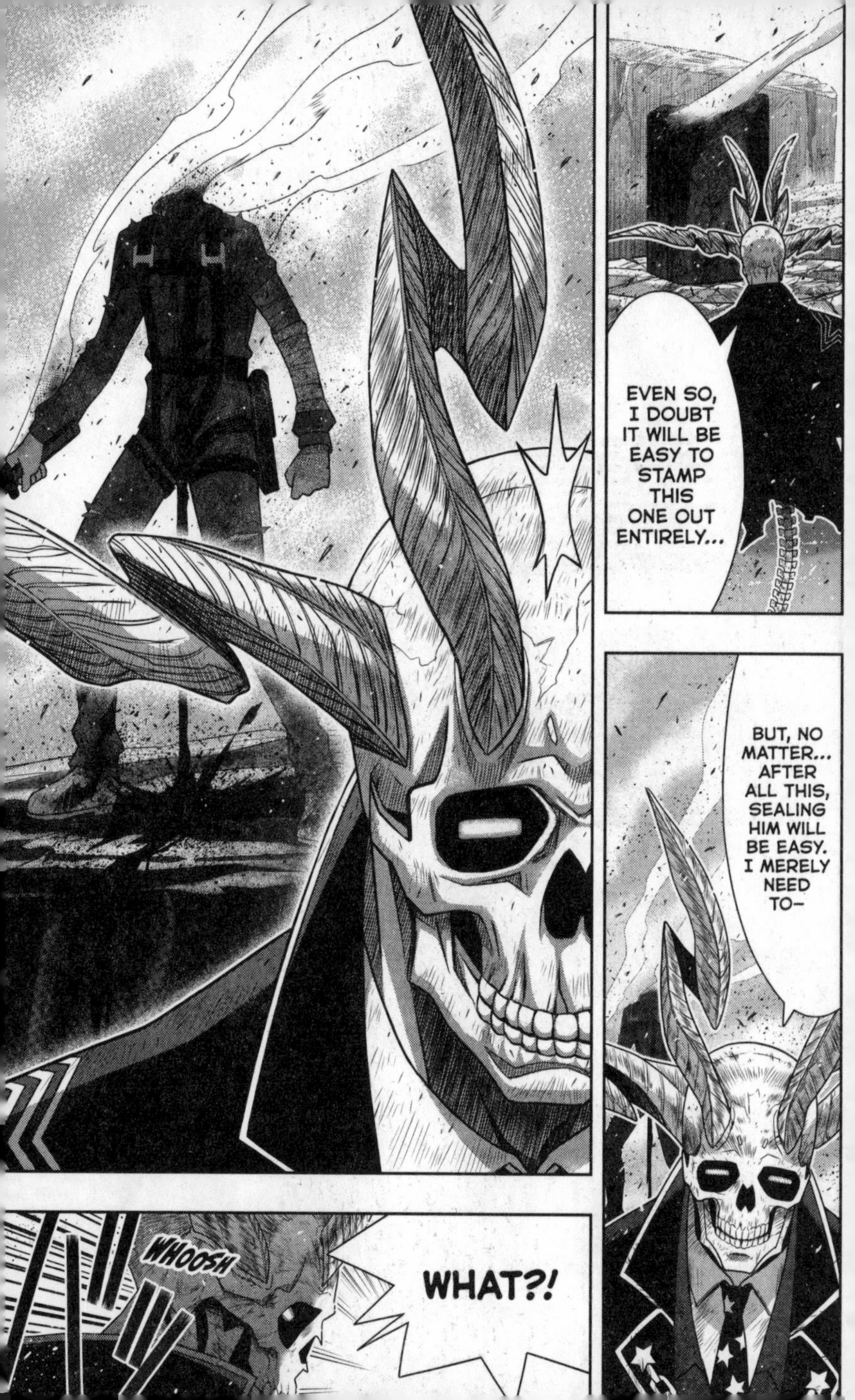
EVEN SO, I DOUBT IT WILL BE EASY TO STAMP THIS ONE OUT ENTIRELY...
BUT, NO MATTER... AFTER ALL THIS, SEALING HIM WILL BE EASY. I MERELY NEED TO–
WHAT?!
WHOOSH

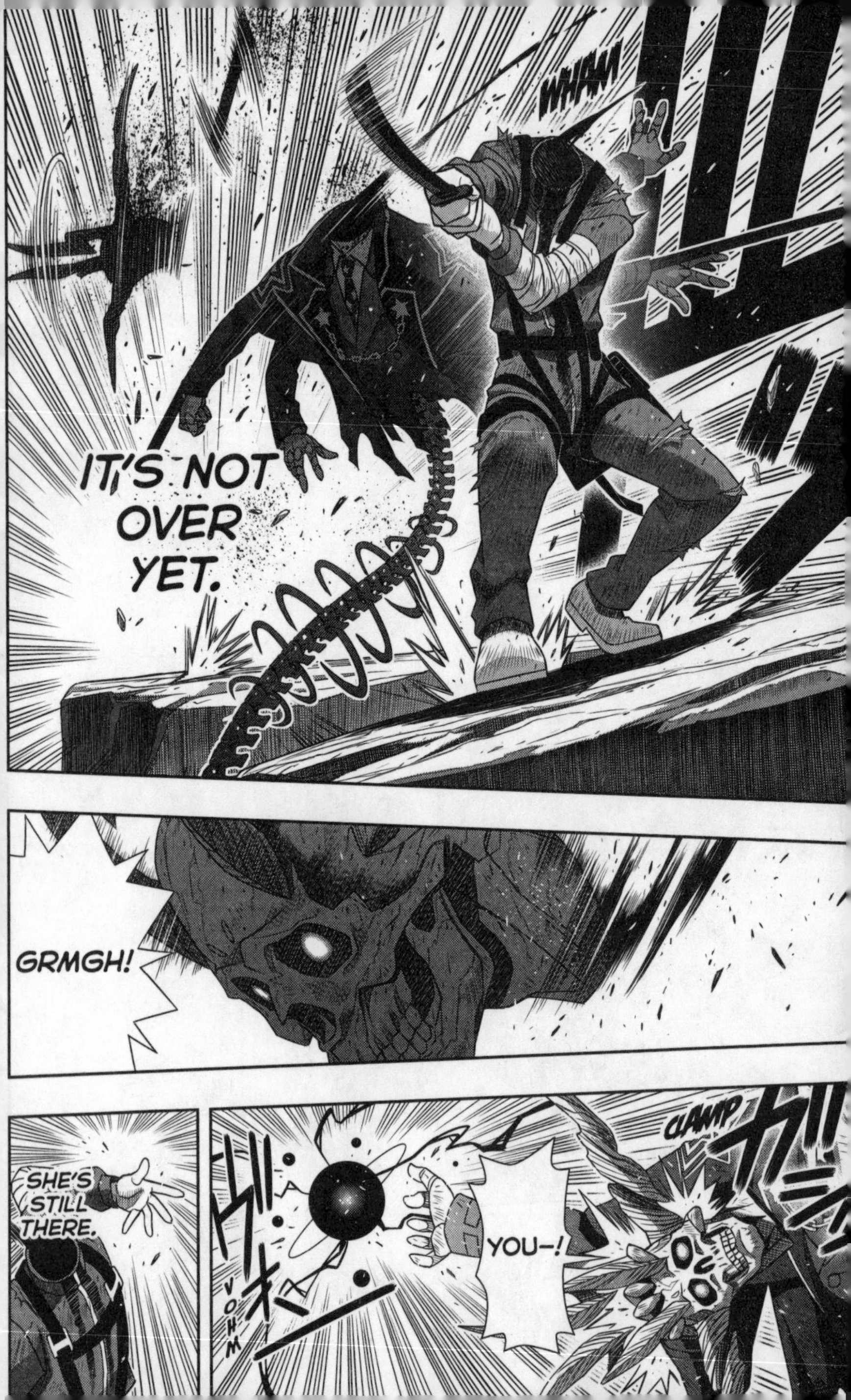
WHAM
IT'S NOT OVER YET.
GRMGH!
CLAMP
YOU–!
VOHM
SHE'S STILL THERE.

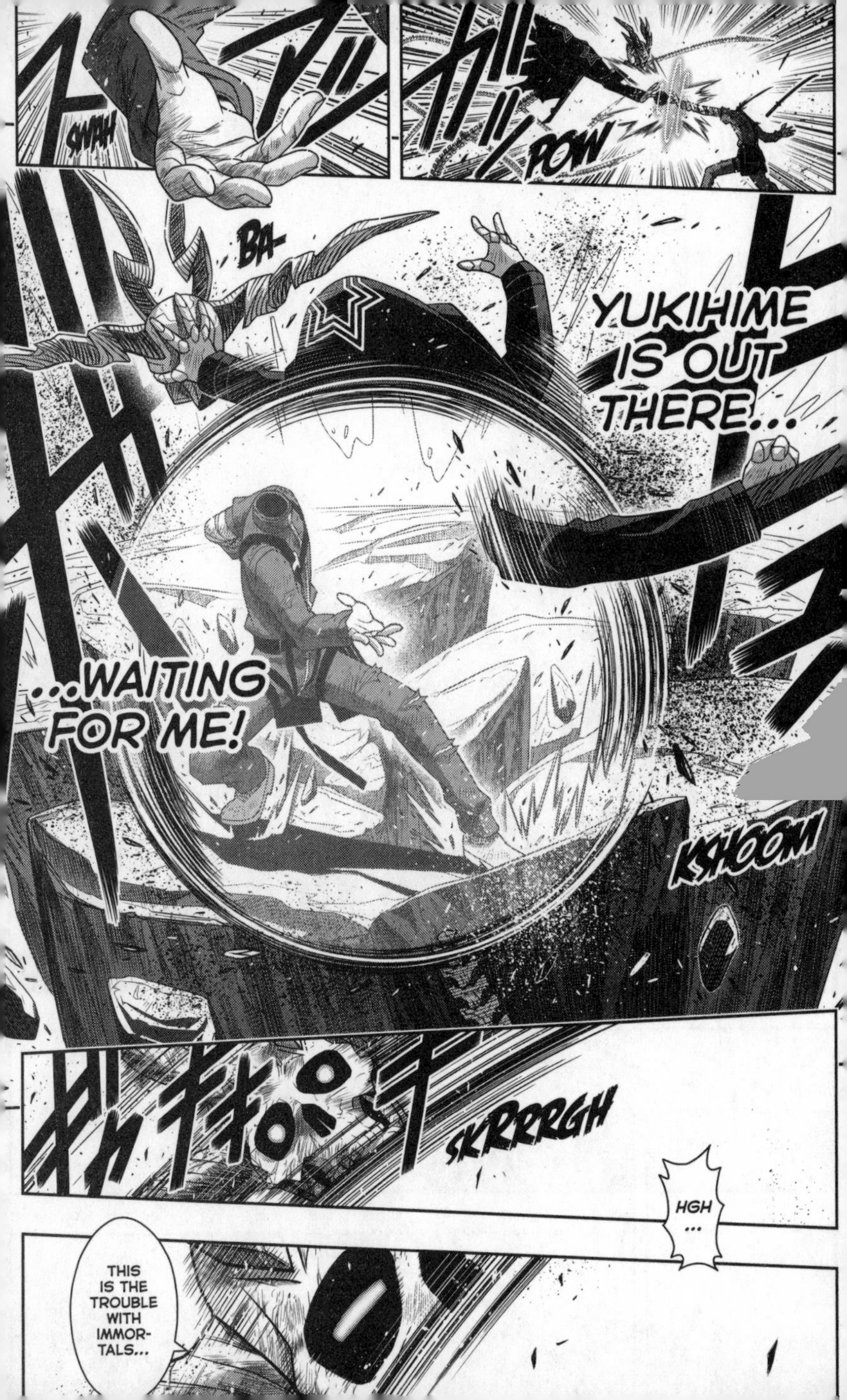
POW
SWAH
YUKIHIME IS OUT THERE...
BA-
...WAITING FOR ME!
KSHOOM
SKRRRGH
HGH...
THIS IS THE TROUBLE WITH IMMORTALS...

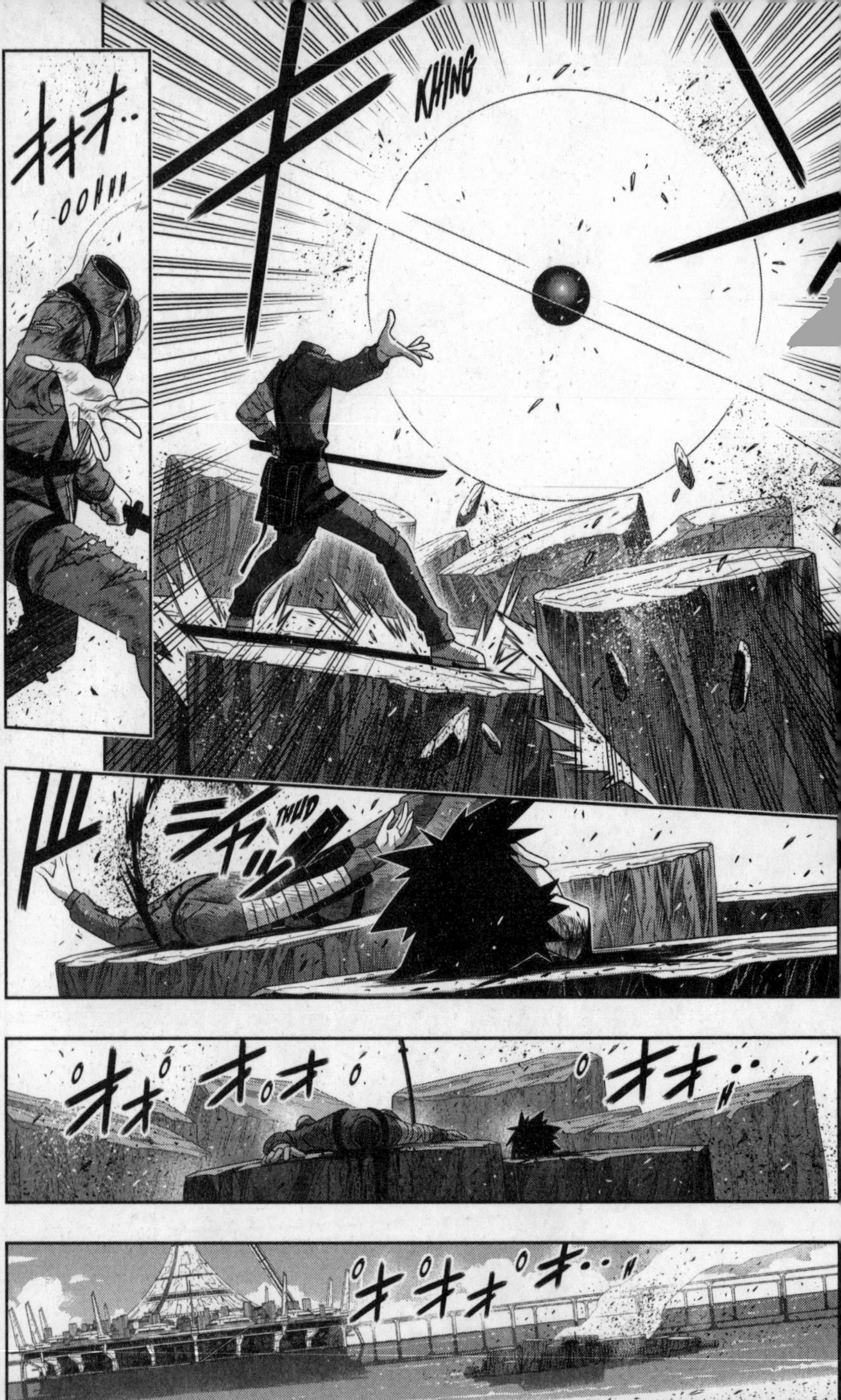
KHING
オオオ‥
OOHHH
ドシャッ
THUD
オオオオオオ‥
オオオオ‥

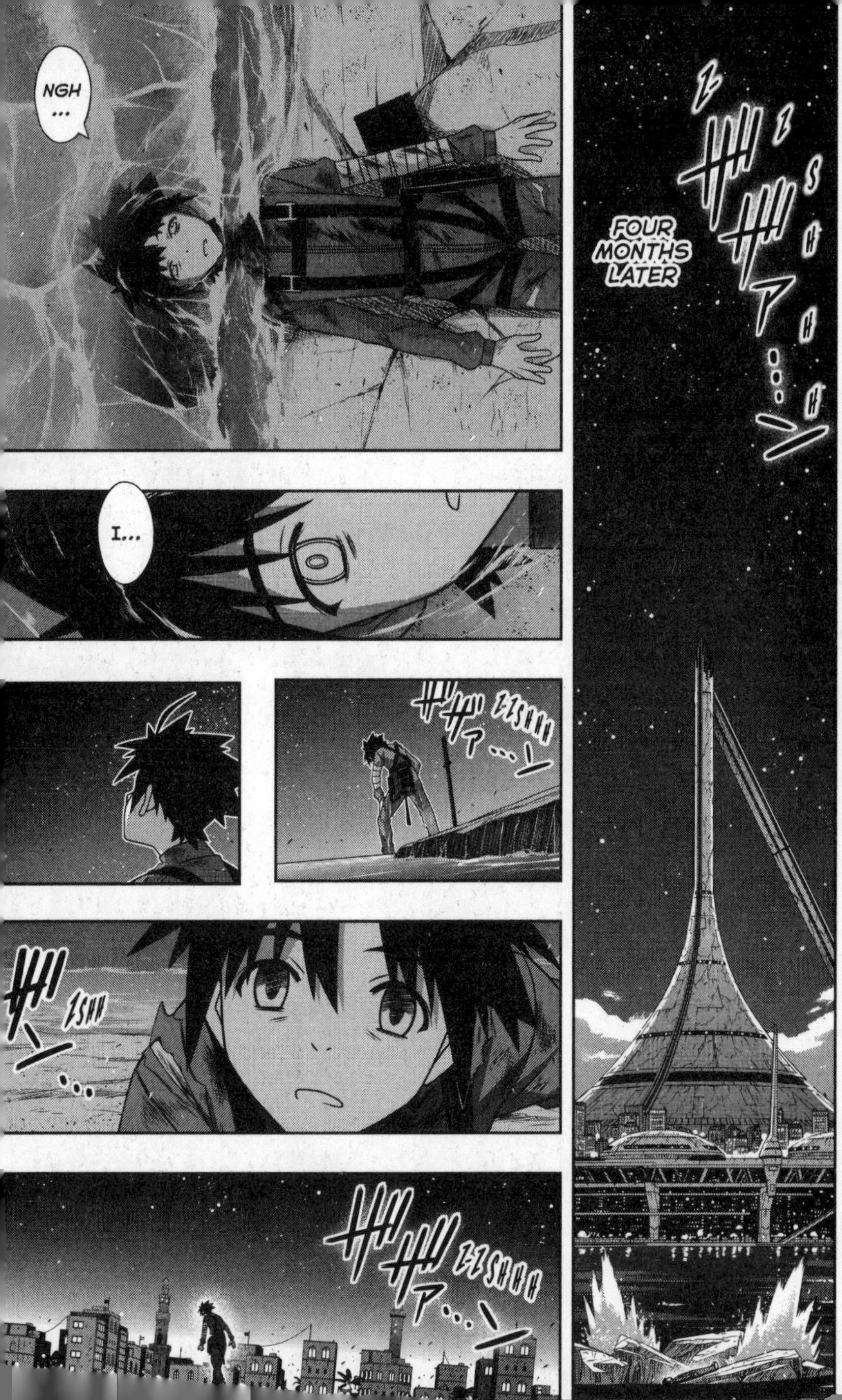
ZZSHHHHH
FOUR MONTHS LATER
NGH...
I...
Z-ZSHHH
ZSHH...
Z-ZSHHH

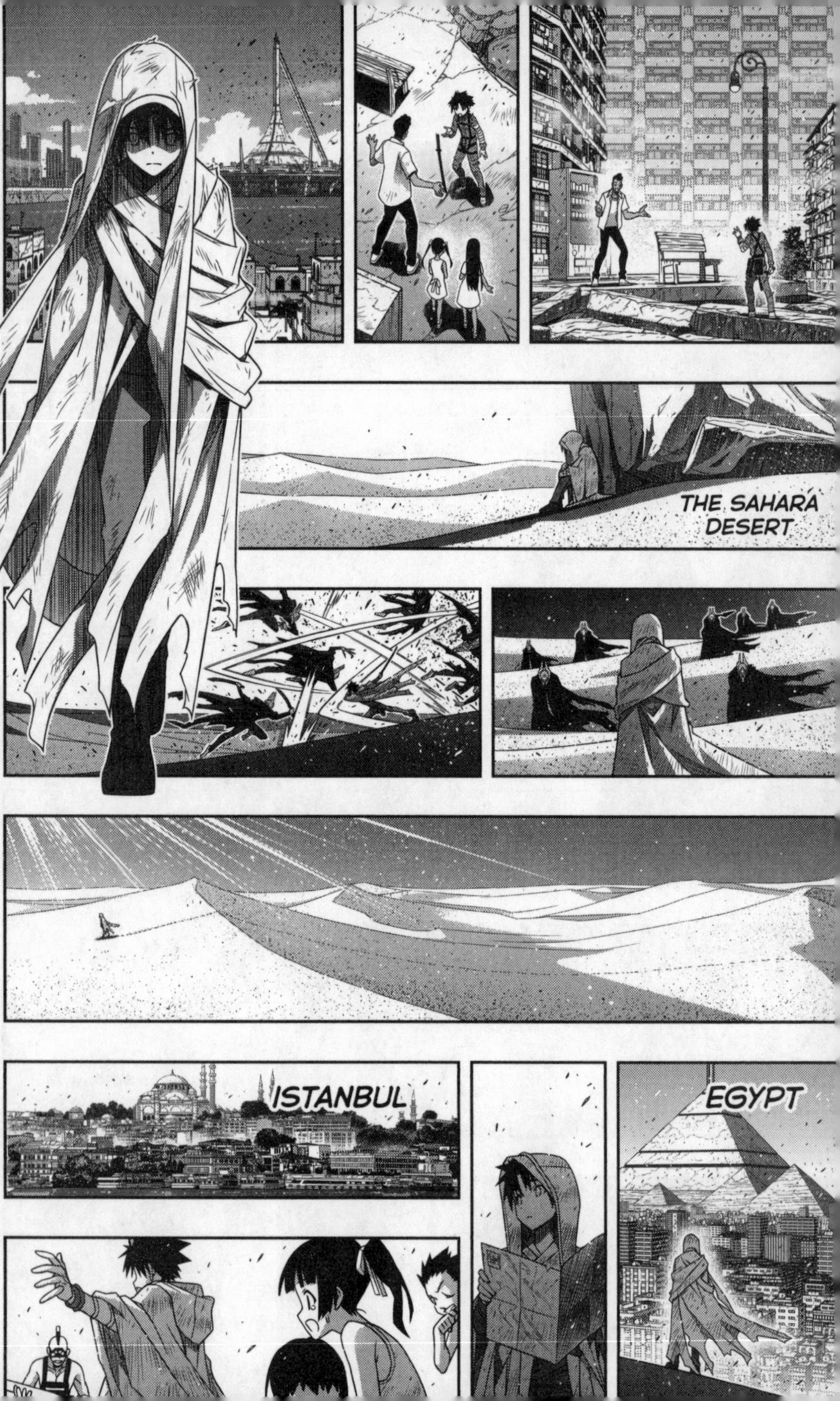
THE SAHARA DESERT
EGYPT
ISTANBUL

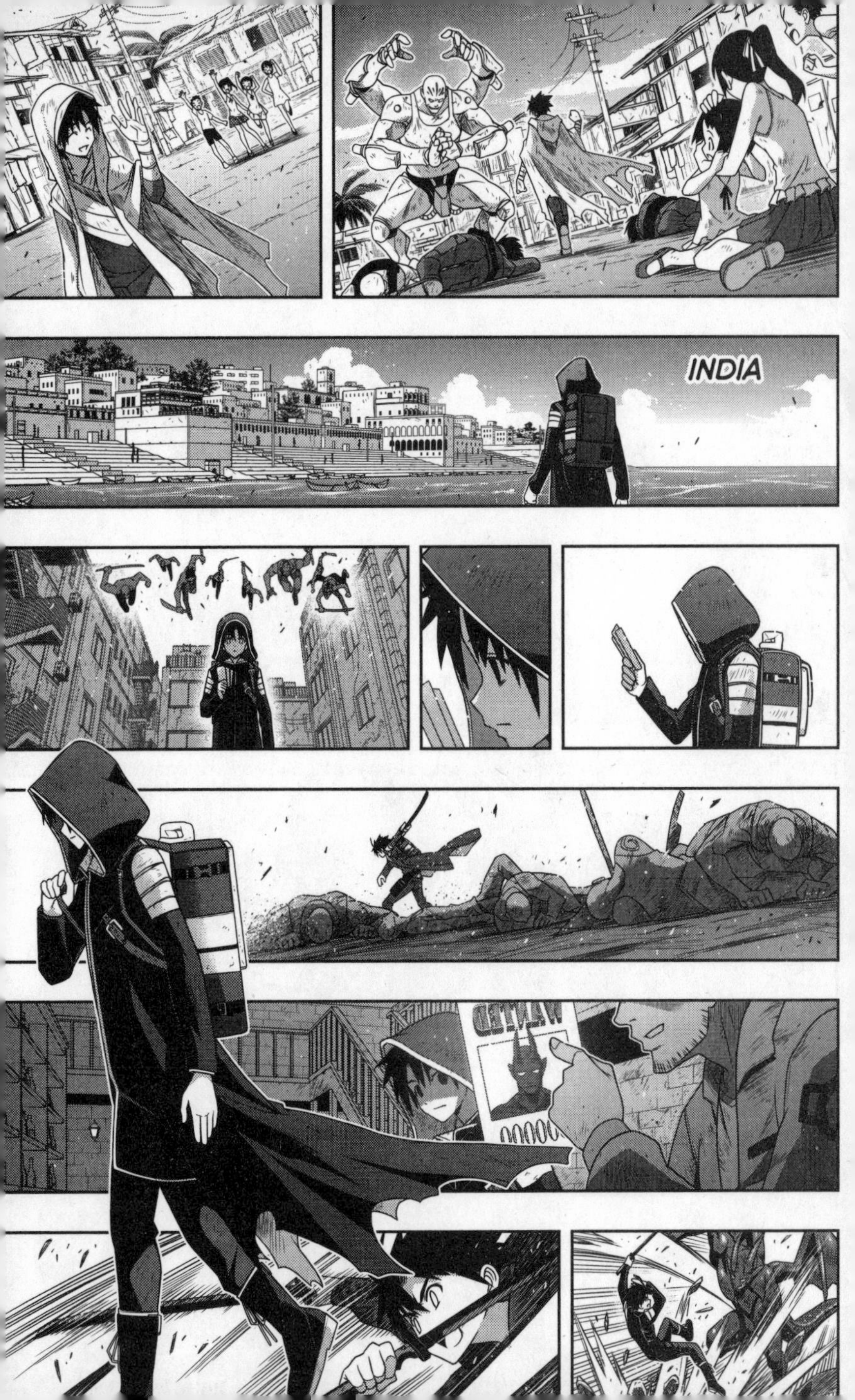
INDIA

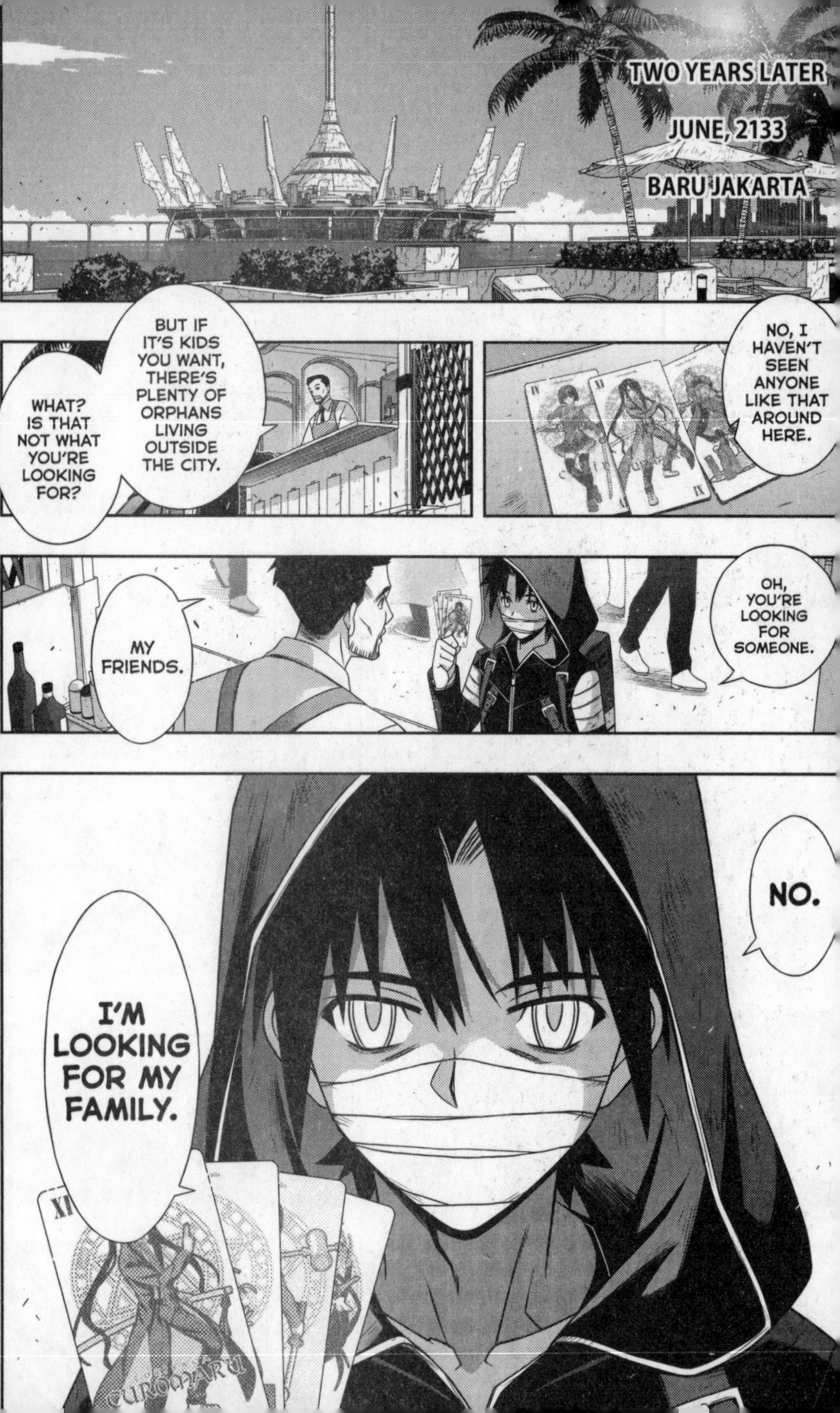
TWO YEARS LATER
JUNE, 2133
BARU JAKARTA
NO, I HAVEN'T SEEN ANYONE LIKE THAT AROUND HERE.
BUT IF IT'S KIDS YOU WANT, THERE'S PLENTY OF ORPHANS LIVING OUTSIDE THE CITY.
WHAT? IS THAT NOT WHAT YOU'RE LOOKING FOR?
OH, YOU'RE LOOKING FOR SOMEONE.
MY FRIENDS.
NO.
I'M LOOKING FOR MY FAMILY.

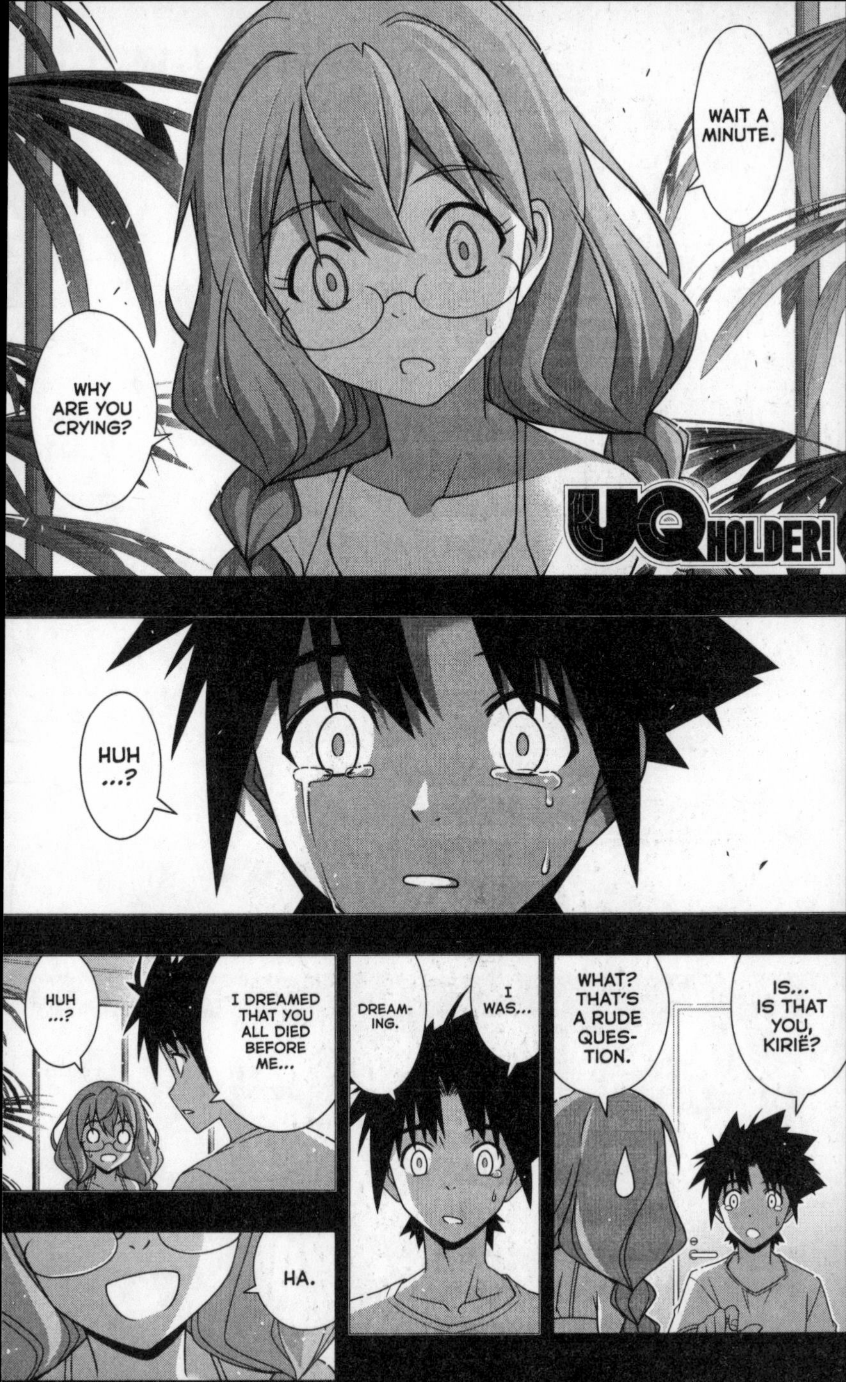
WAIT A MINUTE.
WHY ARE YOU CRYING?
UQ HOLDER!
HUH ...?
IS... IS THAT YOU, KIRIË?
WHAT? THAT'S A RUDE QUES-TION.
I WAS...
DREAM-ING.
I DREAMED THAT YOU ALL DIED BEFORE ME...
HUH ...?
HA.

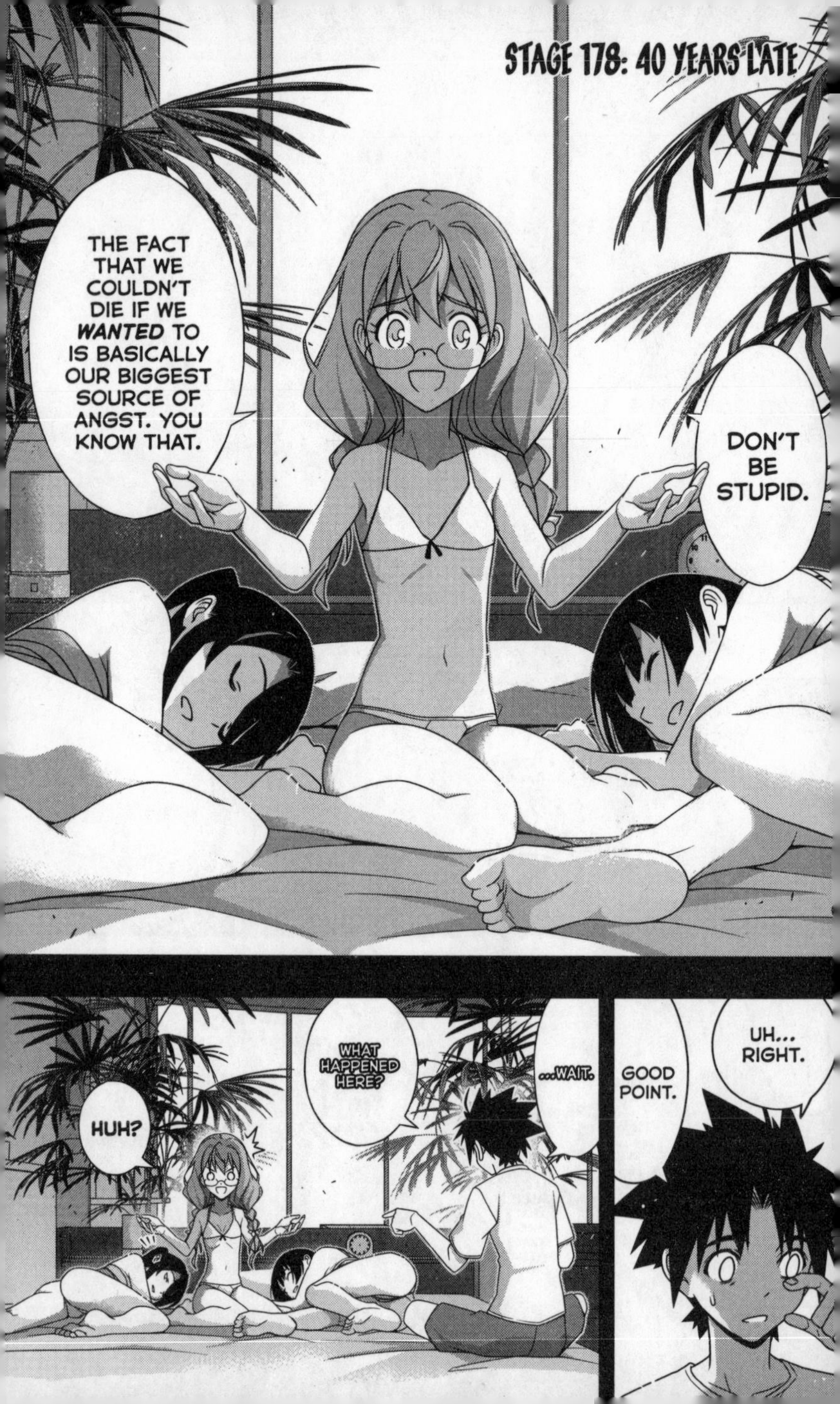
STAGE 178: 40 YEARS LATE
DON'T BE STUPID.
THE FACT THAT WE COULDN'T DIE IF WE *WANTED* TO IS BASICALLY OUR BIGGEST SOURCE OF ANGST. YOU KNOW THAT.
UH... RIGHT.
GOOD POINT.
...WAIT.
WHAT HAPPENED HERE?
HUH?

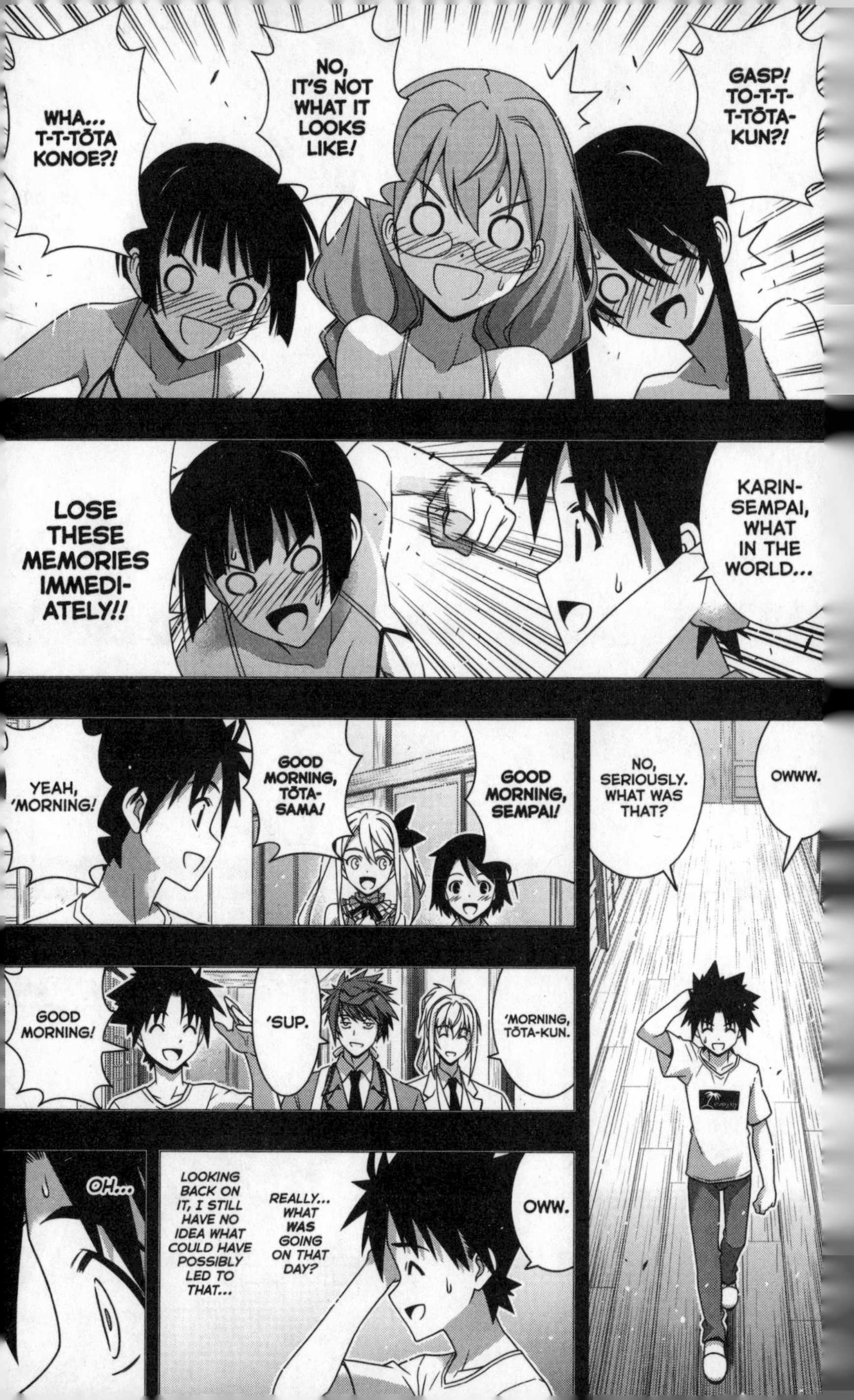
GASP! TO-T-T-T-TŌTA-KUN?!
NO, IT'S NOT WHAT IT LOOKS LIKE!
WHA... T-T-TŌTA KONOE?!
KARIN-SEMPAI, WHAT IN THE WORLD...
LOSE THESE MEMORIES IMMEDIATELY!!
OWWW.
NO, SERIOUSLY. WHAT WAS THAT?
GOOD MORNING, SEMPAI!
GOOD MORNING, TŌTA-SAMA!
YEAH, 'MORNING!
'MORNING, TŌTA-KUN.
'SUP.
GOOD MORNING!
OWW.
REALLY... WHAT WAS GOING ON THAT DAY?
LOOKING BACK ON IT, I STILL HAVE NO IDEA WHAT COULD HAVE POSSIBLY LED TO THAT...
OH...

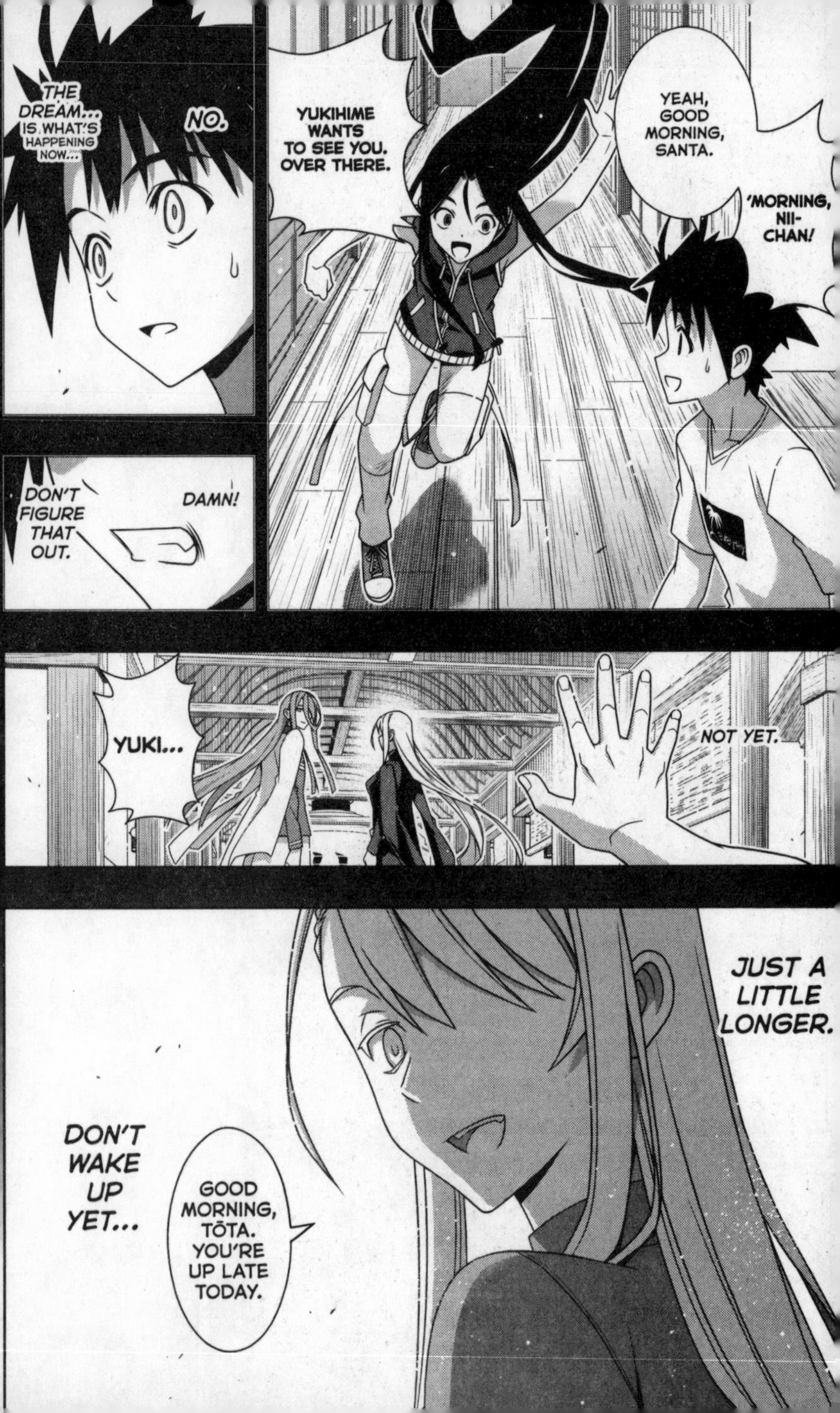
'MORNING, NII-CHAN!
YEAH, GOOD MORNING, SANTA.
YUKIHIME WANTS TO SEE YOU. OVER THERE.
NO.
THE DREAM... IS WHAT'S HAPPENING NOW...
DAMN!
DON'T FIGURE THAT OUT.
NOT YET.
YUKI...
JUST A LITTLE LONGER.
GOOD MORNING, TŌTA. YOU'RE UP LATE TODAY.
DON'T WAKE UP YET...

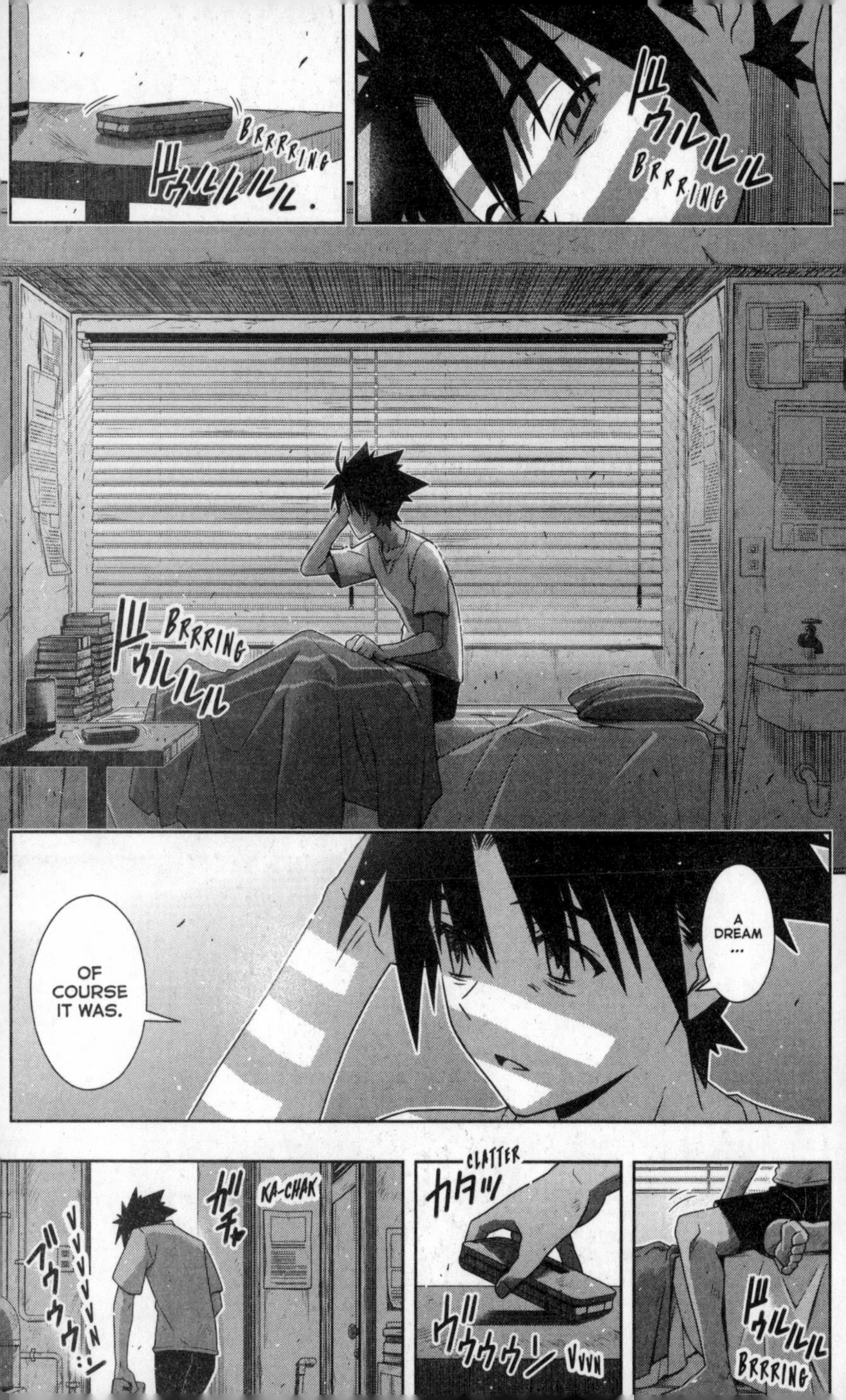
ドゥルルルル
BRRRING
BRRRRING
ドゥルルルル.
ドゥルルル
BRRRING
A DREAM ...
OF COURSE IT WAS.
ドゥルルル
BRRRING
CLATTER
カタッ
ヴゥゥゥン
VVVN
ガチャ
KA-CHAK
VVVVVVVN
ブゥゥゥ…ン

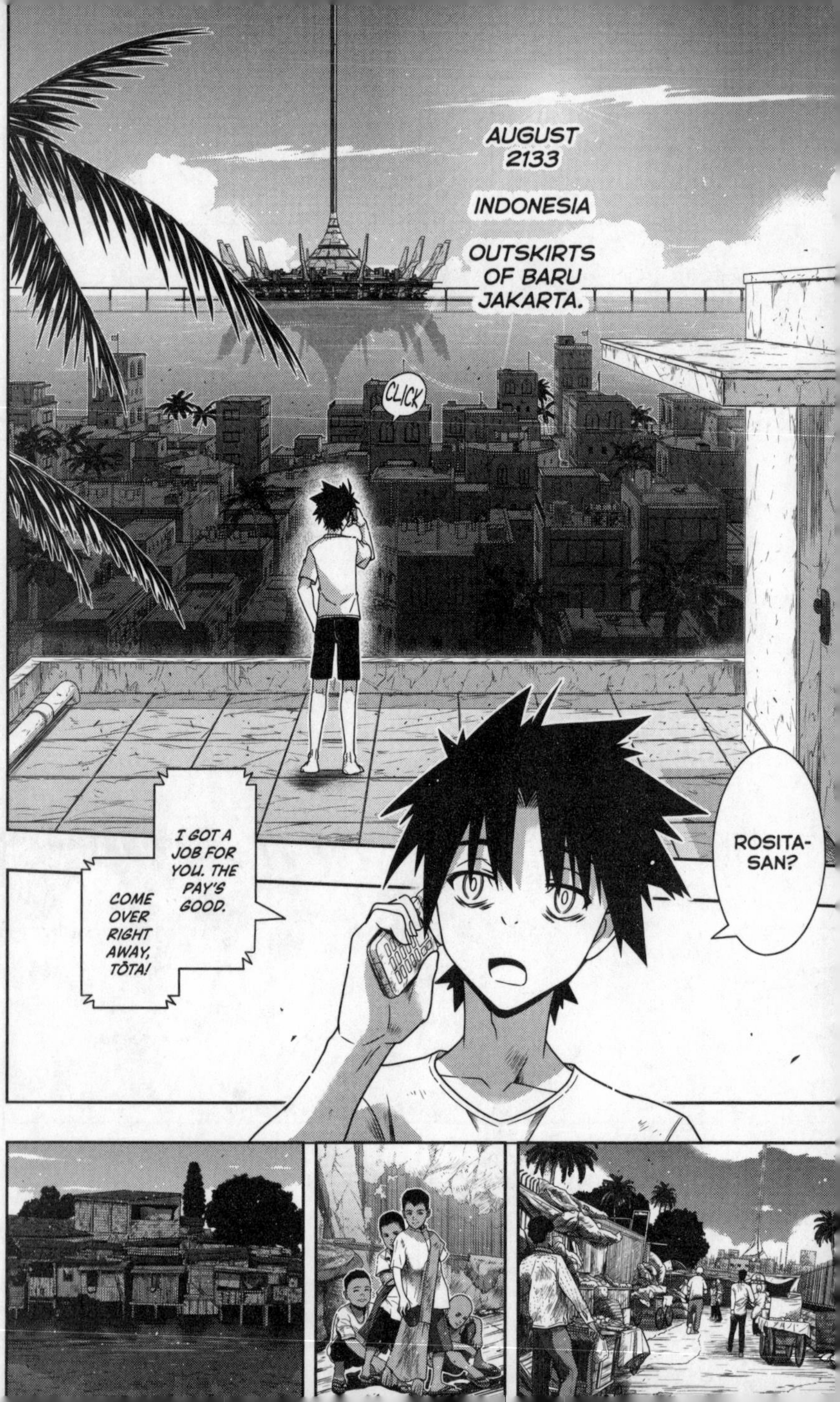
AUGUST 2133
INDONESIA
OUTSKIRTS OF BARU JAKARTA.
CLICK
ROSITA-SAN?
I GOT A JOB FOR YOU. THE PAY'S GOOD.
COME OVER RIGHT AWAY, TŌTA!

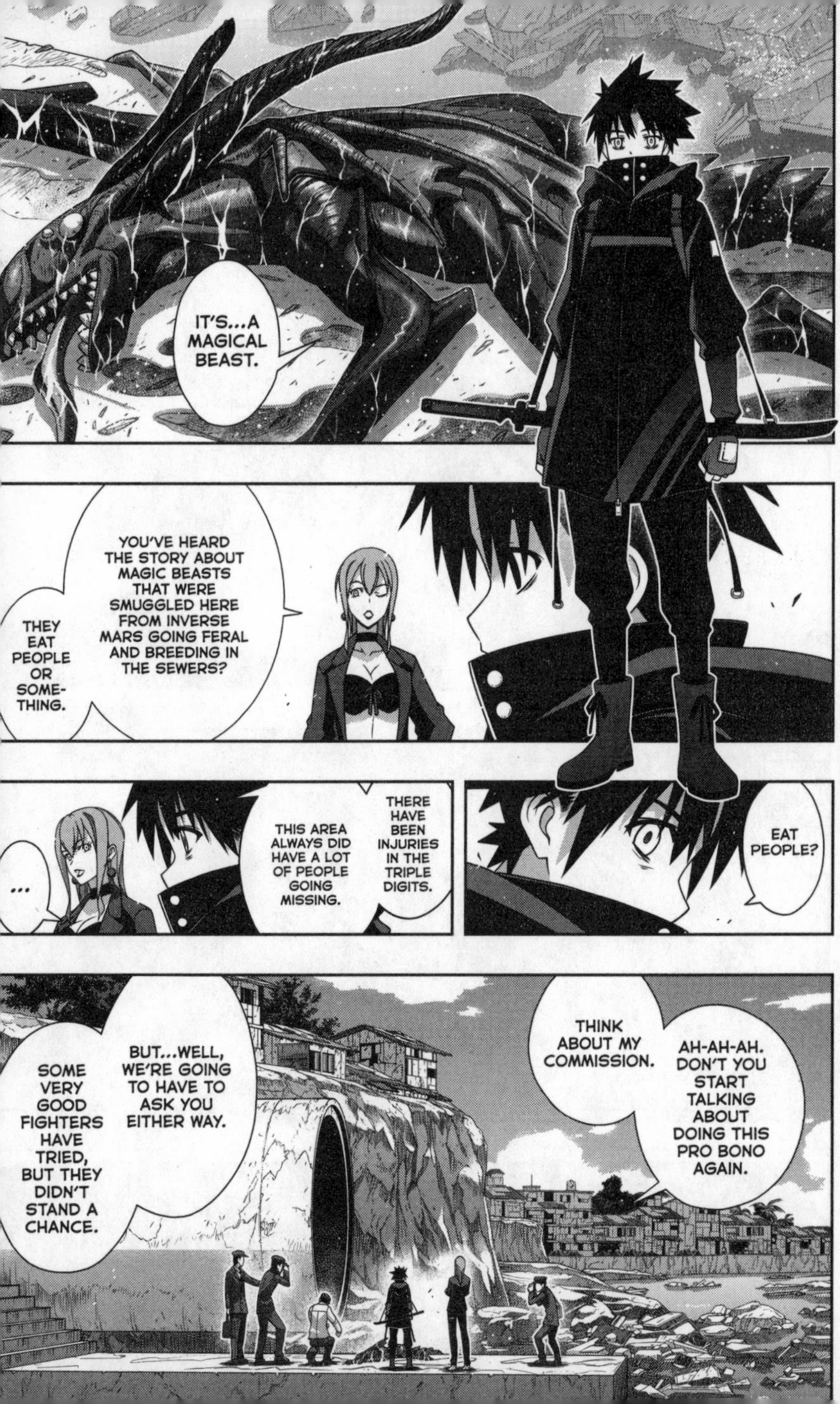
IT'S...A MAGICAL BEAST.
YOU'VE HEARD THE STORY ABOUT MAGIC BEASTS THAT WERE SMUGGLED HERE FROM INVERSE MARS GOING FERAL AND BREEDING IN THE SEWERS?
THEY EAT PEOPLE OR SOME-THING.
EAT PEOPLE?
THERE HAVE BEEN INJURIES IN THE TRIPLE DIGITS.
THIS AREA ALWAYS DID HAVE A LOT OF PEOPLE GOING MISSING.
...
AH-AH-AH. DON'T YOU START TALKING ABOUT DOING THIS PRO BONO AGAIN.
THINK ABOUT MY COMMISSION.
BUT...WELL, WE'RE GOING TO HAVE TO ASK YOU EITHER WAY.
SOME VERY GOOD FIGHTERS HAVE TRIED, BUT THEY DIDN'T STAND A CHANCE.

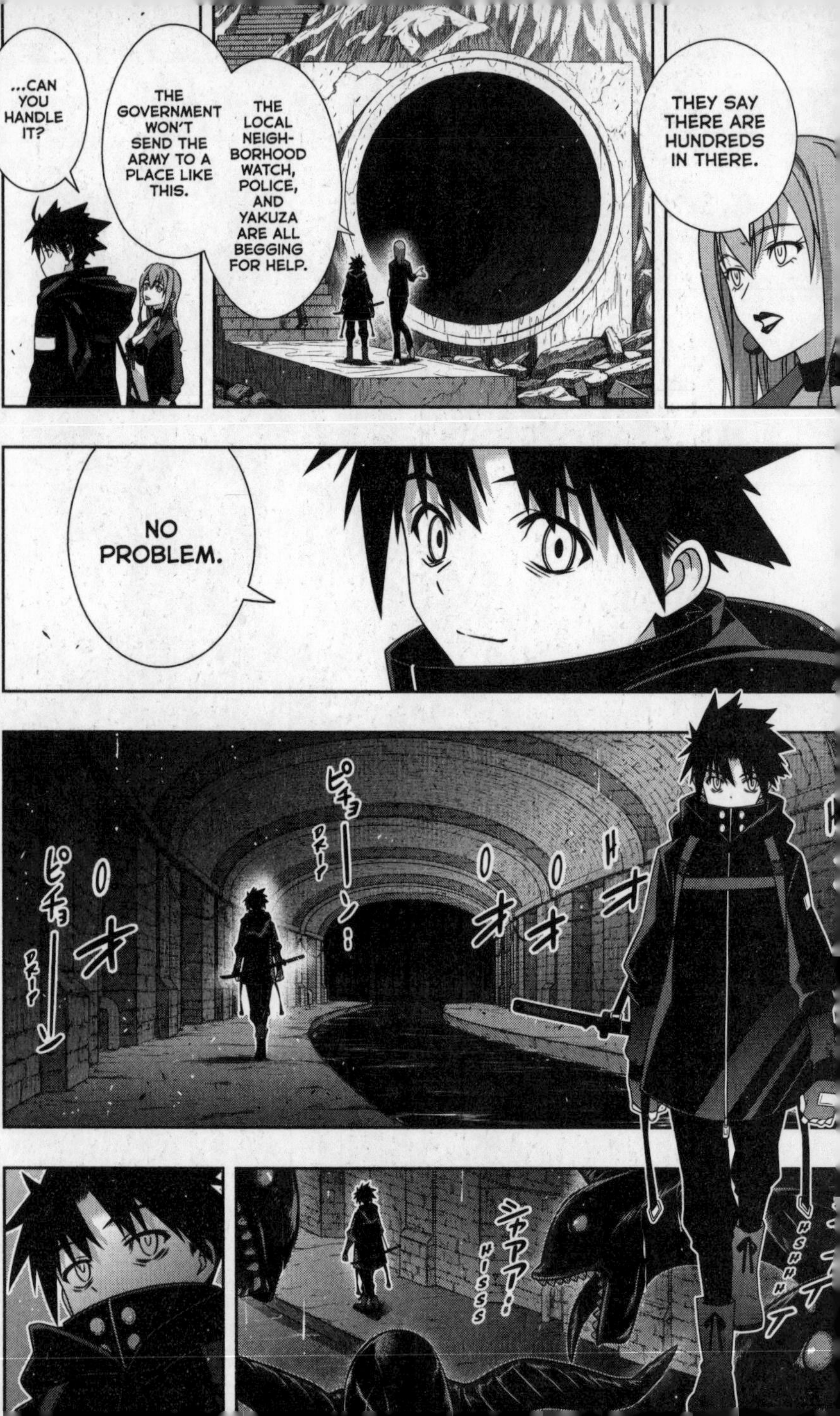
THEY SAY THERE ARE HUNDREDS IN THERE.
THE LOCAL NEIGHBORHOOD WATCH, POLICE, AND YAKUZA ARE ALL BEGGING FOR HELP.
THE GOVERNMENT WON'T SEND THE ARMY TO A PLACE LIKE THIS.
...CAN YOU HANDLE IT?
NO PROBLEM.
オオオオ
HOOO
ピチョーン…
DRIP
ピチョ
DRIP
HSHHH
シャアア‼
HISSS

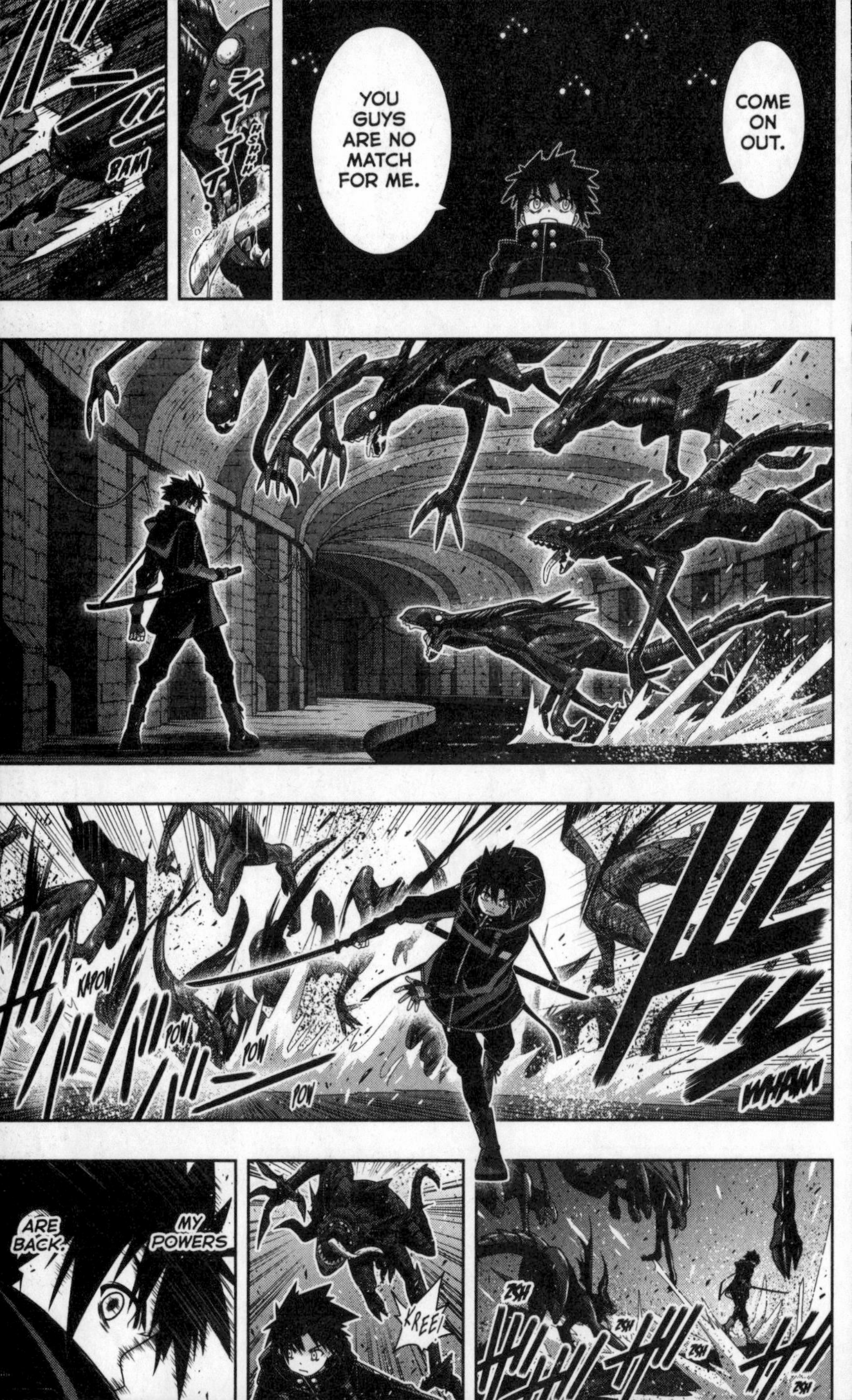
COME ON OUT.
YOU GUYS ARE NO MATCH FOR ME.
HSHHH
BAM
WHAM
POW
POW
POW
KAPOW
ZSH
ZSH
ZSH
ZSH
KREE!
MY POWERS
ARE BACK.

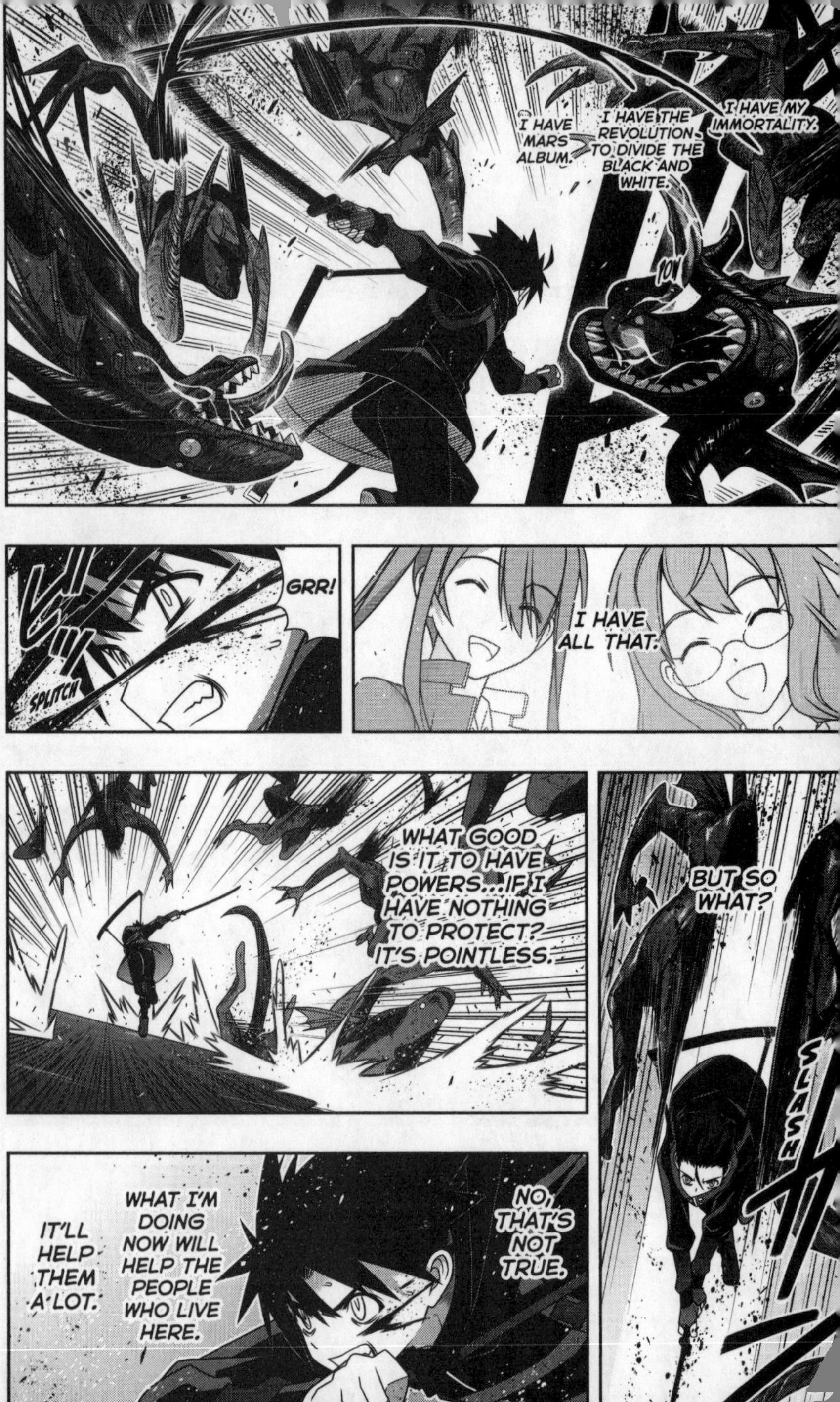
I HAVE MY IMMORTALITY.
I HAVE THE REVOLUTION TO DIVIDE THE BLACK AND WHITE.
I HAVE MARS ALBUM.
I HAVE ALL THAT.
GRR!
SPLITCH
BUT SO WHAT?
SLASH
WHAT GOOD IS IT TO HAVE POWERS...IF I HAVE NOTHING TO PROTECT? IT'S POINTLESS.
NO, THAT'S NOT TRUE.
WHAT I'M DOING NOW WILL HELP THE PEOPLE WHO LIVE HERE.
IT'LL HELP THEM A LOT.

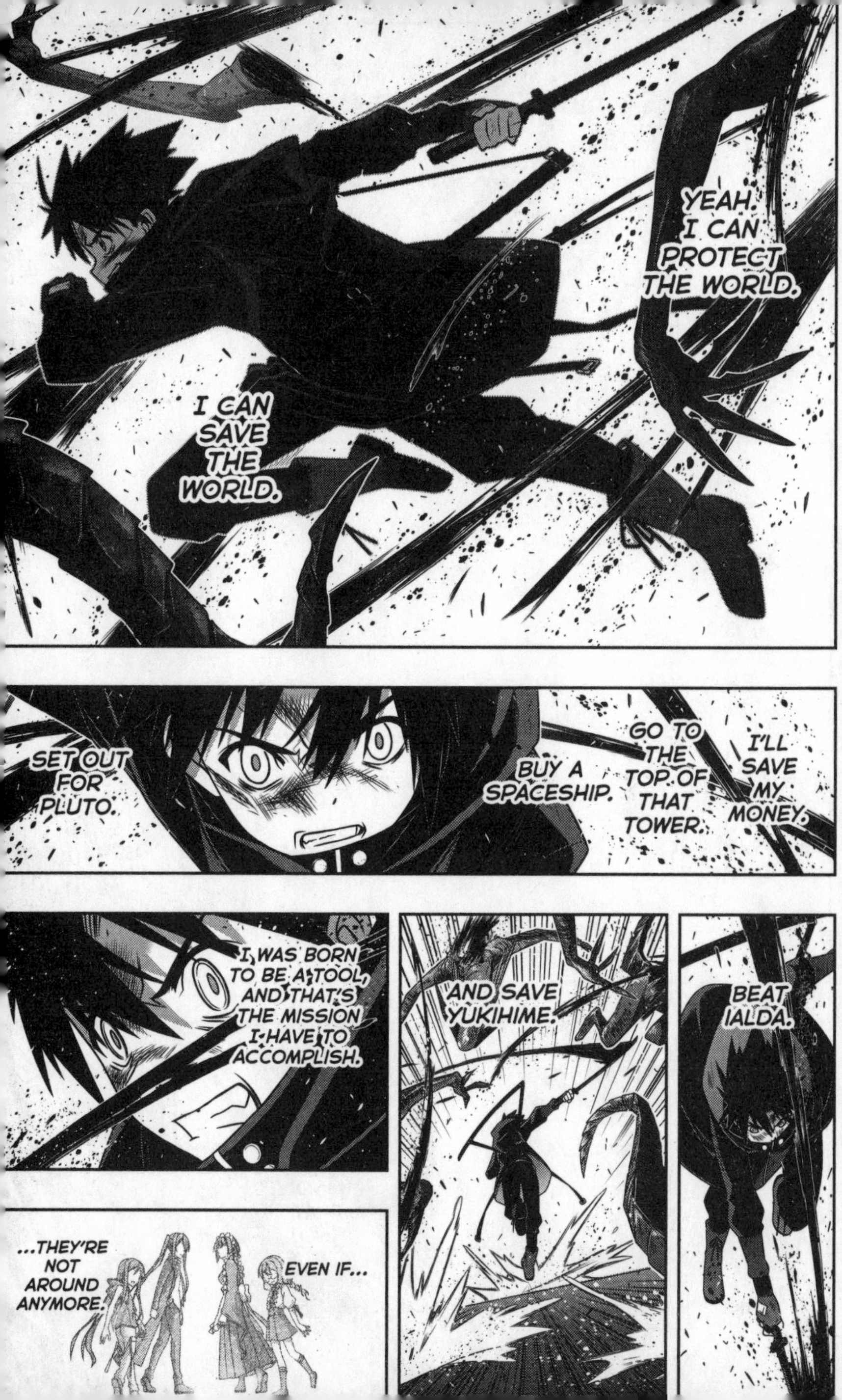
YEAH. I CAN PROTECT THE WORLD.
I CAN SAVE THE WORLD.
I'LL SAVE MY MONEY.
GO TO THE TOP OF THAT TOWER.
BUY A SPACESHIP.
SET OUT FOR PLUTO.
BEAT IALDA.
AND SAVE YUKIHIME.
I WAS BORN TO BE A TOOL, AND THAT'S THE MISSION I HAVE TO ACCOMPLISH.
EVEN IF...
...THEY'RE NOT AROUND ANYMORE.

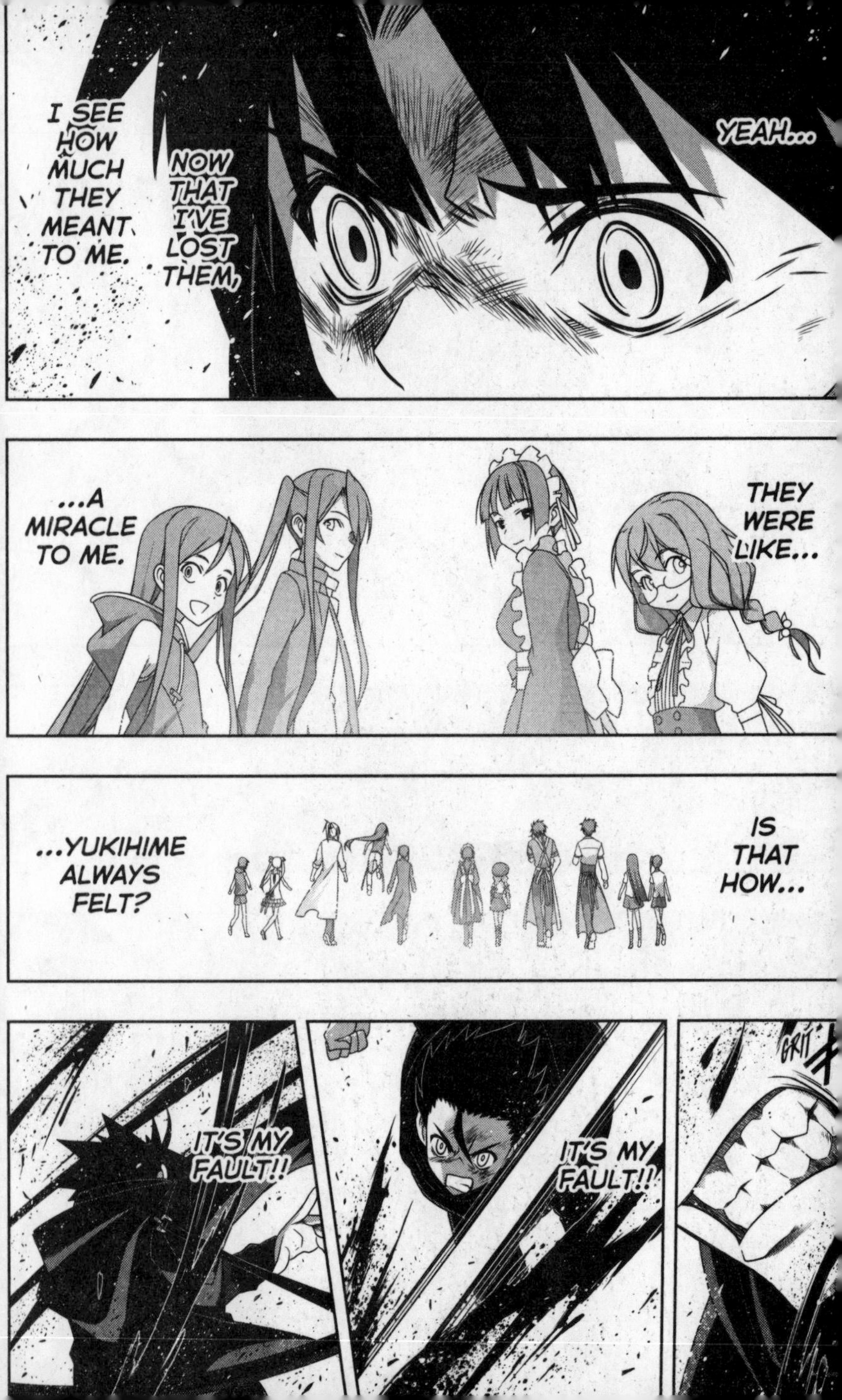
YEAH...
NOW THAT I'VE LOST THEM,
I SEE HOW MUCH THEY MEANT TO ME.
THEY WERE LIKE...
...A MIRACLE TO ME.
IS THAT HOW...
...YUKIHIME ALWAYS FELT?
GRIT
IT'S MY FAULT!!
IT'S MY FAULT!!

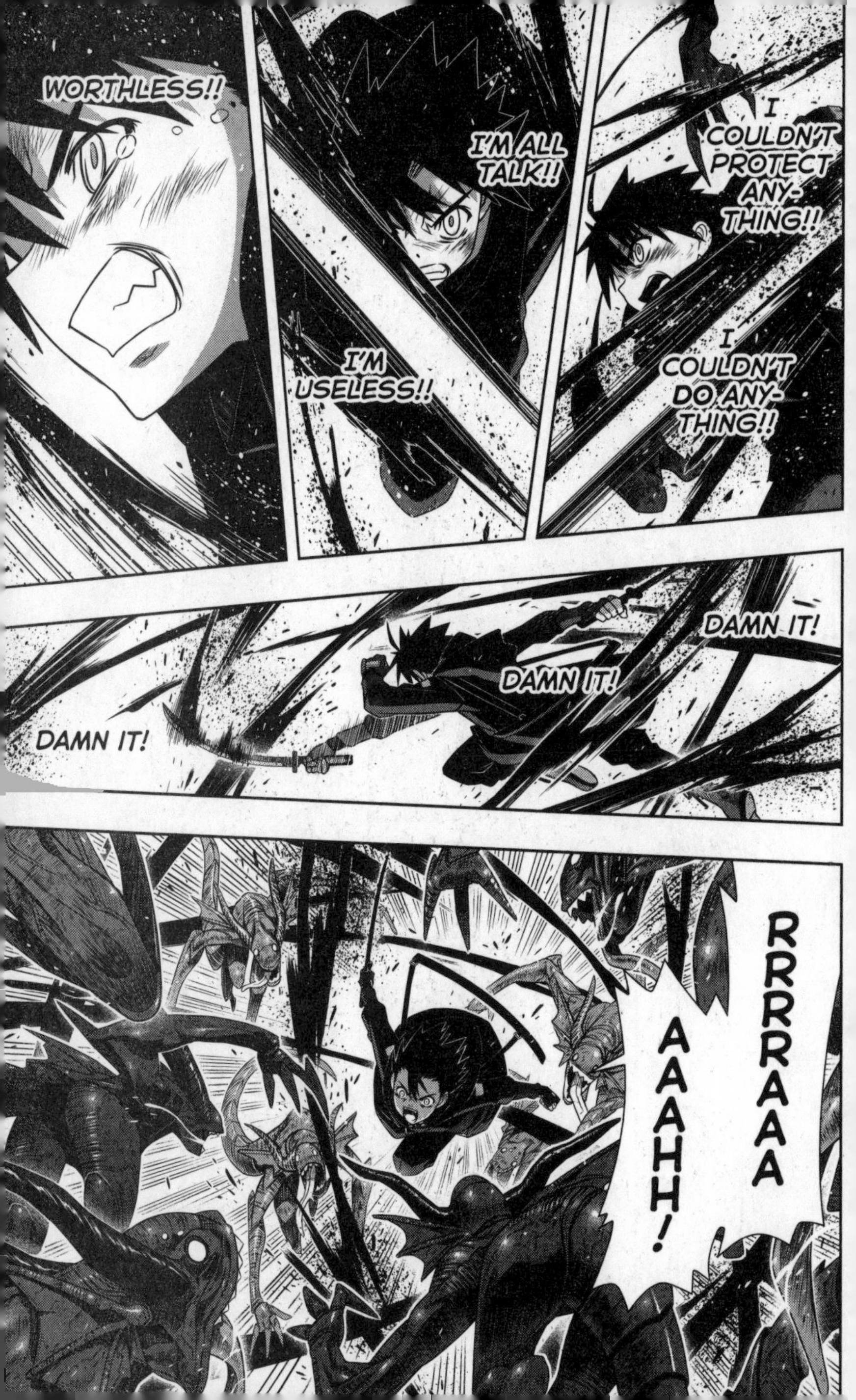
I COULDN'T PROTECT ANYTHING!!
I COULDN'T DO ANYTHING!!
I'M ALL TALK!!
I'M USELESS!!
WORTHLESS!!
DAMN IT!
DAMN IT!
DAMN IT!
RRRAAAAAAHH!

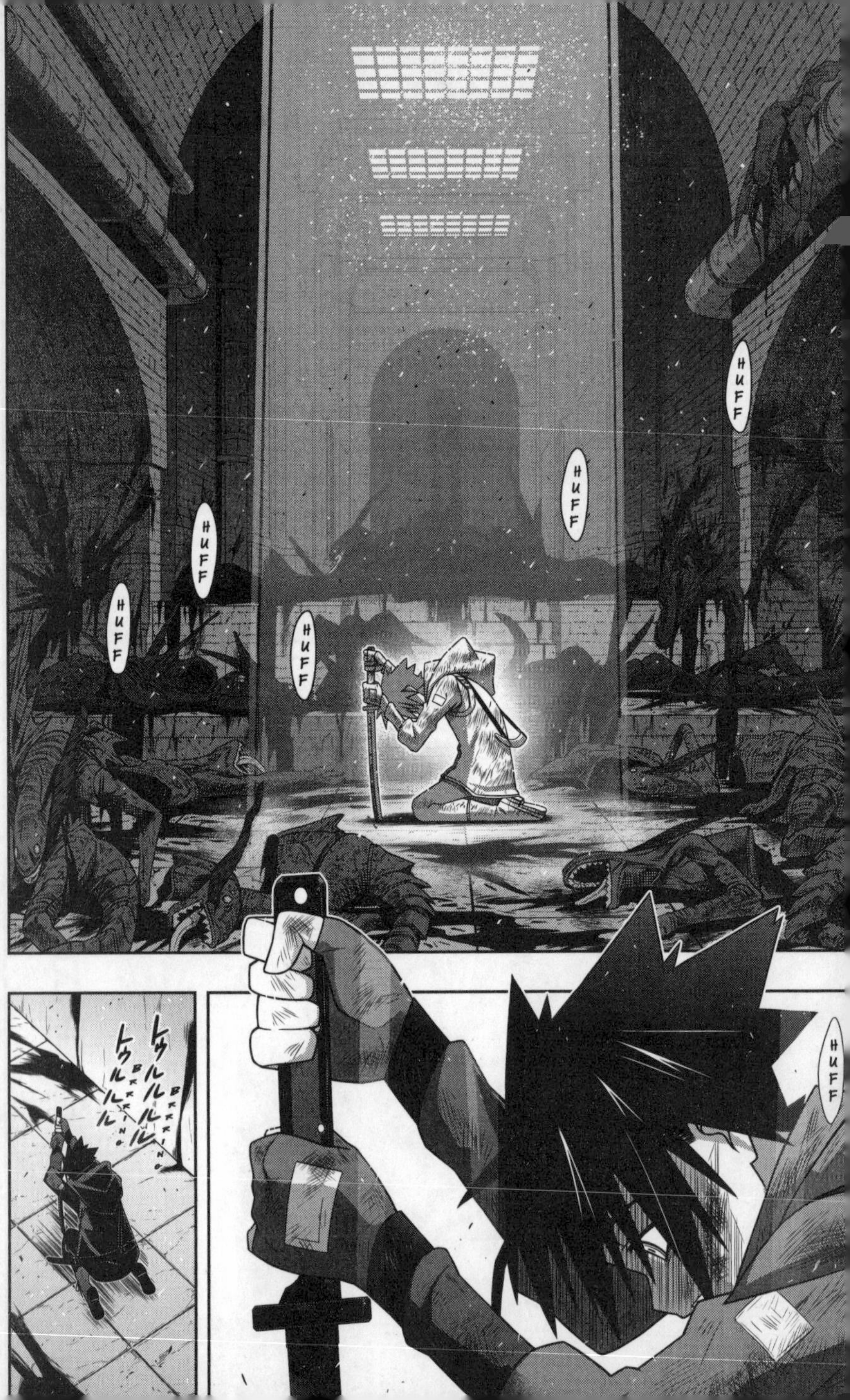
HUFF
HUFF
HUFF
HUFF
HUFF
HUFF
トゥルルルル
BRRRING
トゥルルル
BRRRING

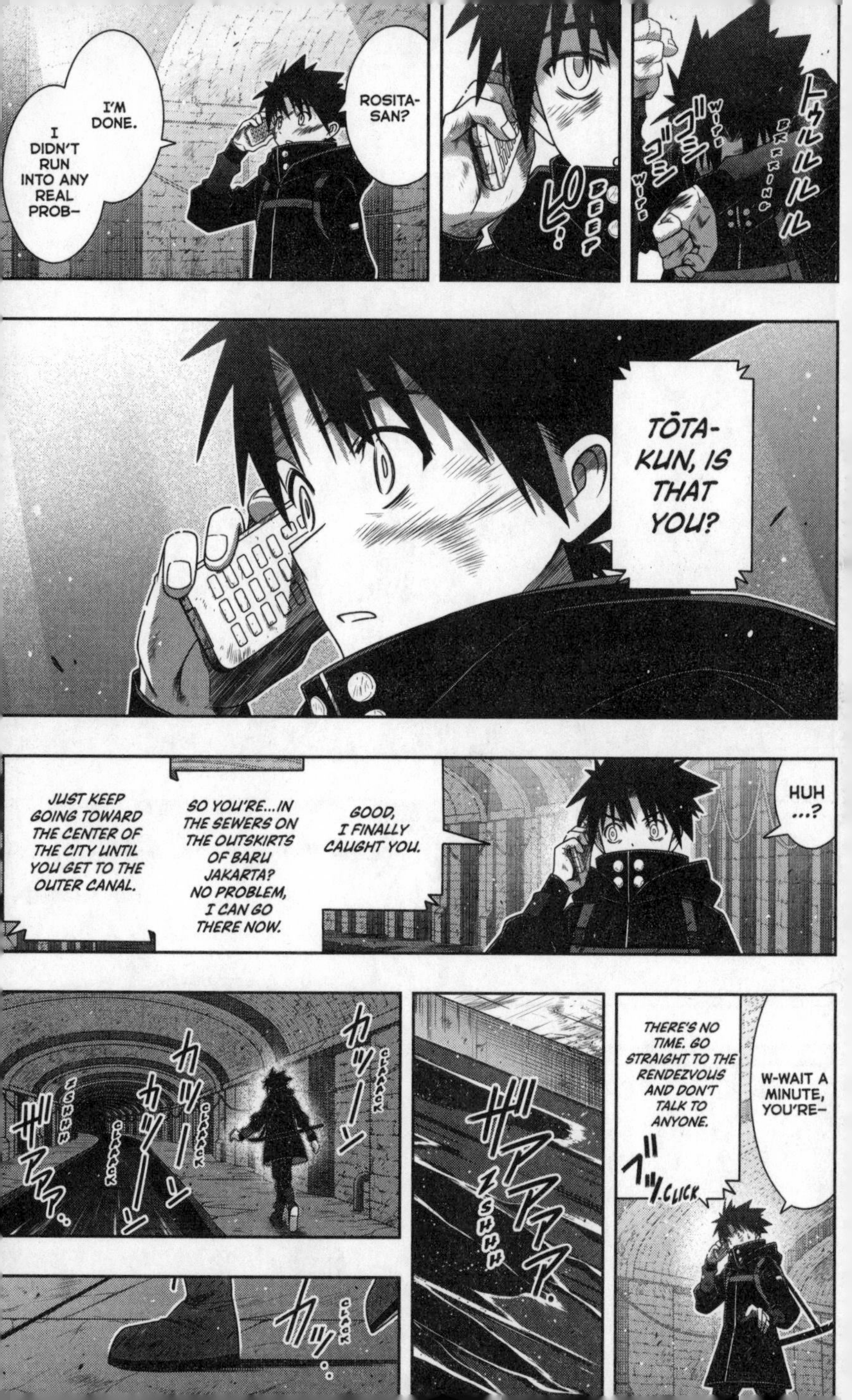

トゥルルル
BRRRING
ゴシゴシ
WIPE WIPE
ピッ
BEEP
ROSITA-SAN?
I'M DONE.
I DIDN'T RUN INTO ANY REAL PROB—
TŌTA-KUN, IS THAT YOU?
HUH ...?
GOOD, I FINALLY CAUGHT YOU.
SO YOU'RE...IN THE SEWERS ON THE OUTSKIRTS OF BARU JAKARTA? NO PROBLEM, I CAN GO THERE NOW.
JUST KEEP GOING TOWARD THE CENTER OF THE CITY UNTIL YOU GET TO THE OUTER CANAL.
THERE'S NO TIME. GO STRAIGHT TO THE RENDEZVOUS AND DON'T TALK TO ANYONE.
W-WAIT A MINUTE, YOU'RE—
ブツッ
CLICK
ザァァァァ
ZSHHH
カツーン
CLAAACK
カツーン
CLAAACK
カツーン
CLAAACK
ザァァァ..
ZSHHH
カッ..
CLACK

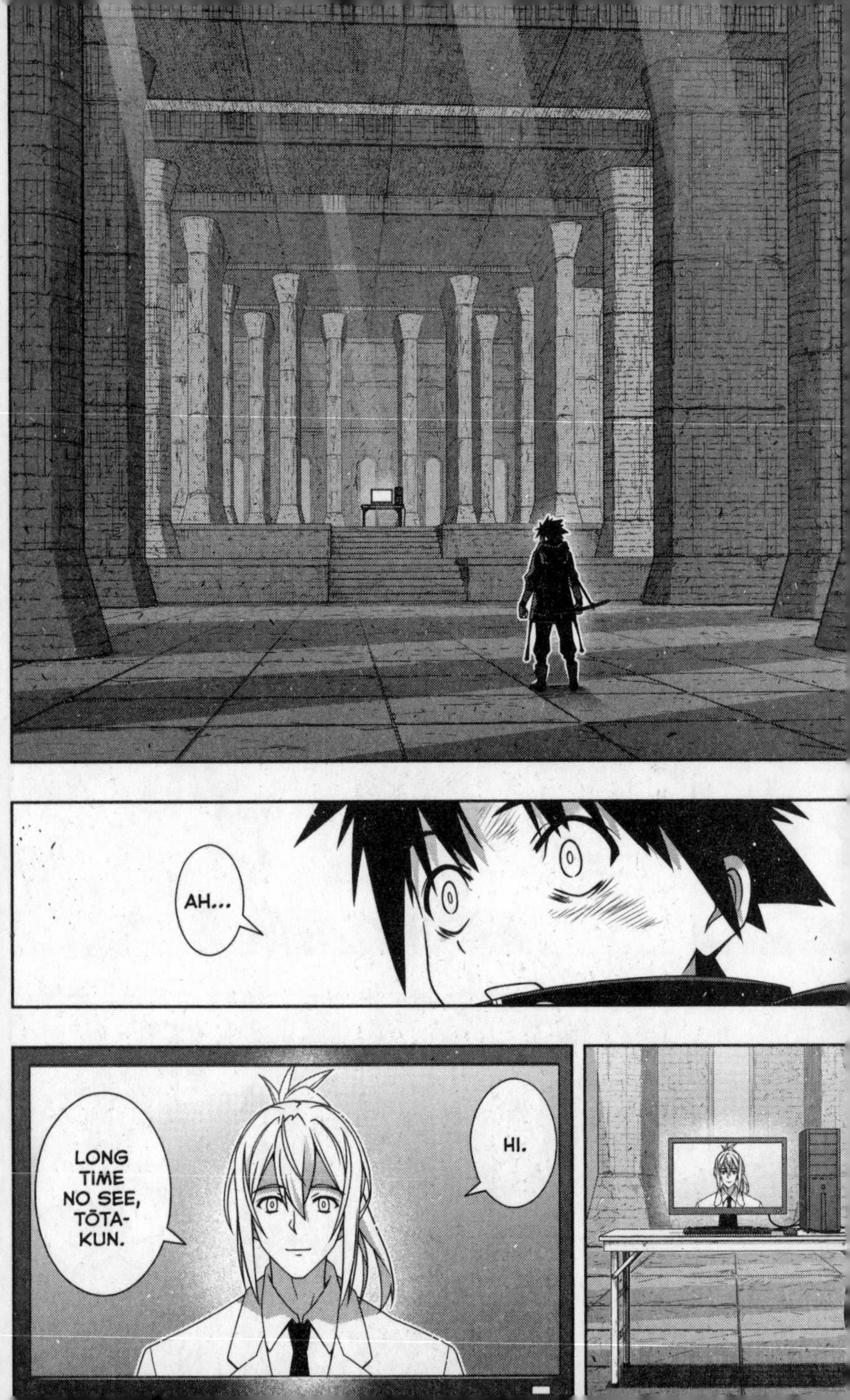
AH...
HI.
LONG TIME NO SEE, TŌTA-KUN.

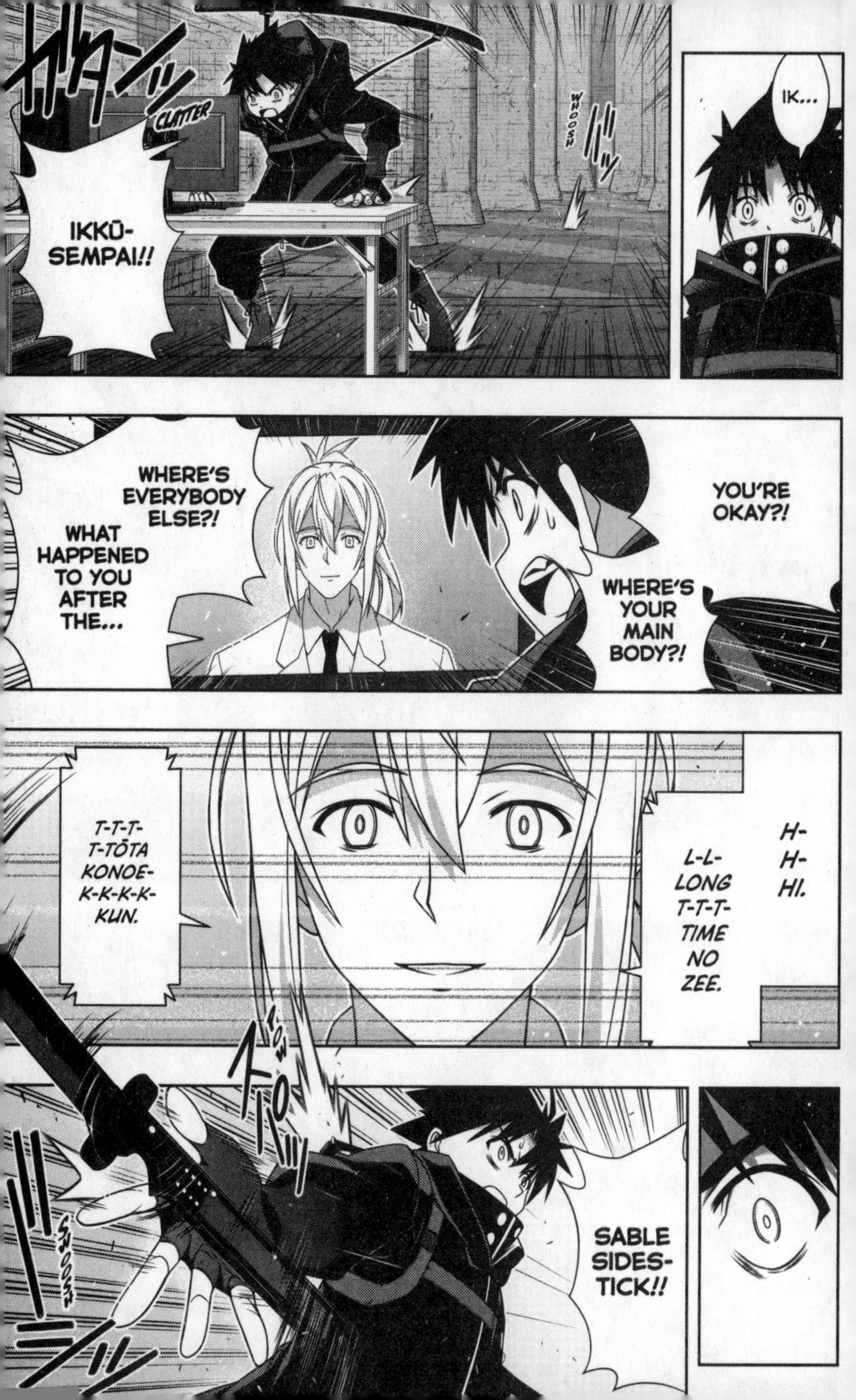
IK...
WHOOSH
CLATTER
IKKŪ-SEMPAI!!
YOU'RE OKAY?!
WHERE'S YOUR MAIN BODY?!
WHERE'S EVERYBODY ELSE?!
WHAT HAPPENED TO YOU AFTER THE...
H-H-HI.
L-L-LONG T-T-T-TIME NO ZEE.
T-T-T-T-TŌTA KONOE-K-K-K-K-KUN.
SABLE SIDES-TICK!!
SWOOSH

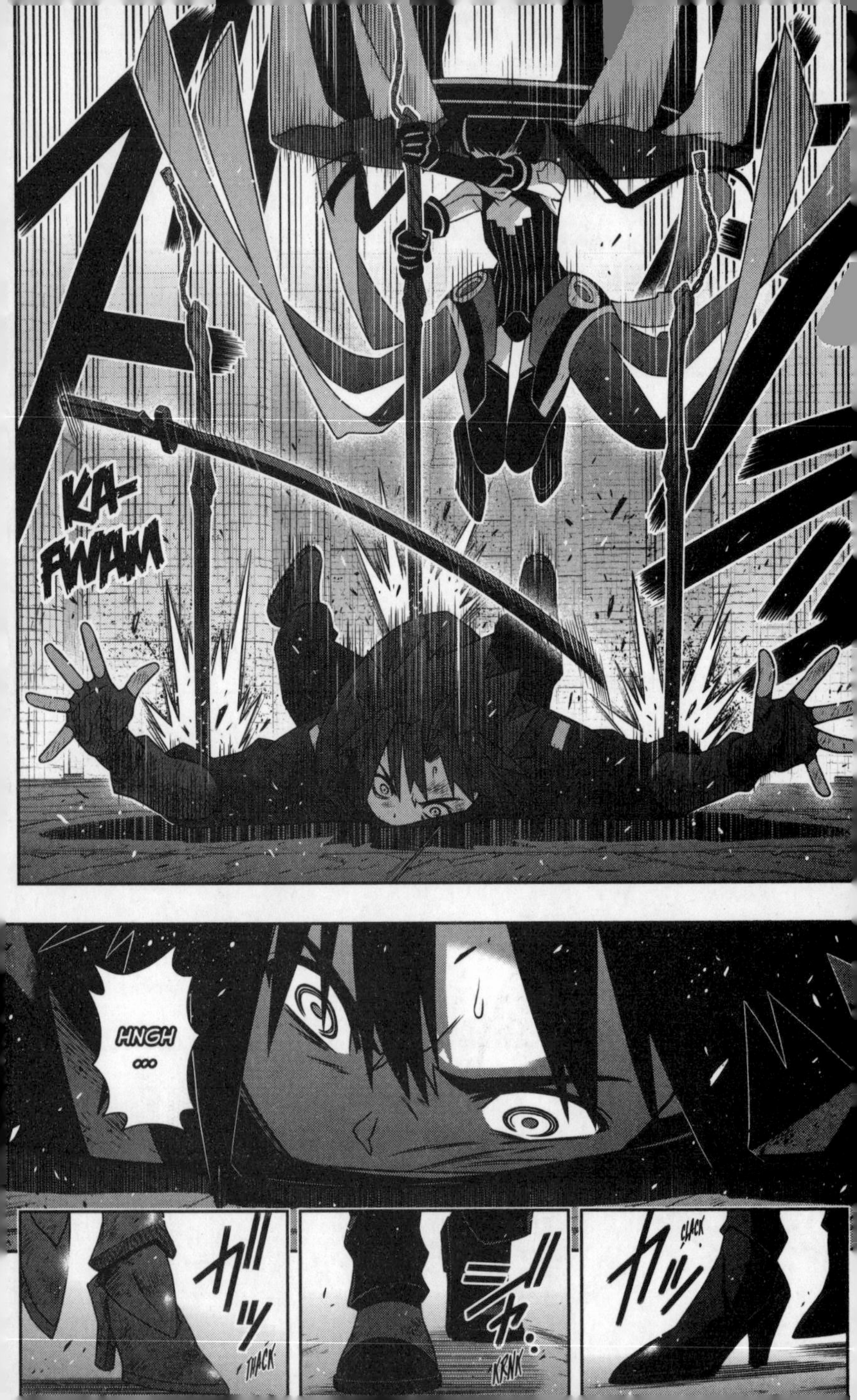
KA-FWAM
HNGH...
CLACK
KRNK
THACK

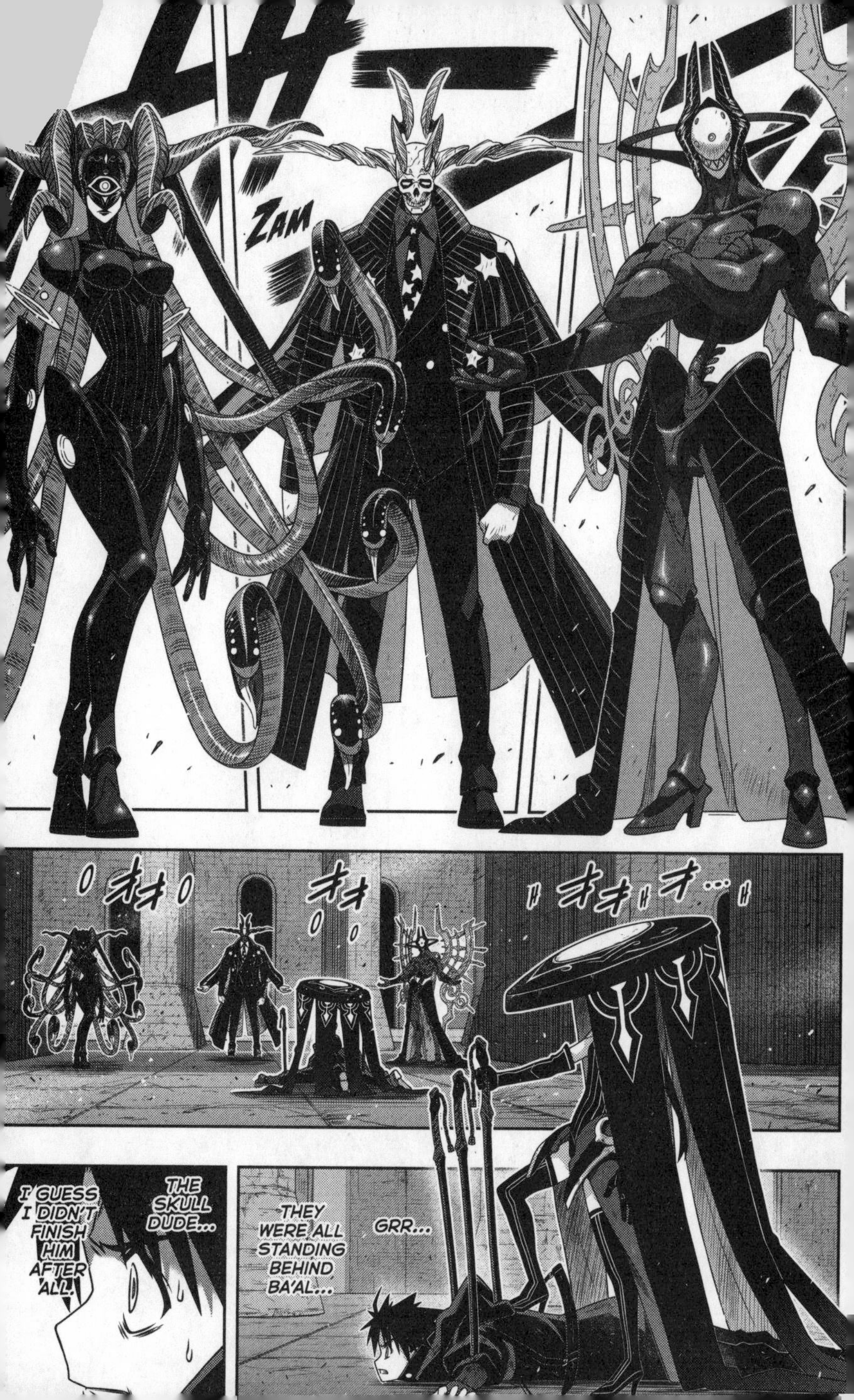
ZAM
O オオ O
オオ O O
H オオ H オ… H
GRR…
THEY WERE ALL STANDING BEHIND BA'AL…
THE SKULL DUDE…
I GUESS I DIDN'T FINISH HIM AFTER ALL.

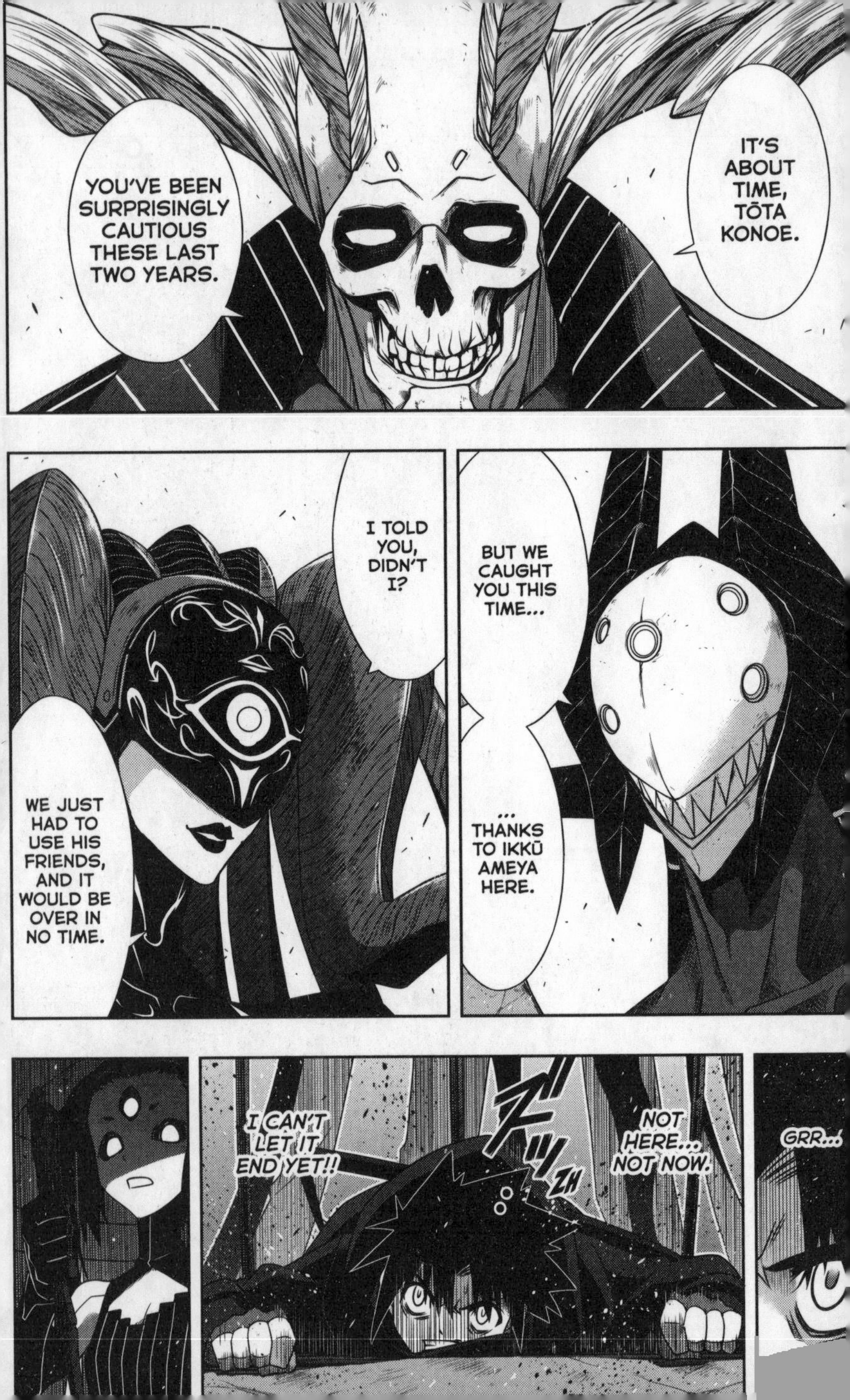
IT'S ABOUT TIME, TŌTA KONOE.
YOU'VE BEEN SURPRISINGLY CAUTIOUS THESE LAST TWO YEARS.
BUT WE CAUGHT YOU THIS TIME...
...THANKS TO IKKŪ AMEYA HERE.
I TOLD YOU, DIDN'T I?
WE JUST HAD TO USE HIS FRIENDS, AND IT WOULD BE OVER IN NO TIME.
GRR...
NOT HERE... NOT NOW.
I CAN'T LET IT END YET!!

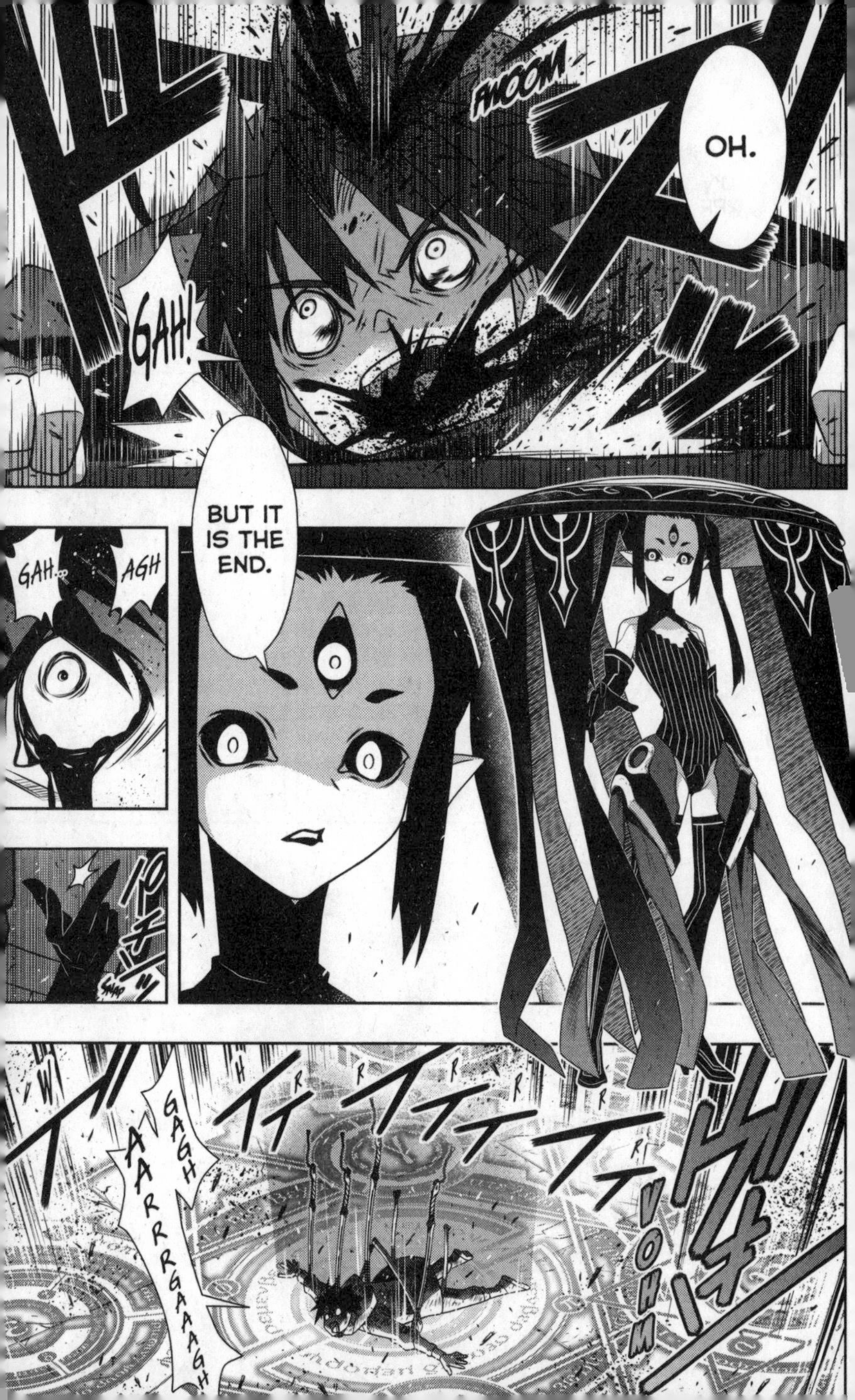
OH.
FWOOM
GAH!
BUT IT IS THE END.
GAH... AGH
SNAP
VOHM
GAGH
AARRRRGAAAAGH

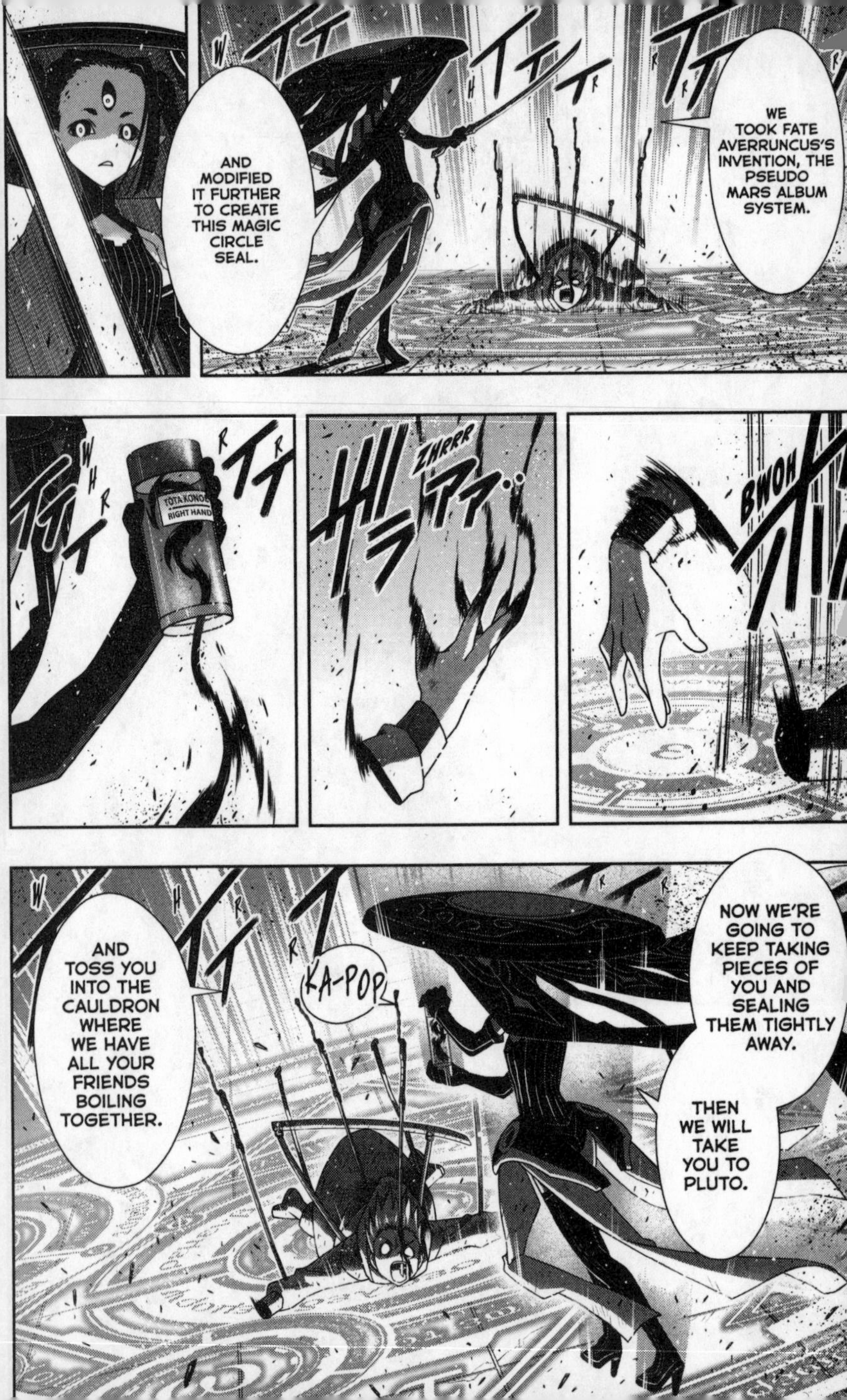
WHIRR
WE TOOK FATE AVERRUNCUS'S INVENTION, THE PSEUDO MARS ALBUM SYSTEM.
AND MODIFIED IT FURTHER TO CREATE THIS MAGIC CIRCLE SEAL.
BWOH
ZHRRR
WHIRR
TŌTA KONOE RIGHT HAND
WHIRR
NOW WE'RE GOING TO KEEP TAKING PIECES OF YOU AND SEALING THEM TIGHTLY AWAY.
KA-POP
AND TOSS YOU INTO THE CAULDRON WHERE WE HAVE ALL YOUR FRIENDS BOILING TOGETHER.
THEN WE WILL TAKE YOU TO PLUTO.

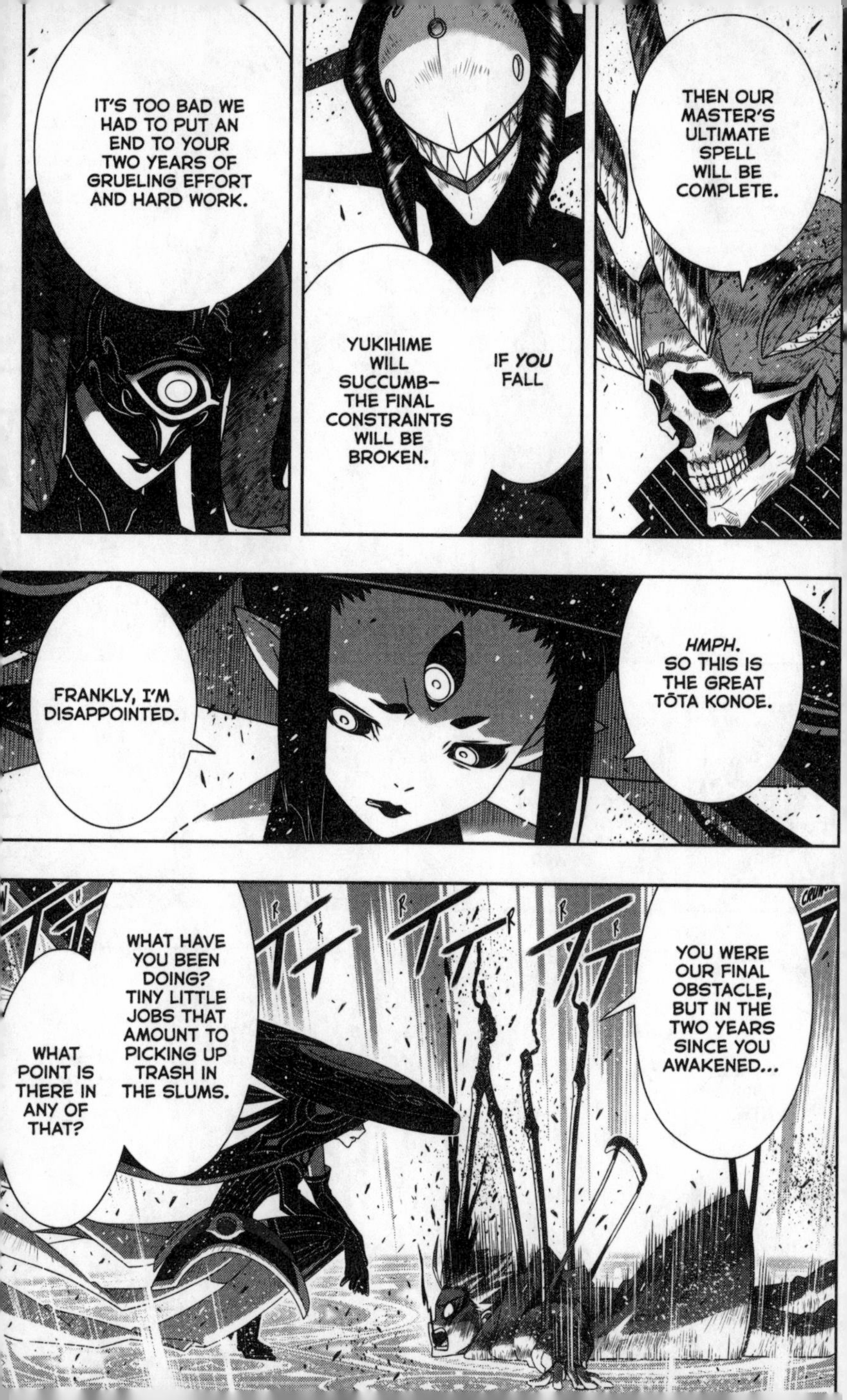
THEN OUR MASTER'S ULTIMATE SPELL WILL BE COMPLETE.
IF *YOU* FALL
YUKIHIME WILL SUCCUMB– THE FINAL CONSTRAINTS WILL BE BROKEN.
IT'S TOO BAD WE HAD TO PUT AN END TO YOUR TWO YEARS OF GRUELING EFFORT AND HARD WORK.
HMPH. SO THIS IS THE GREAT TŌTA KONOE.
FRANKLY, I'M DISAPPOINTED.
YOU WERE OUR FINAL OBSTACLE, BUT IN THE TWO YEARS SINCE YOU AWAKENED...
WHAT HAVE YOU BEEN DOING? TINY LITTLE JOBS THAT AMOUNT TO PICKING UP TRASH IN THE SLUMS.
WHAT POINT IS THERE IN ANY OF THAT?

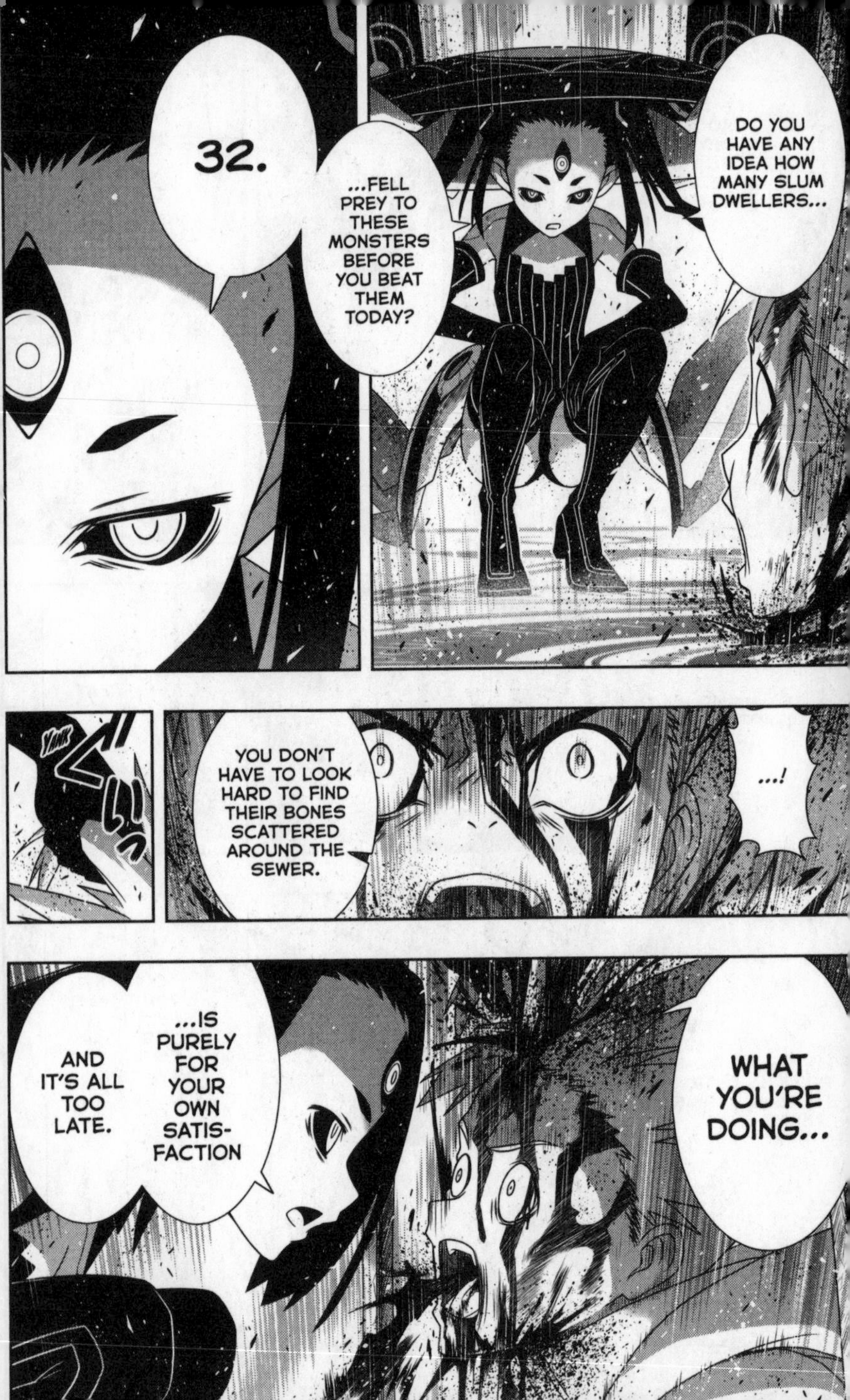
DO YOU HAVE ANY IDEA HOW MANY SLUM DWELLERS...
...FELL PREY TO THESE MONSTERS BEFORE YOU BEAT THEM TODAY?
32.
...!
YOU DON'T HAVE TO LOOK HARD TO FIND THEIR BONES SCATTERED AROUND THE SEWER.
YANK
WHAT YOU'RE DOING...
...IS PURELY FOR YOUR OWN SATISFACTION
AND IT'S ALL TOO LATE.

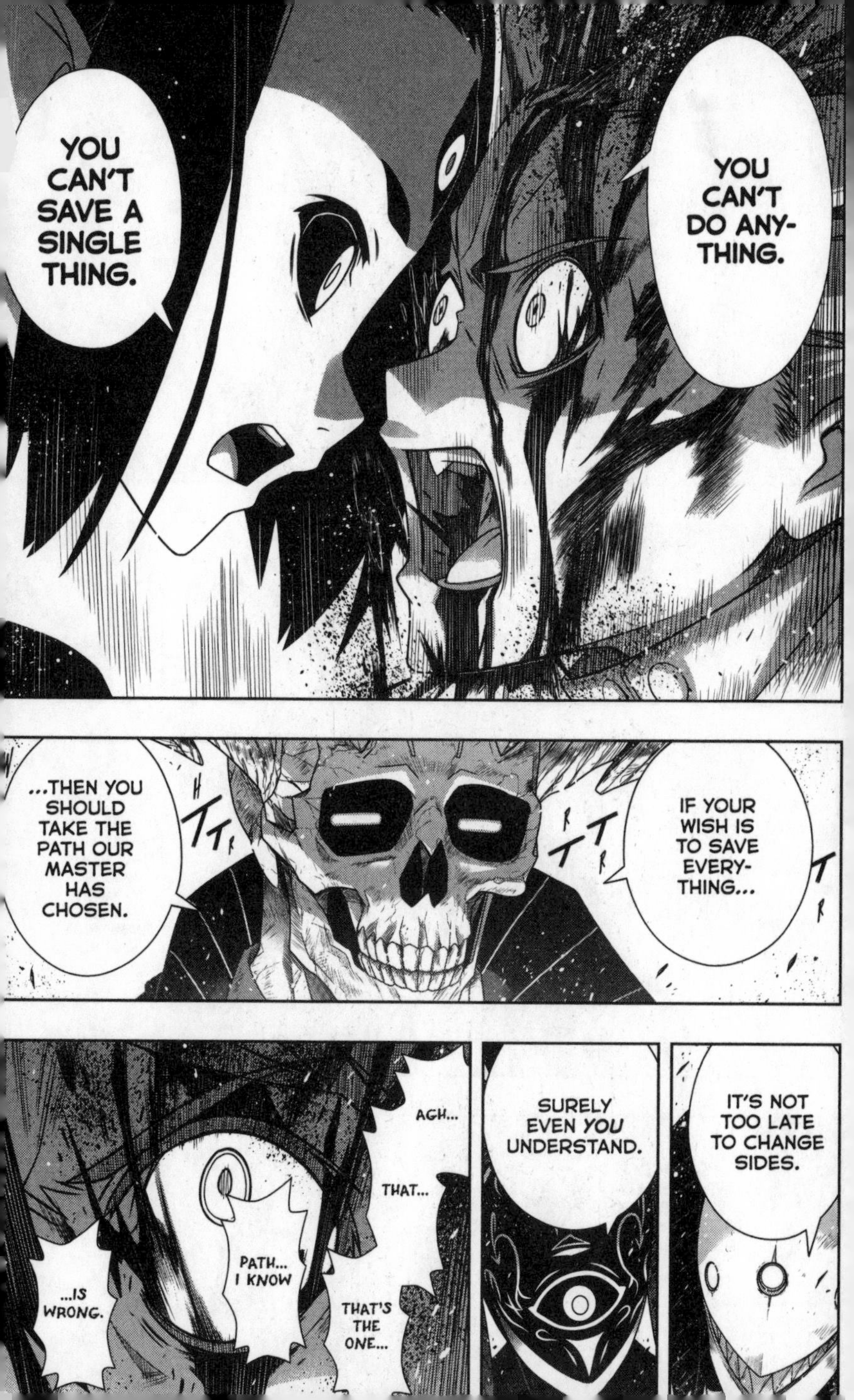
YOU CAN'T DO ANYTHING.
YOU CAN'T SAVE A SINGLE THING.
IF YOUR WISH IS TO SAVE EVERYTHING...
...THEN YOU SHOULD TAKE THE PATH OUR MASTER HAS CHOSEN.
IT'S NOT TOO LATE TO CHANGE SIDES.
SURELY EVEN *YOU* UNDERSTAND.
AGH...
THAT...
THAT'S THE ONE...
PATH... I KNOW
...IS WRONG.

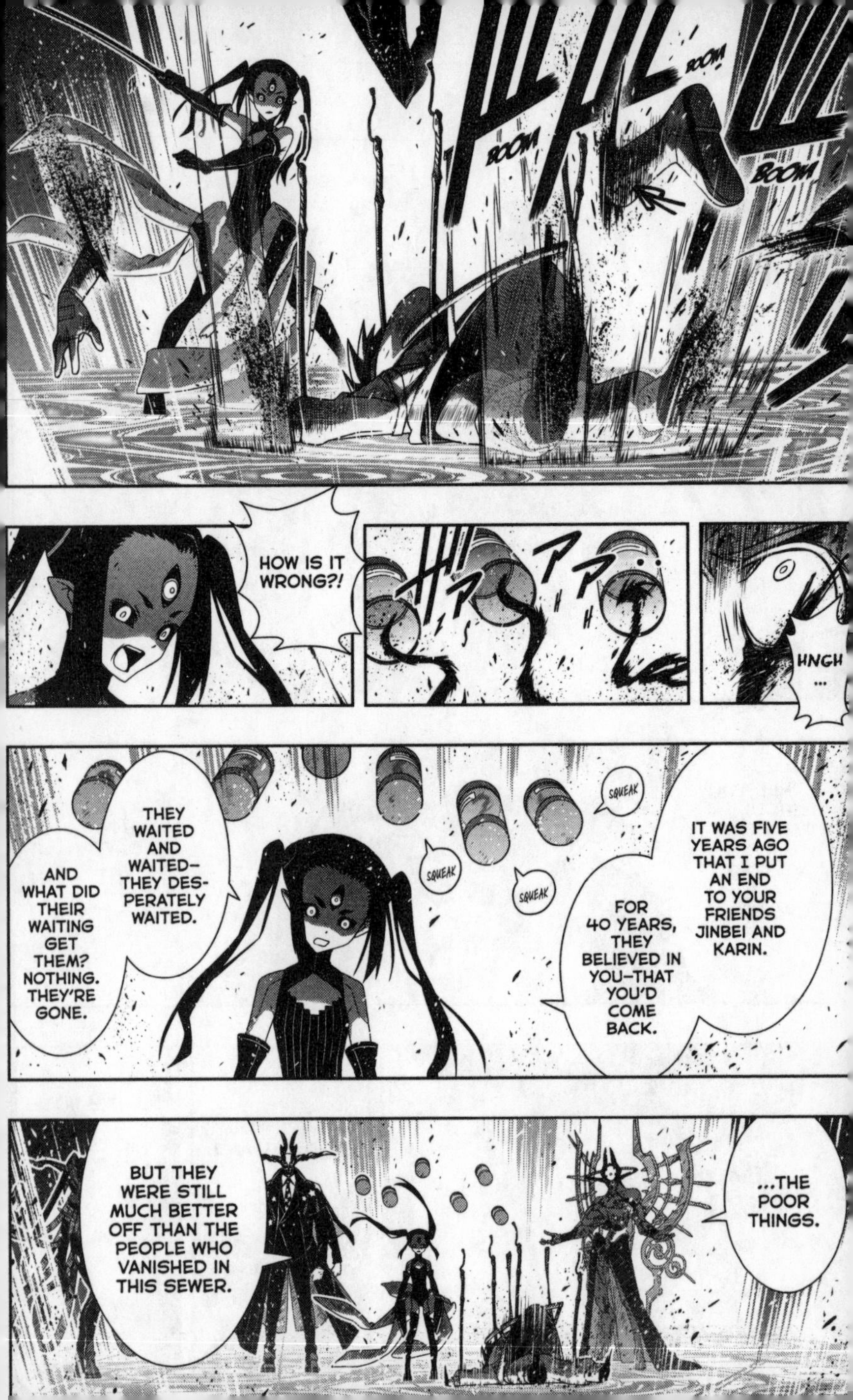
BOOM
BOOM
BOOM
UNGH ...
HOW IS IT WRONG?!
IT WAS FIVE YEARS AGO THAT I PUT AN END TO YOUR FRIENDS JINBEI AND KARIN.
FOR 40 YEARS, THEY BELIEVED IN YOU—THAT YOU'D COME BACK.
SQUEAK
SQUEAK
SQUEAK
THEY WAITED AND WAITED—THEY DES-PERATELY WAITED.
AND WHAT DID THEIR WAITING GET THEM? NOTHING. THEY'RE GONE.
...THE POOR THINGS.
BUT THEY WERE STILL MUCH BETTER OFF THAN THE PEOPLE WHO VANISHED IN THIS SEWER.

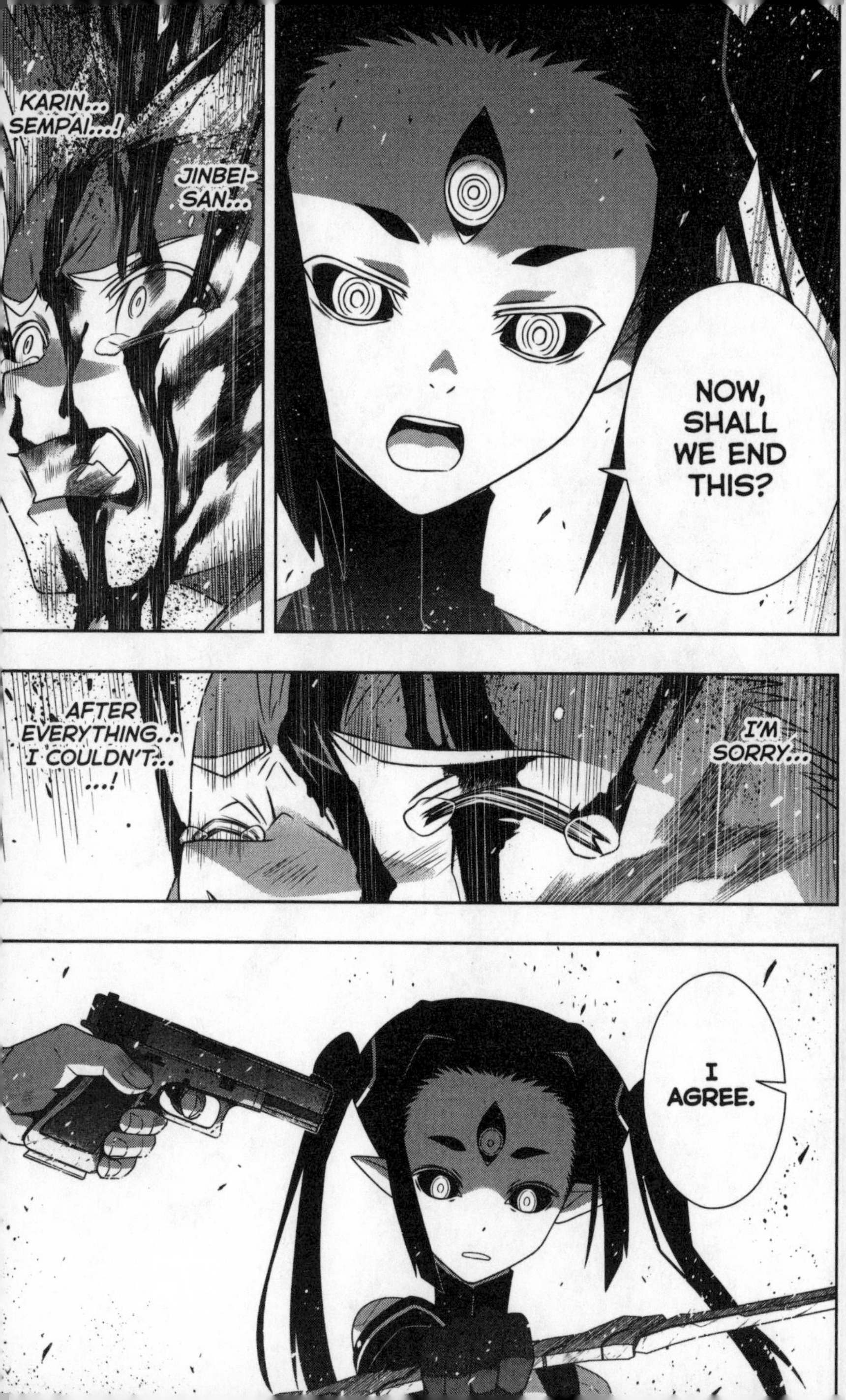
NOW, SHALL WE END THIS?
KARIN... SEMPAI...!
JINBEI-SAN...
I'M SORRY...
AFTER EVERYTHING... I COULDN'T... ...!
I AGREE.

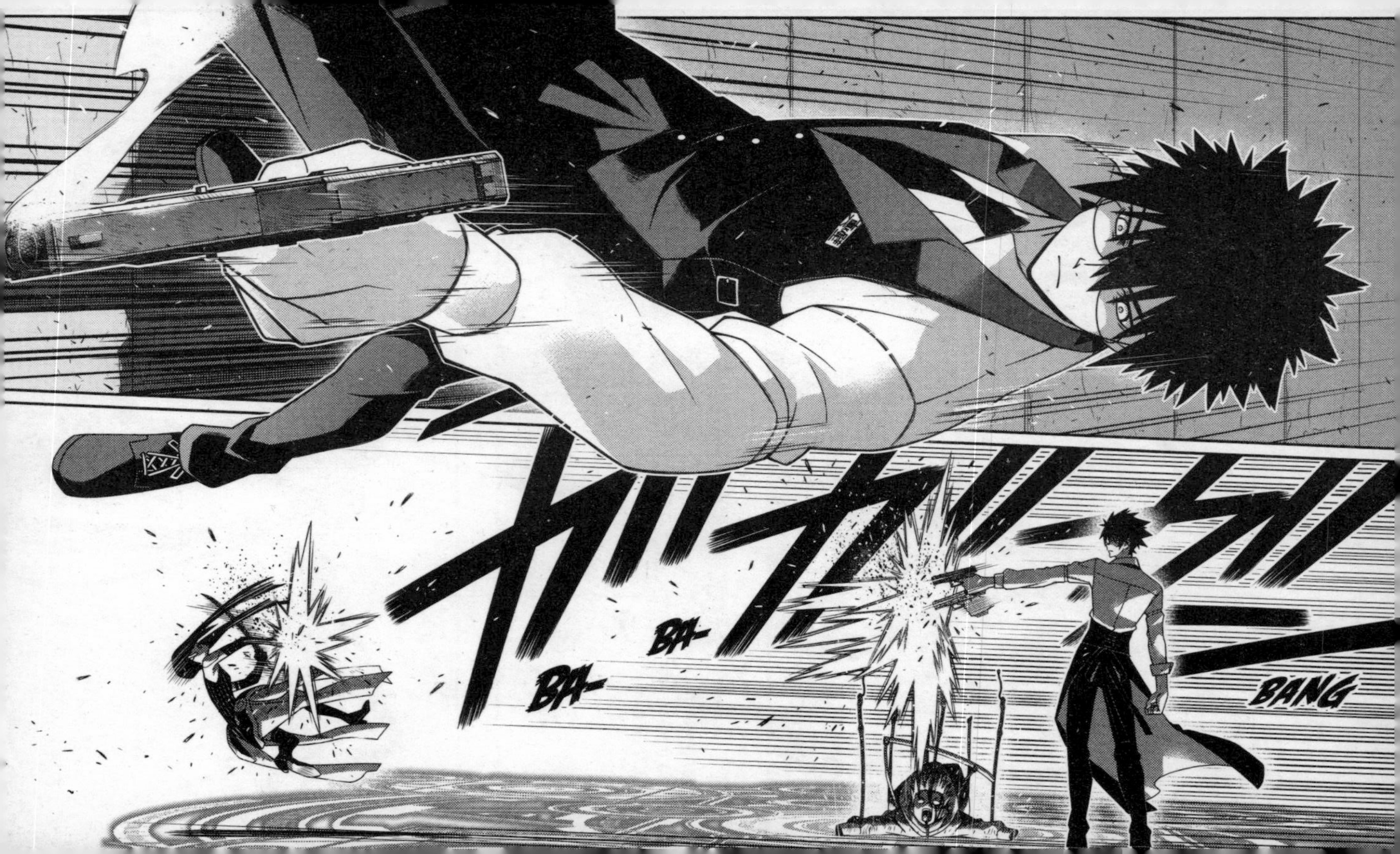
BANG
BA-
BA-

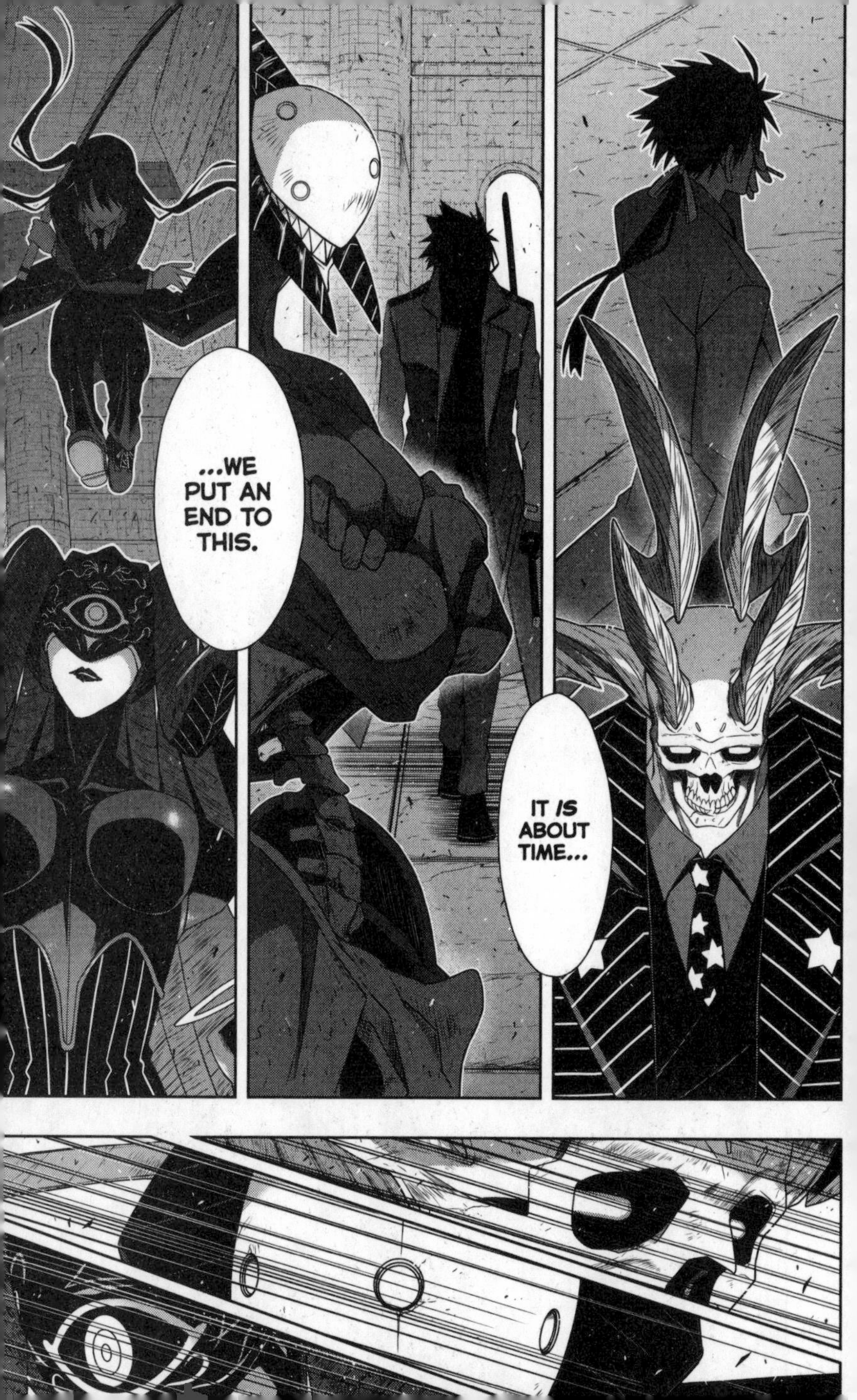
IT IS ABOUT TIME...
...WE PUT AN END TO THIS.

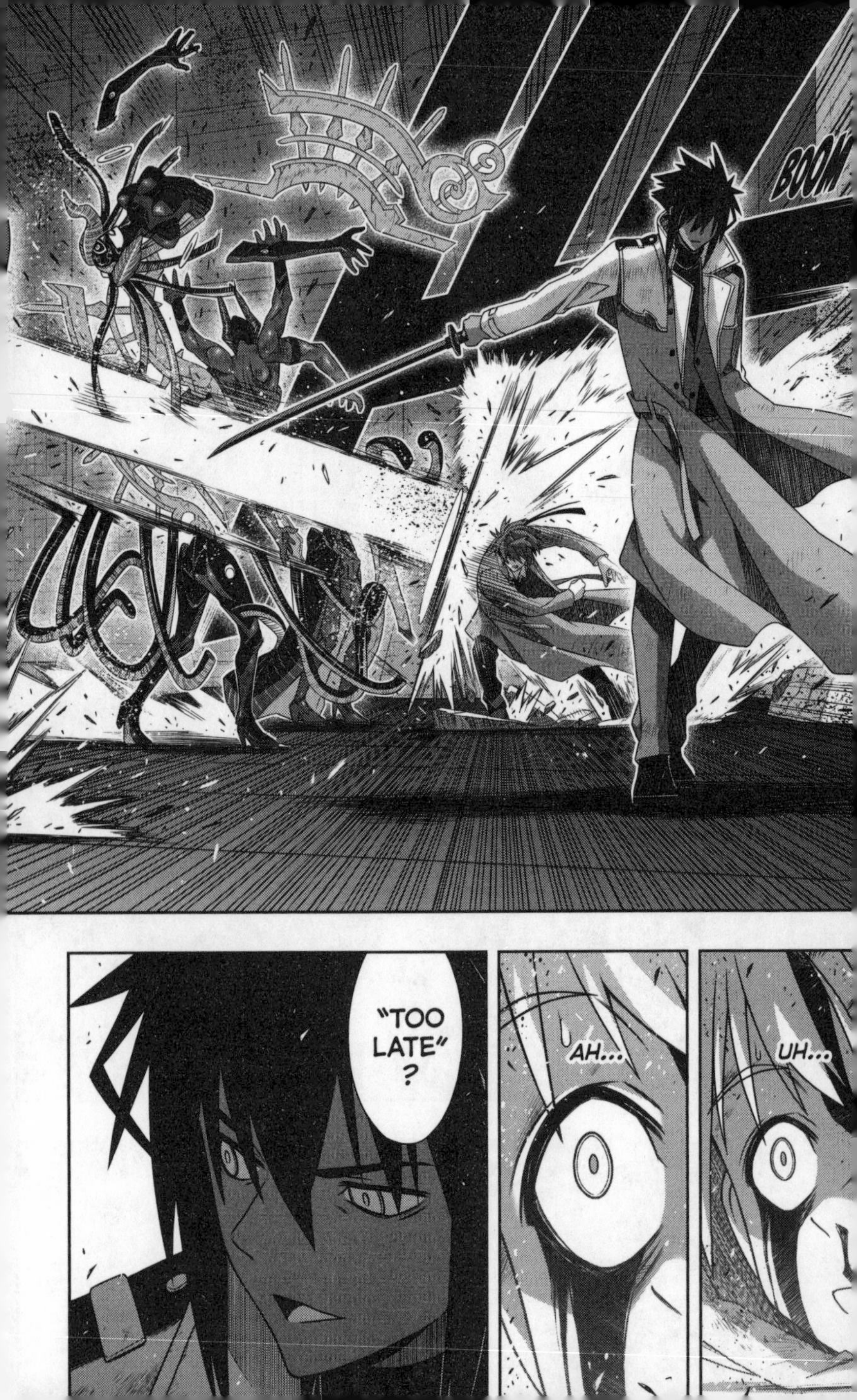
BOOM
UH...
AH...
"TOO LATE"?

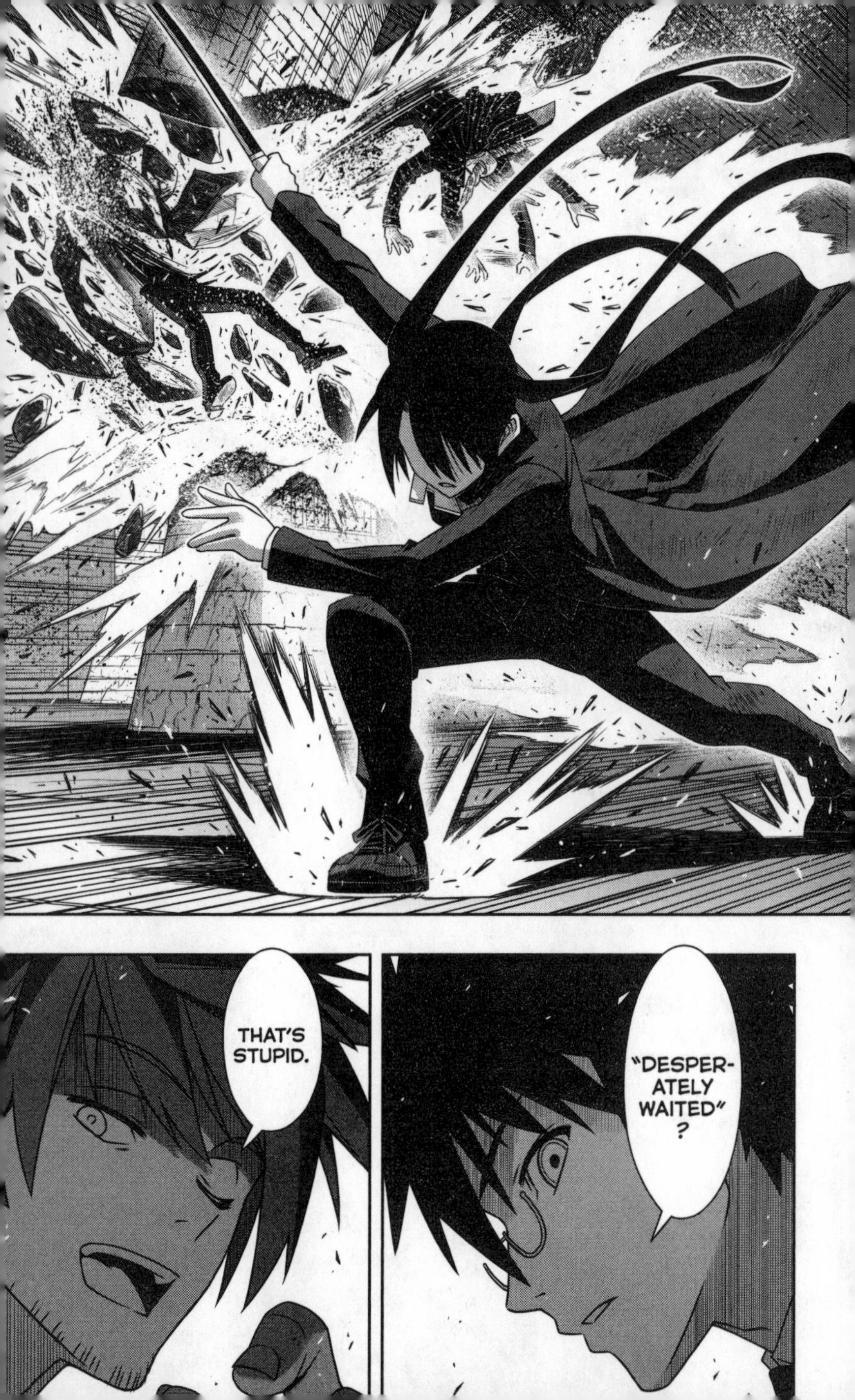
"DESPER-ATELY WAITED"?
THAT'S STUPID.

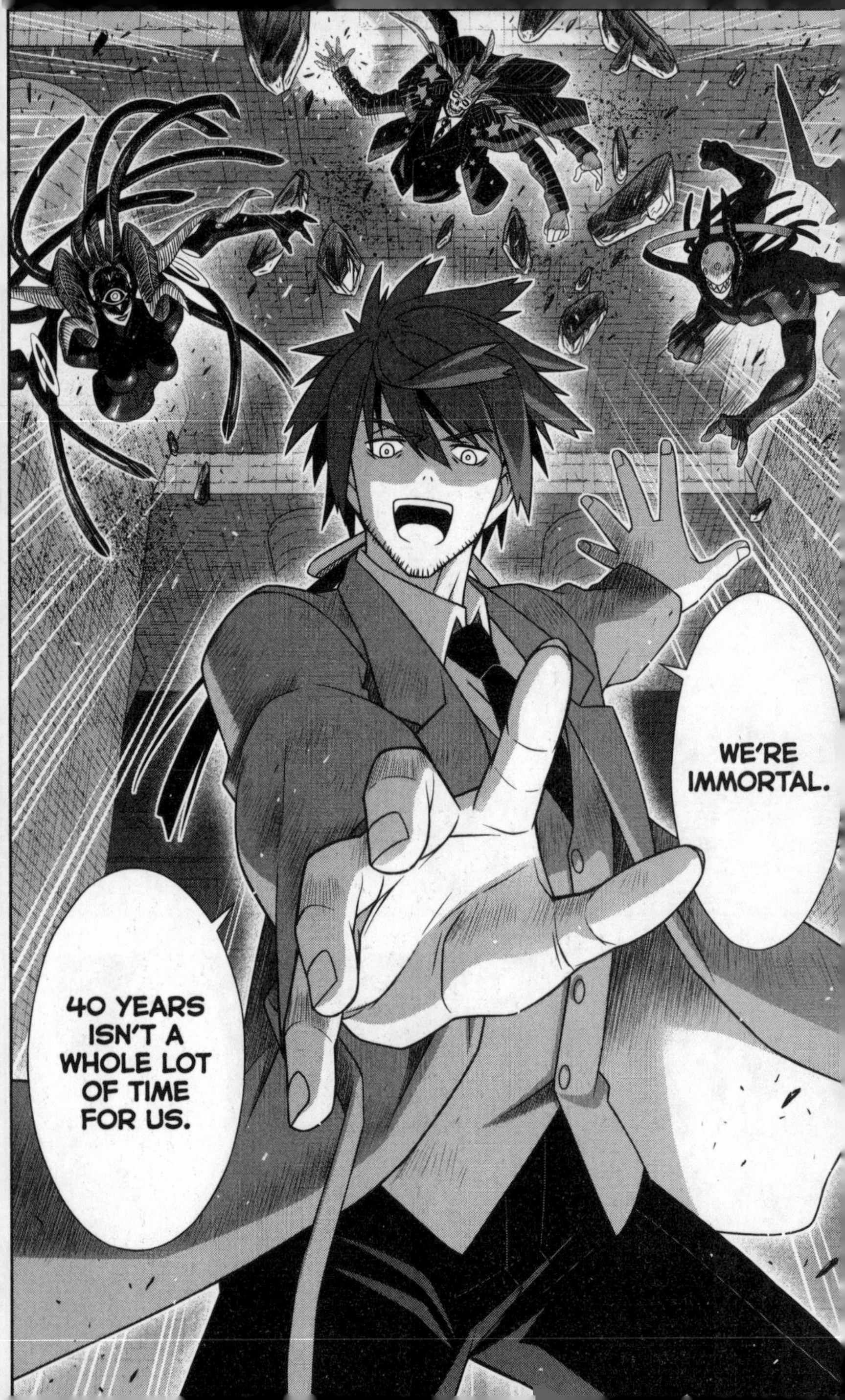
WE'RE IMMORTAL.
40 YEARS ISN'T A WHOLE LOT OF TIME FOR US.

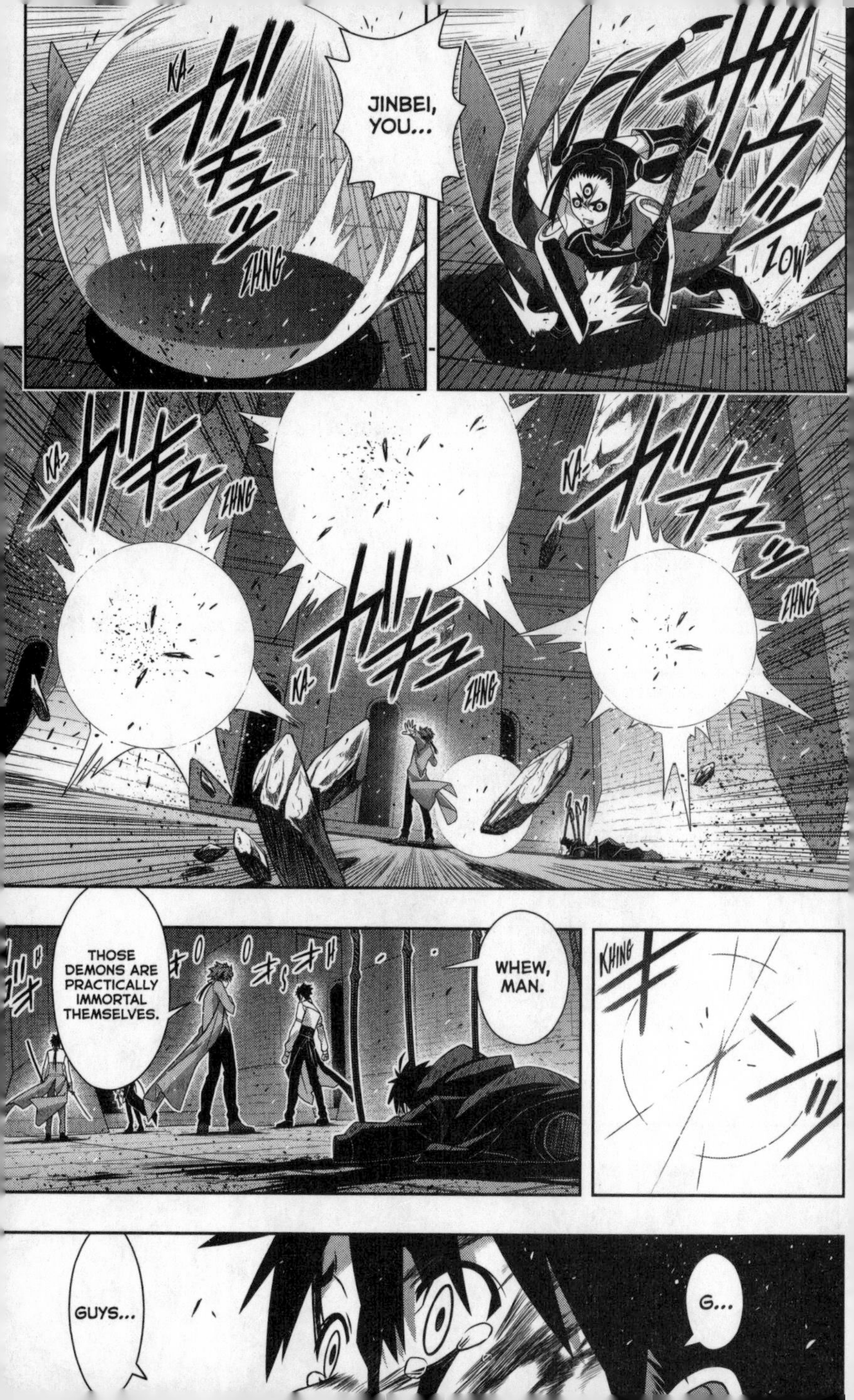
ZOW
JINBEI, YOU...
KA-
ZHNG
KA-
ZHNG
KA-
ZHNG
KA-
ZHNG
KHING
WHEW, MAN.
THOSE DEMONS ARE PRACTICALLY IMMORTAL THEMSELVES.
G...
GUYS...

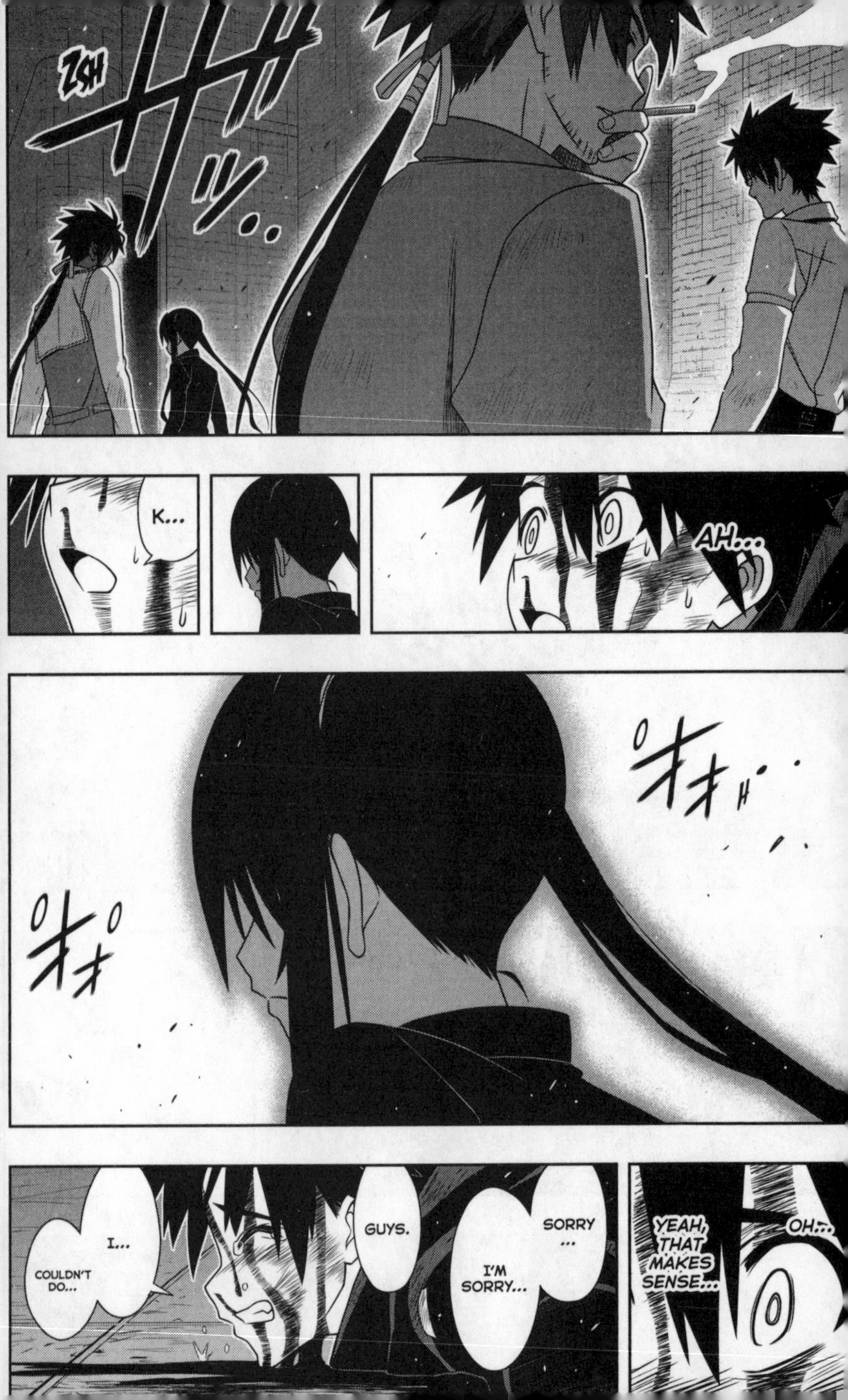
ZSH
AH...
K...
OH...
YEAH, THAT MAKES SENSE...
SORRY ...
I'M SORRY...
GUYS.
I...
COULDN'T DO...

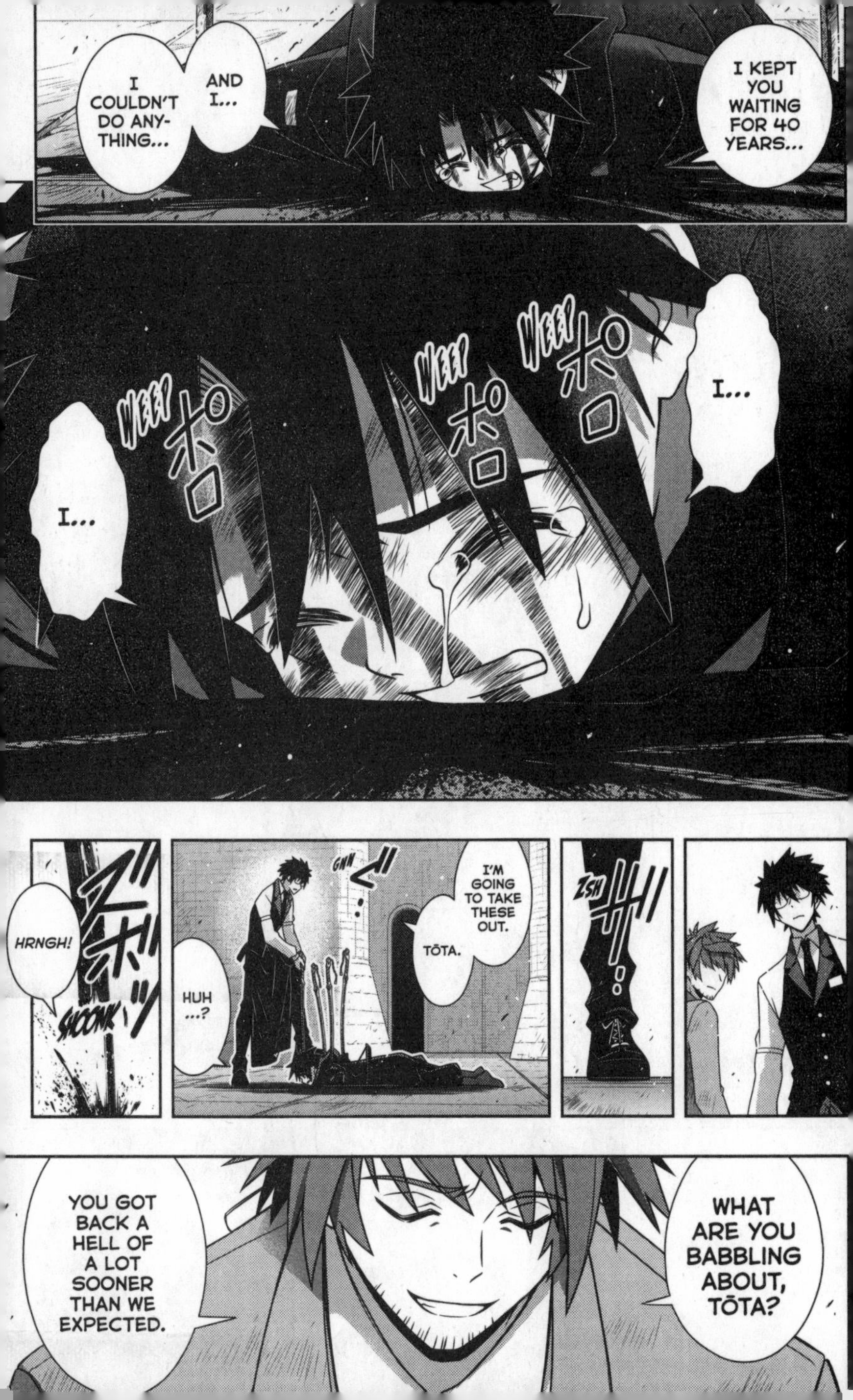
I KEPT YOU WAITING FOR 40 YEARS...
AND I...
I COULDN'T DO ANYTHING...
I...
WEEP
ポロ
WEEP
ポロ
WEEP
ポロ
I...
ZSH
I'M GOING TO TAKE THESE OUT.
TŌTA.
GNN
HUH...?
HRNGH!
SHOONK
WHAT ARE YOU BABBLING ABOUT, TŌTA?
YOU GOT BACK A HELL OF A LOT SOONER THAN WE EXPECTED.

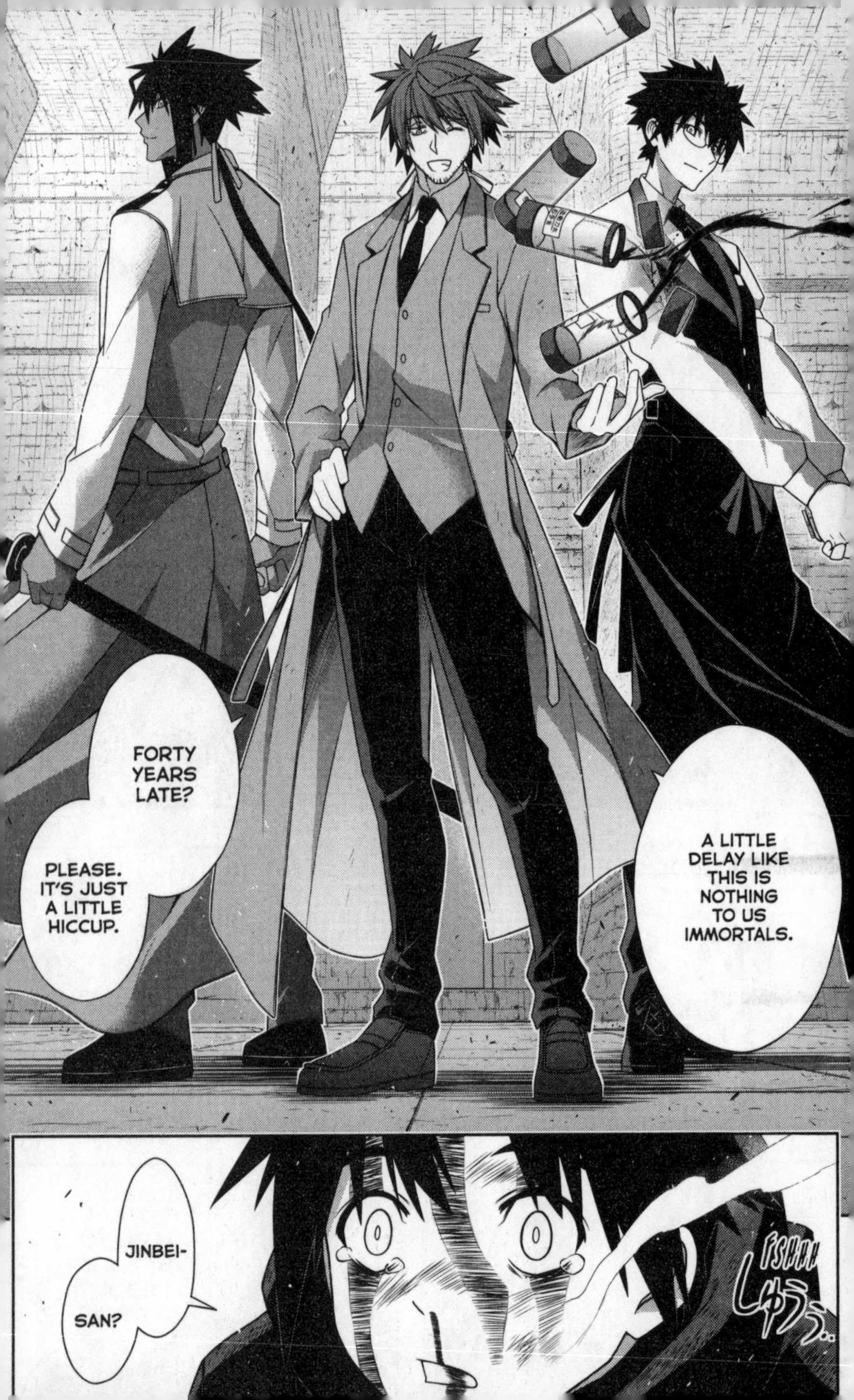
A LITTLE DELAY LIKE THIS IS NOTHING TO US IMMORTALS.
FORTY YEARS LATE?
PLEASE. IT'S JUST A LITTLE HICCUP.
FSHHH
JINBEI-
SAN?

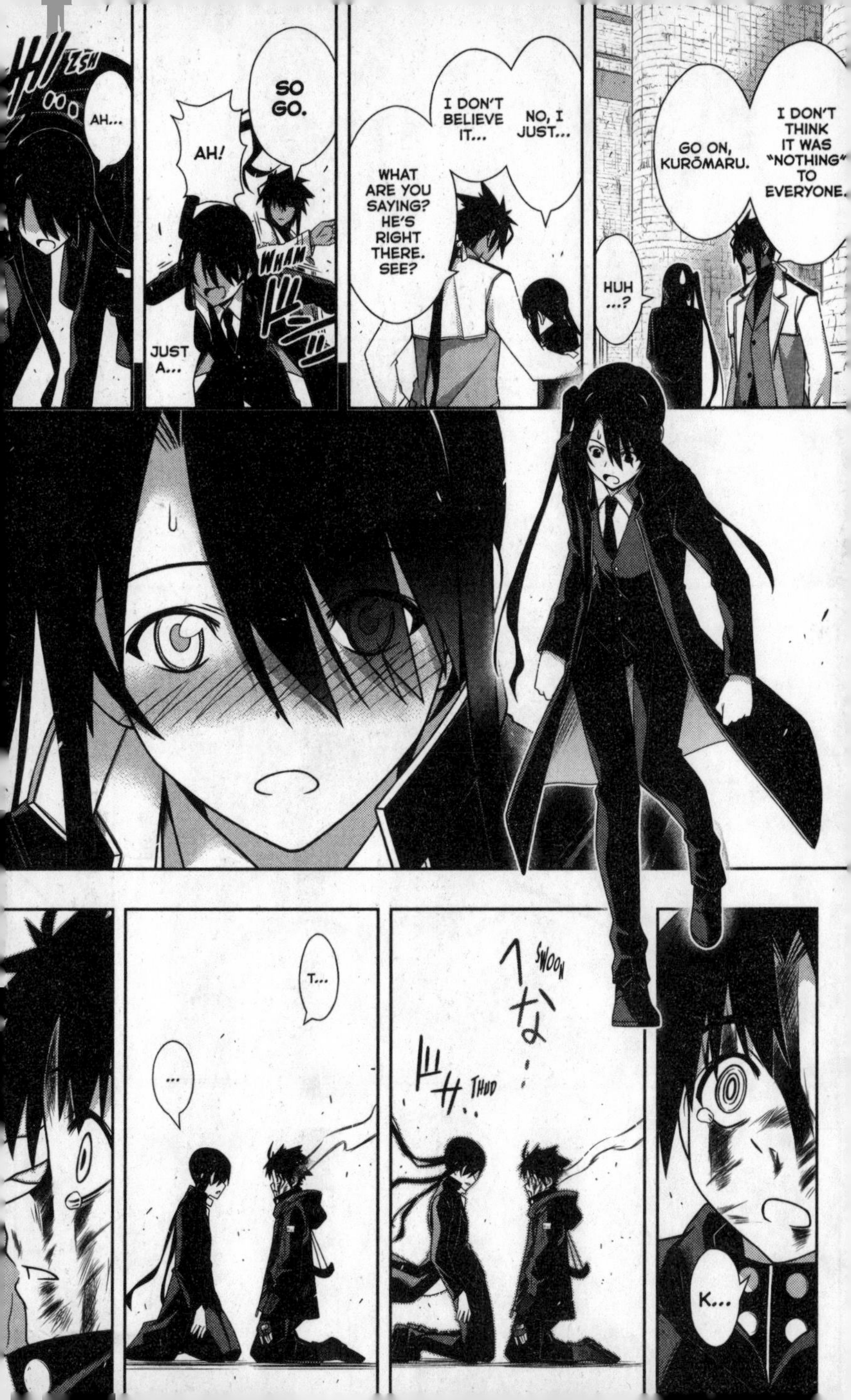
I DON'T THINK IT WAS "NOTHING" TO EVERYONE.
GO ON, KURŌMARU.
HUH ...?
NO, I JUST...
I DON'T BELIEVE IT...
WHAT ARE YOU SAYING? HE'S RIGHT THERE. SEE?
SO GO.
AH!
WHAM
JUST A...
ZSH
AH...
K...
SWOON
THUD
T...
...

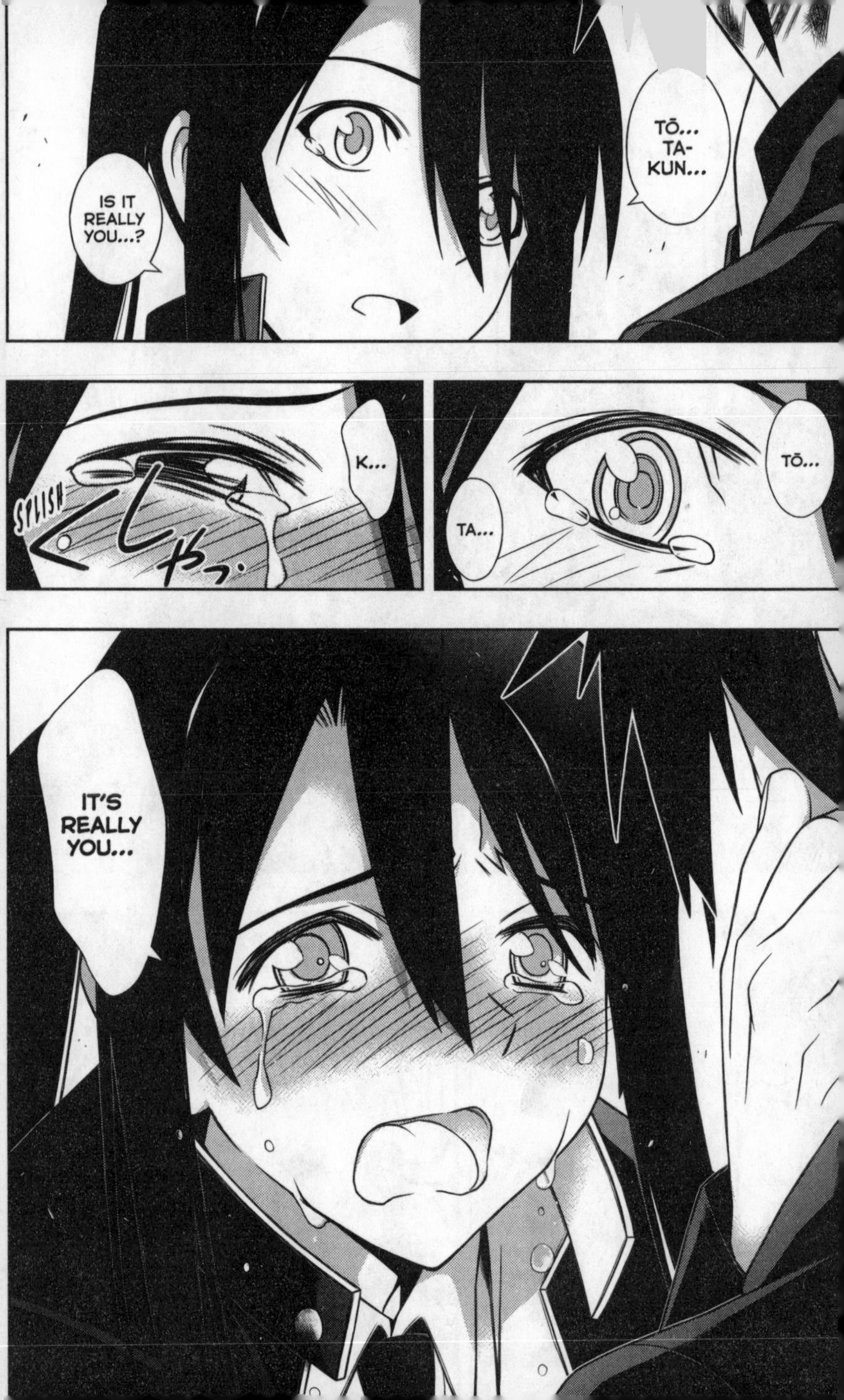
TŌ... TA-KUN...
IS IT REALLY YOU...?
TŌ...
TA...
K...
SPLISH
IT'S REALLY YOU...

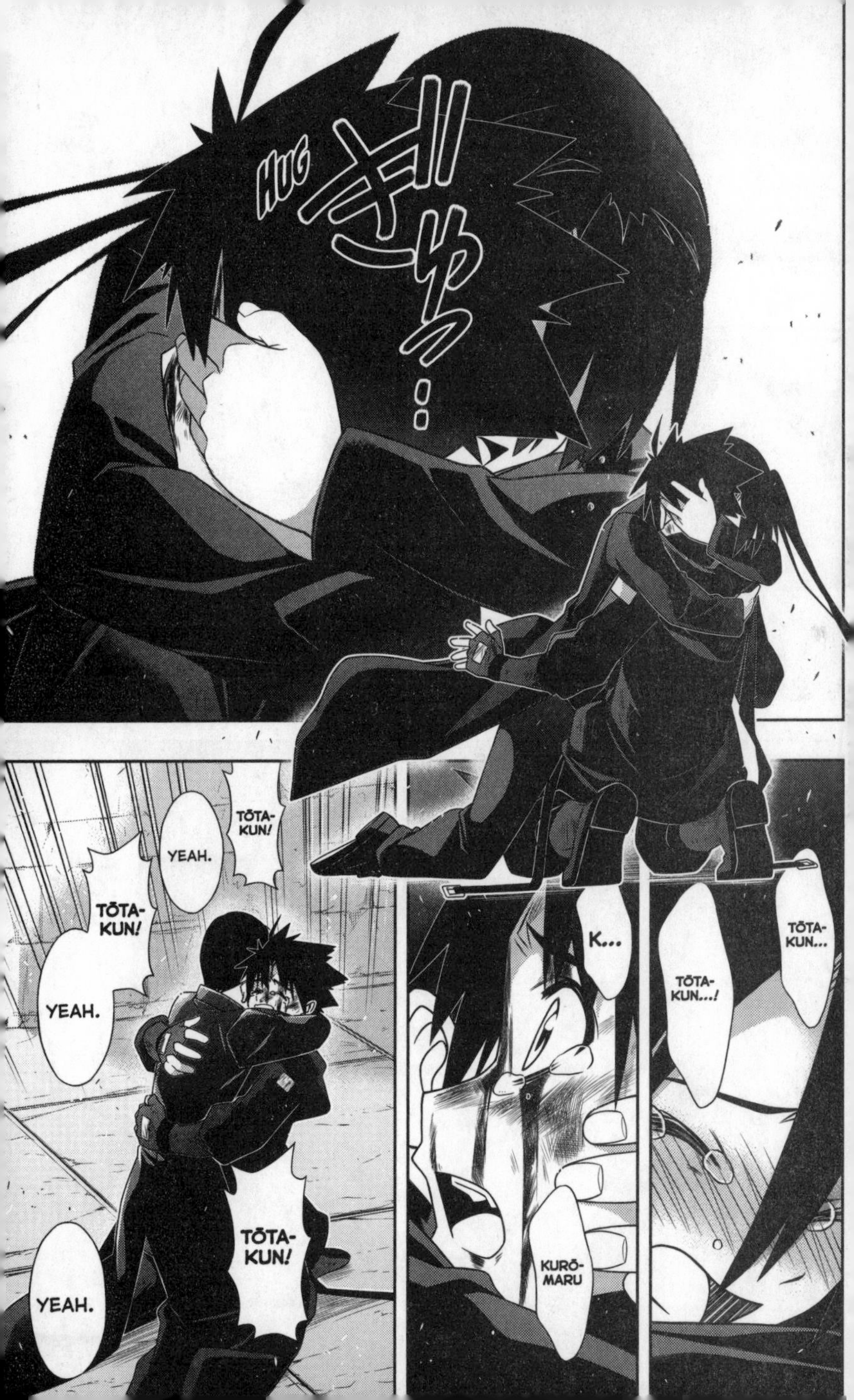
HUG
ぎゅう!!
TŌTA-KUN...
TŌTA-KUN...!
K...
KURŌMARU
TŌTA-KUN!
YEAH.
TŌTA-KUN!
YEAH.
TŌTA-KUN!
YEAH.

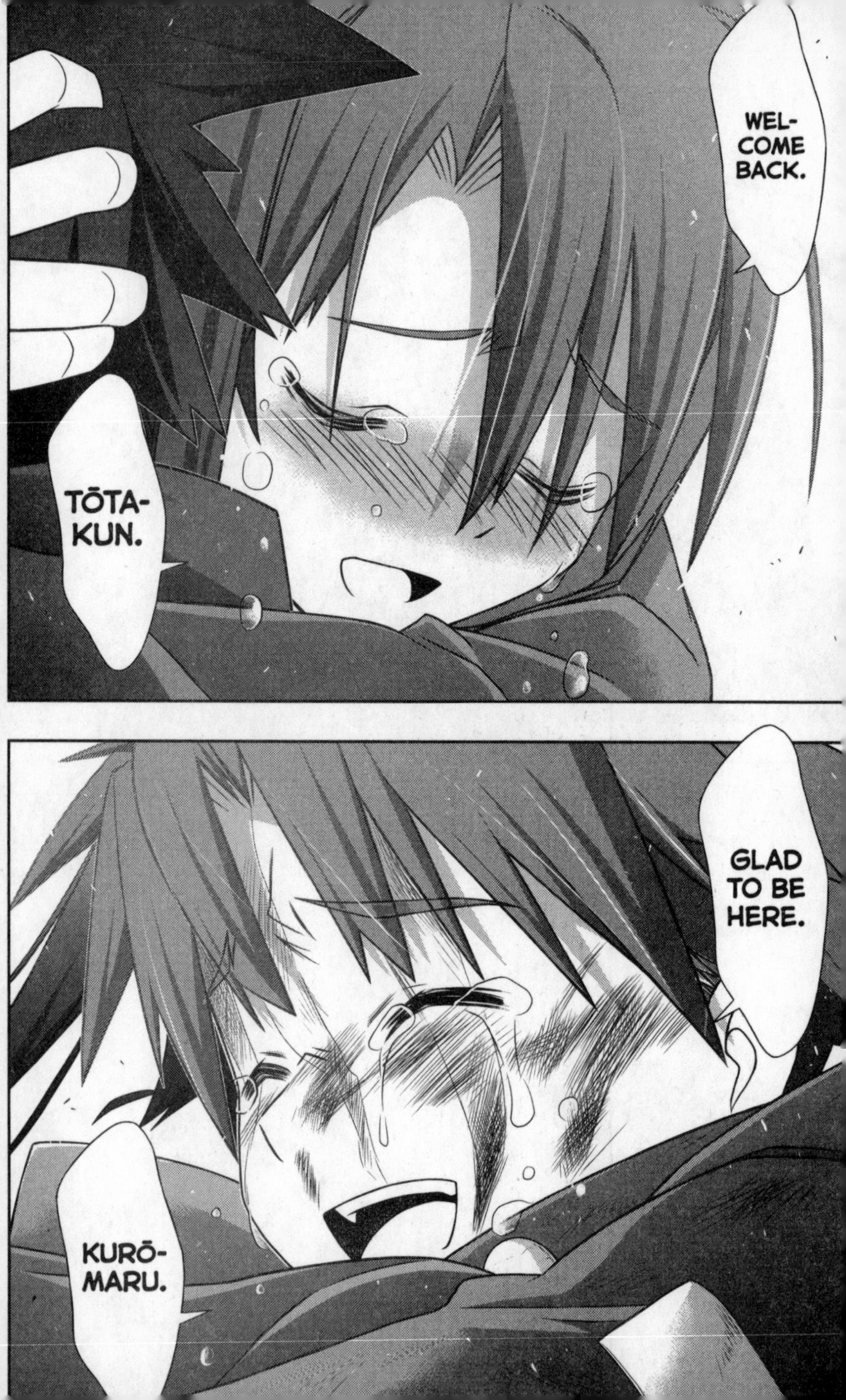
WEL-COME BACK.
TŌTA-KUN.
GLAD TO BE HERE.
KURŌ-MARU.

悠UQ HOLDER!

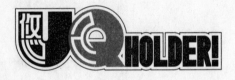

UQ HOLDER!

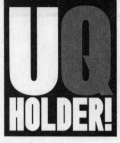

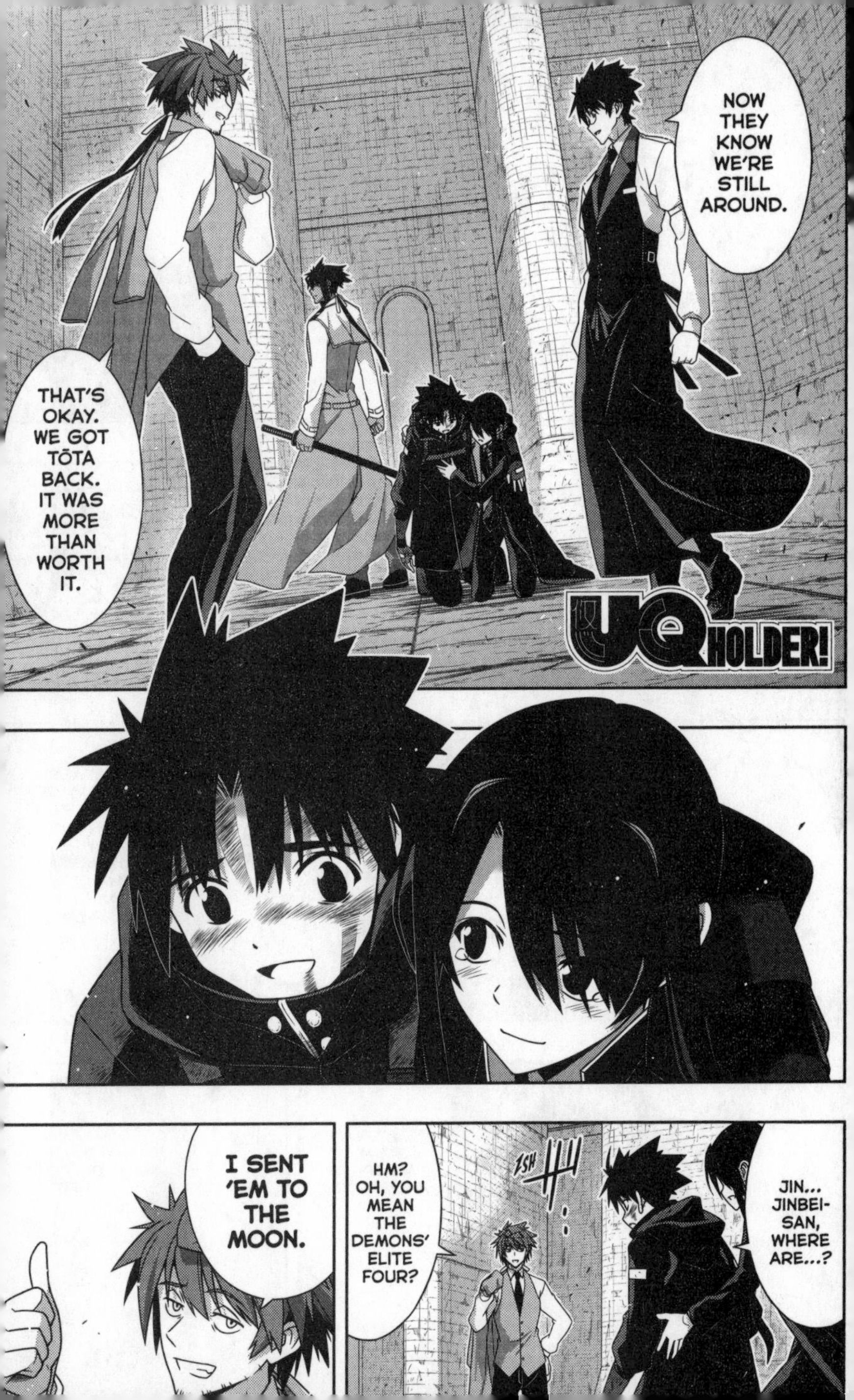
NOW THEY KNOW WE'RE STILL AROUND.
THAT'S OKAY. WE GOT TŌTA BACK. IT WAS MORE THAN WORTH IT.
UQ HOLDER!
JIN... JINBEI-SAN, WHERE ARE...?
ISH
HM? OH, YOU MEAN THE DEMONS' ELITE FOUR?
I SENT 'EM TO THE MOON.

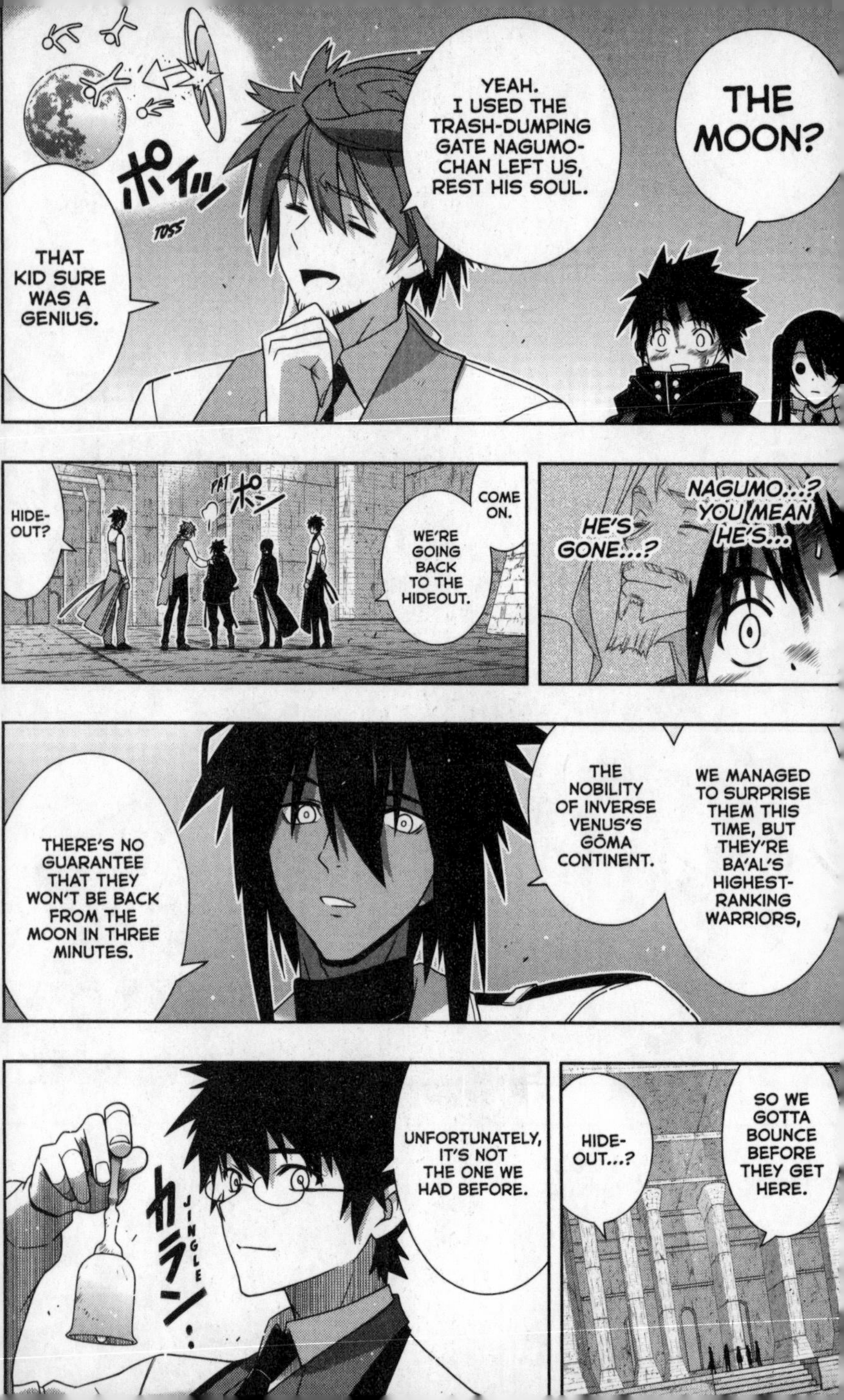
THE MOON?
YEAH. I USED THE TRASH-DUMPING GATE NAGUMO-CHAN LEFT US, REST HIS SOUL.
ポイッ
TOSS
THAT KID SURE WAS A GENIUS.
NAGUMO...? YOU MEAN HE'S...
HE'S GONE...?
COME ON.
WE'RE GOING BACK TO THE HIDEOUT.
PAT
ポン
HIDE-OUT?
WE MANAGED TO SURPRISE THEM THIS TIME, BUT THEY'RE BA'AL'S HIGHEST-RANKING WARRIORS,
THE NOBILITY OF INVERSE VENUS'S GŌMA CONTINENT.
THERE'S NO GUARANTEE THAT THEY WON'T BE BACK FROM THE MOON IN THREE MINUTES.
SO WE GOTTA BOUNCE BEFORE THEY GET HERE.
HIDE-OUT...?
UNFORTUNATELY, IT'S NOT THE ONE WE HAD BEFORE.
カラン
JINGLE

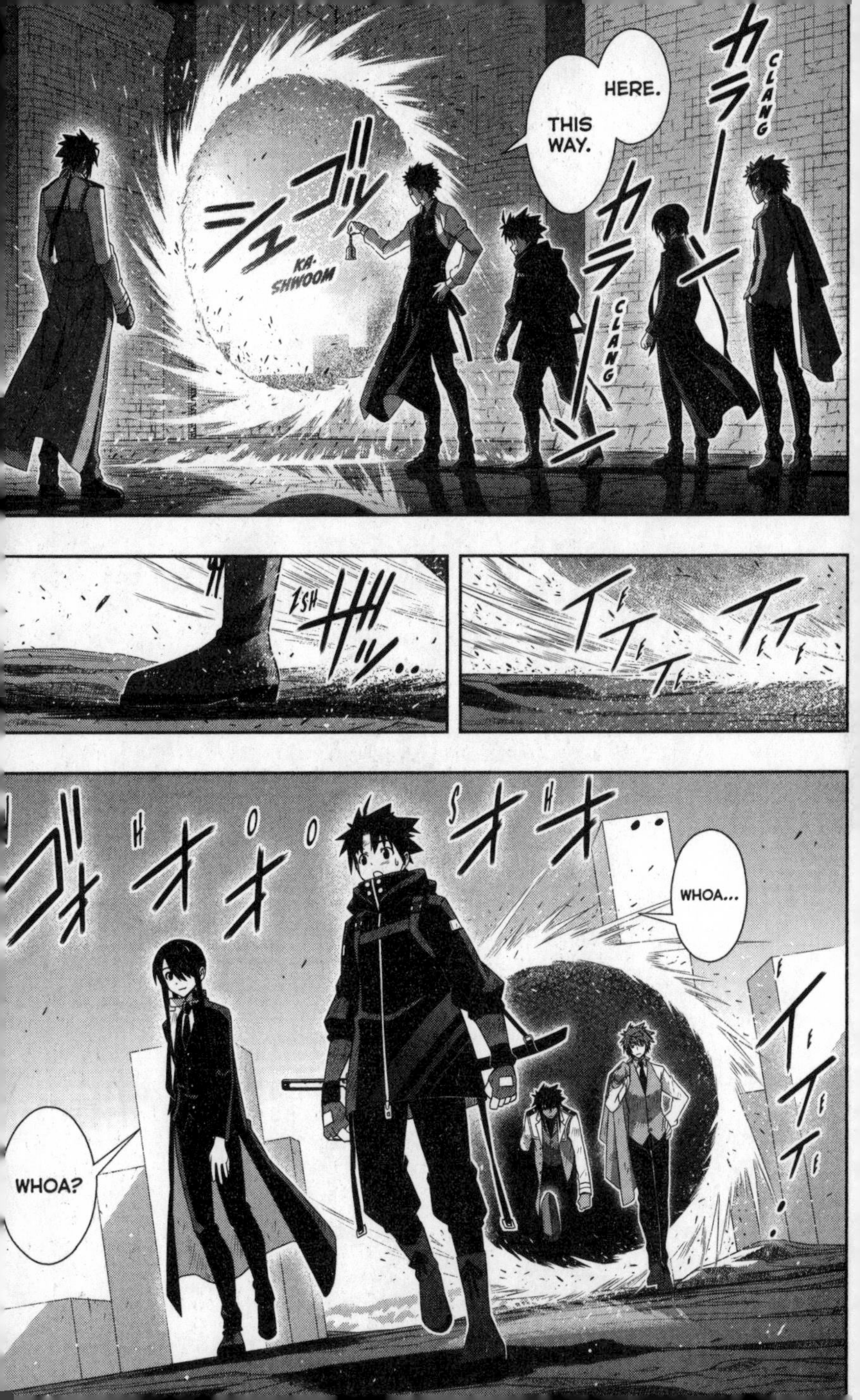
カラーン
CLANG
HERE.
THIS WAY.
カラーン
CLANG
シュゴッ
KA-SHWOOM
イイイイ
ザッ..
ZSH
WHOA...
イイイ..
ゴォオオオオ
SHHOOO
WHOA?

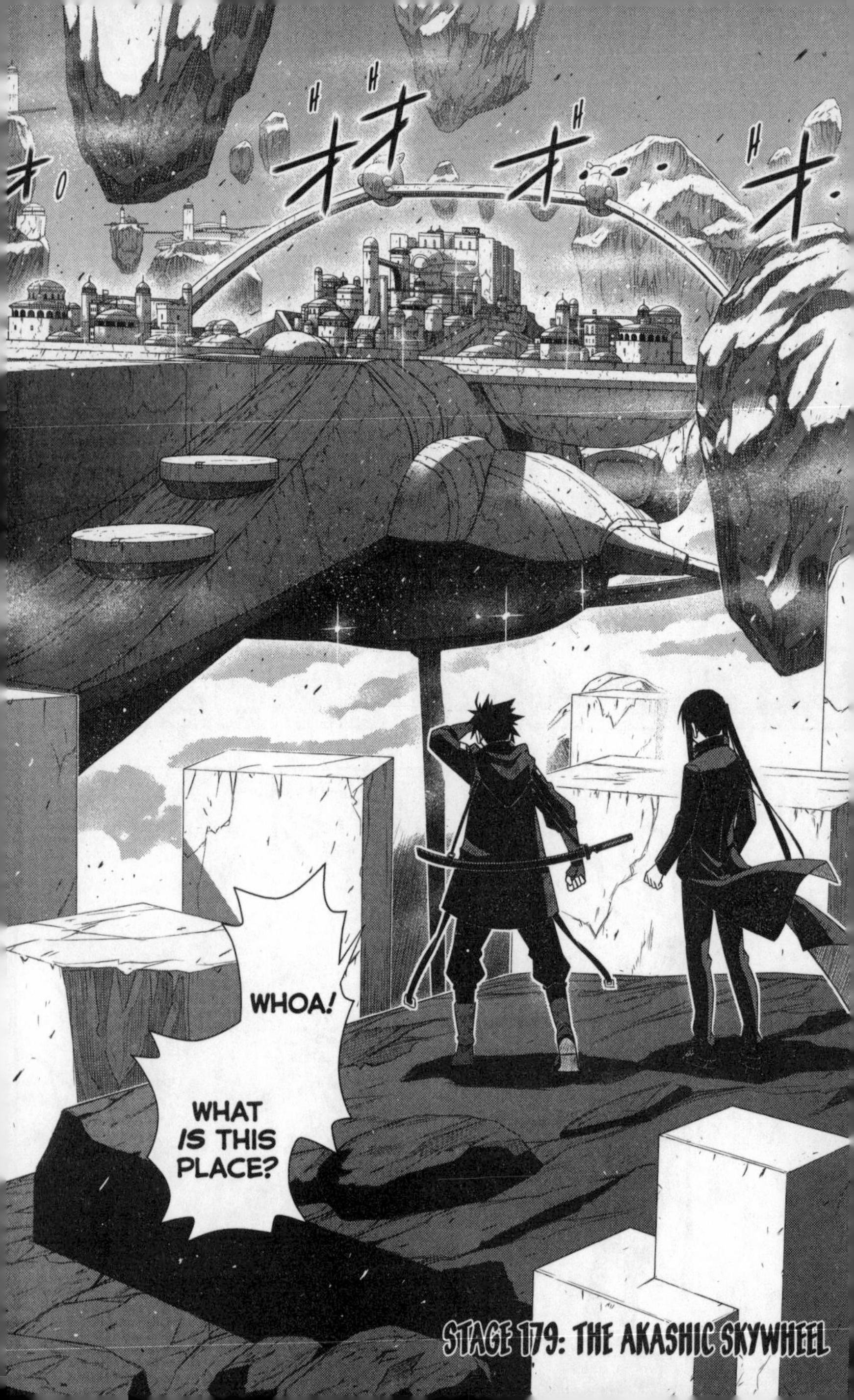
WHOA!
WHAT IS THIS PLACE?
STAGE 179: THE AKASHIC SKYWHEEL

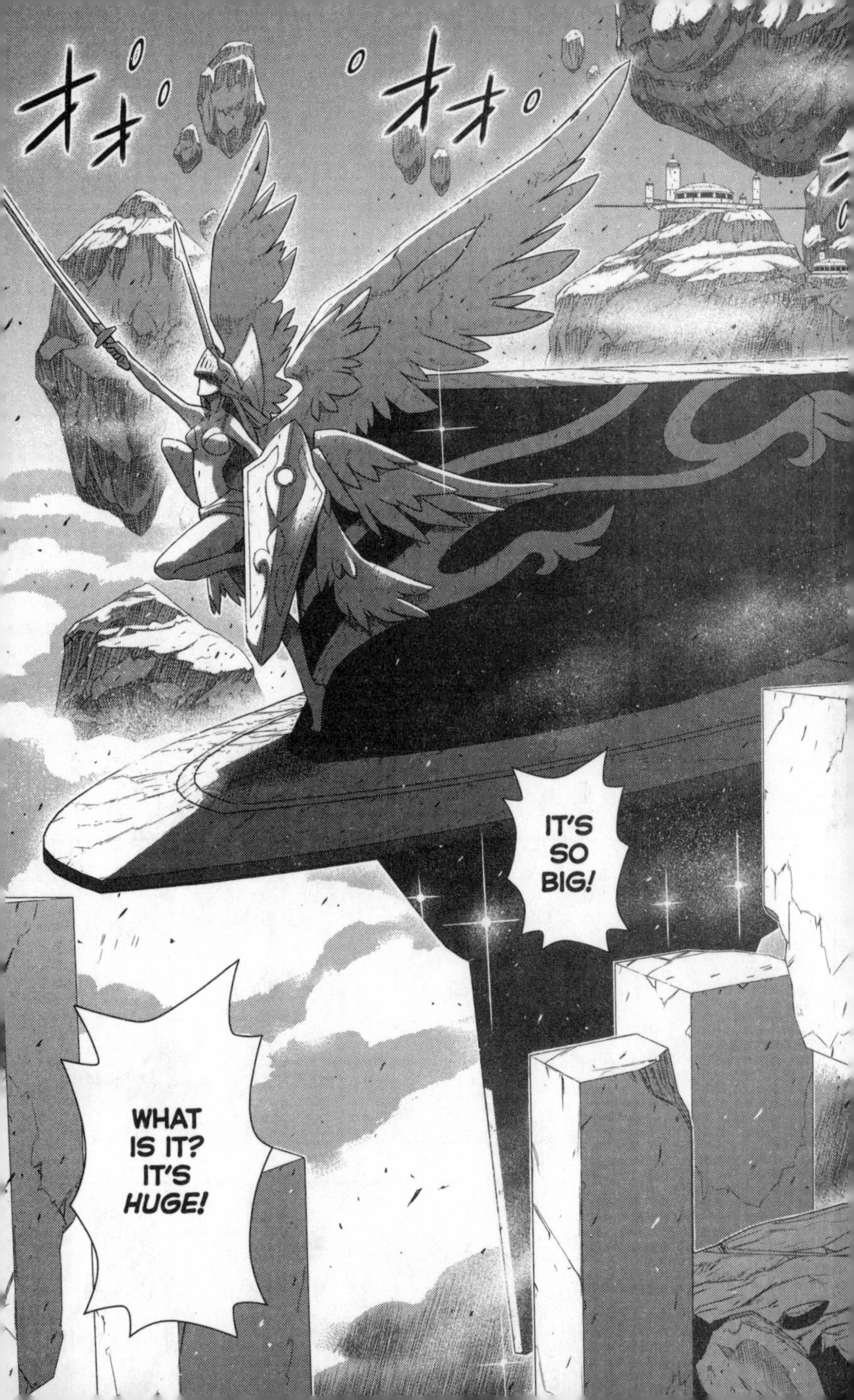
オオ
オオ
IT'S SO BIG!
WHAT IS IT? IT'S HUGE!

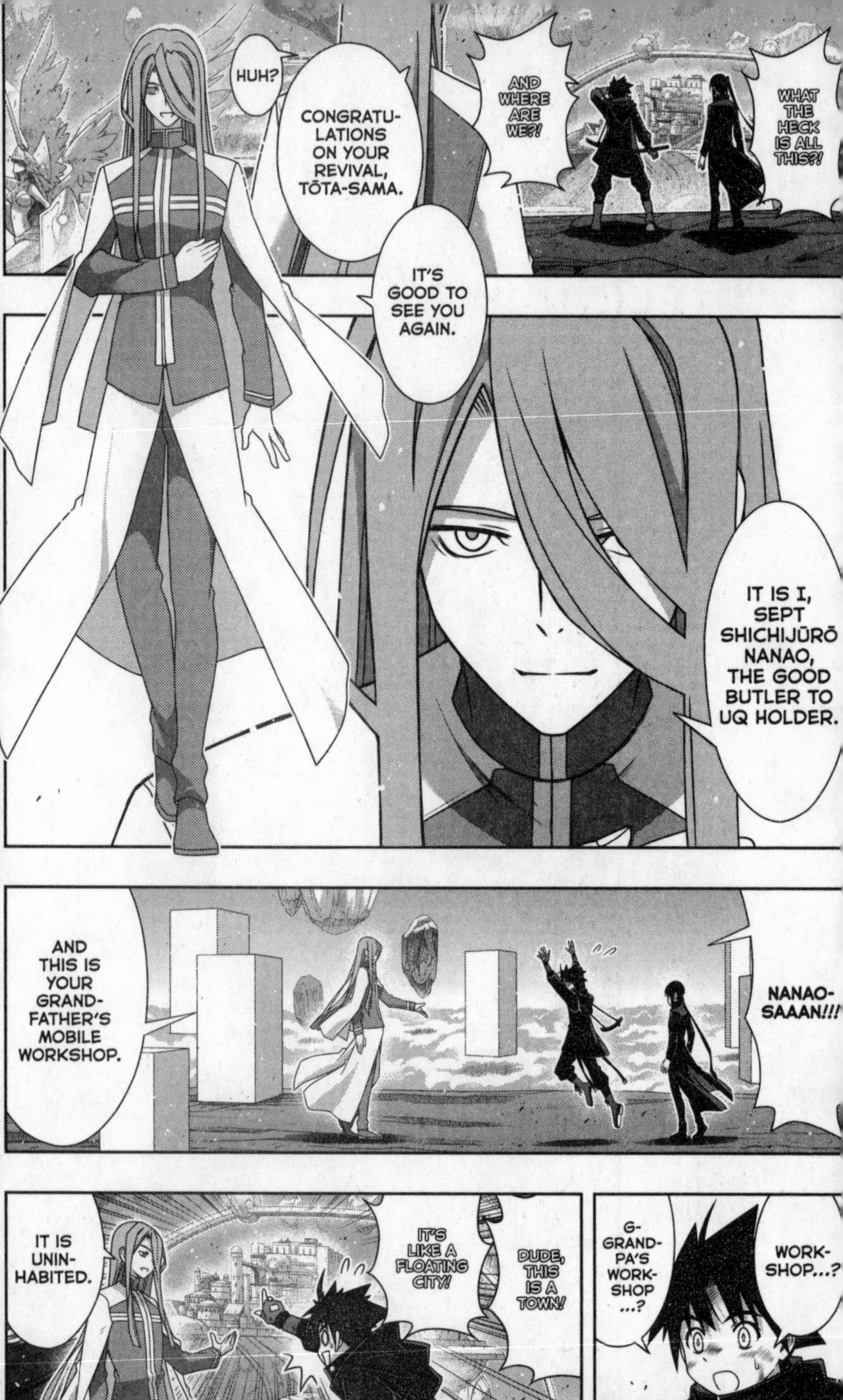
WHAT THE HECK IS ALL THIS?!
AND WHERE ARE WE?!
HUH?
CONGRATULATIONS ON YOUR REVIVAL, TŌTA-SAMA.
IT'S GOOD TO SEE YOU AGAIN.
IT IS I, SEPT SHICHIJŪRŌ NANAO, THE GOOD BUTLER TO UQ HOLDER.
NANAO-SAAAN!!!
AND THIS IS YOUR GRANDFATHER'S MOBILE WORKSHOP.
WORKSHOP...?
G-GRANDPA'S WORKSHOP...?
DUDE, THIS IS A TOWN!
IT'S LIKE A FLOATING CITY!
IT IS UNINHABITED.

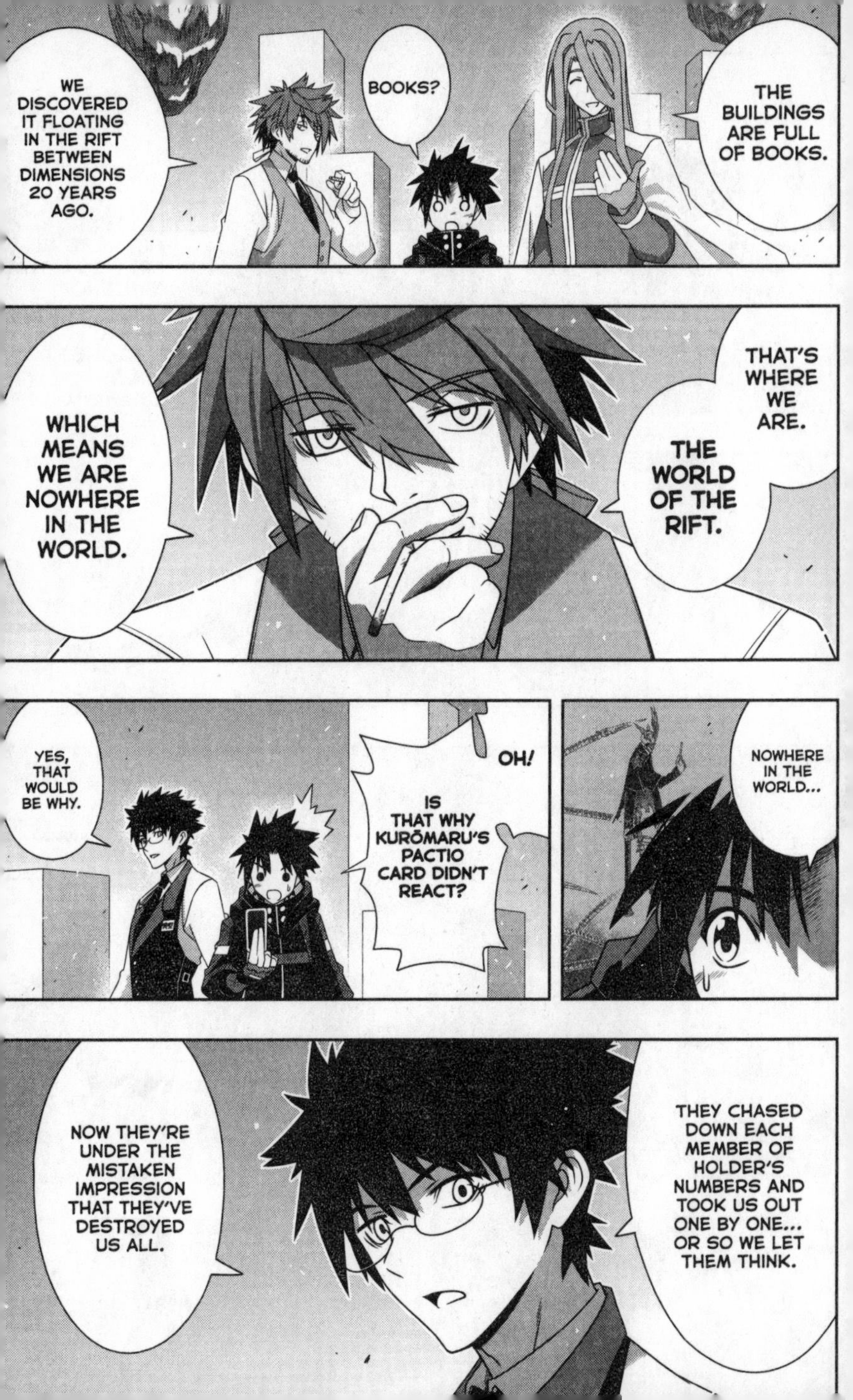
THE BUILDINGS ARE FULL OF BOOKS.
BOOKS?
WE DISCOVERED IT FLOATING IN THE RIFT BETWEEN DIMENSIONS 20 YEARS AGO.
THAT'S WHERE WE ARE.
THE WORLD OF THE RIFT.
WHICH MEANS WE ARE NOWHERE IN THE WORLD.
NOWHERE IN THE WORLD...
OH!
IS THAT WHY KURŌMARU'S PACTIO CARD DIDN'T REACT?
YES, THAT WOULD BE WHY.
THEY CHASED DOWN EACH MEMBER OF HOLDER'S NUMBERS AND TOOK US OUT ONE BY ONE... OR SO WE LET THEM THINK.
NOW THEY'RE UNDER THE MISTAKEN IMPRESSION THAT THEY'VE DESTROYED US ALL.

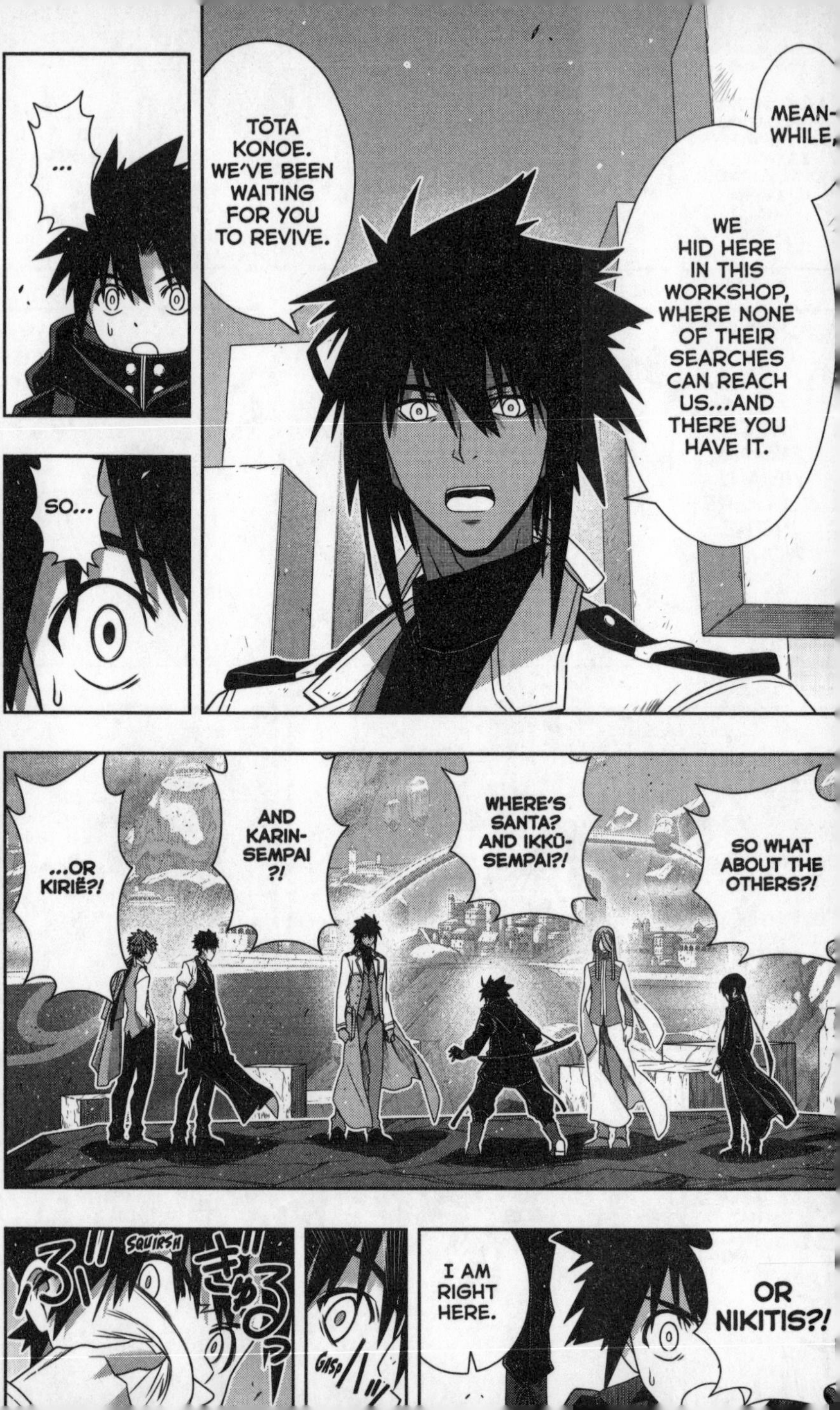
MEAN-WHILE,
WE HID HERE IN THIS WORKSHOP, WHERE NONE OF THEIR SEARCHES CAN REACH US...AND THERE YOU HAVE IT.
TŌTA KONOE. WE'VE BEEN WAITING FOR YOU TO REVIVE.
...
SO...
SO WHAT ABOUT THE OTHERS?!
WHERE'S SANTA? AND IKKŪ-SEMPAI?!
AND KARIN-SEMPAI ?!
...OR KIRIË?!
OR NIKITIS?!
I AM RIGHT HERE.
GASP
SQUIRSH

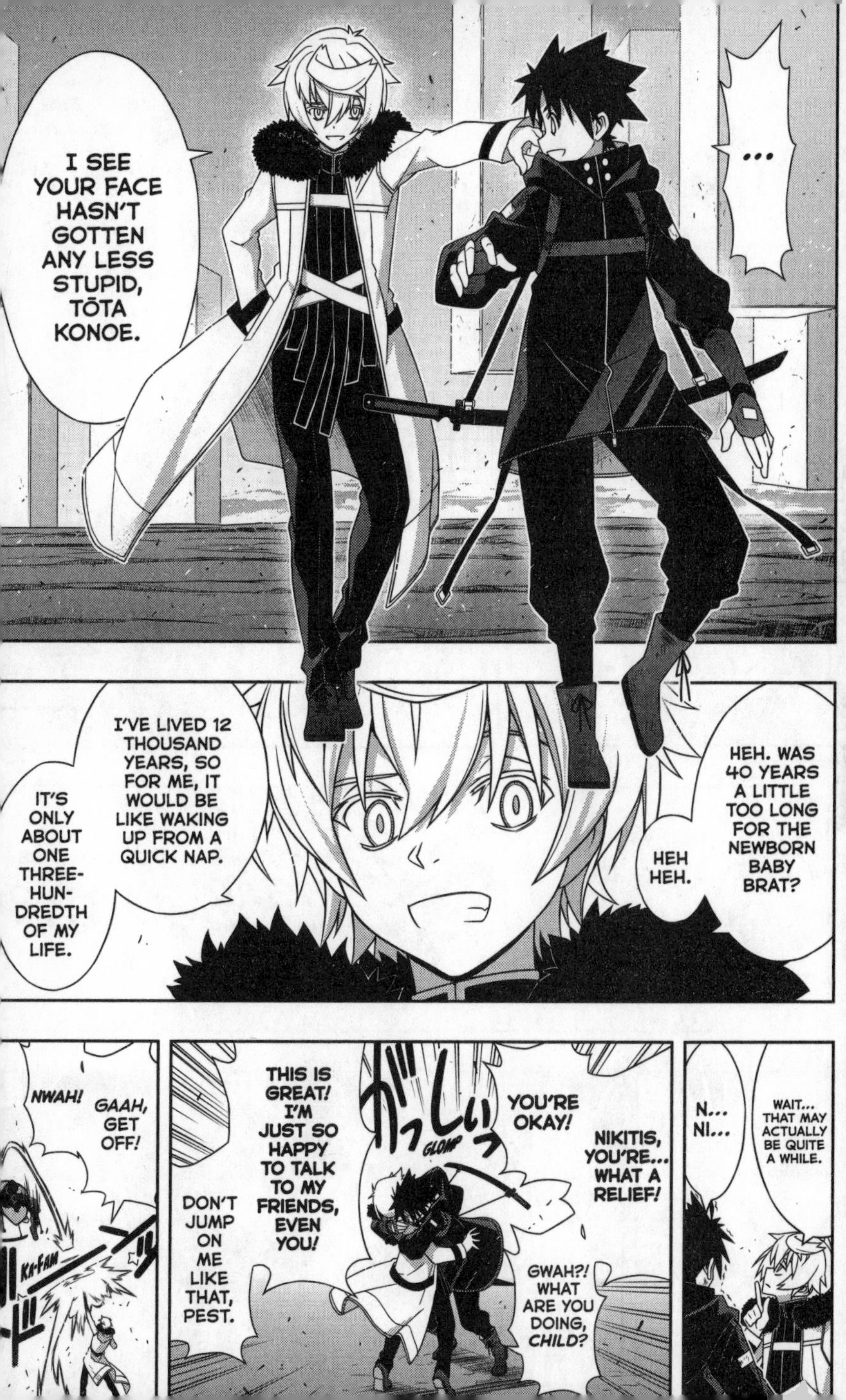
...
I SEE YOUR FACE HASN'T GOTTEN ANY LESS STUPID, TŌTA KONOE.
HEH. WAS 40 YEARS A LITTLE TOO LONG FOR THE NEWBORN BABY BRAT?
HEH HEH.
I'VE LIVED 12 THOUSAND YEARS, SO FOR ME, IT WOULD BE LIKE WAKING UP FROM A QUICK NAP.
IT'S ONLY ABOUT ONE THREE-HUNDREDTH OF MY LIFE.
WAIT... THAT MAY ACTUALLY BE QUITE A WHILE.
N... NI...
YOU'RE OKAY!
NIKITIS, YOU'RE... WHAT A RELIEF!
THIS IS GREAT! I'M JUST SO HAPPY TO TALK TO MY FRIENDS, EVEN YOU!
GLOMP
GWAH?! WHAT ARE YOU DOING, CHILD?
DON'T JUMP ON ME LIKE THAT, PEST.
GAAH, GET OFF!
NWAH!
KA-FAM

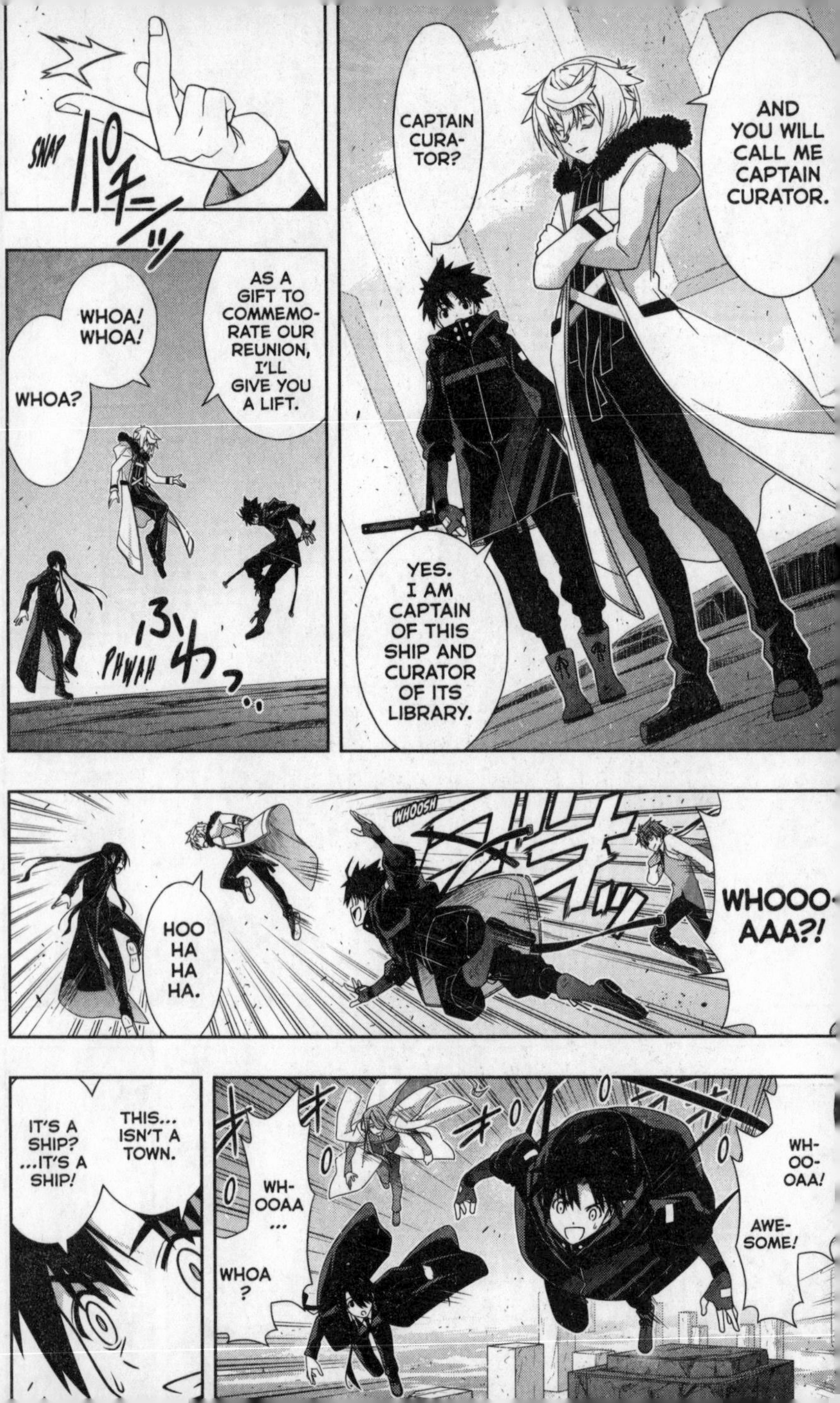
AND YOU WILL CALL ME CAPTAIN CURATOR.
CAPTAIN CURA-TOR?
YES. I AM CAPTAIN OF THIS SHIP AND CURATOR OF ITS LIBRARY.
SNAP
パチーンッ
AS A GIFT TO COMMEMO-RATE OUR REUNION, I'LL GIVE YOU A LIFT.
WHOA! WHOA!
WHOA?
PHWAH
ふわっ
WHOOO-AAA?!
WHOOSH
HOO HA HA HA.
WH-OO-OAA!
AWE-SOME!
WH-OOAA ...
WHOA ?
THIS... ISN'T A TOWN.
IT'S A SHIP? ...IT'S A SHIP!

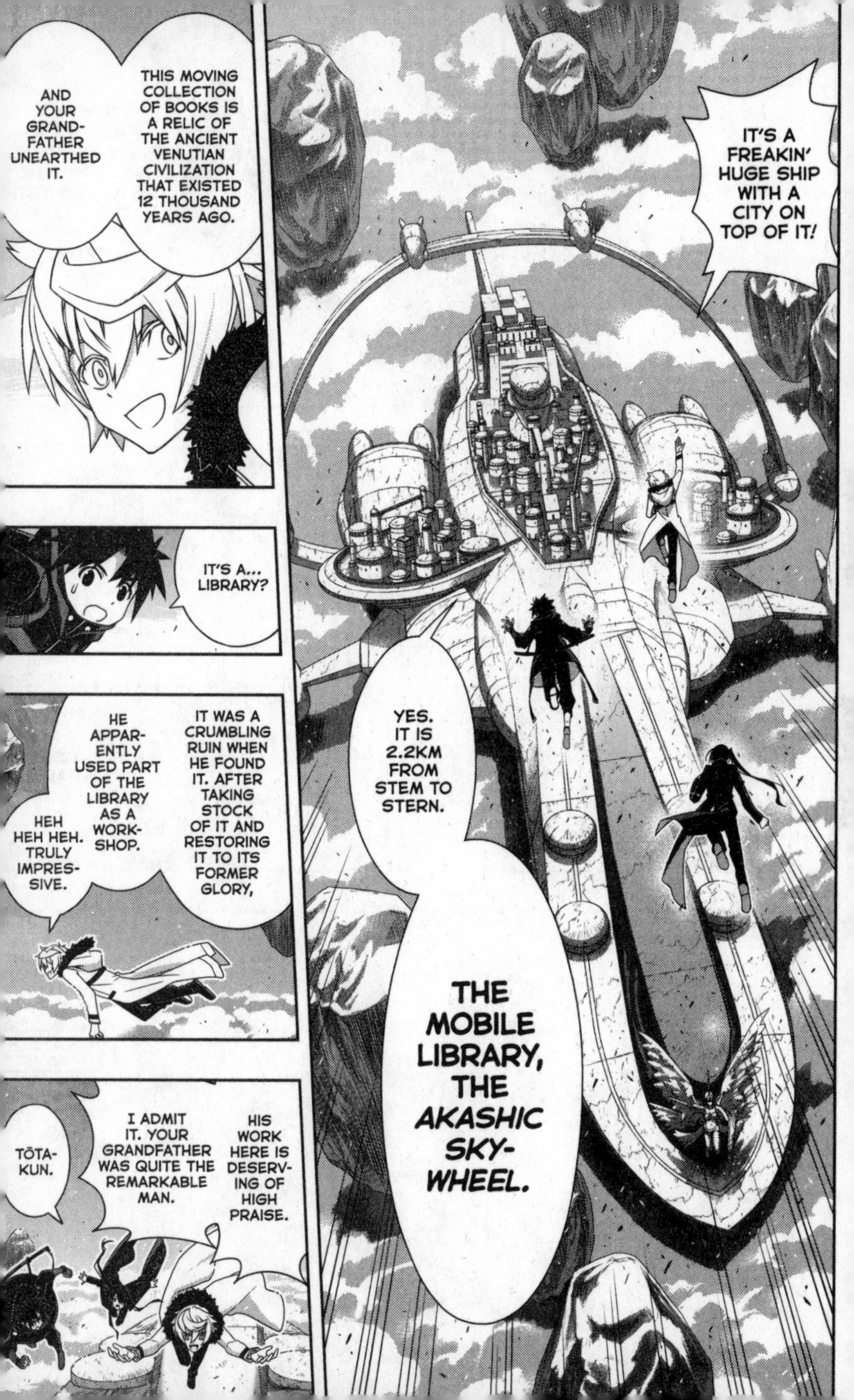
IT'S A FREAKIN' HUGE SHIP WITH A CITY ON TOP OF IT!
YES. IT IS 2.2KM FROM STEM TO STERN.
THE MOBILE LIBRARY, THE *AKASHIC SKY-WHEEL.*
THIS MOVING COLLECTION OF BOOKS IS A RELIC OF THE ANCIENT VENUTIAN CIVILIZATION THAT EXISTED 12 THOUSAND YEARS AGO.
AND YOUR GRAND-FATHER UNEARTHED IT.
IT'S A... LIBRARY?
IT WAS A CRUMBLING RUIN WHEN HE FOUND IT. AFTER TAKING STOCK OF IT AND RESTORING IT TO ITS FORMER GLORY,
HE APPAR-ENTLY USED PART OF THE LIBRARY AS A WORK-SHOP.
HEH HEH HEH. TRULY IMPRES-SIVE.
HIS WORK HERE IS DESERV-ING OF HIGH PRAISE.
I ADMIT IT. YOUR GRANDFATHER WAS QUITE THE REMARKABLE MAN.
TŌTA-KUN.

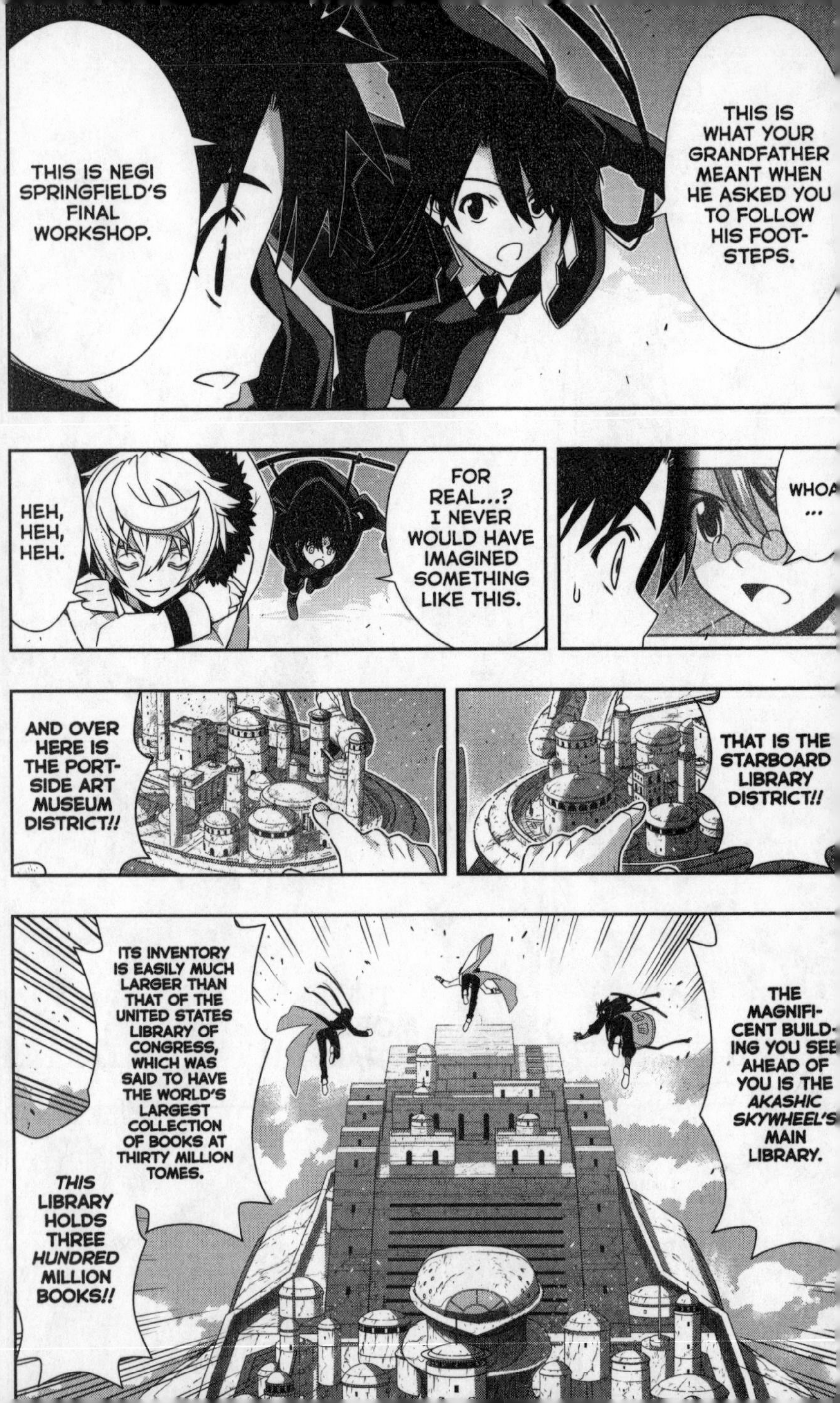
THIS IS WHAT YOUR GRANDFATHER MEANT WHEN HE ASKED YOU TO FOLLOW HIS FOOT-STEPS.
THIS IS NEGI SPRINGFIELD'S FINAL WORKSHOP.
WHOA...
FOR REAL...? I NEVER WOULD HAVE IMAGINED SOMETHING LIKE THIS.
HEH, HEH, HEH.
THAT IS THE STARBOARD LIBRARY DISTRICT!!
AND OVER HERE IS THE PORT-SIDE ART MUSEUM DISTRICT!!
THE MAGNIFI-CENT BUILD-ING YOU SEE AHEAD OF YOU IS THE *AKASHIC SKYWHEEL'S* MAIN LIBRARY.
ITS INVENTORY IS EASILY MUCH LARGER THAN THAT OF THE UNITED STATES LIBRARY OF CONGRESS, WHICH WAS SAID TO HAVE THE WORLD'S LARGEST COLLECTION OF BOOKS AT THIRTY MILLION TOMES.
THIS LIBRARY HOLDS THREE *HUNDRED* MILLION BOOKS!!

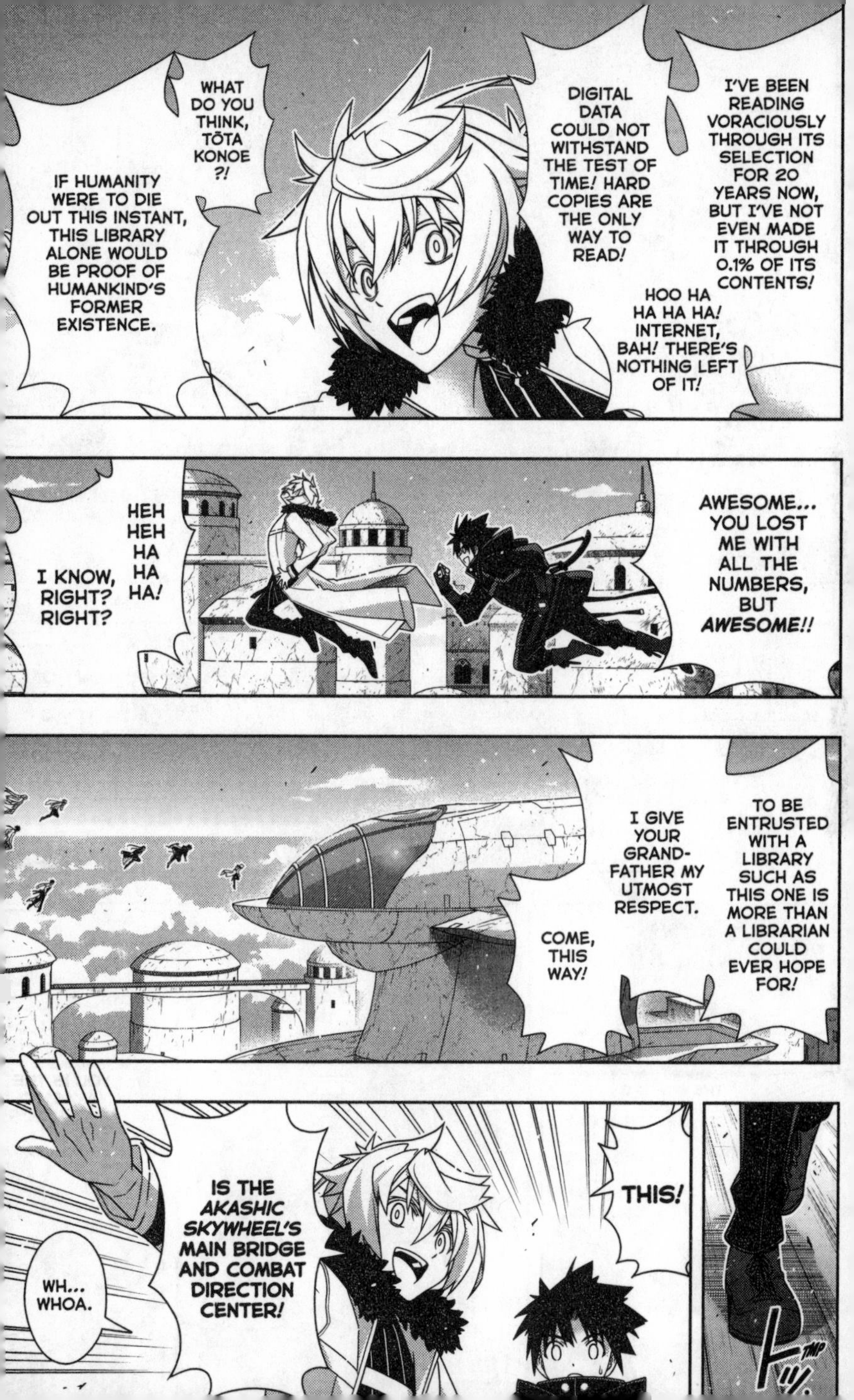

I'VE BEEN READING VORACIOUSLY THROUGH ITS SELECTION FOR 20 YEARS NOW, BUT I'VE NOT EVEN MADE IT THROUGH 0.1% OF ITS CONTENTS!
DIGITAL DATA COULD NOT WITHSTAND THE TEST OF TIME! HARD COPIES ARE THE ONLY WAY TO READ!
HOO HA HA HA HA! INTERNET, BAH! THERE'S NOTHING LEFT OF IT!
WHAT DO YOU THINK, TŌTA KONOE?!
IF HUMANITY WERE TO DIE OUT THIS INSTANT, THIS LIBRARY ALONE WOULD BE PROOF OF HUMANKIND'S FORMER EXISTENCE.
AWESOME... YOU LOST ME WITH ALL THE NUMBERS, BUT *AWESOME!!*
HEH HEH HA HA HA!
I KNOW, RIGHT? RIGHT?
TO BE ENTRUSTED WITH A LIBRARY SUCH AS THIS ONE IS MORE THAN A LIBRARIAN COULD EVER HOPE FOR!
I GIVE YOUR GRANDFATHER MY UTMOST RESPECT.
COME, THIS WAY!
TMP
THIS!
IS THE *AKASHIC SKYWHEEL'S* MAIN BRIDGE AND COMBAT DIRECTION CENTER!
WH... WHOA.

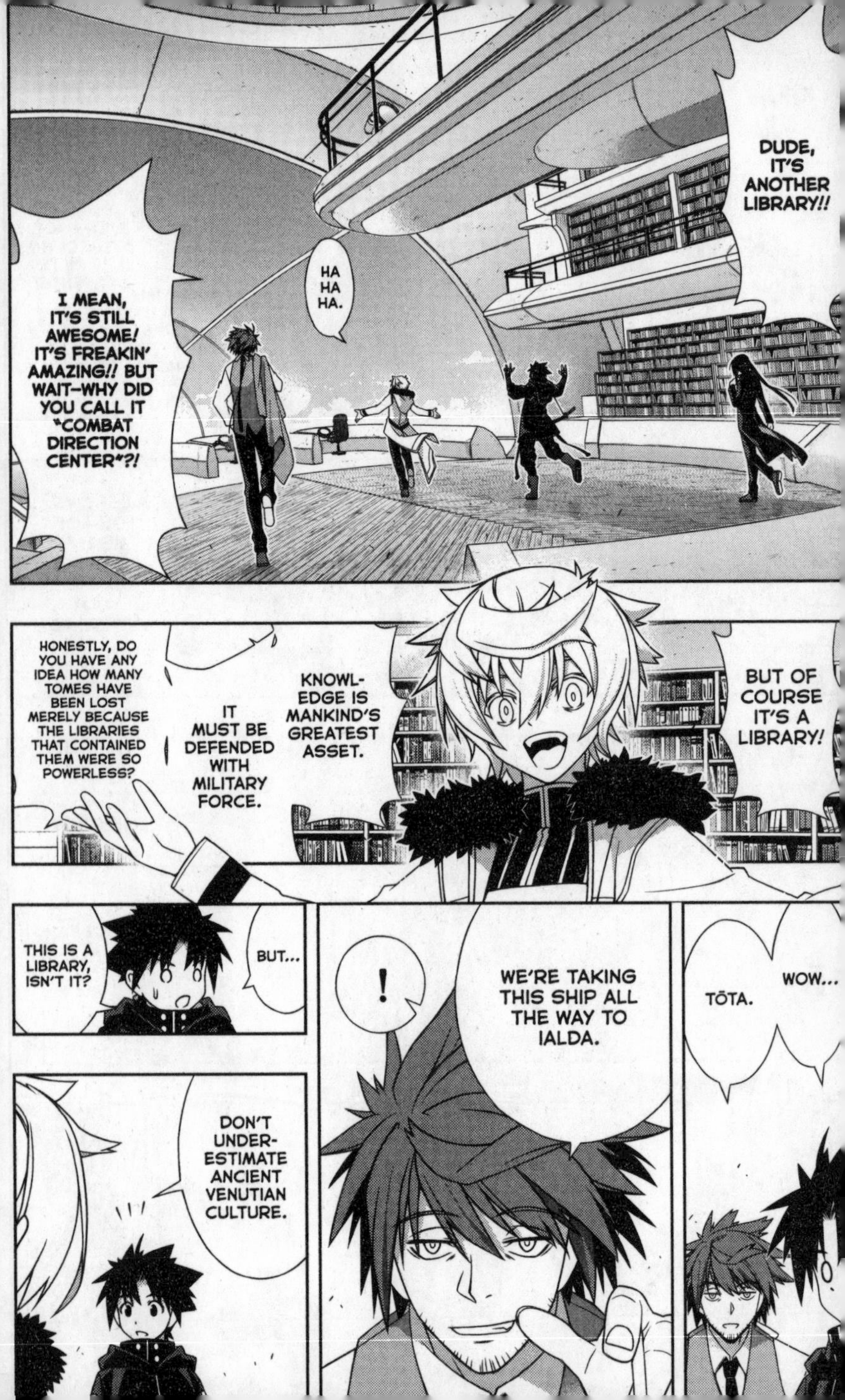

DUDE, IT'S ANOTHER LIBRARY!!
HA HA HA.
I MEAN, IT'S STILL AWESOME! IT'S FREAKIN' AMAZING!! BUT WAIT—WHY DID YOU CALL IT "COMBAT DIRECTION CENTER"?!
BUT OF COURSE IT'S A LIBRARY!
KNOWL-EDGE IS MANKIND'S GREATEST ASSET.
IT MUST BE DEFENDED WITH MILITARY FORCE.
HONESTLY, DO YOU HAVE ANY IDEA HOW MANY TOMES HAVE BEEN LOST MERELY BECAUSE THE LIBRARIES THAT CONTAINED THEM WERE SO POWERLESS?
WOW...
TŌTA.
!
WE'RE TAKING THIS SHIP ALL THE WAY TO IALDA.
BUT...
THIS IS A LIBRARY, ISN'T IT?
DON'T UNDER-ESTIMATE ANCIENT VENUTIAN CULTURE.

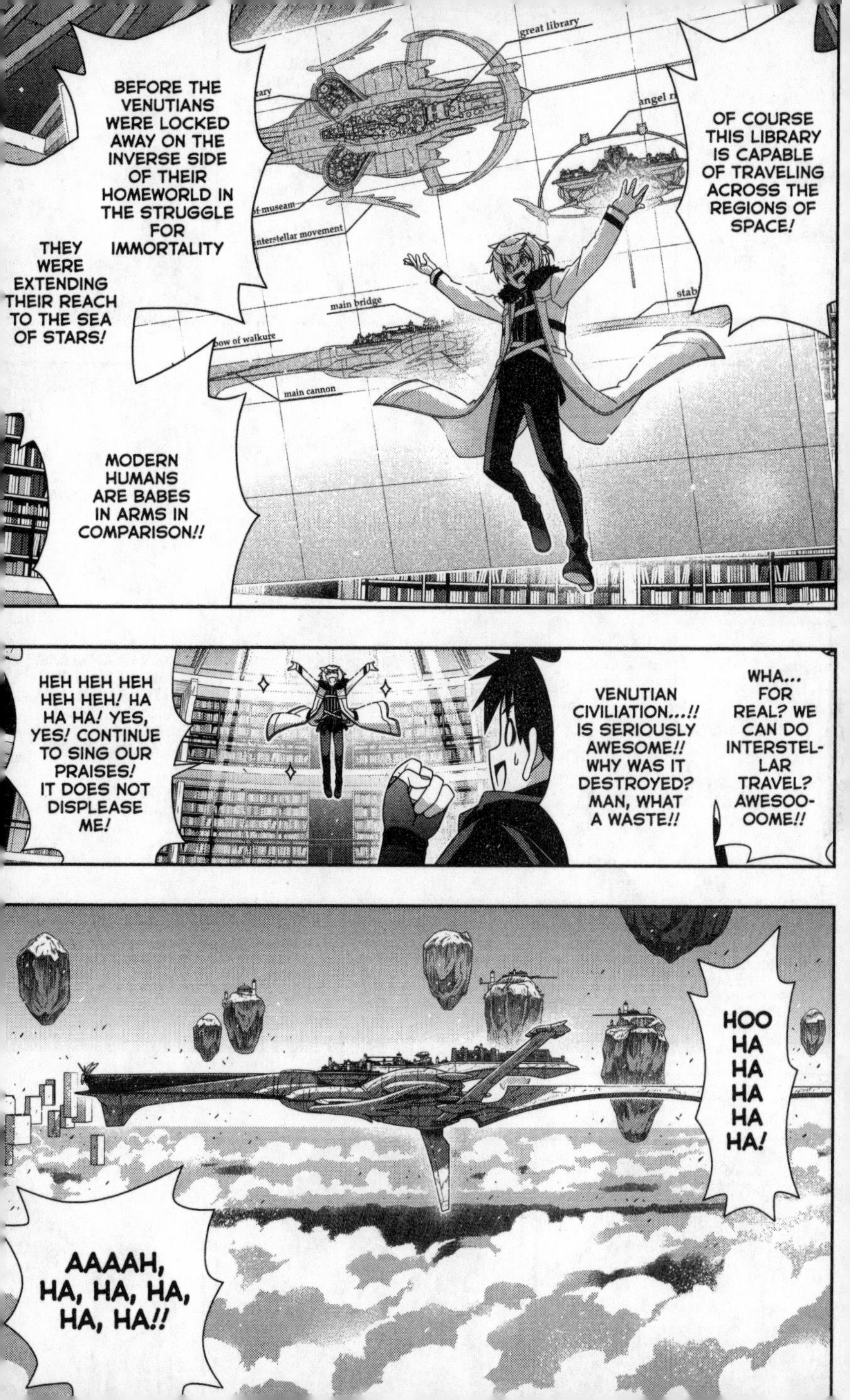
great library
interstellar movement
main bridge
main cannon
OF COURSE THIS LIBRARY IS CAPABLE OF TRAVELING ACROSS THE REGIONS OF SPACE!
BEFORE THE VENUTIANS WERE LOCKED AWAY ON THE INVERSE SIDE OF THEIR HOMEWORLD IN THE STRUGGLE FOR IMMORTALITY
THEY WERE EXTENDING THEIR REACH TO THE SEA OF STARS!
MODERN HUMANS ARE BABES IN ARMS IN COMPARISON!!
WHA... FOR REAL? WE CAN DO INTERSTEL-LAR TRAVEL? AWESOO-OOME!!
VENUTIAN CIVILIATION...!! IS SERIOUSLY AWESOME!! WHY WAS IT DESTROYED? MAN, WHAT A WASTE!!
HEH HEH HEH HEH HEH! HA HA HA! YES, YES! CONTINUE TO SING OUR PRAISES! IT DOES NOT DISPLEASE ME!
HOO HA HA HA HA HA!
AAAAH, HA, HA, HA, HA, HA!!

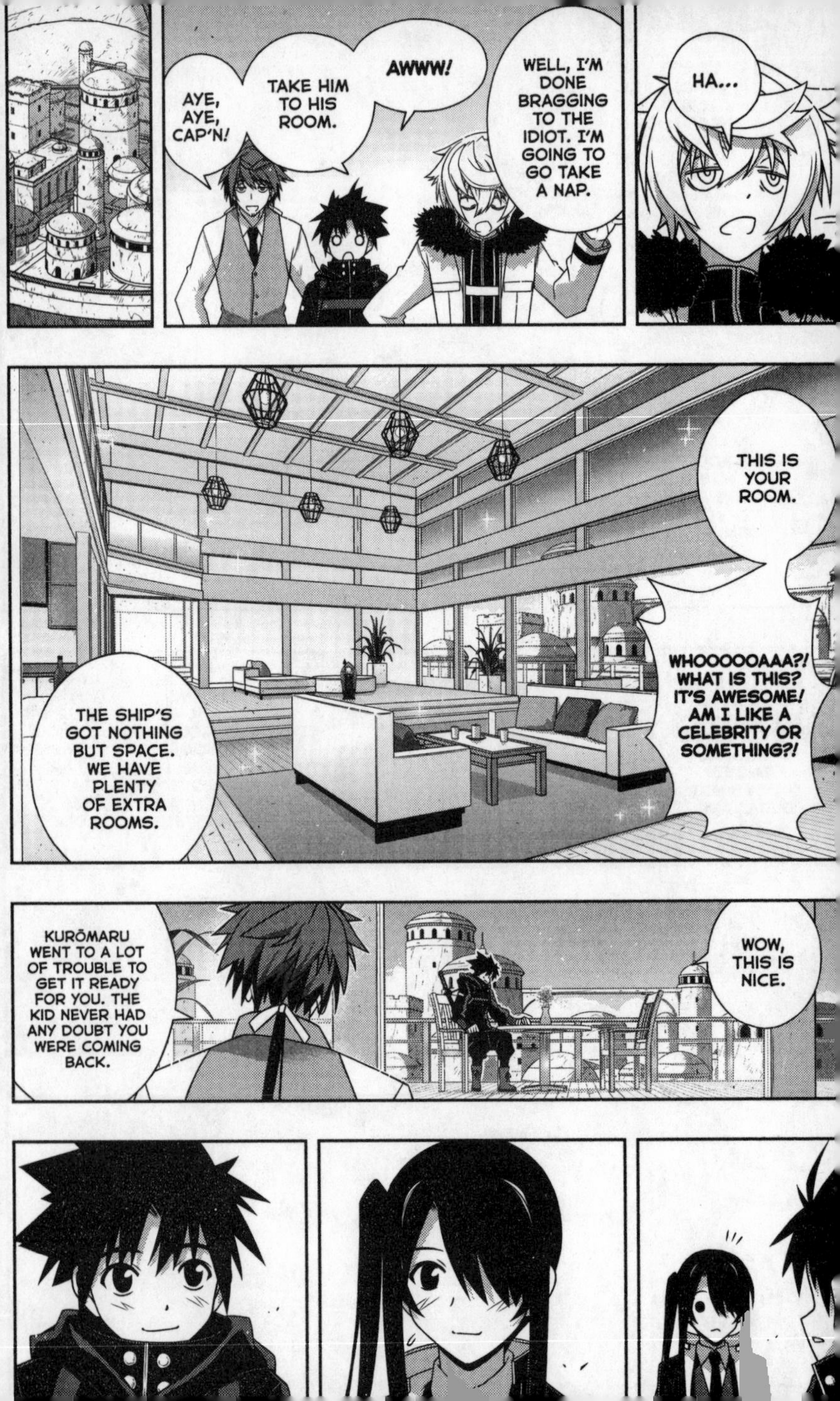
HA...
WELL, I'M DONE BRAGGING TO THE IDIOT. I'M GOING TO GO TAKE A NAP.
AWWW!
TAKE HIM TO HIS ROOM.
AYE, AYE, CAP'N!
THIS IS YOUR ROOM.
WHOOOOOAAA?! WHAT IS THIS? IT'S AWESOME! AM I LIKE A CELEBRITY OR SOMETHING?!
THE SHIP'S GOT NOTHING BUT SPACE. WE HAVE PLENTY OF EXTRA ROOMS.
WOW, THIS IS NICE.
KURŌMARU WENT TO A LOT OF TROUBLE TO GET IT READY FOR YOU. THE KID NEVER HAD ANY DOUBT YOU WERE COMING BACK.

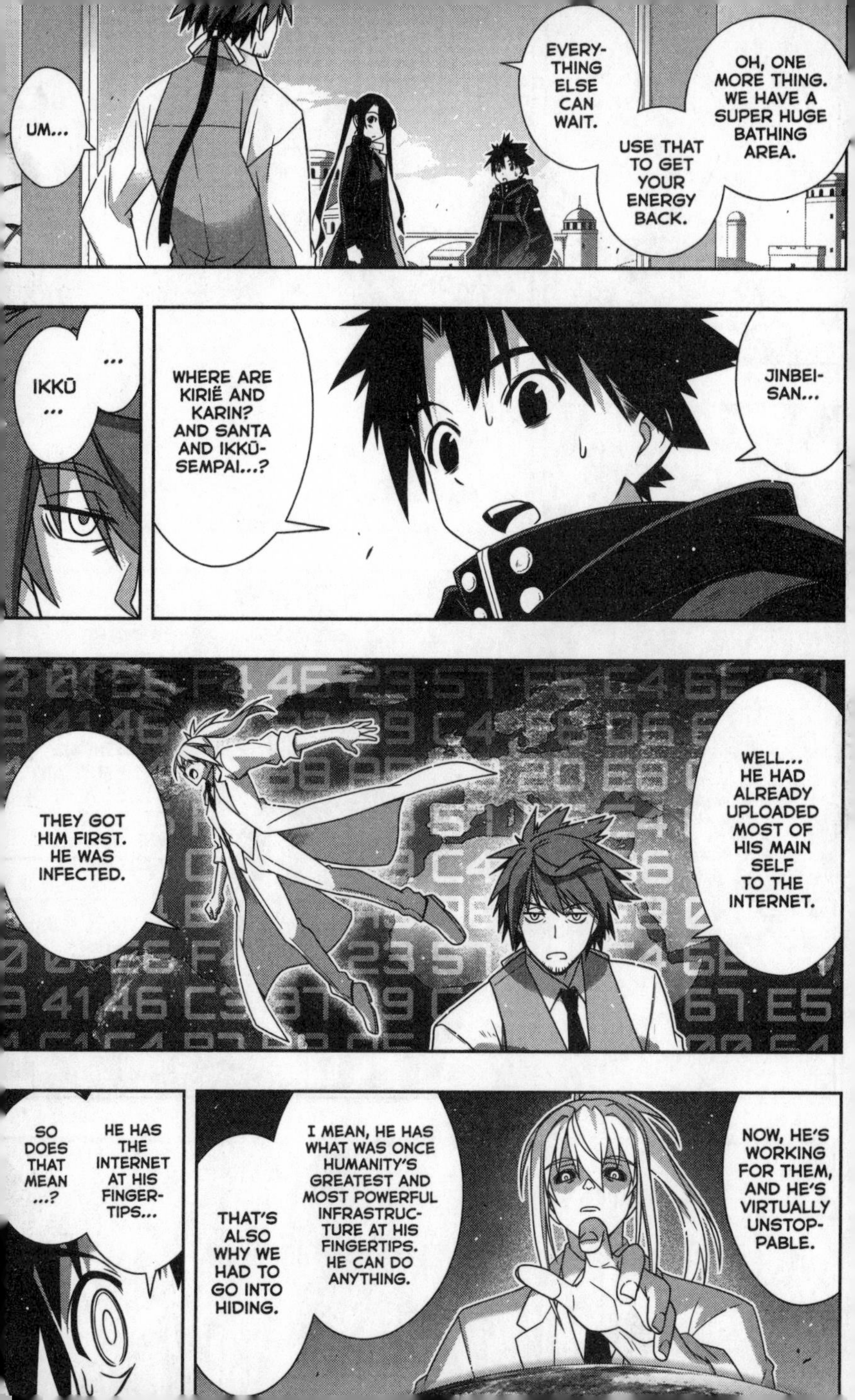

OH, ONE MORE THING. WE HAVE A SUPER HUGE BATHING AREA.
USE THAT TO GET YOUR ENERGY BACK.
EVERYTHING ELSE CAN WAIT.
UM...
JINBEI-SAN...
WHERE ARE KIRIË AND KARIN? AND SANTA AND IKKŪ-SEMPAI...?
... IKKŪ ...
WELL... HE HAD ALREADY UPLOADED MOST OF HIS MAIN SELF TO THE INTERNET.
THEY GOT HIM FIRST. HE WAS INFECTED.
NOW, HE'S WORKING FOR THEM, AND HE'S VIRTUALLY UNSTOPPABLE.
I MEAN, HE HAS WHAT WAS ONCE HUMANITY'S GREATEST AND MOST POWERFUL INFRASTRUCTURE AT HIS FINGERTIPS. HE CAN DO ANYTHING.
THAT'S ALSO WHY WE HAD TO GO INTO HIDING.
HE HAS THE INTERNET AT HIS FINGERTIPS...
SO DOES THAT MEAN ...?

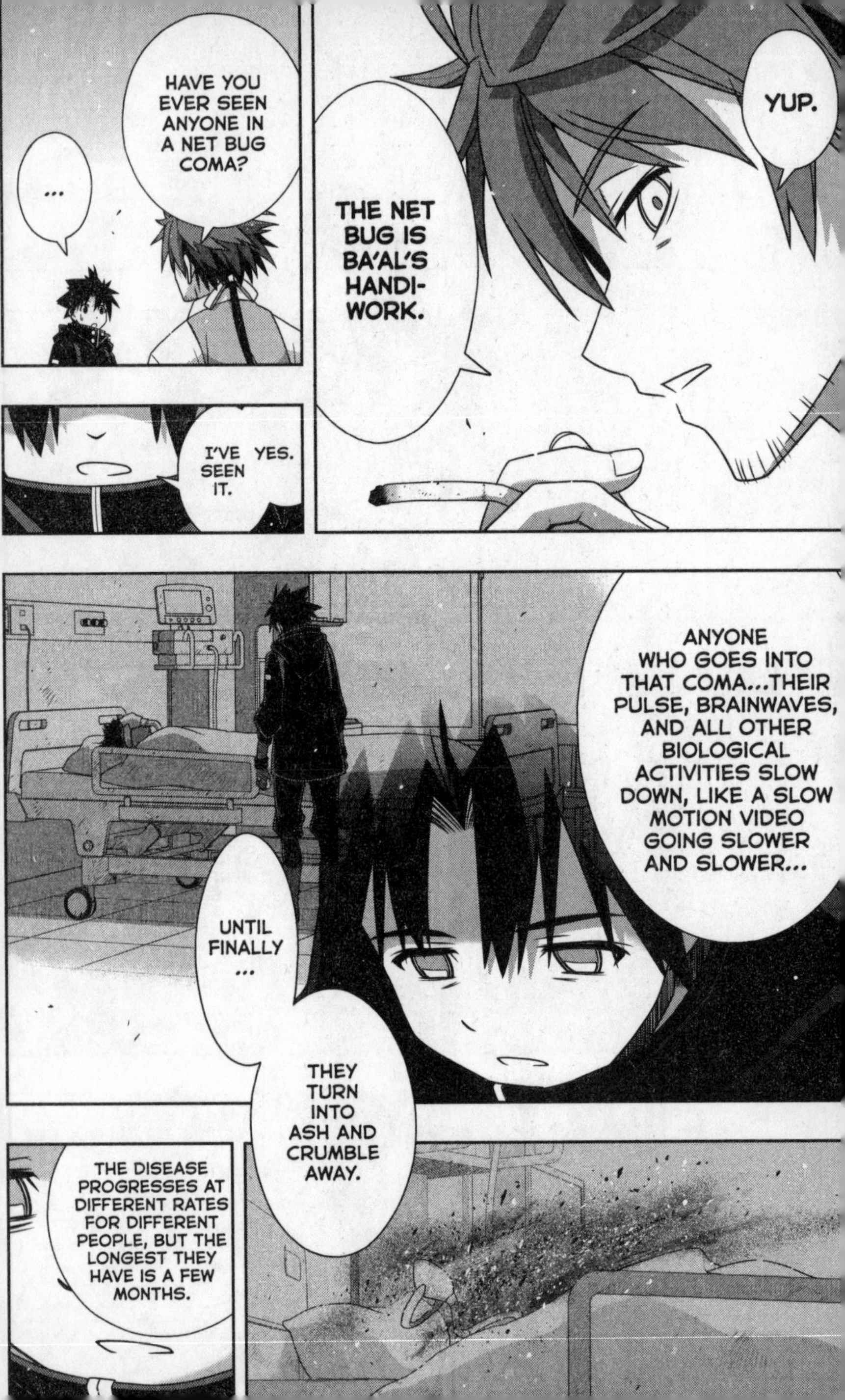
YUP.
THE NET BUG IS BA'AL'S HANDIWORK.
HAVE YOU EVER SEEN ANYONE IN A NET BUG COMA?
...
YES.
I'VE SEEN IT.
ANYONE WHO GOES INTO THAT COMA...THEIR PULSE, BRAINWAVES, AND ALL OTHER BIOLOGICAL ACTIVITIES SLOW DOWN, LIKE A SLOW MOTION VIDEO GOING SLOWER AND SLOWER...
UNTIL FINALLY ...
THEY TURN INTO ASH AND CRUMBLE AWAY.
THE DISEASE PROGRESSES AT DIFFERENT RATES FOR DIFFERENT PEOPLE, BUT THE LONGEST THEY HAVE IS A FEW MONTHS.

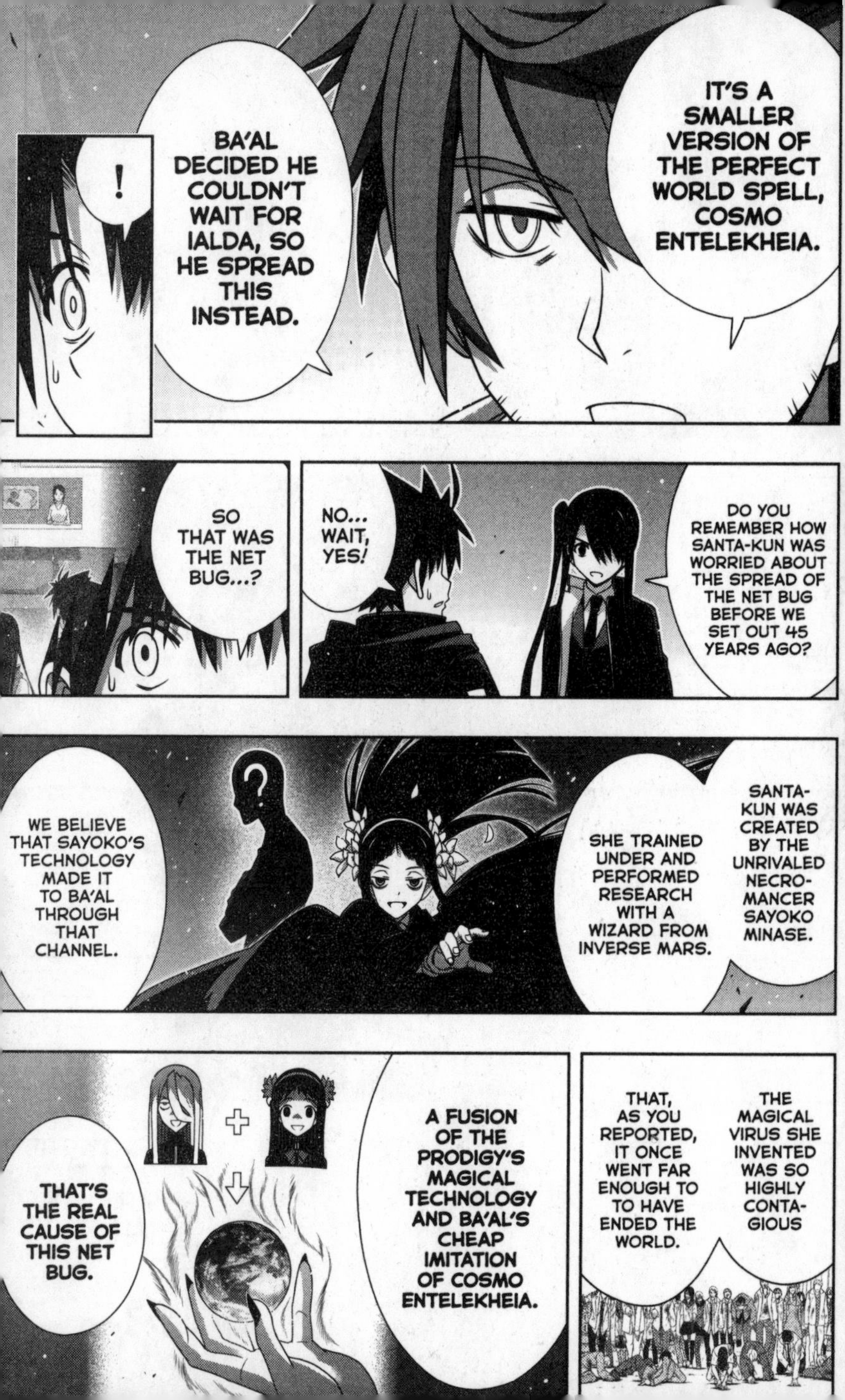
IT'S A SMALLER VERSION OF THE PERFECT WORLD SPELL, COSMO ENTELEKHEIA.
BA'AL DECIDED HE COULDN'T WAIT FOR IALDA, SO HE SPREAD THIS INSTEAD.
!
DO YOU REMEMBER HOW SANTA-KUN WAS WORRIED ABOUT THE SPREAD OF THE NET BUG BEFORE WE SET OUT 45 YEARS AGO?
NO... WAIT, YES!
SO THAT WAS THE NET BUG...?
SANTA-KUN WAS CREATED BY THE UNRIVALED NECRO-MANCER SAYOKO MINASE.
SHE TRAINED UNDER AND PERFORMED RESEARCH WITH A WIZARD FROM INVERSE MARS.
WE BELIEVE THAT SAYOKO'S TECHNOLOGY MADE IT TO BA'AL THROUGH THAT CHANNEL.
THE MAGICAL VIRUS SHE INVENTED WAS SO HIGHLY CONTA-GIOUS
THAT, AS YOU REPORTED, IT ONCE WENT FAR ENOUGH TO TO HAVE ENDED THE WORLD.
A FUSION OF THE PRODIGY'S MAGICAL TECHNOLOGY AND BA'AL'S CHEAP IMITATION OF COSMO ENTELEKHEIA.
THAT'S THE REAL CAUSE OF THIS NET BUG.

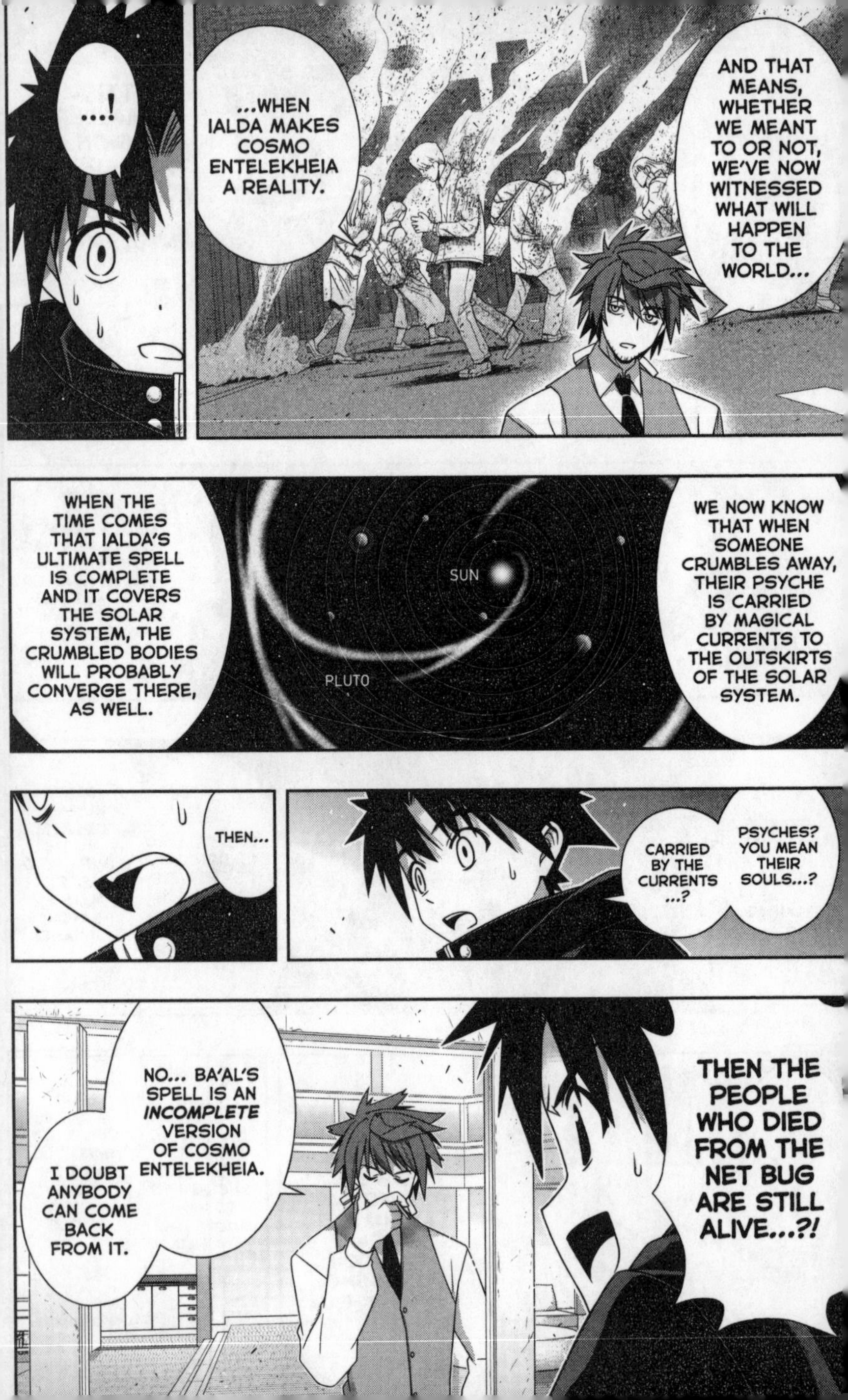
AND THAT MEANS, WHETHER WE MEANT TO OR NOT, WE'VE NOW WITNESSED WHAT WILL HAPPEN TO THE WORLD...
...WHEN IALDA MAKES COSMO ENTELEKHEIA A REALITY.
...!
WE NOW KNOW THAT WHEN SOMEONE CRUMBLES AWAY, THEIR PSYCHE IS CARRIED BY MAGICAL CURRENTS TO THE OUTSKIRTS OF THE SOLAR SYSTEM.
SUN
PLUTO
WHEN THE TIME COMES THAT IALDA'S ULTIMATE SPELL IS COMPLETE AND IT COVERS THE SOLAR SYSTEM, THE CRUMBLED BODIES WILL PROBABLY CONVERGE THERE, AS WELL.
PSYCHES? YOU MEAN THEIR SOULS...?
CARRIED BY THE CURRENTS ...?
THEN...
THEN THE PEOPLE WHO DIED FROM THE NET BUG ARE STILL ALIVE...?!
NO... BA'AL'S SPELL IS AN *INCOMPLETE* VERSION OF COSMO ENTELEKHEIA.
I DOUBT ANYBODY CAN COME BACK FROM IT.

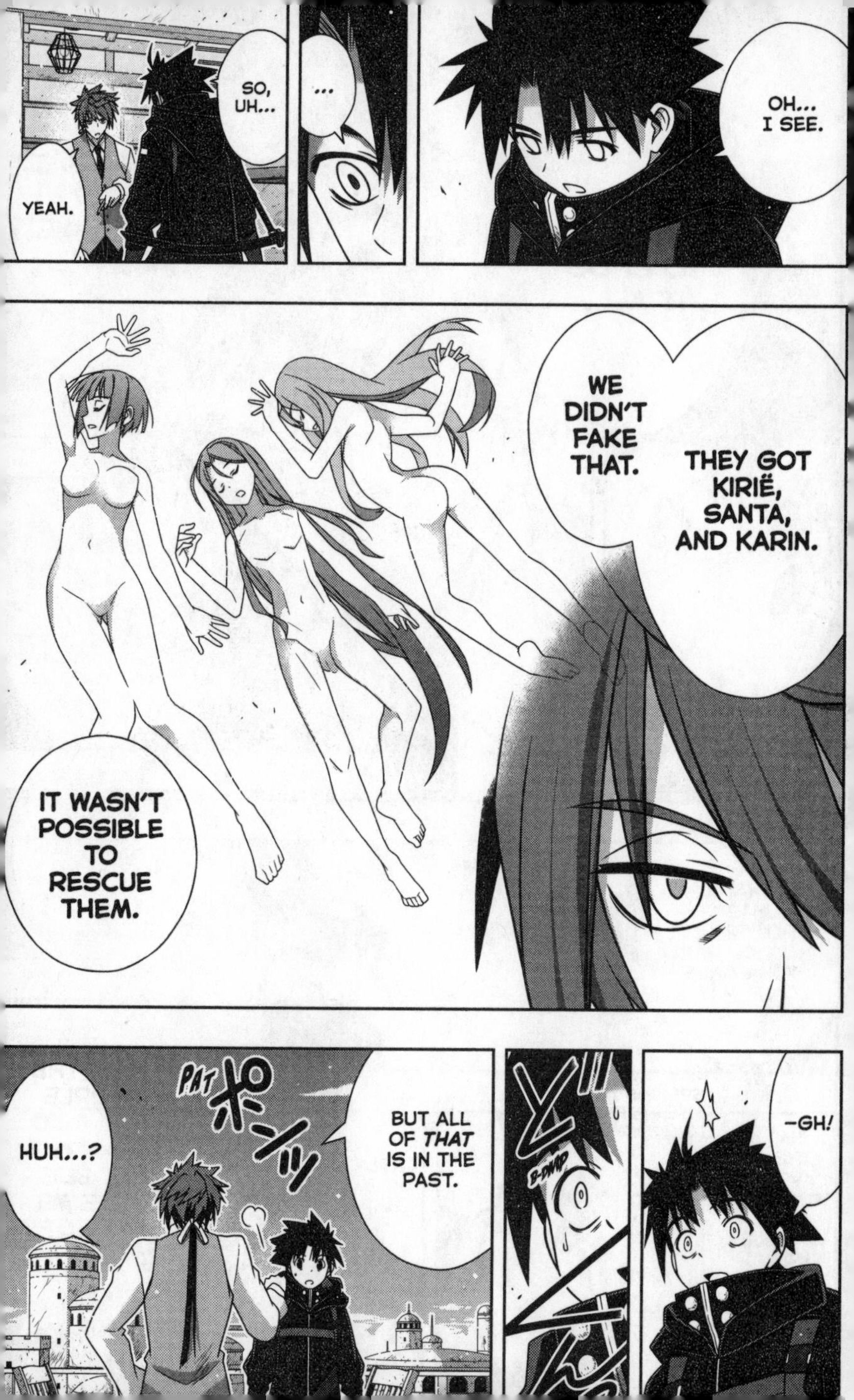
OH... I SEE.
...
SO, UH...
YEAH.
THEY GOT KIRIË, SANTA, AND KARIN.
WE DIDN'T FAKE THAT.
IT WASN'T POSSIBLE TO RESCUE THEM.
-GH!
BUT ALL OF *THAT* IS IN THE PAST.
PAT
HUH...?

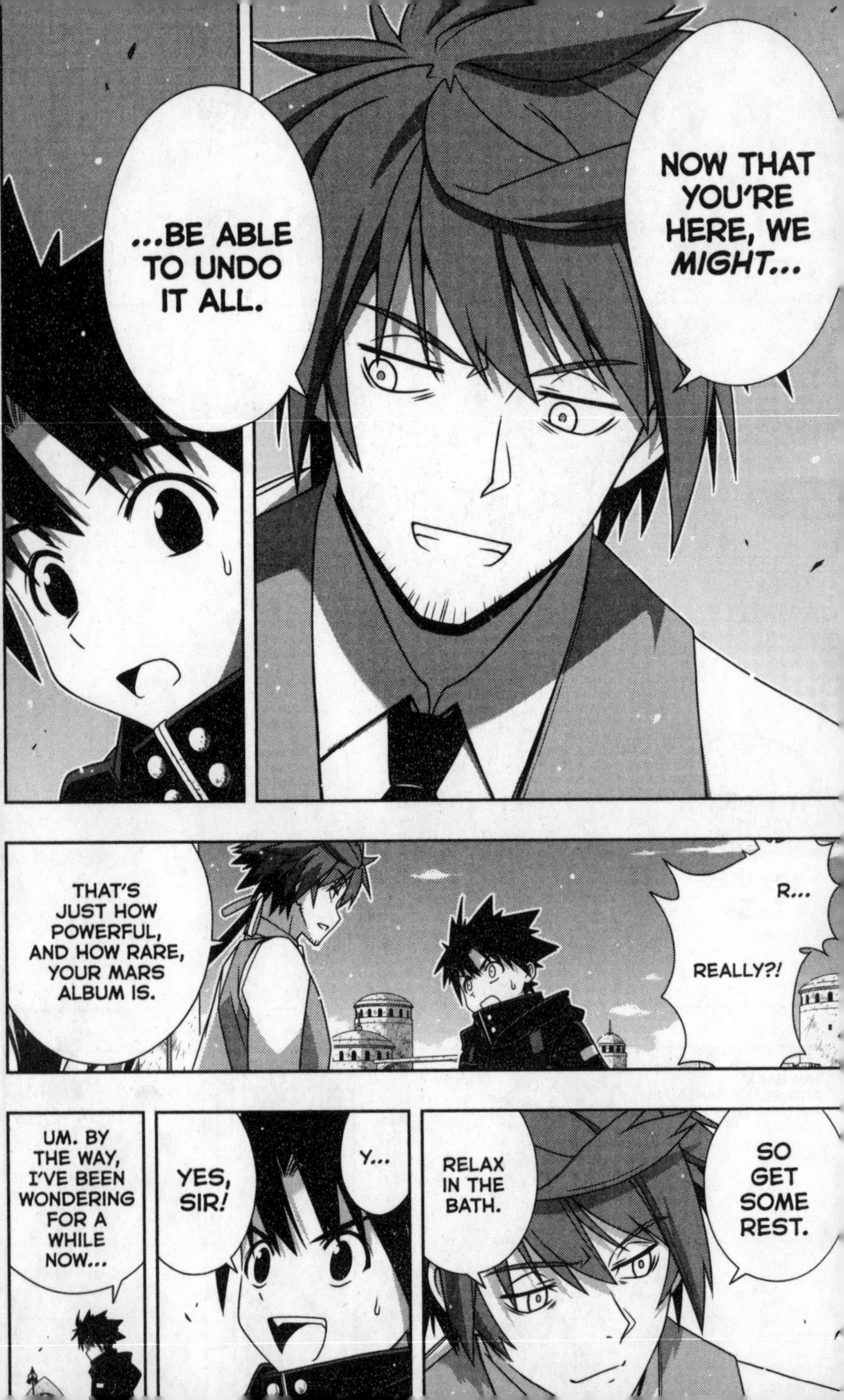
NOW THAT YOU'RE HERE, WE *MIGHT*...
...BE ABLE TO UNDO IT ALL.
R...
REALLY?!
THAT'S JUST HOW POWERFUL, AND HOW RARE, YOUR MARS ALBUM IS.
SO GET SOME REST.
RELAX IN THE BATH.
Y...
YES, SIR!
UM. BY THE WAY, I'VE BEEN WONDERING FOR A WHILE NOW...

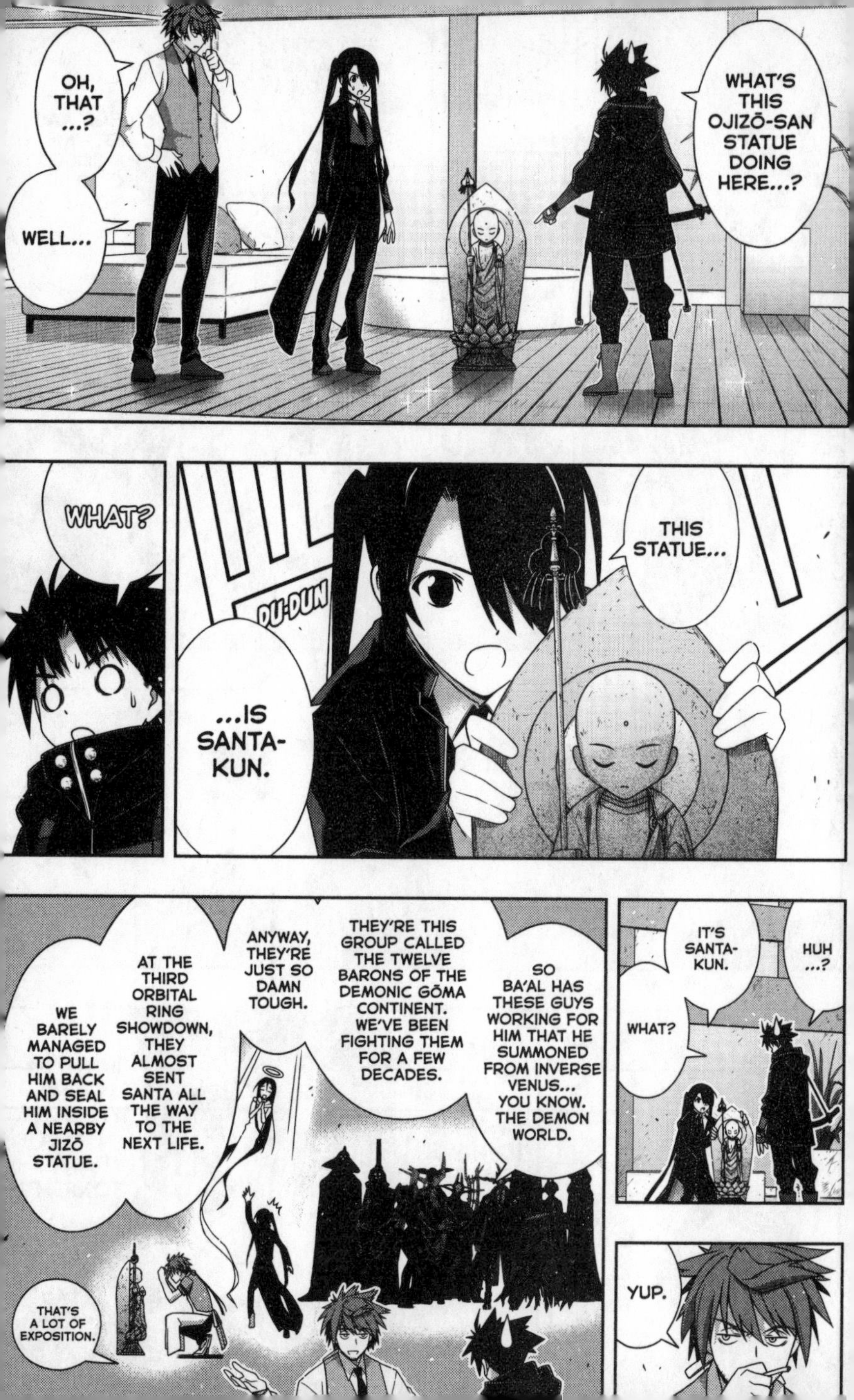
WHAT'S THIS OJIZŌ-SAN STATUE DOING HERE...?
OH, THAT ...?
WELL...
THIS STATUE...
DU-DUN
...IS SANTA-KUN.
WHAT?
IT'S SANTA-KUN.
HUH ...?
WHAT?
YUP.
SO BA'AL HAS THESE GUYS WORKING FOR HIM THAT HE SUMMONED FROM INVERSE VENUS... YOU KNOW. THE DEMON WORLD.
THEY'RE THIS GROUP CALLED THE TWELVE BARONS OF THE DEMONIC GŌMA CONTINENT. WE'VE BEEN FIGHTING THEM FOR A FEW DECADES.
ANYWAY, THEY'RE JUST SO DAMN TOUGH.
AT THE THIRD ORBITAL RING SHOWDOWN, THEY ALMOST SENT SANTA ALL THE WAY TO THE NEXT LIFE.
WE BARELY MANAGED TO PULL HIM BACK AND SEAL HIM INSIDE A NEARBY JIZŌ STATUE.
THAT'S A LOT OF EXPOSITION.

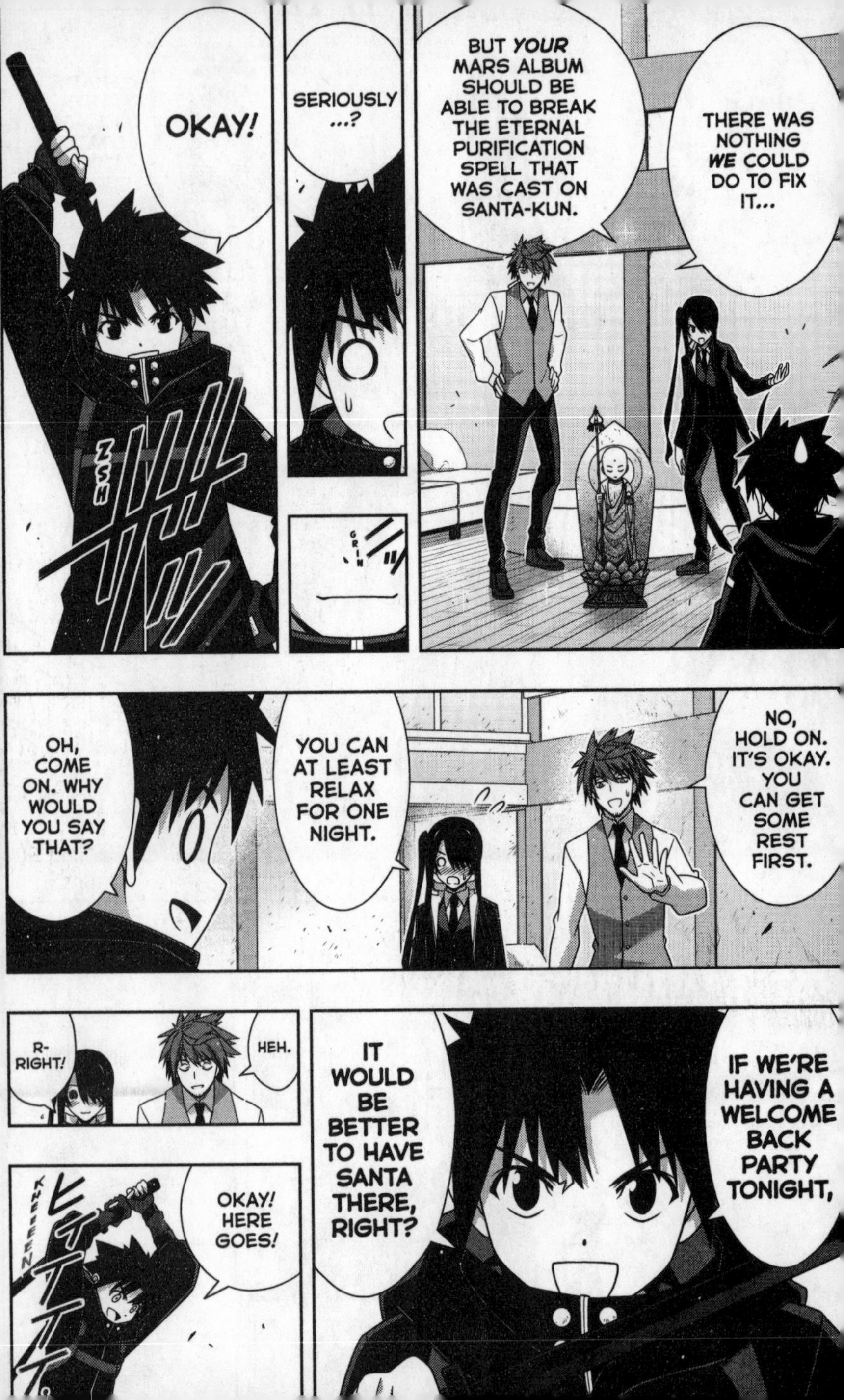
THERE WAS NOTHING WE COULD DO TO FIX IT...
BUT YOUR MARS ALBUM SHOULD BE ABLE TO BREAK THE ETERNAL PURIFICATION SPELL THAT WAS CAST ON SANTA-KUN.
SERIOUSLY ...?
GRIN
OKAY!
ZSH
NO, HOLD ON. IT'S OKAY. YOU CAN GET SOME REST FIRST.
YOU CAN AT LEAST RELAX FOR ONE NIGHT.
OH, COME ON. WHY WOULD YOU SAY THAT?
IF WE'RE HAVING A WELCOME BACK PARTY TONIGHT,
IT WOULD BE BETTER TO HAVE SANTA THERE, RIGHT?
HEH.
R-RIGHT!
OKAY! HERE GOES!
KWEEEEN

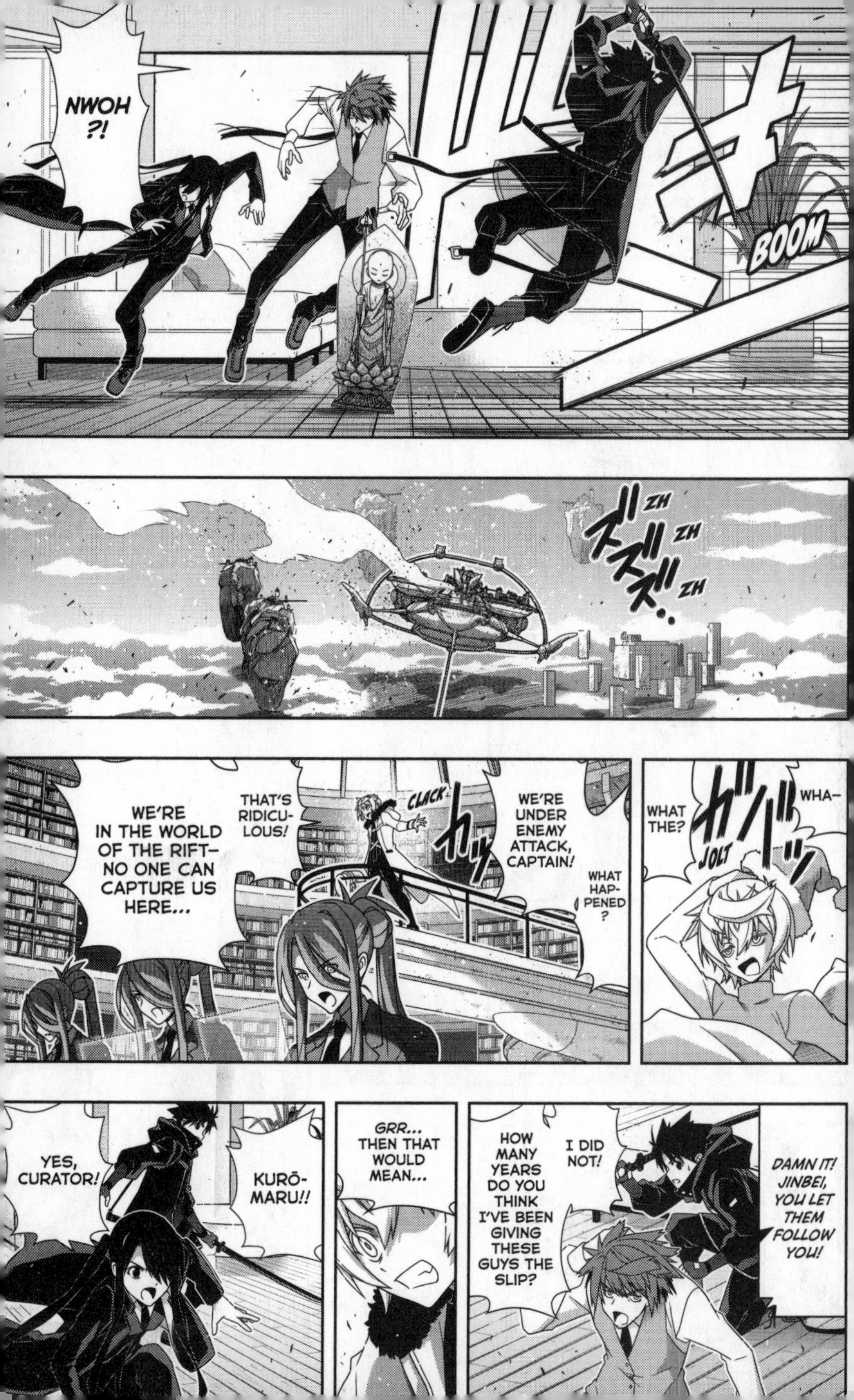
BOOM
NWOH ?!
ZH
ZH
ZH
WHA-
WHAT THE?
JOLT
WHAT HAPPENED?
WE'RE UNDER ENEMY ATTACK, CAPTAIN!
CLACK
THAT'S RIDICULOUS!
WE'RE IN THE WORLD OF THE RIFT— NO ONE CAN CAPTURE US HERE...
DAMN IT! JINBEI, YOU LET THEM FOLLOW YOU!
I DID NOT!
HOW MANY YEARS DO YOU THINK I'VE BEEN GIVING THESE GUYS THE SLIP?
GRR... THEN THAT WOULD MEAN...
KURŌ-MARU!!
YES, CURATOR!

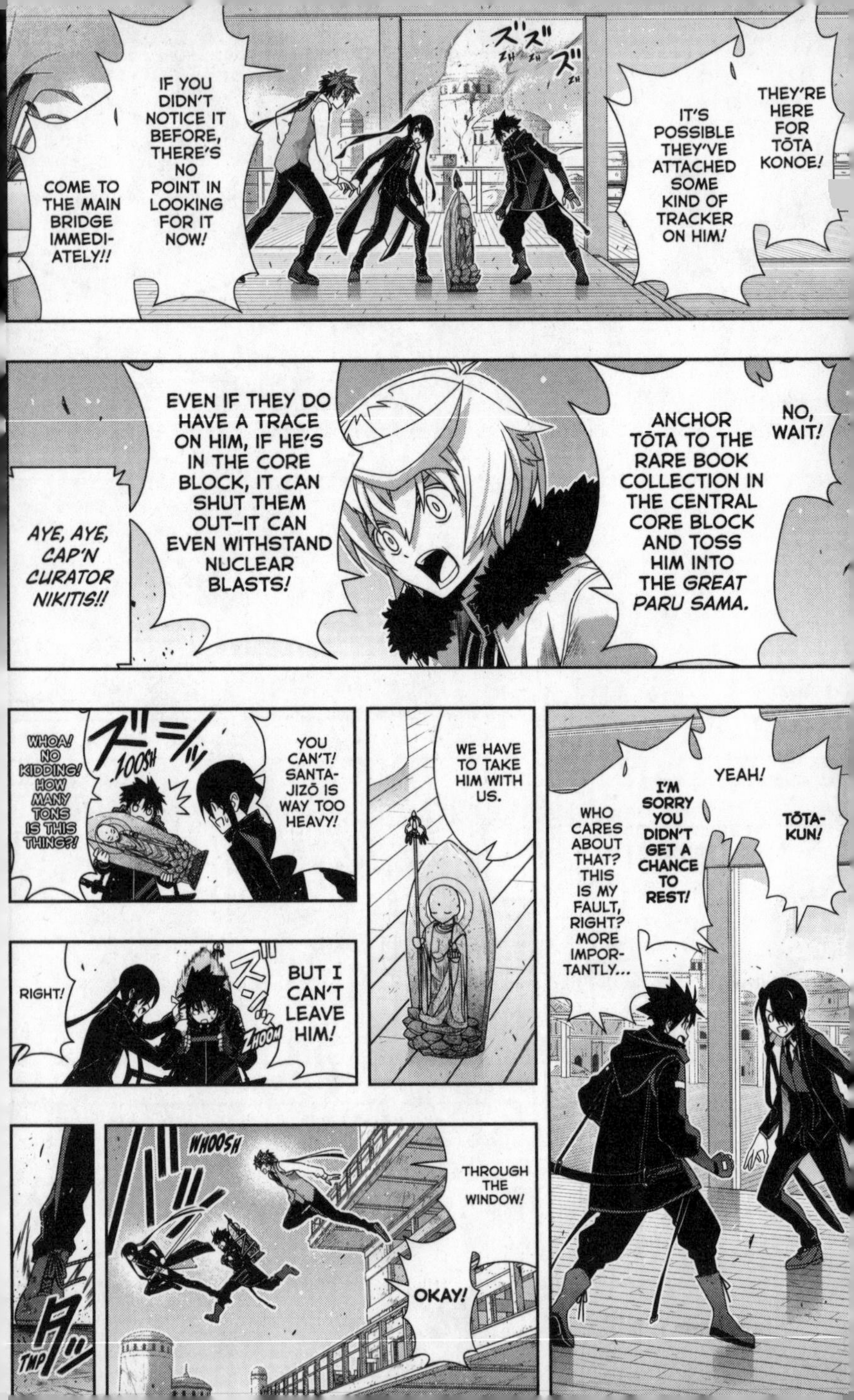
THEY'RE HERE FOR TŌTA KONOE!
IT'S POSSIBLE THEY'VE ATTACHED SOME KIND OF TRACKER ON HIM!
ZH ZH ZH
IF YOU DIDN'T NOTICE IT BEFORE, THERE'S NO POINT IN LOOKING FOR IT NOW!
COME TO THE MAIN BRIDGE IMMEDIATELY!!
NO, WAIT!
ANCHOR TŌTA TO THE RARE BOOK COLLECTION IN THE CENTRAL CORE BLOCK AND TOSS HIM INTO THE *GREAT PARU SAMA*.
EVEN IF THEY DO HAVE A TRACE ON HIM, IF HE'S IN THE CORE BLOCK, IT CAN SHUT THEM OUT—IT CAN EVEN WITHSTAND NUCLEAR BLASTS!
AYE, AYE, CAP'N CURATOR NIKITIS!!
TŌTA-KUN!
YEAH!
I'M SORRY YOU DIDN'T GET A CHANCE TO REST!
WHO CARES ABOUT THAT? THIS IS MY FAULT, RIGHT? MORE IMPORTANTLY...
WE HAVE TO TAKE HIM WITH US.
YOU CAN'T! SANTA-JIZŌ IS WAY TOO HEAVY!
ZOOSH
WHOA! NO KIDDING! HOW MANY TONS IS THIS THING?!
BUT I CAN'T LEAVE HIM!
ZHOOM
RIGHT!
THROUGH THE WINDOW!
WHOOSH
OKAY!
TMP

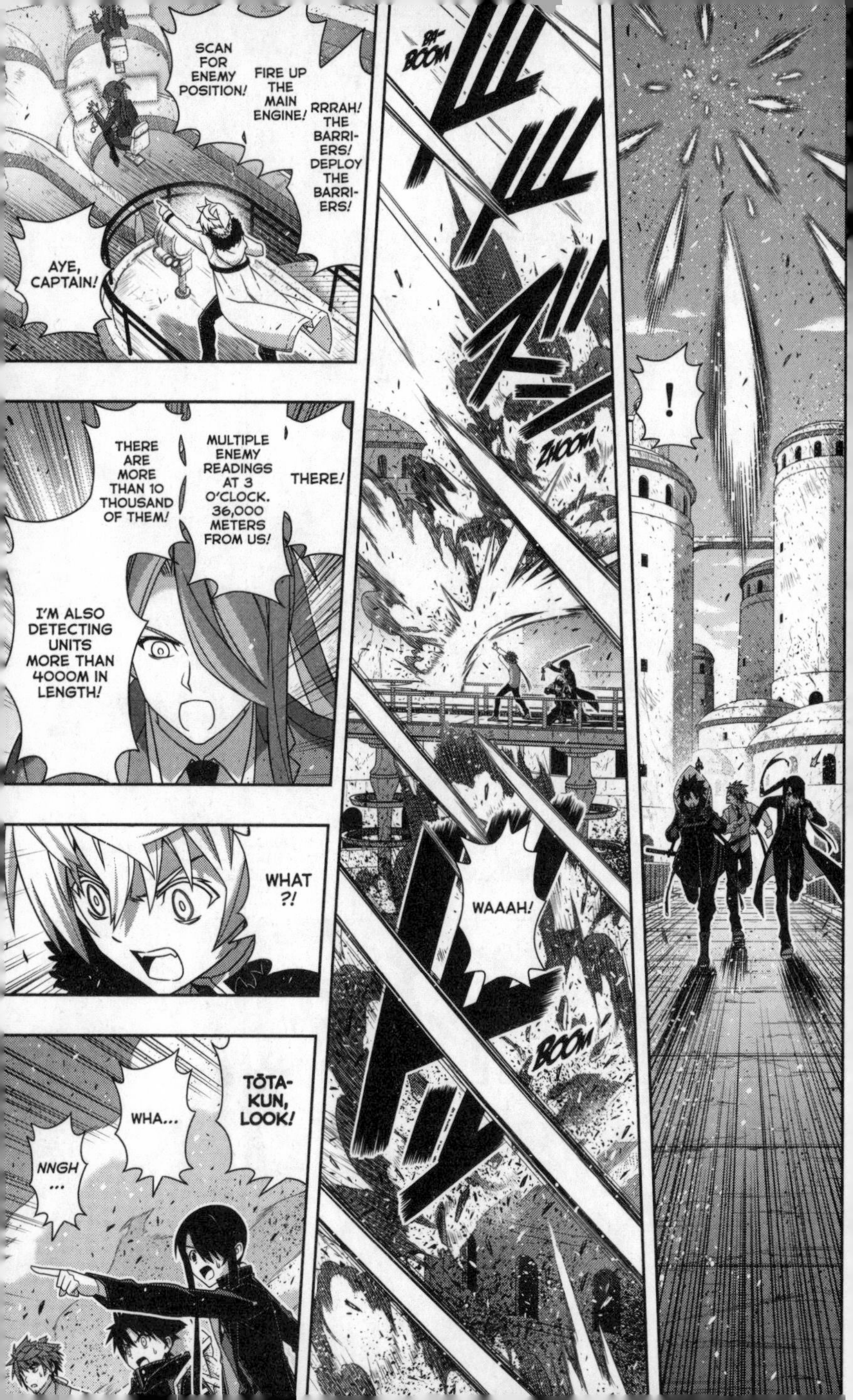
!
BA-BOOM
ZHOOM
WAAAH!
BOOM
RRRAH! THE BARRI-ERS! DEPLOY THE BARRI-ERS!
FIRE UP THE MAIN ENGINE!
SCAN FOR ENEMY POSITION!
AYE, CAPTAIN!
THERE!
MULTIPLE ENEMY READINGS AT 3 O'CLOCK. 36,000 METERS FROM US!
THERE ARE MORE THAN 10 THOUSAND OF THEM!
I'M ALSO DETECTING UNITS MORE THAN 4000M IN LENGTH!
WHAT ?!
TŌTA-KUN, LOOK!
WHA...
NNGH ...

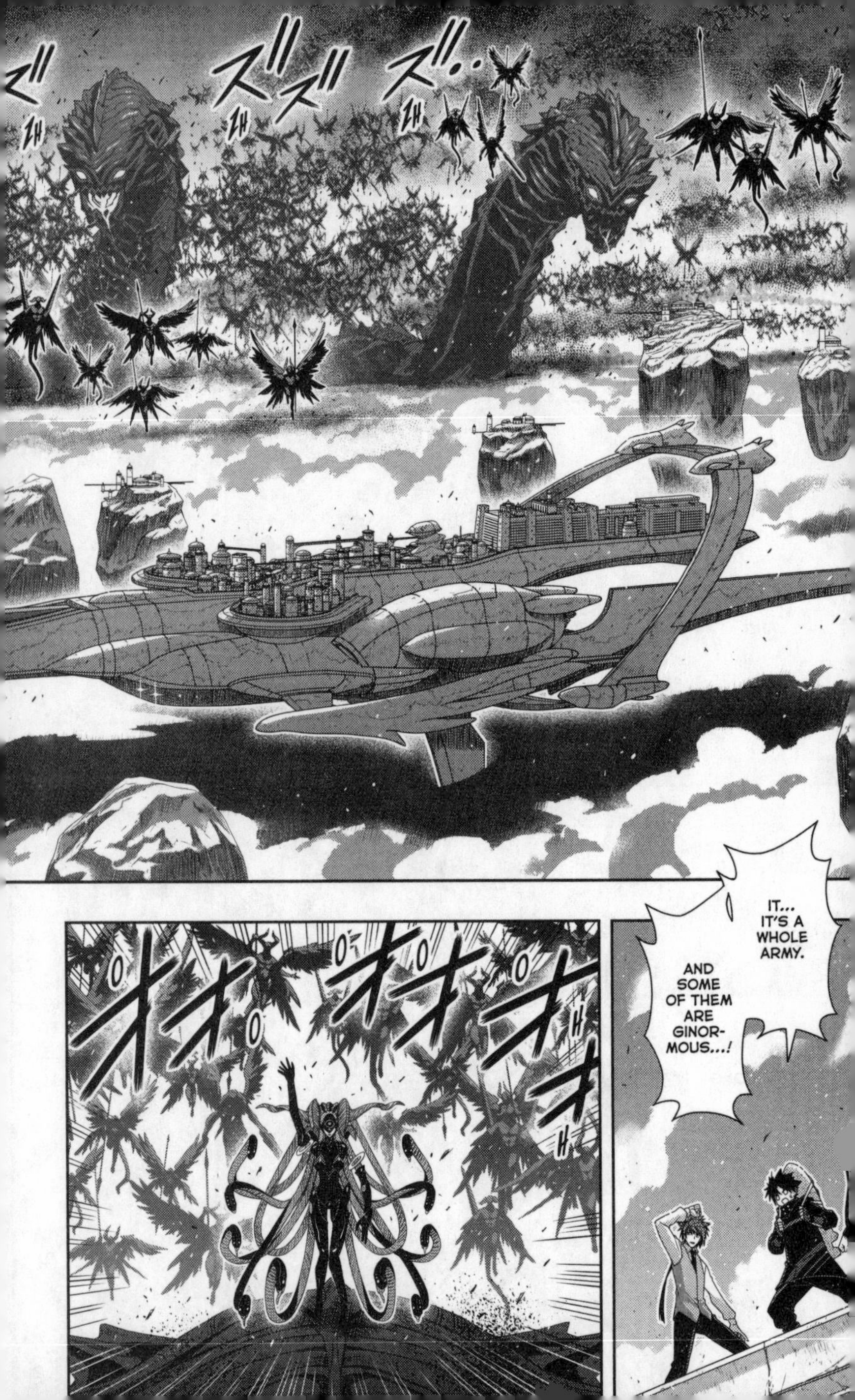
ZH
ZH
ZH
IT... IT'S A WHOLE ARMY.
AND SOME OF THEM ARE GINOR-MOUS...!
O
O
O
O
O
H
H

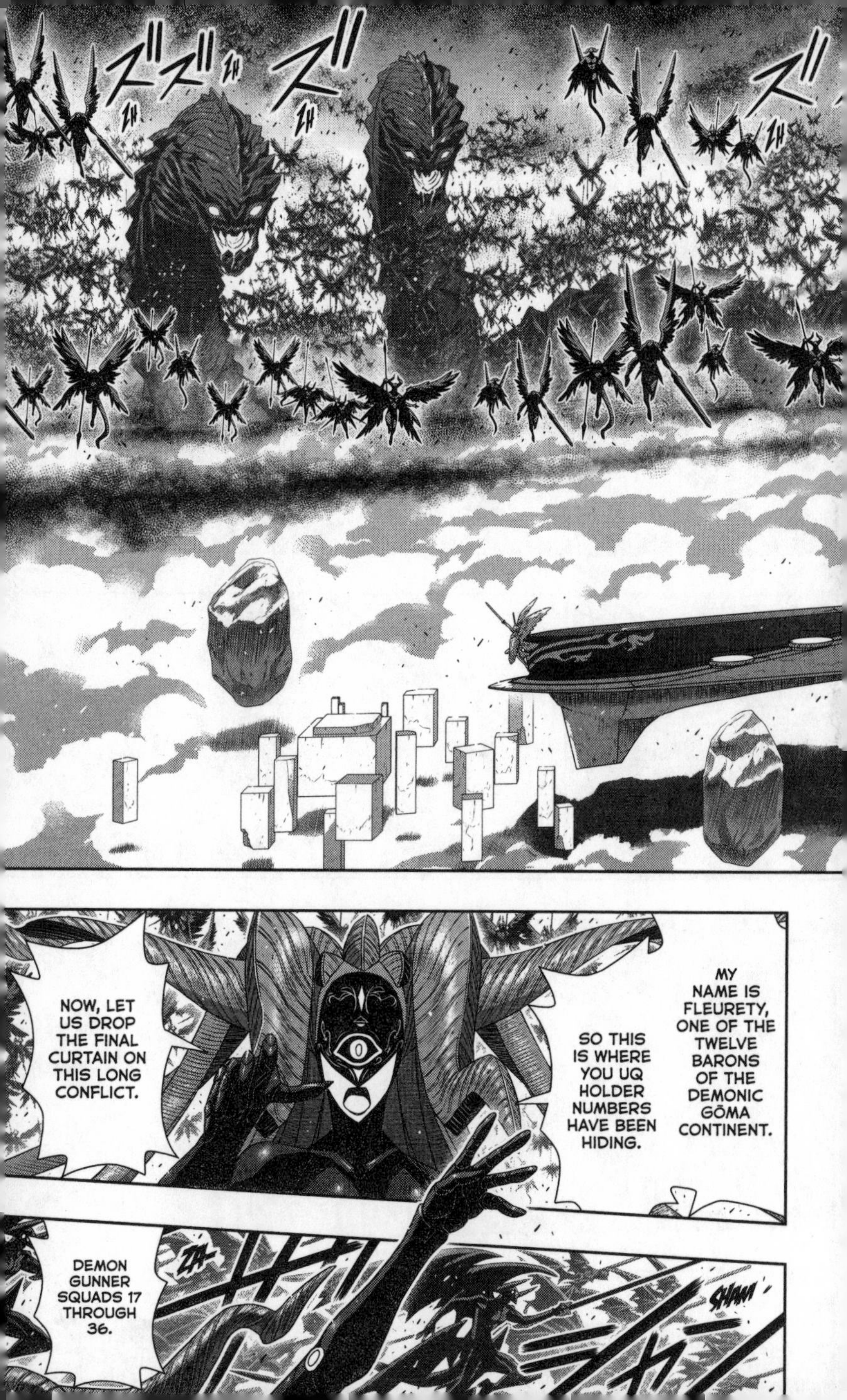
ズ
ZH
ズ
ZH
ズ
ZH
ズ
ZH
MY NAME IS FLEURETY, ONE OF THE TWELVE BARONS OF THE DEMONIC GŌMA CONTINENT.
SO THIS IS WHERE YOU UQ HOLDER NUMBERS HAVE BEEN HIDING.
NOW, LET US DROP THE FINAL CURTAIN ON THIS LONG CONFLICT.
SHAM
ZA
DEMON GUNNER SQUADS 17 THROUGH 36.

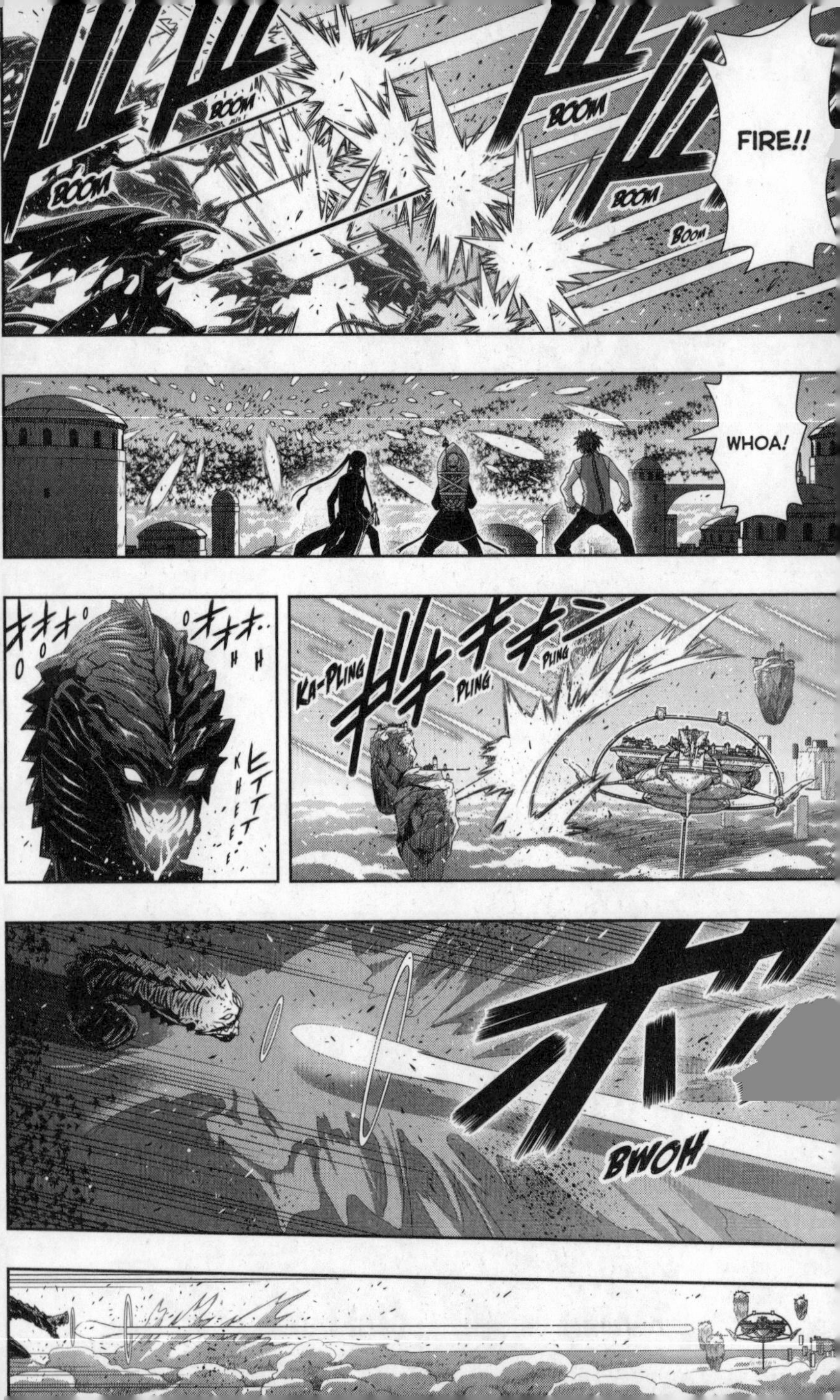
FIRE!!
BOOM
BOOM
Boom
BOOM
BOOM
WHOA!
PLING
PLING
KA-PLING
BWOH

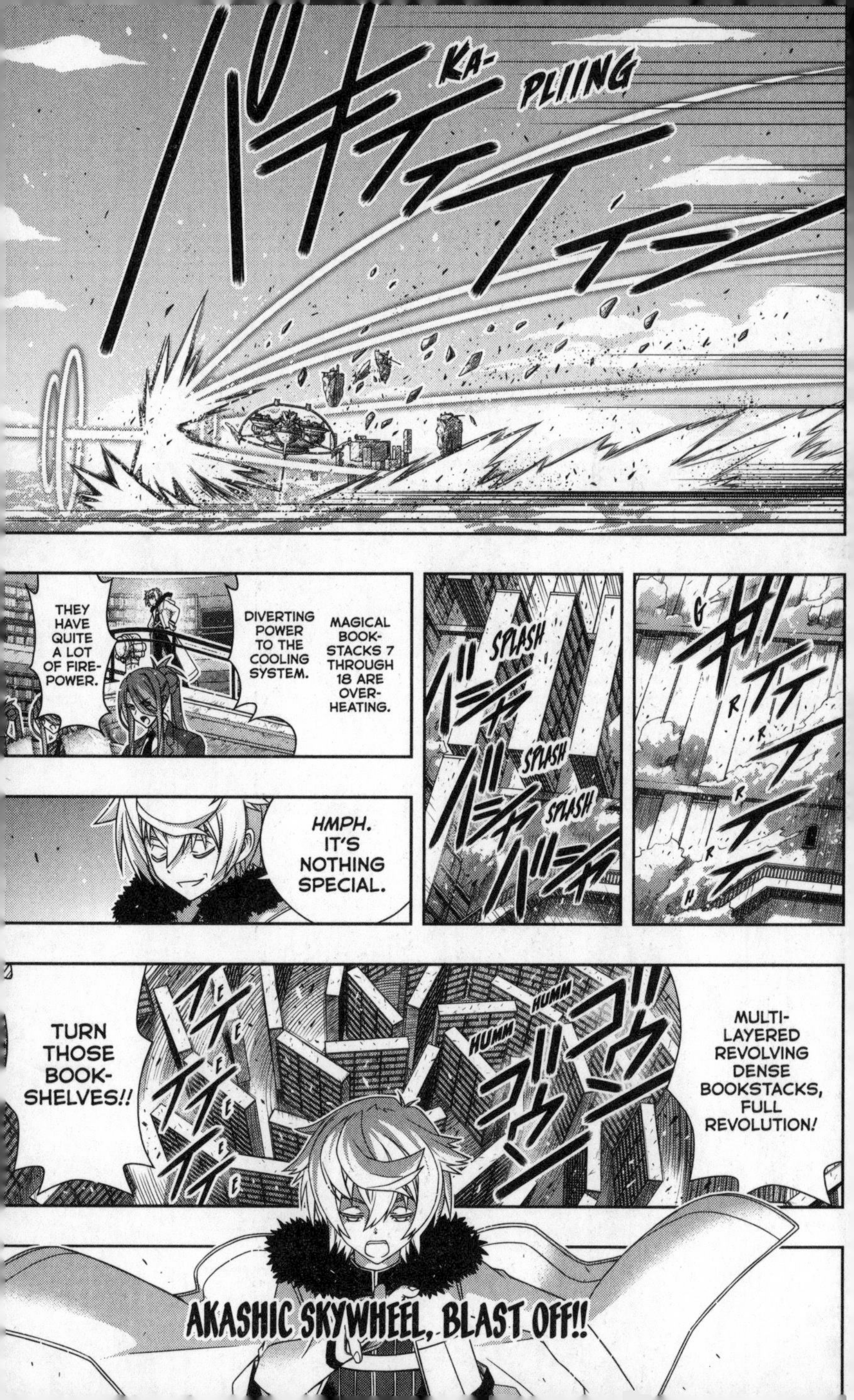
KA-
PLIING
GRRRRH
SPLASH
SPLASH
SPLASH
MAGICAL BOOK-STACKS 7 THROUGH 18 ARE OVER-HEATING.
DIVERTING POWER TO THE COOLING SYSTEM.
THEY HAVE QUITE A LOT OF FIRE-POWER.
HMPH. IT'S NOTHING SPECIAL.
MULTI-LAYERED REVOLVING DENSE BOOKSTACKS, FULL REVOLUTION!
HUMM
HUMM
EEEEEE
TURN THOSE BOOK-SHELVES!!
AKASHIC SKYWHEEL, BLAST OFF!!

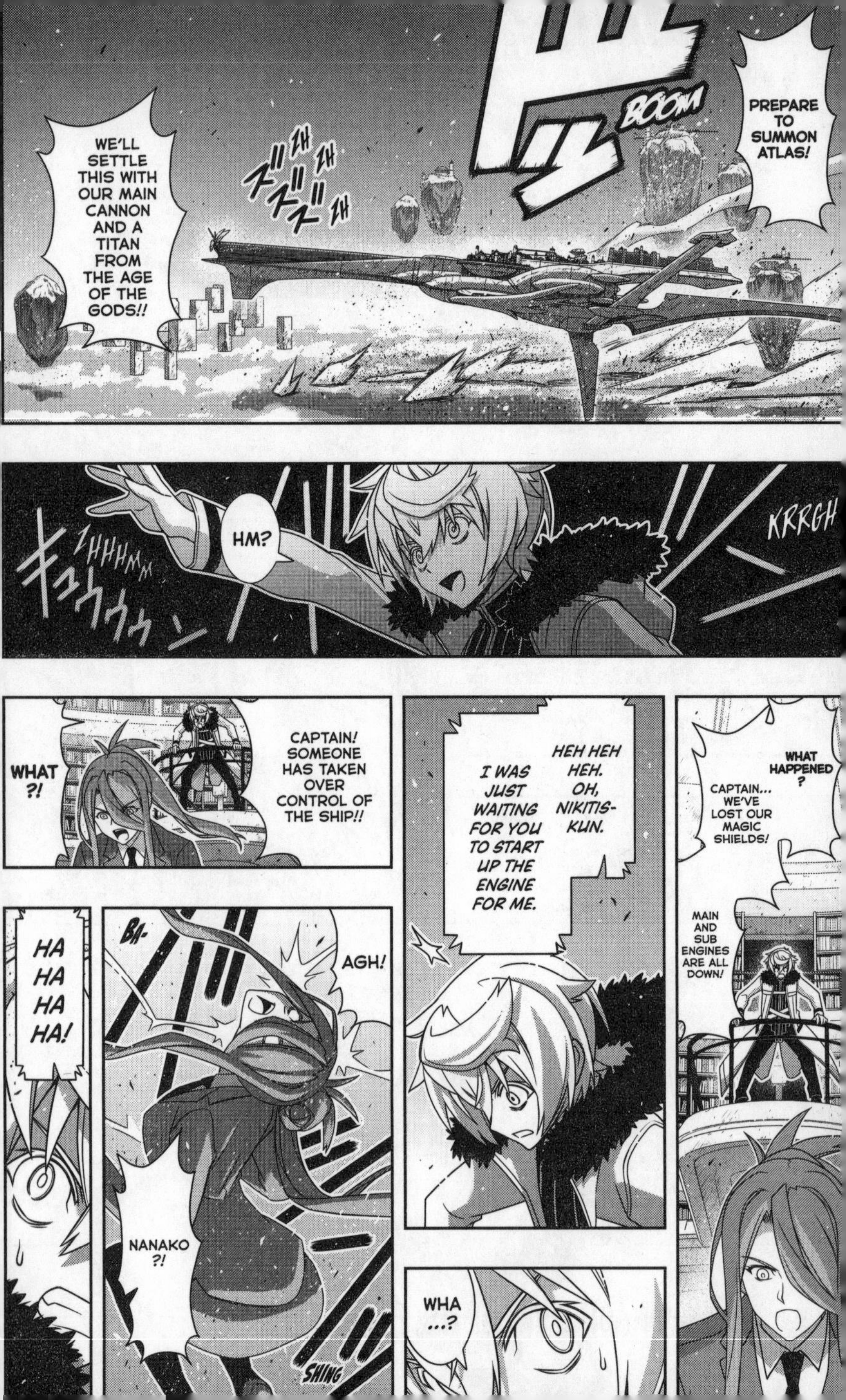

PREPARE TO SUMMON ATLAS!
BOOM
ZH
ZH
ZH
WE'LL SETTLE THIS WITH OUR MAIN CANNON AND A TITAN FROM THE AGE OF THE GODS!!
KRRGH
HM?
ZHHHMM
WHAT HAPPENED?
CAPTAIN... WE'VE LOST OUR MAGIC SHIELDS!
MAIN AND SUB ENGINES ARE ALL DOWN!
HEH HEH HEH. OH, NIKITIS-KUN.
I WAS JUST WAITING FOR YOU TO START UP THE ENGINE FOR ME.
CAPTAIN! SOMEONE HAS TAKEN OVER CONTROL OF THE SHIP!!
WHAT?!
WHA...?
SHING
AGH!
BA-
NANAKO?!
HA HA HA HA!

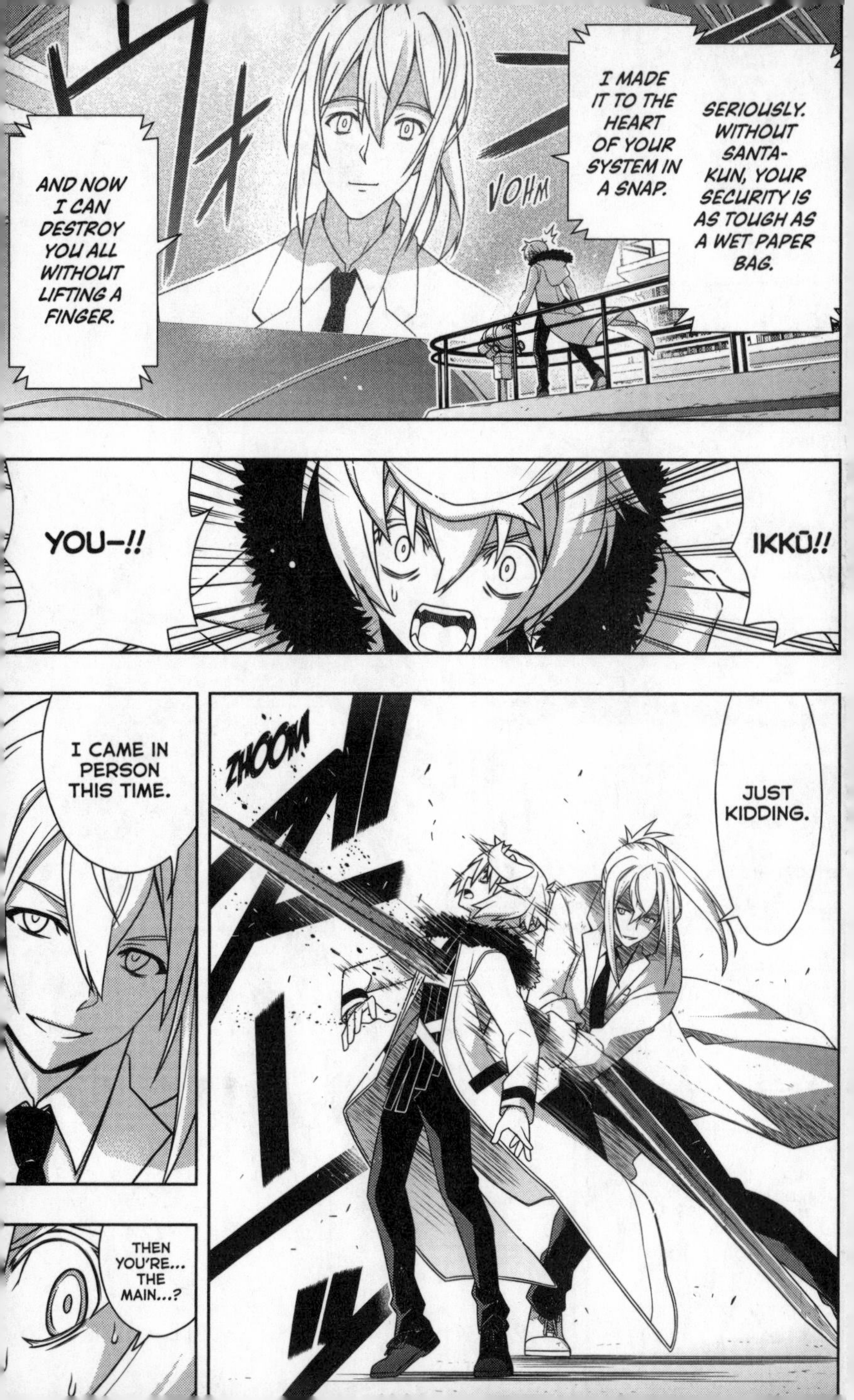
SERIOUSLY. WITHOUT SANTA-KUN, YOUR SECURITY IS AS TOUGH AS A WET PAPER BAG.
I MADE IT TO THE HEART OF YOUR SYSTEM IN A SNAP.
VOHM
AND NOW I CAN DESTROY YOU ALL WITHOUT LIFTING A FINGER.
IKKŪ!!
YOU–!!
JUST KIDDING.
ZHOOM
I CAME IN PERSON THIS TIME.
THEN YOU'RE... THE MAIN...?

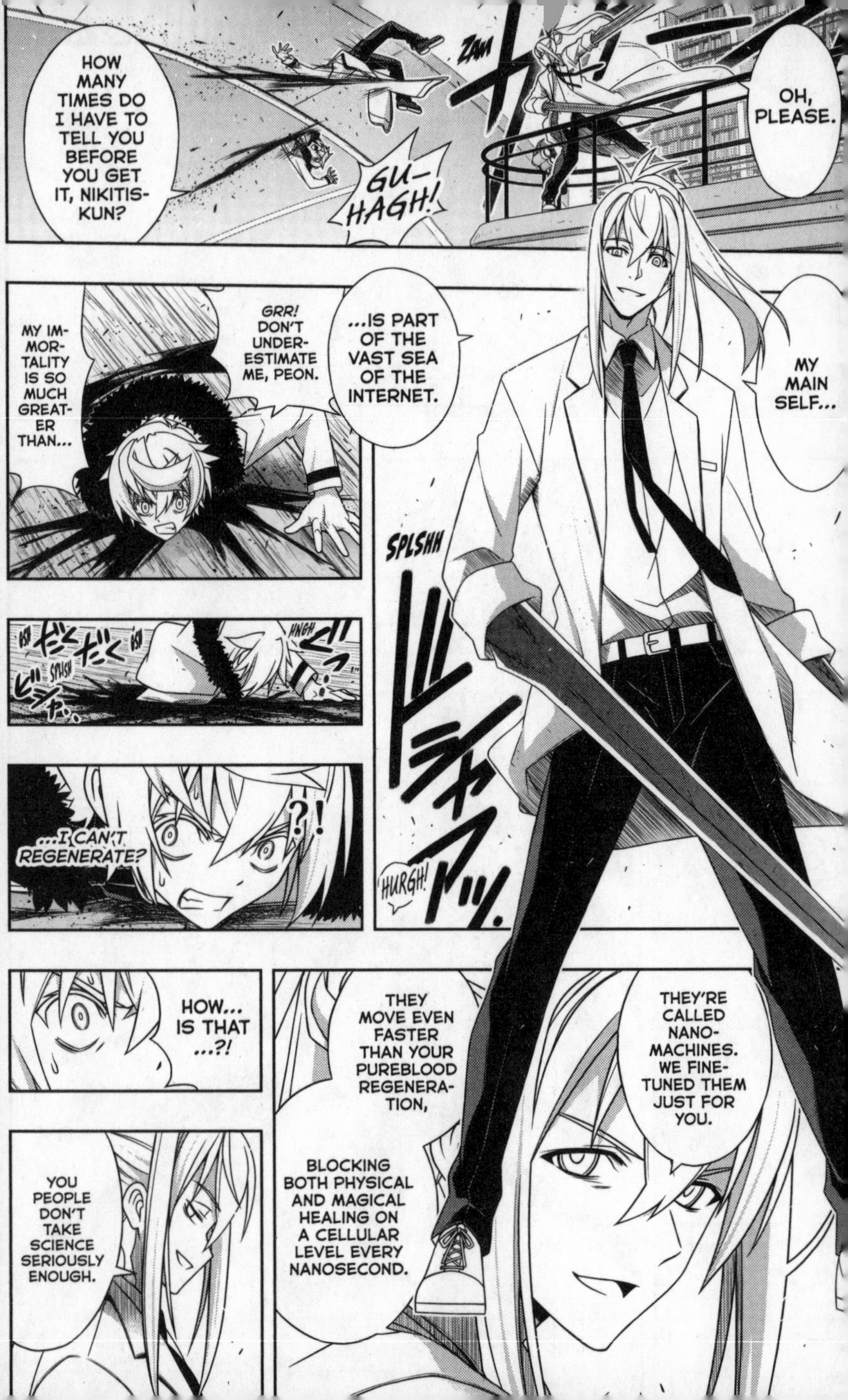
OH, PLEASE.
ZAN
HOW MANY TIMES DO I HAVE TO TELL YOU BEFORE YOU GET IT, NIKITIS-KUN?
GU-HAGH!
MY MAIN SELF...
...IS PART OF THE VAST SEA OF THE INTERNET.
SPLSHH
HURGH!
GRR! DON'T UNDER-ESTIMATE ME, PEON.
MY IM-MOR-TALITY IS SO MUCH GREAT-ER THAN...
HNGH
SPLUSH
?!
...I CAN'T REGENERATE?
THEY'RE CALLED NANO-MACHINES. WE FINE-TUNED THEM JUST FOR YOU.
THEY MOVE EVEN FASTER THAN YOUR PUREBLOOD REGENERA-TION,
BLOCKING BOTH PHYSICAL AND MAGICAL HEALING ON A CELLULAR LEVEL EVERY NANOSECOND.
HOW... IS THAT ...?!
YOU PEOPLE DON'T TAKE SCIENCE SERIOUSLY ENOUGH.

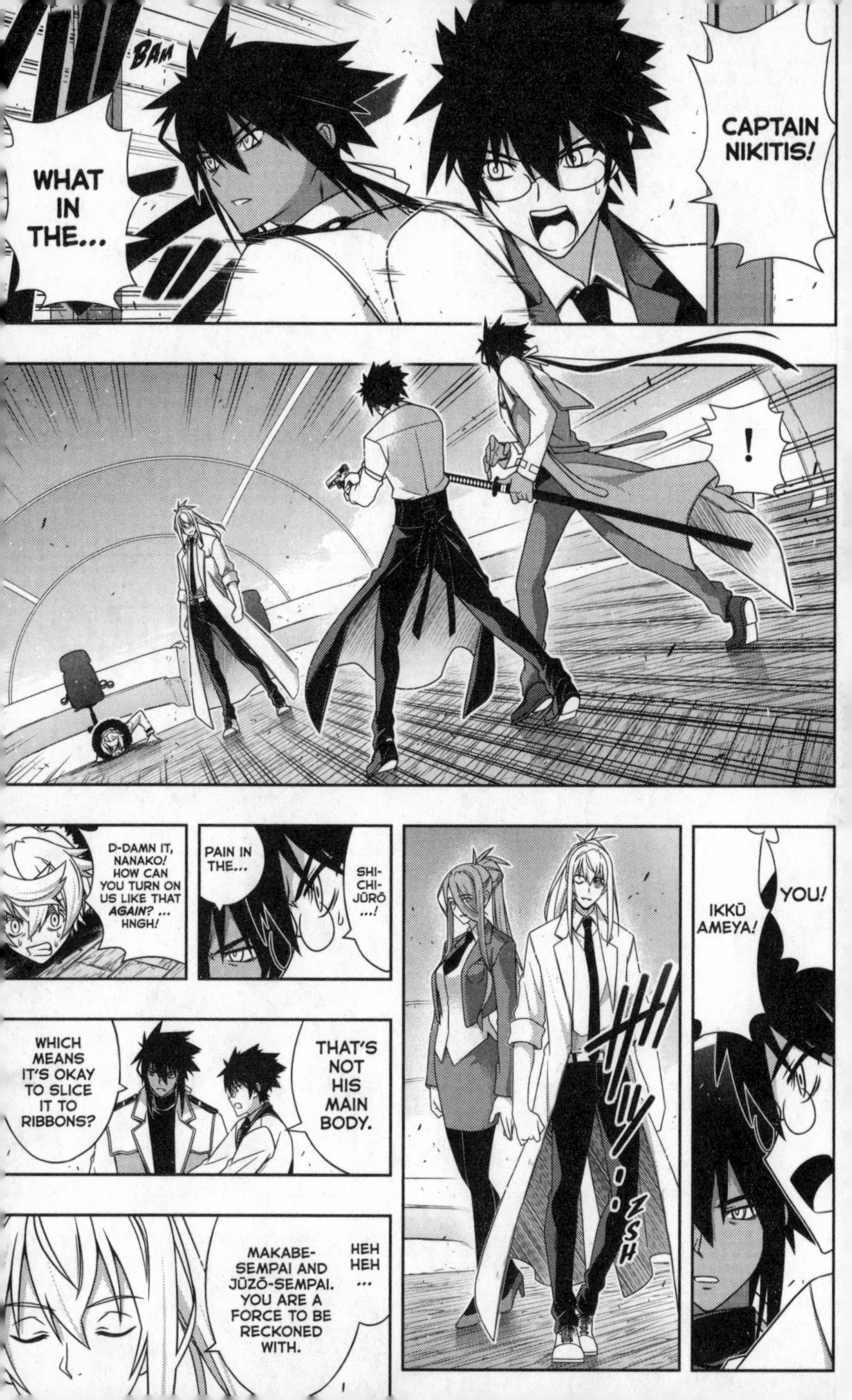
CAPTAIN NIKITIS!
BAM
WHAT IN THE...
!
YOU!
IKKŪ AMEYA!
ZSH
SHI-CHIJŪRŌ...!
PAIN IN THE...
D-DAMN IT, NANAKO! HOW CAN YOU TURN ON US LIKE THAT *AGAIN*? ... HNGH!
THAT'S NOT HIS MAIN BODY.
WHICH MEANS IT'S OKAY TO SLICE IT TO RIBBONS?
HEH HEH ...
MAKABE-SEMPAI AND JŪZŌ-SEMPAI. YOU ARE A FORCE TO BE RECKONED WITH.

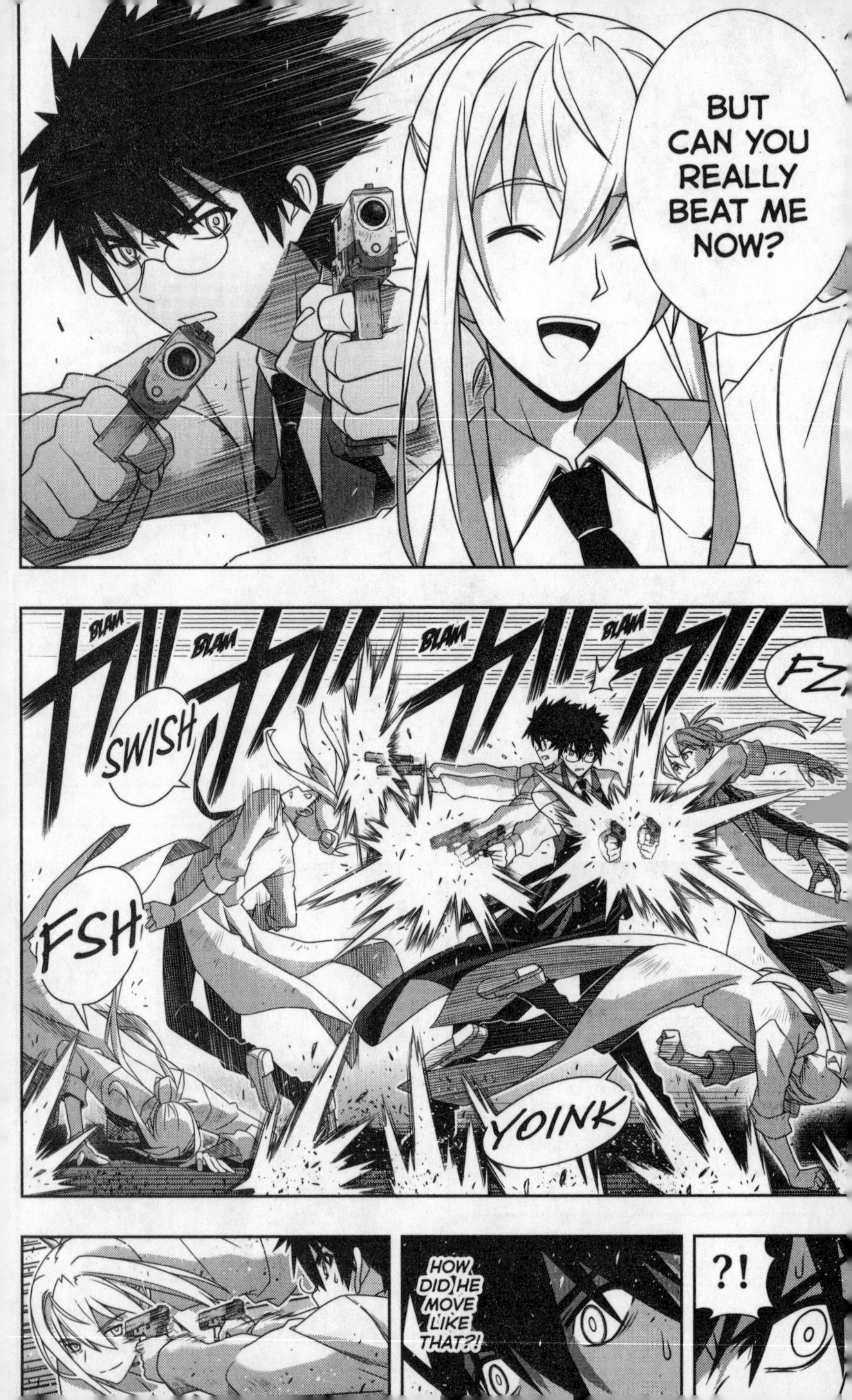
BUT CAN YOU REALLY BEAT ME NOW?
FZ
BLAM
BLAM
BLAM
BLAM
SWISH
FSH
YOINK
?!
HOW DID HE MOVE LIKE THAT?!

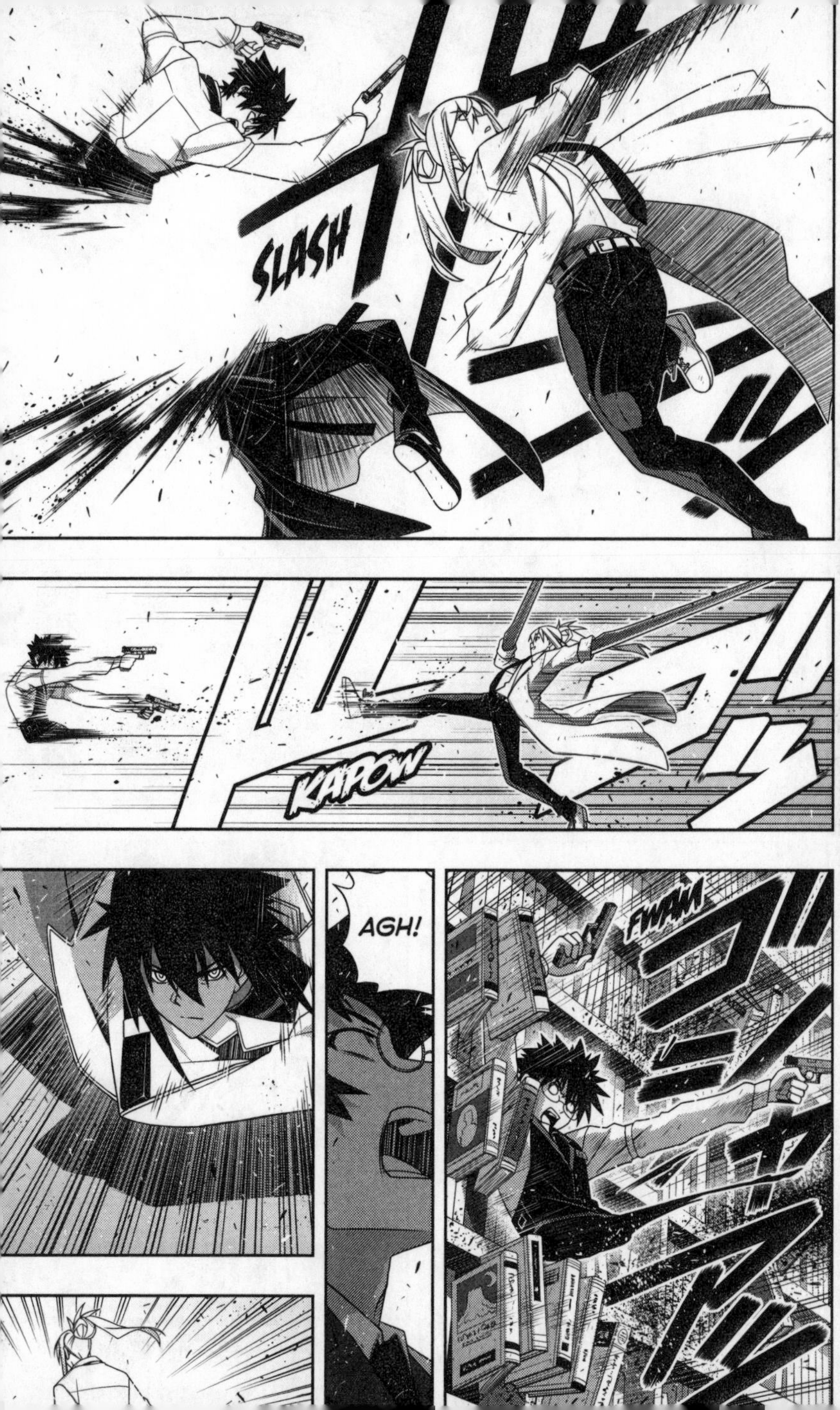
SLASH
KAPOW
FWAM
AGH!

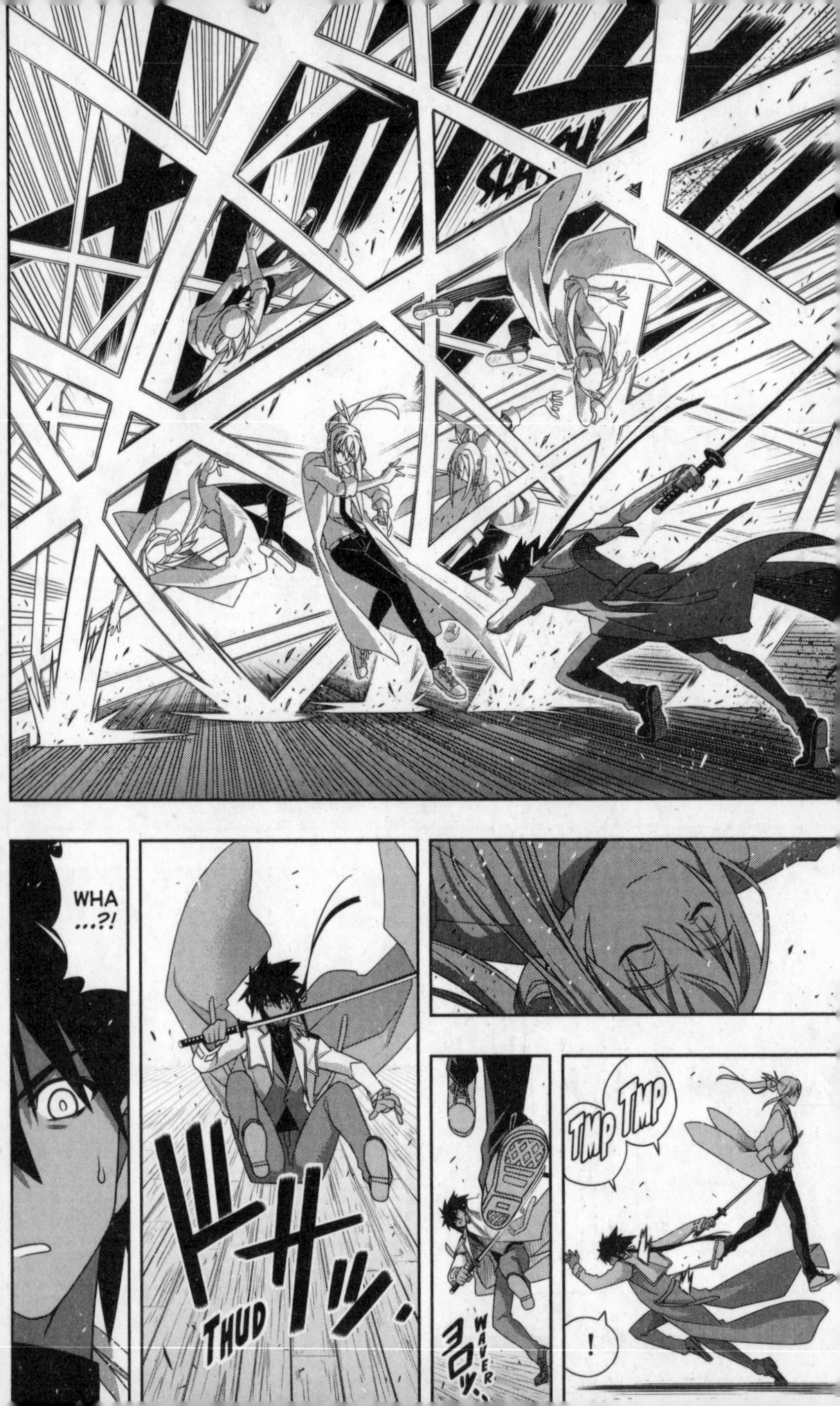
TMP TMP
!
ヨロッ
WAVER
ドサッ
THUD
WHA
...?!

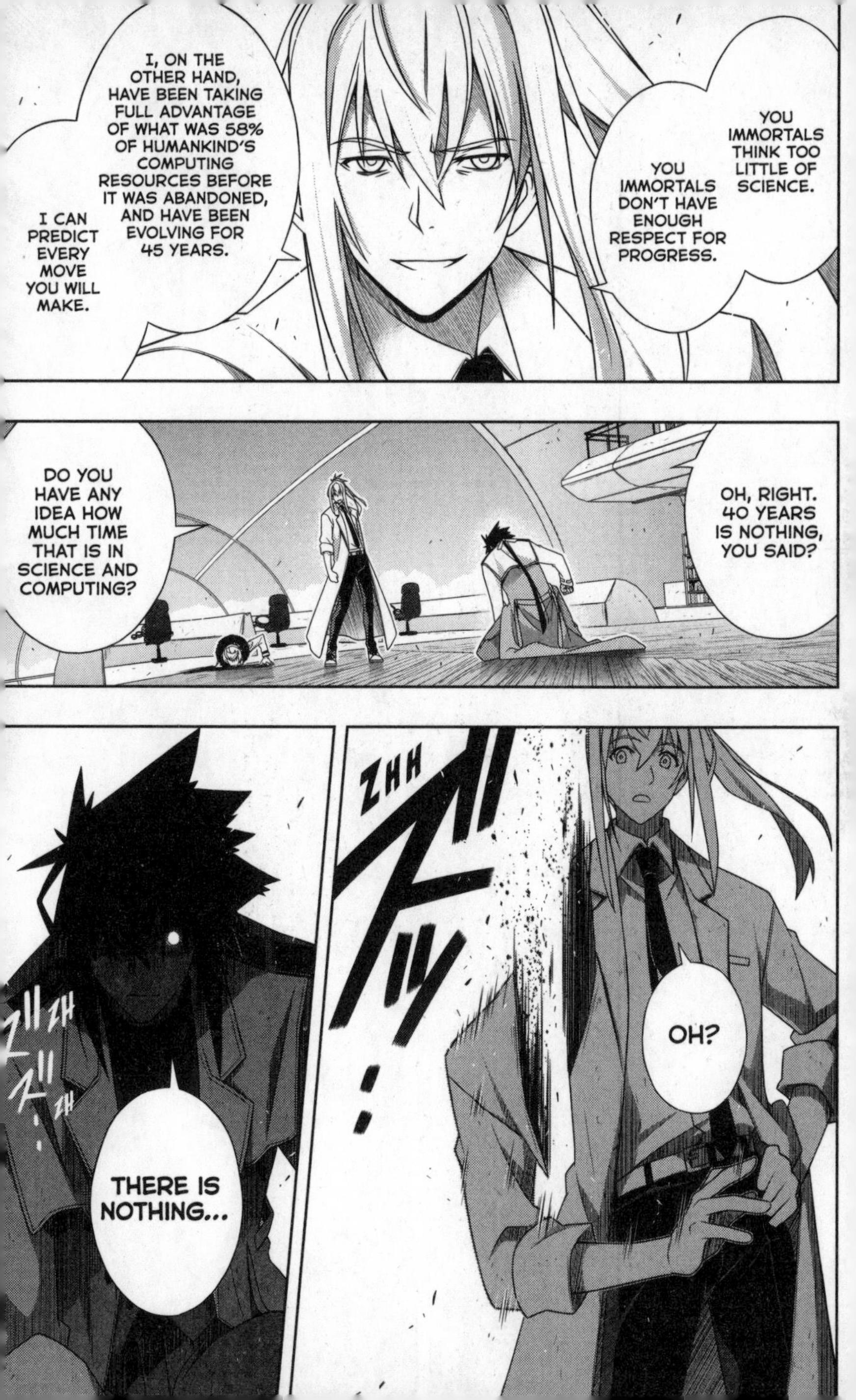
YOU IMMORTALS THINK TOO LITTLE OF SCIENCE.
YOU IMMORTALS DON'T HAVE ENOUGH RESPECT FOR PROGRESS.
I, ON THE OTHER HAND, HAVE BEEN TAKING FULL ADVANTAGE OF WHAT WAS 58% OF HUMANKIND'S COMPUTING RESOURCES BEFORE IT WAS ABANDONED, AND HAVE BEEN EVOLVING FOR 45 YEARS.
I CAN PREDICT EVERY MOVE YOU WILL MAKE.
OH, RIGHT. 40 YEARS IS NOTHING, YOU SAID?
DO YOU HAVE ANY IDEA HOW MUCH TIME THAT IS IN SCIENCE AND COMPUTING?
ZHH
OH?
ZH
ZH
THERE IS NOTHING...

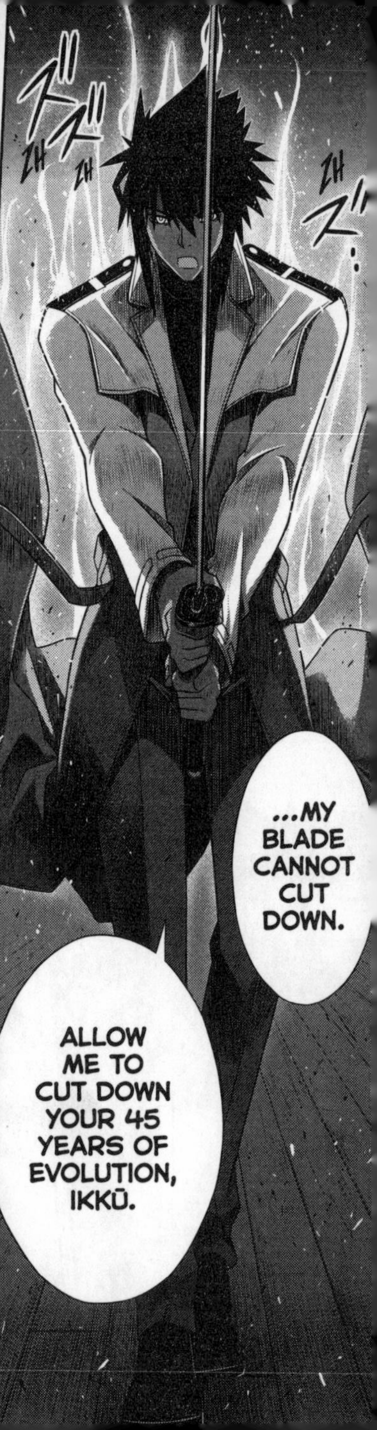
ズ ZH
ズ ZH
ズ ZH
...MY BLADE CANNOT CUT DOWN.
ALLOW ME TO CUT DOWN YOUR 45 YEARS OF EVOLUTION, IKKŪ.
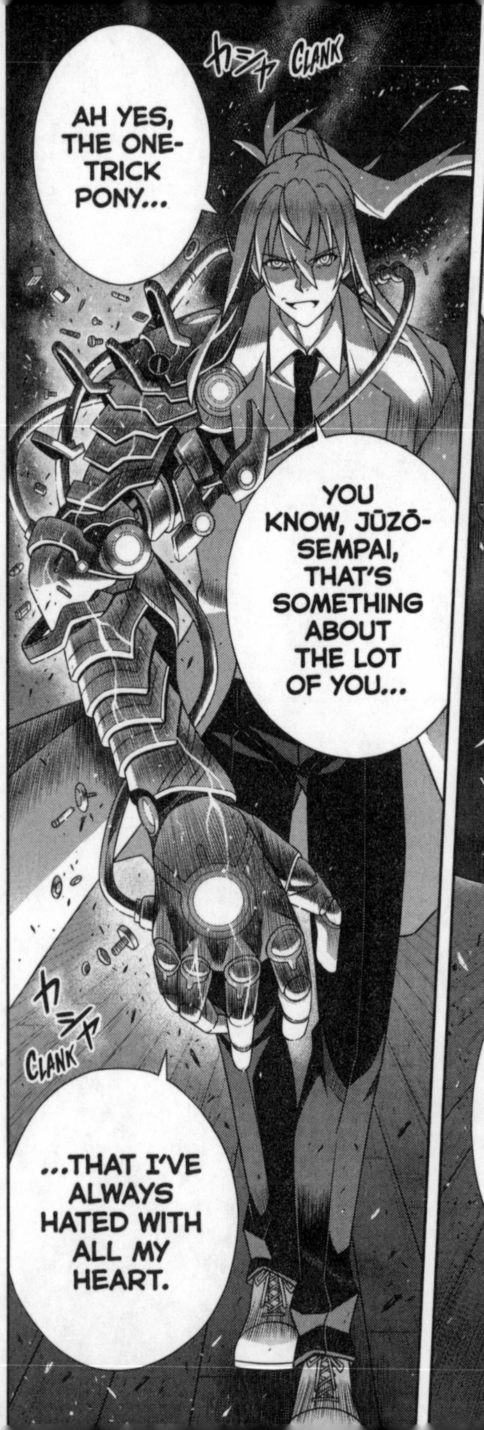
カシャ CLANK
AH YES, THE ONE-TRICK PONY...
YOU KNOW, JŪZŌ-SEMPAI, THAT'S SOMETHING ABOUT THE LOT OF YOU...
カシャ CLANK
...THAT I'VE ALWAYS HATED WITH ALL MY HEART.

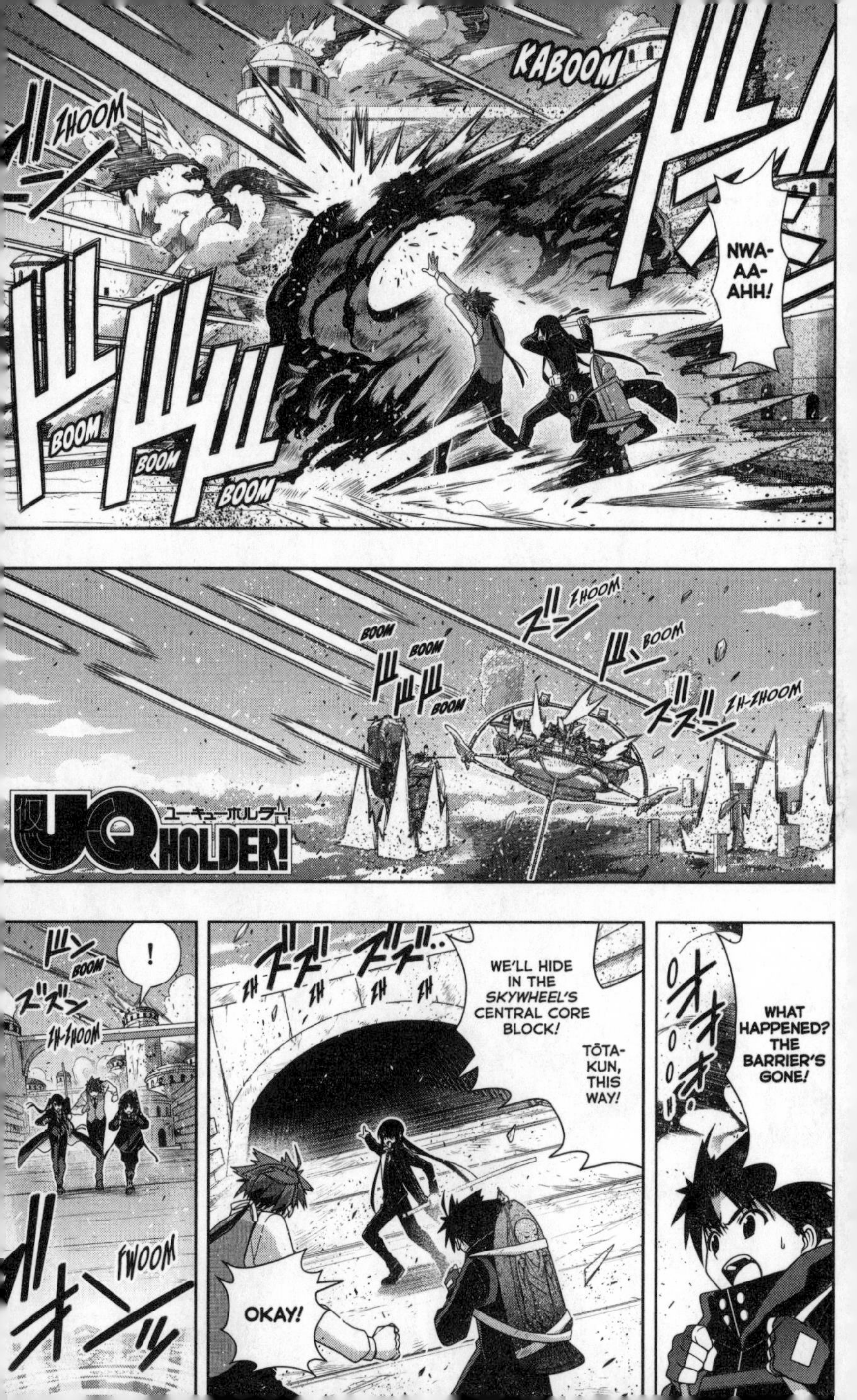
KABOOM
ZHOOM
NWA-AA-AHH!
BOOM
BOOM
BOOM
ZHOOM
BOOM
BOOM
BOOM
BOOM
ZH-ZHOOM
UQ HOLDER!
WHAT HAPPENED? THE BARRIER'S GONE!
ZH ZH ZH ZH
WE'LL HIDE IN THE *SKYWHEEL'S* CENTRAL CORE BLOCK!
TŌTA-KUN, THIS WAY!
OKAY!
!
BOOM
ZH-ZHOOM
FWOOM

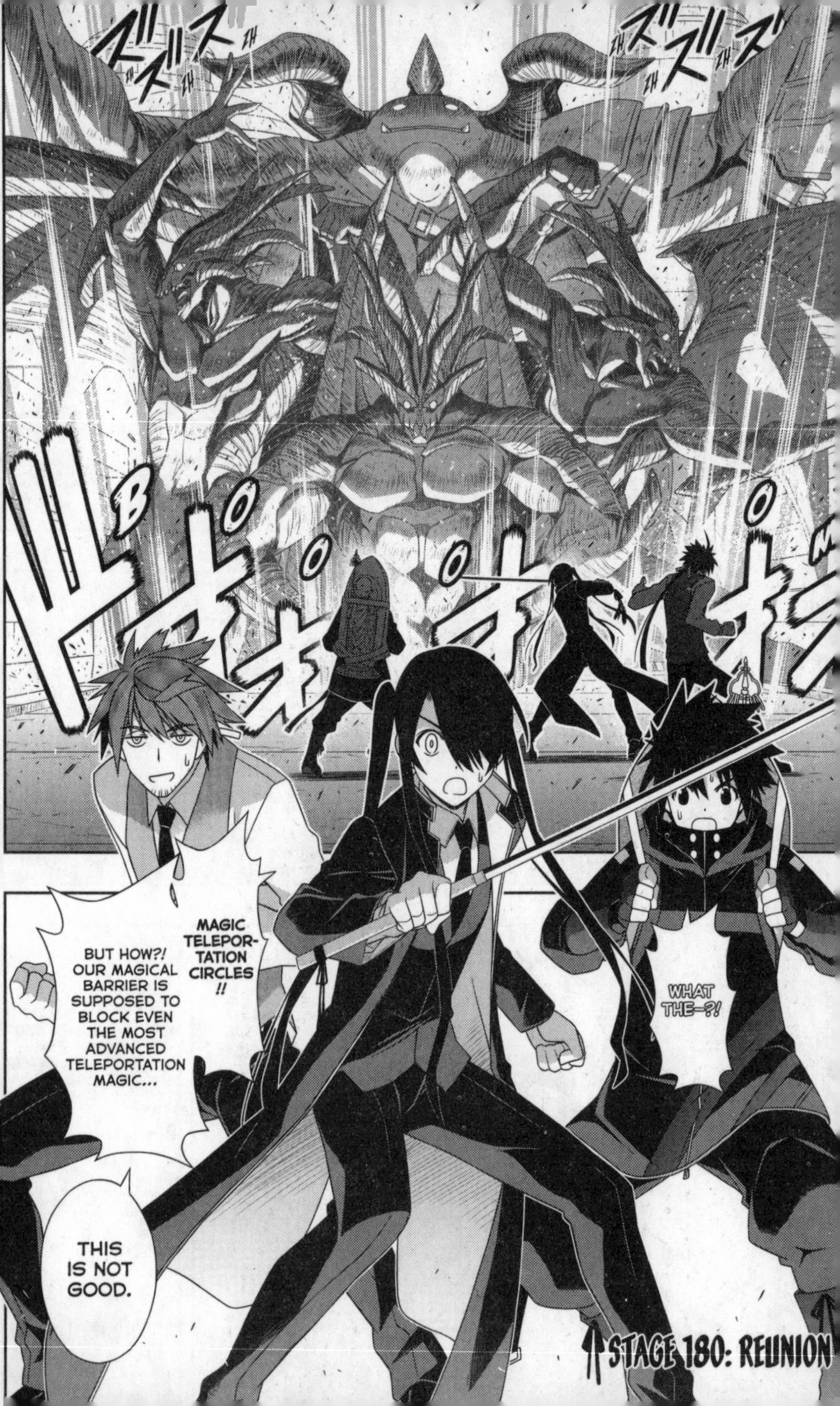
ZH ZH ZH
ZH ZH ZH
BOOOM
WHAT THE--?!
MAGIC TELEPORTATION CIRCLES!!
BUT HOW?! OUR MAGICAL BARRIER IS SUPPOSED TO BLOCK EVEN THE MOST ADVANCED TELEPORTATION MAGIC...
THIS IS NOT GOOD.

STAGE 180: REUNION

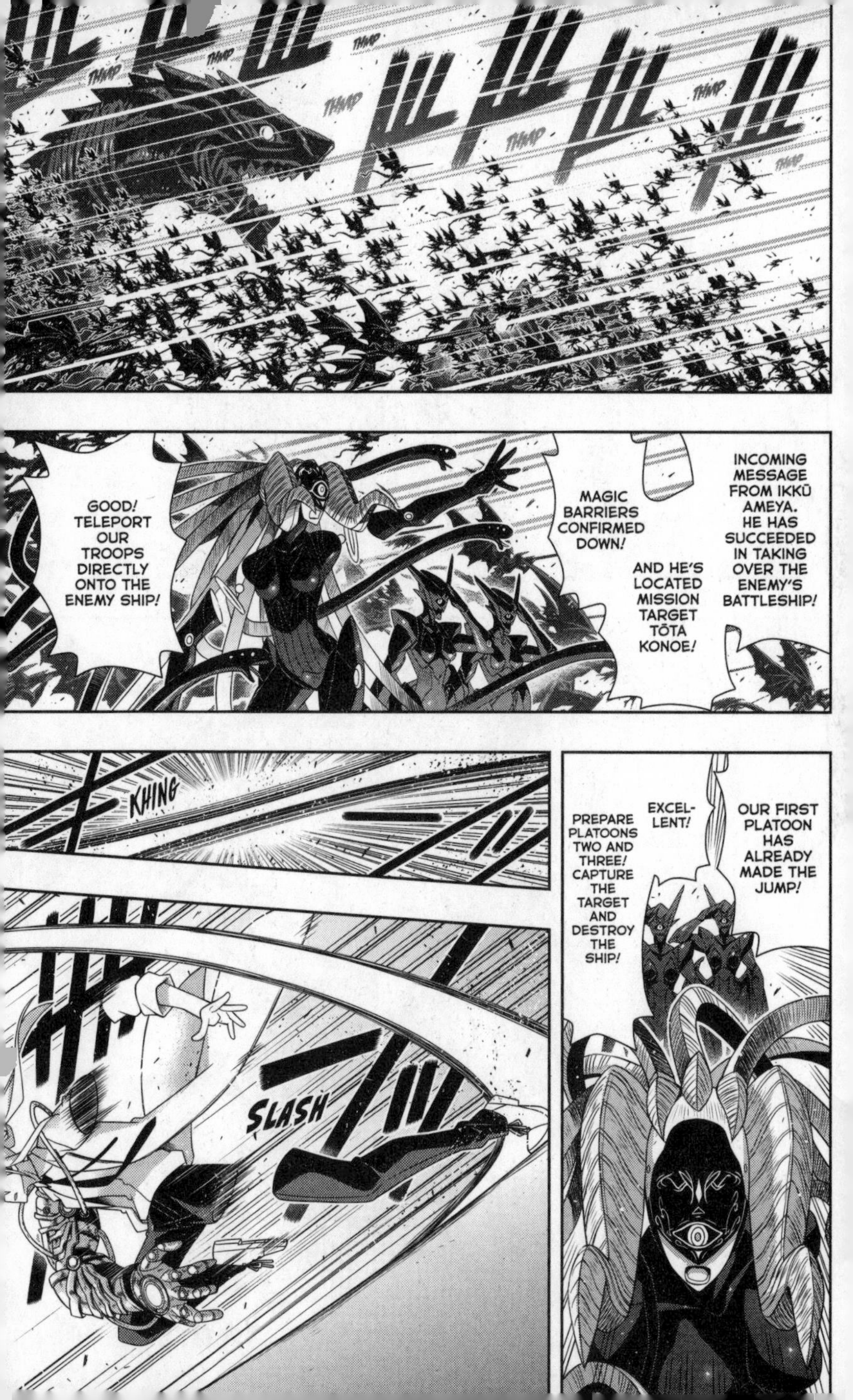
THMP
THMP
THMP
THMP
THMP
THMP
THMP
INCOMING MESSAGE FROM IKKŪ AMEYA. HE HAS SUCCEEDED IN TAKING OVER THE ENEMY'S BATTLESHIP!
MAGIC BARRIERS CONFIRMED DOWN!
AND HE'S LOCATED MISSION TARGET TŌTA KONOE!
GOOD! TELEPORT OUR TROOPS DIRECTLY ONTO THE ENEMY SHIP!
OUR FIRST PLATOON HAS ALREADY MADE THE JUMP!
EXCEL-LENT!
PREPARE PLATOONS TWO AND THREE! CAPTURE THE TARGET AND DESTROY THE SHIP!
KHING
SLASH

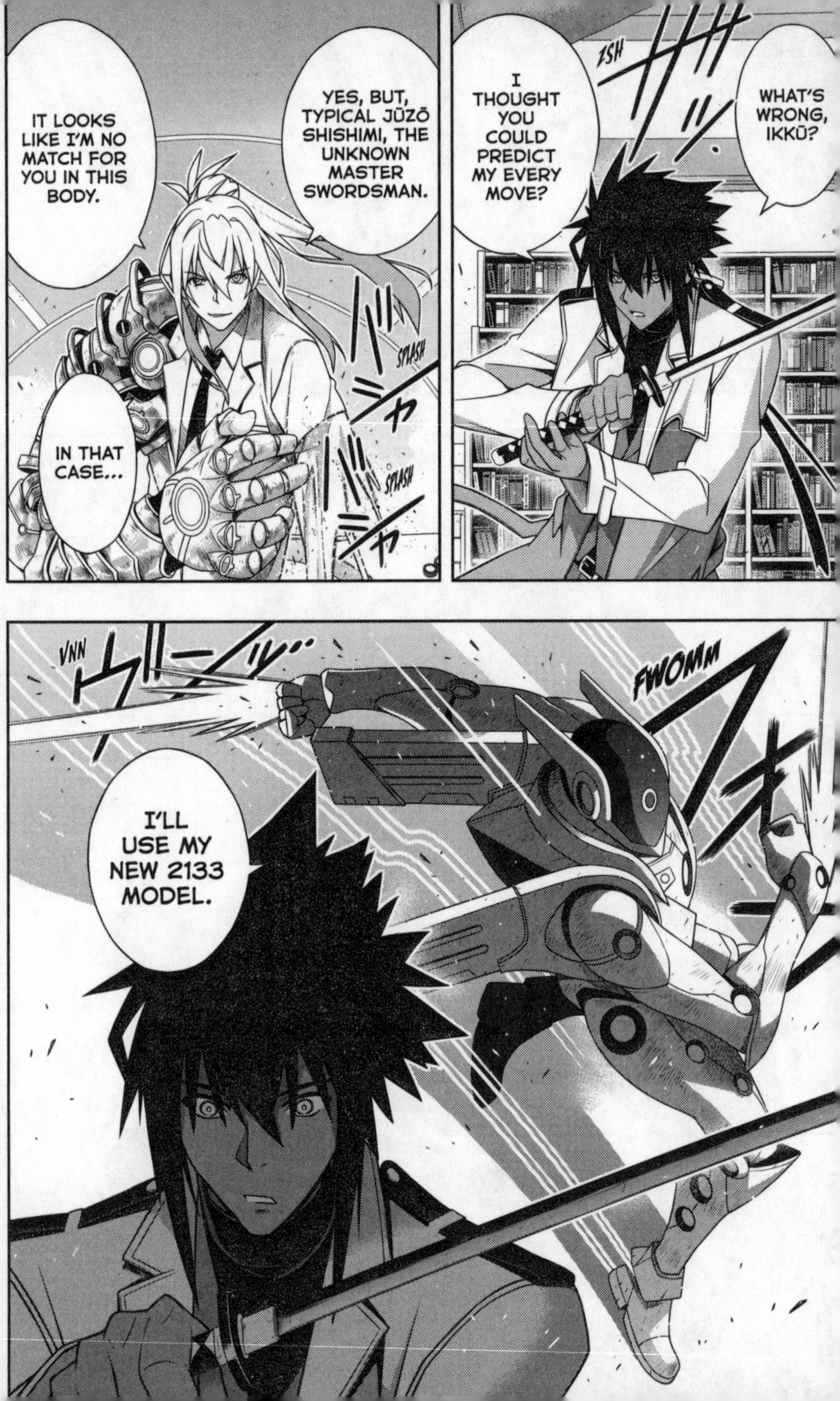
WHAT'S WRONG, IKKŪ?
ZSH
I THOUGHT YOU COULD PREDICT MY EVERY MOVE?
YES, BUT, TYPICAL JŪZŌ SHISHIMI, THE UNKNOWN MASTER SWORDSMAN.
IT LOOKS LIKE I'M NO MATCH FOR YOU IN THIS BODY.
SPLASH
SPLASH
IN THAT CASE...
FWOMM
VNN
I'LL USE MY NEW 2133 MODEL.

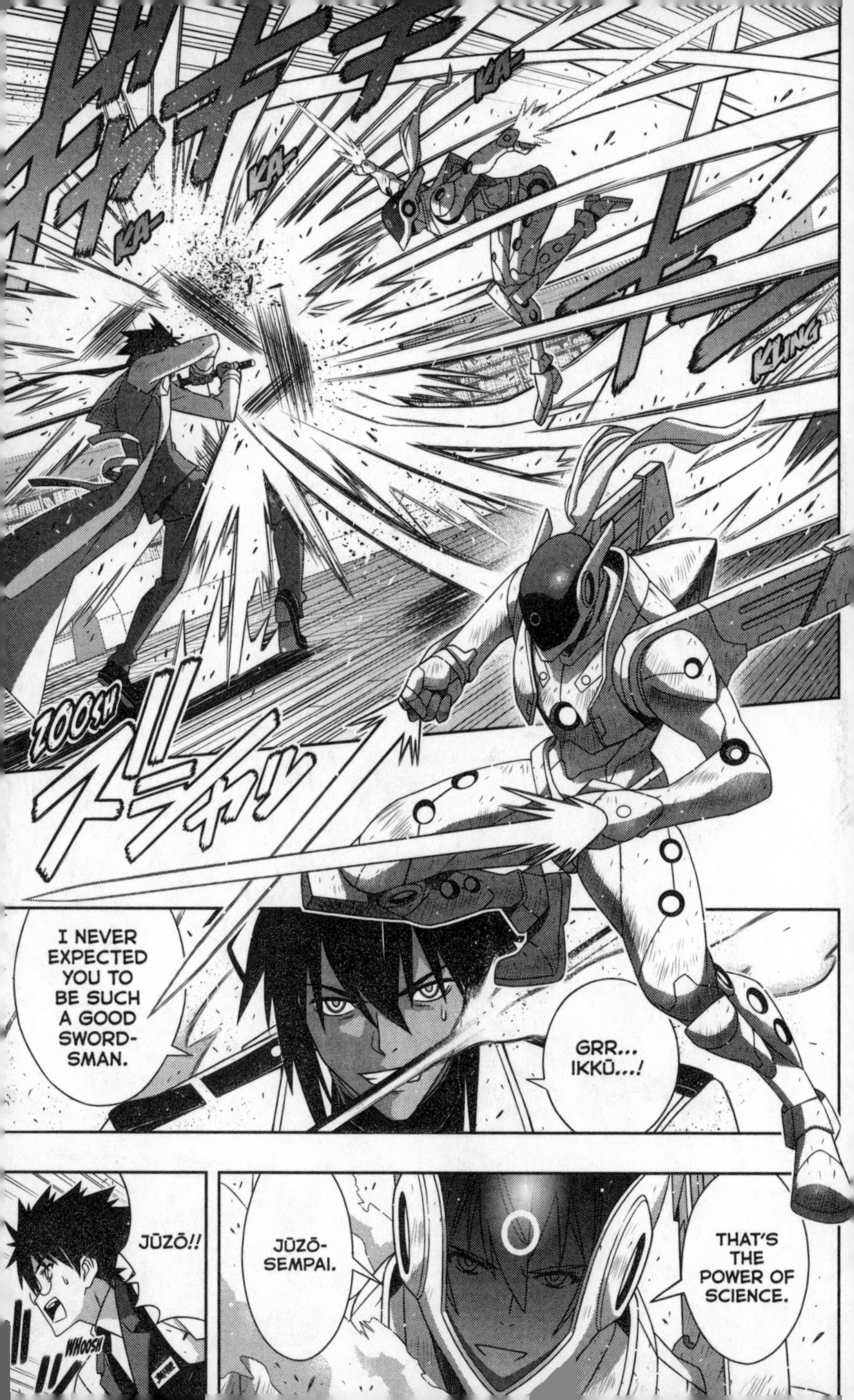
KA-
KA-
KA-
KA-LING
ZOOSH
GRR... IKKŪ...!
I NEVER EXPECTED YOU TO BE SUCH A GOOD SWORD-SMAN.
THAT'S THE POWER OF SCIENCE.
JŪZŌ-SEMPAI.
JŪZŌ!!
WHOOSH

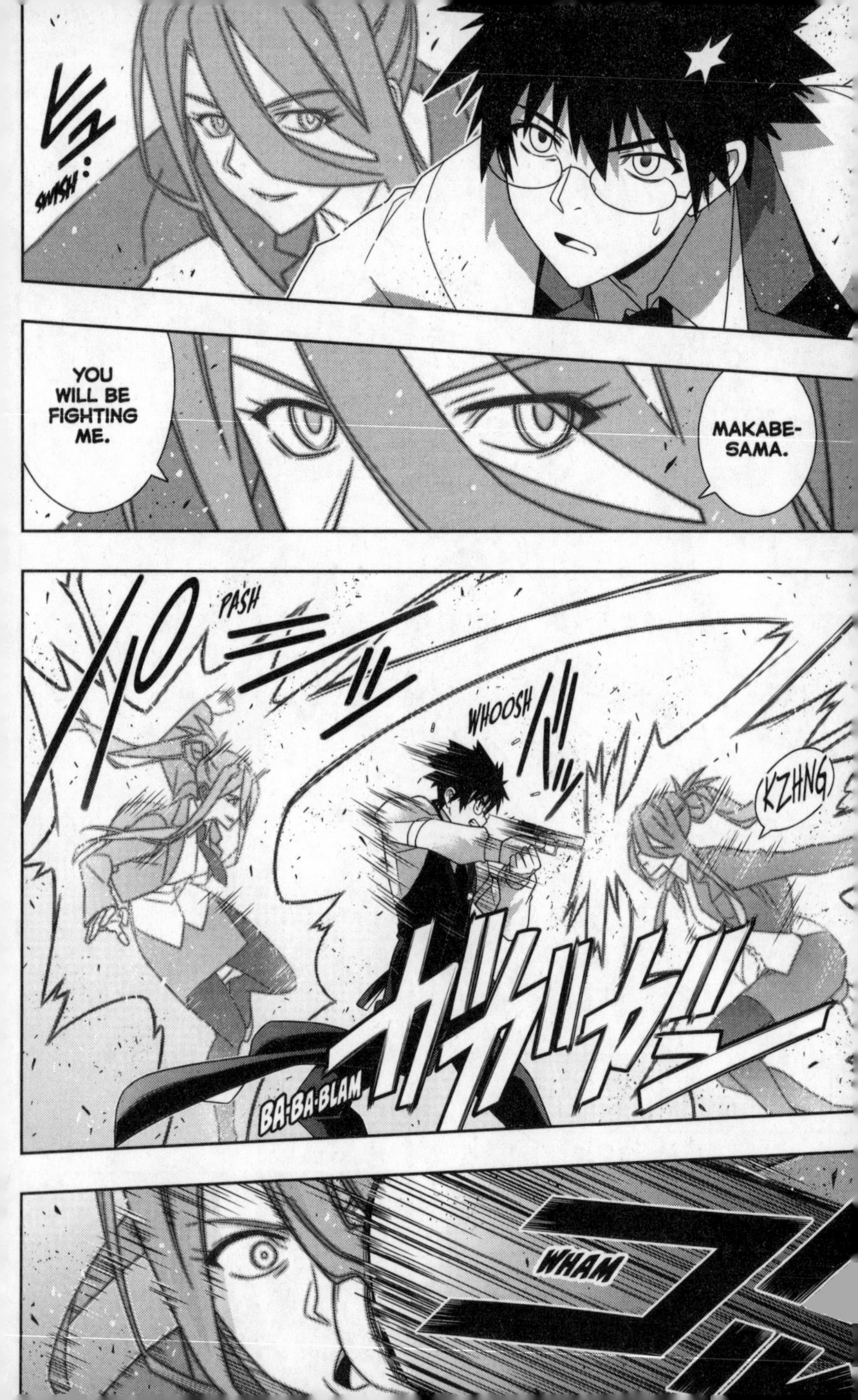
SWISH
YOU WILL BE FIGHTING ME.
MAKABE-SAMA.
PASH
WHOOSH
(KZHNG)
BA-BA-BLAM
WHAM

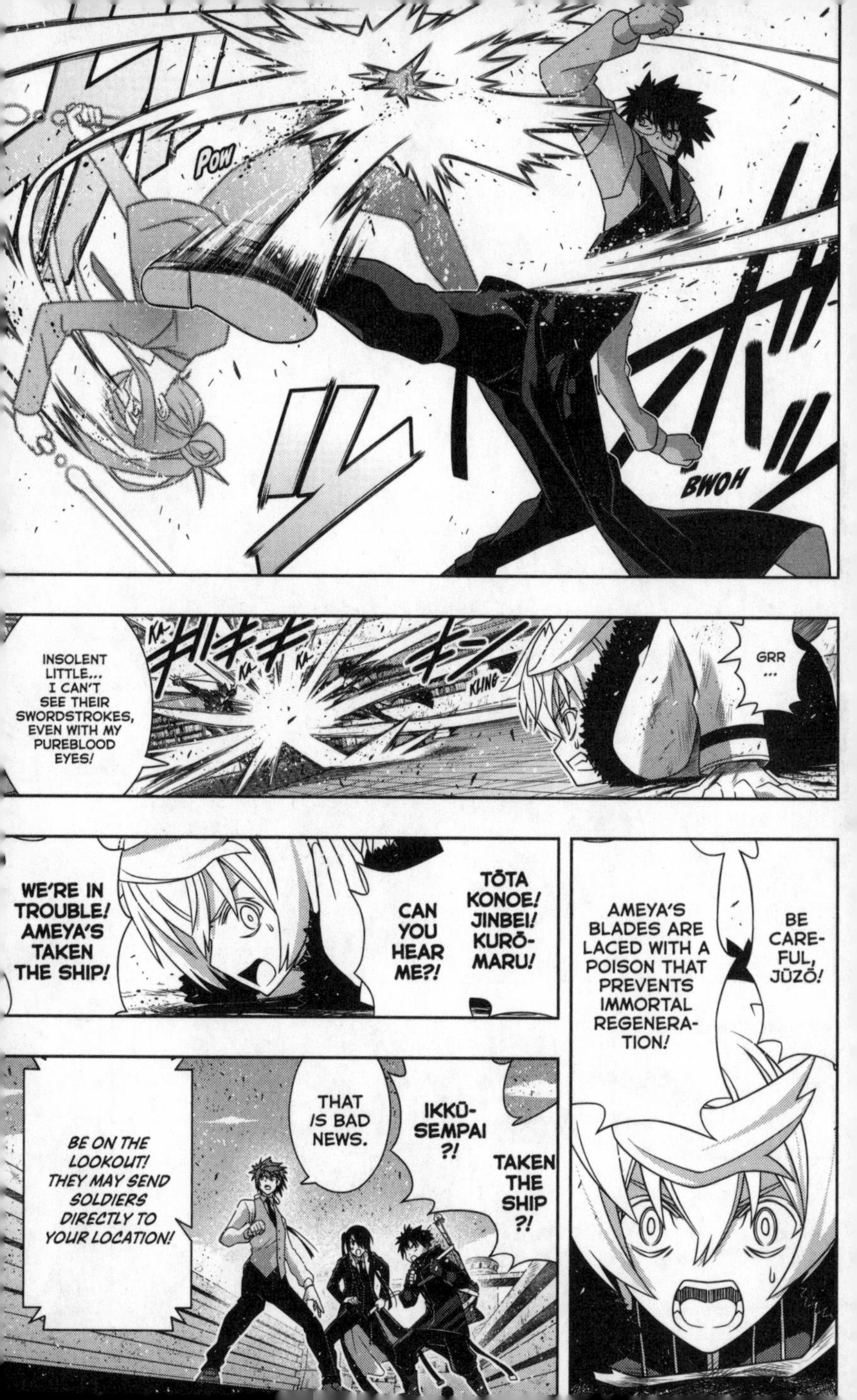
BWOH
POW
GRR...
KLING
KA
KA
KA
INSOLENT LITTLE... I CAN'T SEE THEIR SWORDSTROKES, EVEN WITH MY PUREBLOOD EYES!
BE CAREFUL, JŪZŌ!
AMEYA'S BLADES ARE LACED WITH A POISON THAT PREVENTS IMMORTAL REGENERATION!
TŌTA KONOE! JINBEI! KURŌMARU!
CAN YOU HEAR ME?!
WE'RE IN TROUBLE! AMEYA'S TAKEN THE SHIP!
TAKEN THE SHIP?!
IKKŪ-SEMPAI?!
THAT IS BAD NEWS.
BE ON THE LOOKOUT! THEY MAY SEND SOLDIERS DIRECTLY TO YOUR LOCATION!

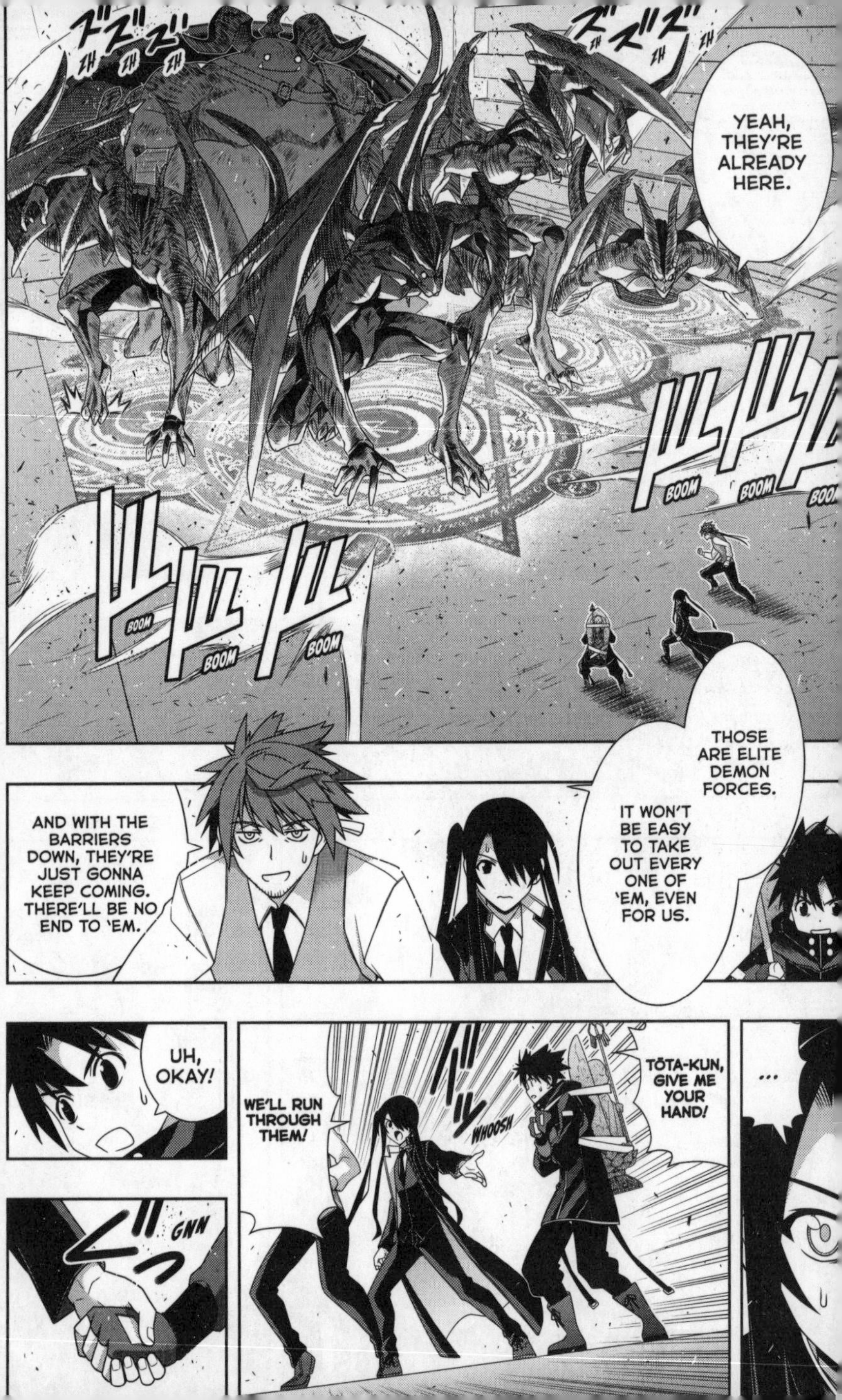
ZH ZH ZH
YEAH, THEY'RE ALREADY HERE.
ZH ZH ZH
BOOM BOOM BOOM
BOOM BOOM BOOM
THOSE ARE ELITE DEMON FORCES.
IT WON'T BE EASY TO TAKE OUT EVERY ONE OF 'EM, EVEN FOR US.
AND WITH THE BARRIERS DOWN, THEY'RE JUST GONNA KEEP COMING. THERE'LL BE NO END TO 'EM.
...
TŌTA-KUN, GIVE ME YOUR HAND!
WHOOSH
WE'LL RUN THROUGH THEM!
UH, OKAY!
GNN

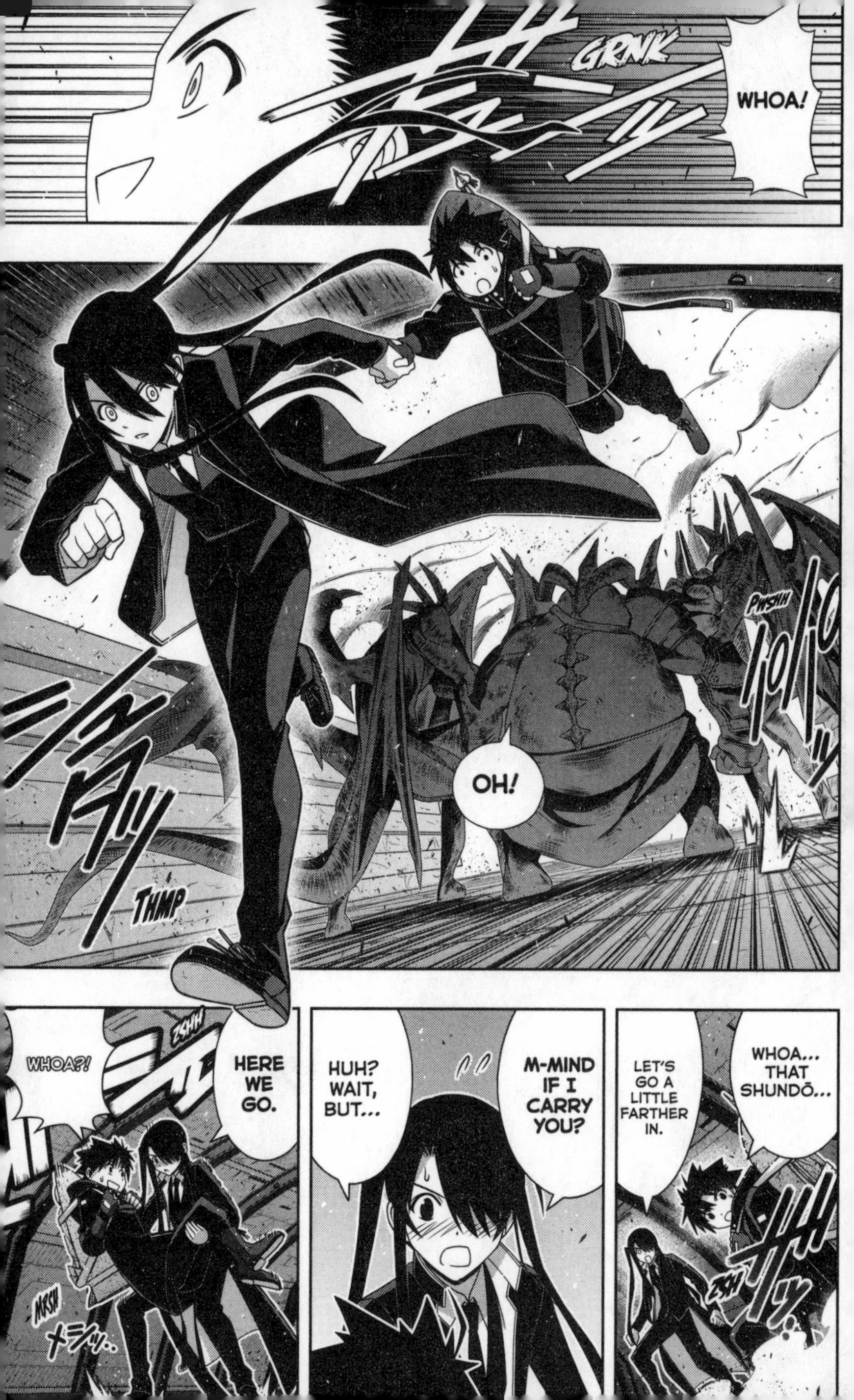
WHOA!
GRNK
PWSHH
OH!
THMP
WHOA... THAT SHUNDŌ...
LET'S GO A LITTLE FARTHER IN.
ZSH
M-MIND IF I CARRY YOU?
HUH? WAIT, BUT...
HERE WE GO.
ZSHH
WHOA?!
MRSH

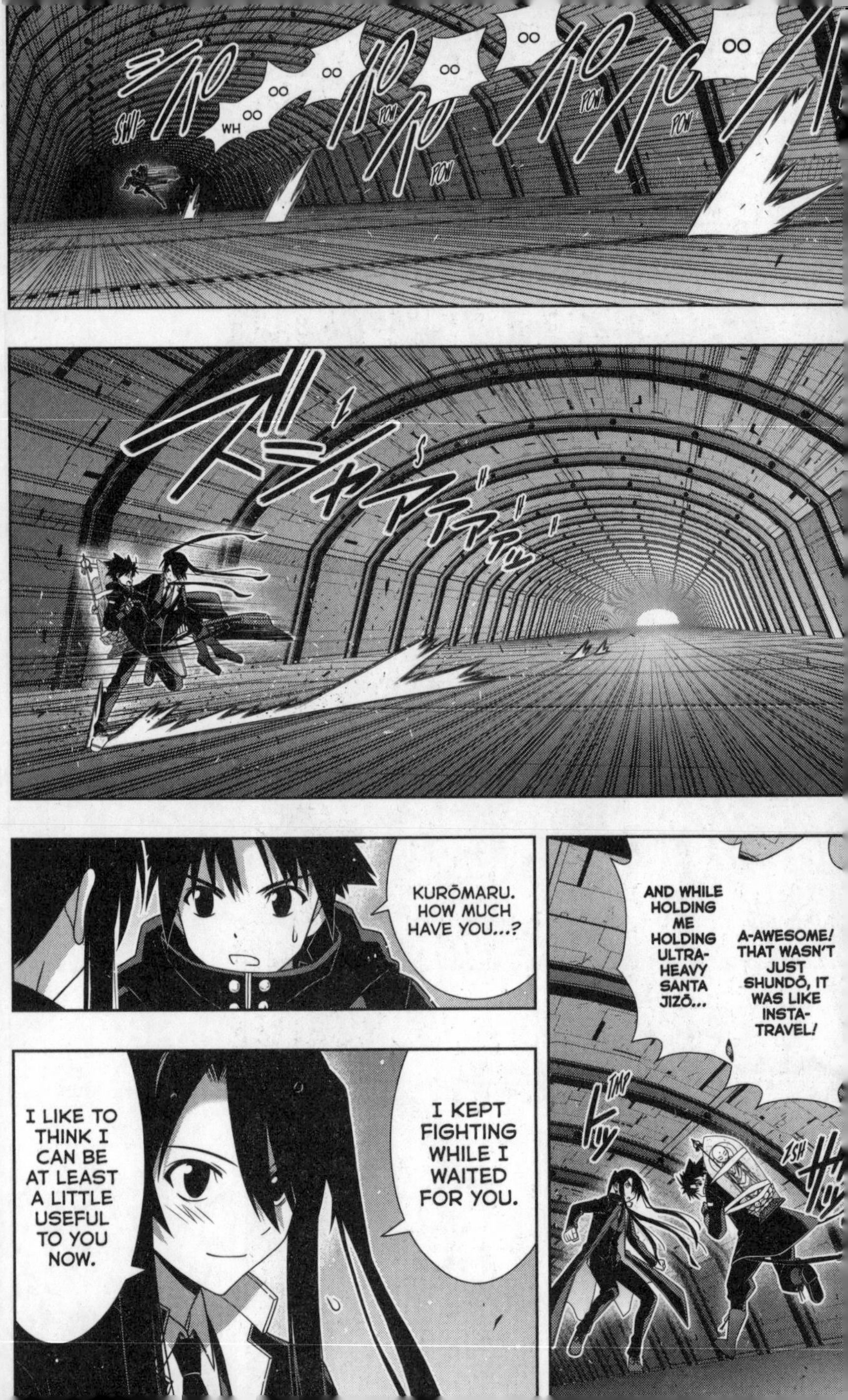
SWI-
WH
OO
OO
OO
OO
OO
POW
POW
POW
POW
A-AWESOME! THAT WASN'T JUST SHUNDŌ, IT WAS LIKE INSTA-TRAVEL!
AND WHILE HOLDING ME HOLDING ULTRA-HEAVY SANTA JIZŌ...
TMP
TSH
KURŌMARU. HOW MUCH HAVE YOU...?
I KEPT FIGHTING WHILE I WAITED FOR YOU.
I LIKE TO THINK I CAN BE AT LEAST A LITTLE USEFUL TO YOU NOW.

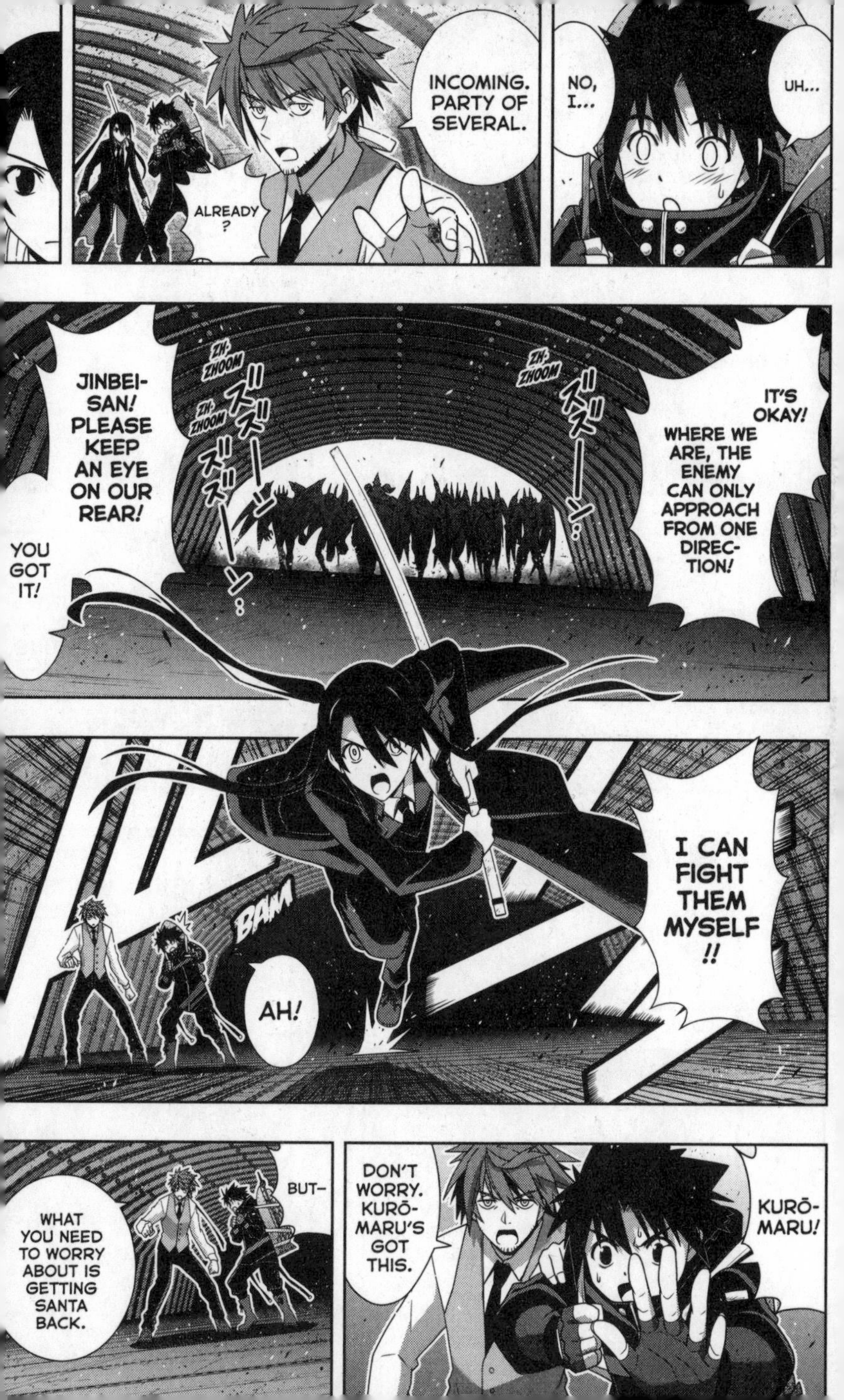
UH...
NO, I...
INCOMING. PARTY OF SEVERAL.
ALREADY?
IT'S OKAY! WHERE WE ARE, THE ENEMY CAN ONLY APPROACH FROM ONE DIREC-TION!
ZH-ZHOOM
ZH-ZHOOM
ZH-ZHOOM
JINBEI-SAN! PLEASE KEEP AN EYE ON OUR REAR!
YOU GOT IT!
I CAN FIGHT THEM MYSELF!!
BAM
AH!
KURŌ-MARU!
DON'T WORRY. KURŌ-MARU'S GOT THIS.
BUT-
WHAT YOU NEED TO WORRY ABOUT IS GETTING SANTA BACK.

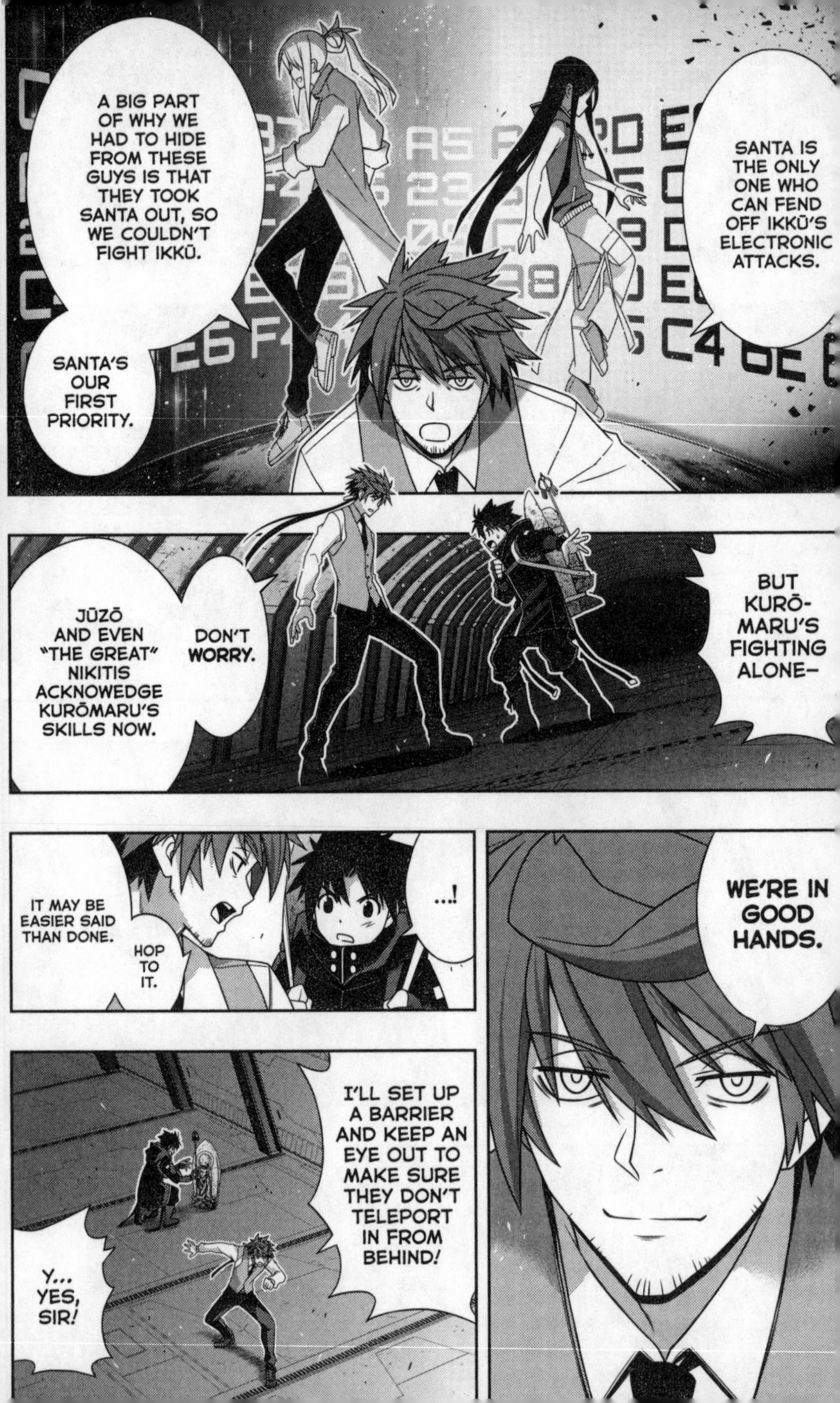
SANTA IS THE ONLY ONE WHO CAN FEND OFF IKKŪ'S ELECTRONIC ATTACKS.
A BIG PART OF WHY WE HAD TO HIDE FROM THESE GUYS IS THAT THEY TOOK SANTA OUT, SO WE COULDN'T FIGHT IKKŪ.
SANTA'S OUR FIRST PRIORITY.
BUT KURŌ-MARU'S FIGHTING ALONE—
DON'T WORRY.
JŪZŌ AND EVEN "THE GREAT" NIKITIS ACKNOWEDGE KURŌMARU'S SKILLS NOW.
WE'RE IN GOOD HANDS.
...!
IT MAY BE EASIER SAID THAN DONE.
HOP TO IT.
I'LL SET UP A BARRIER AND KEEP AN EYE OUT TO MAKE SURE THEY DON'T TELEPORT IN FROM BEHIND!
Y... YES, SIR!

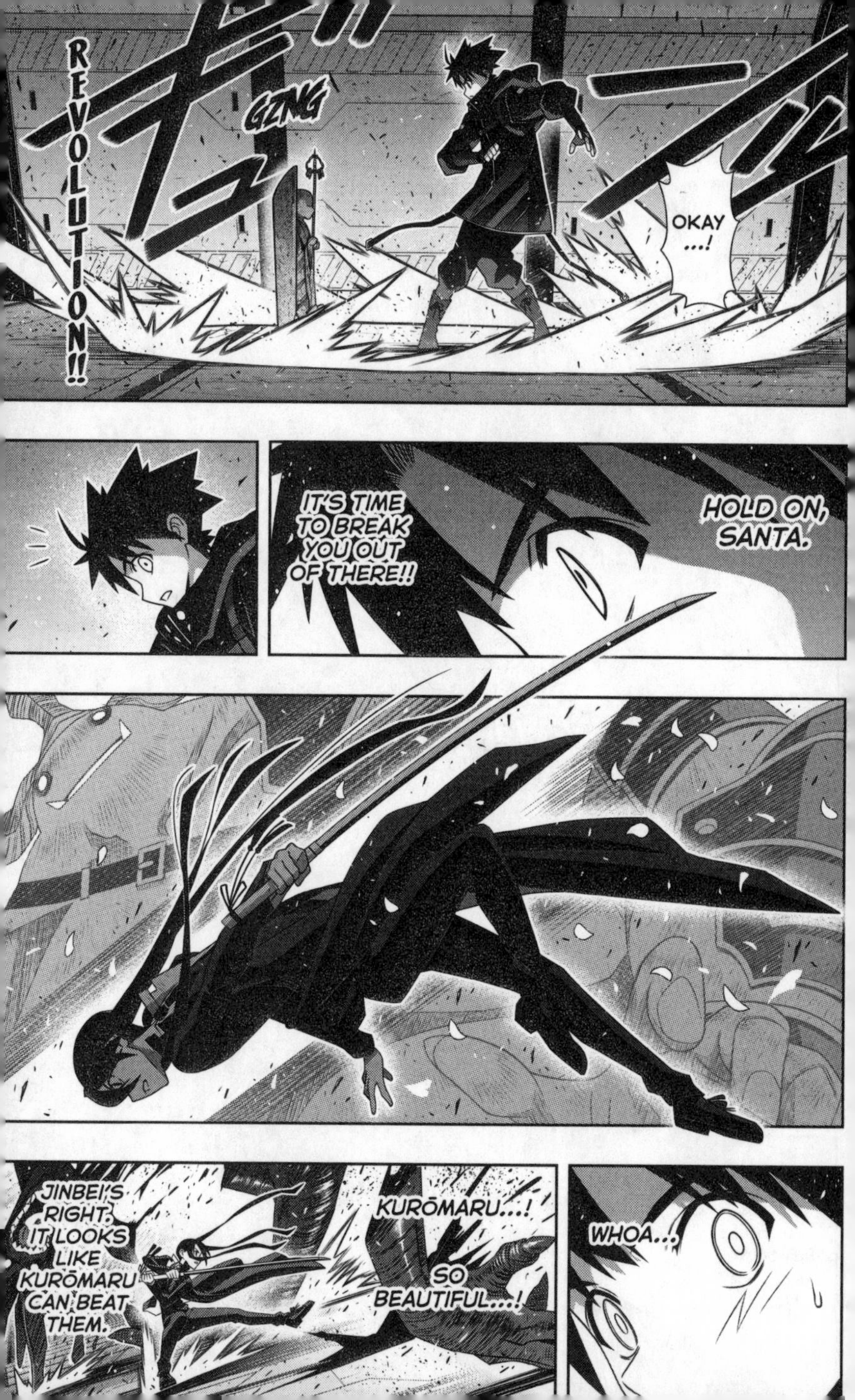
OKAY ...!
GZNG
REVOLUTION!!
HOLD ON, SANTA.
IT'S TIME TO BREAK YOU OUT OF THERE!!
WHOA...
KURŌMARU...!
SO BEAUTIFUL...!
JINBEI'S RIGHT. IT LOOKS LIKE KURŌMARU CAN BEAT THEM.

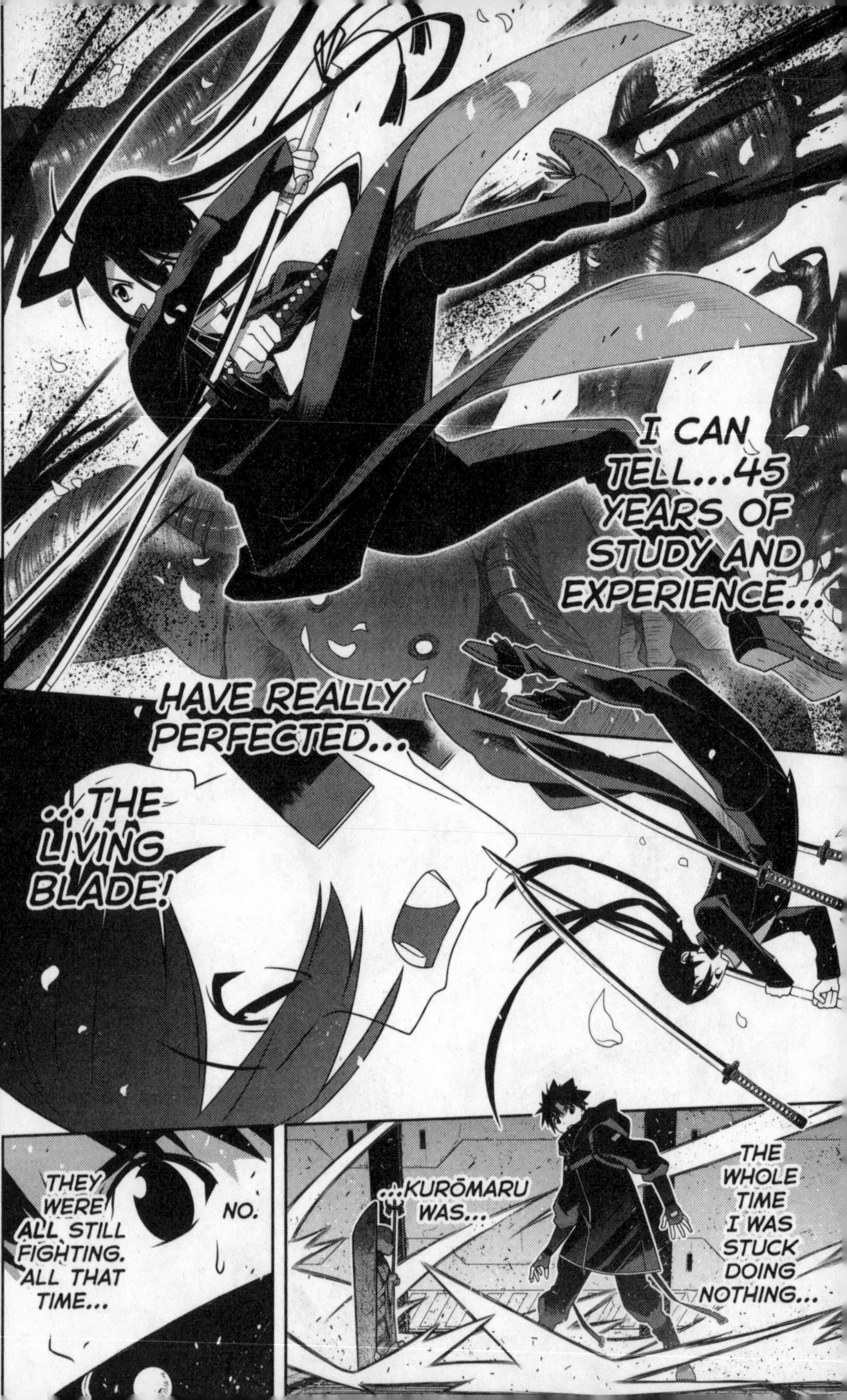
I CAN TELL...45 YEARS OF STUDY AND EXPERIENCE...
HAVE REALLY PERFECTED...
...THE LIVING BLADE!
THE WHOLE TIME I WAS STUCK DOING NOTHING...
...KURŌMARU WAS...
NO.
THEY WERE ALL STILL FIGHTING. ALL THAT TIME...

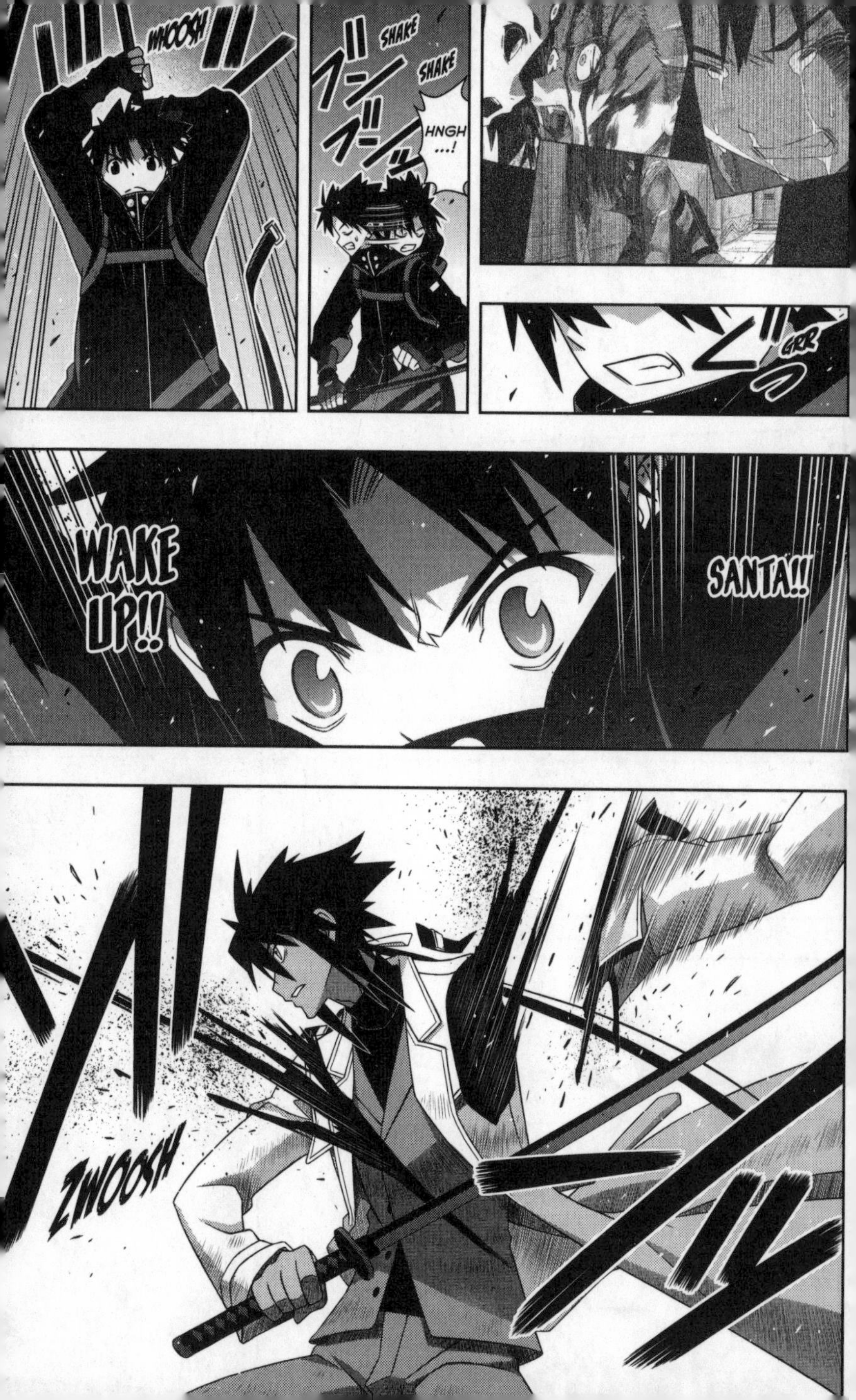
GRR
SHAKE
SHAKE
HNGH...!
WHOOSH
WAKE UP!!
SANTA!!
ZWOOSH

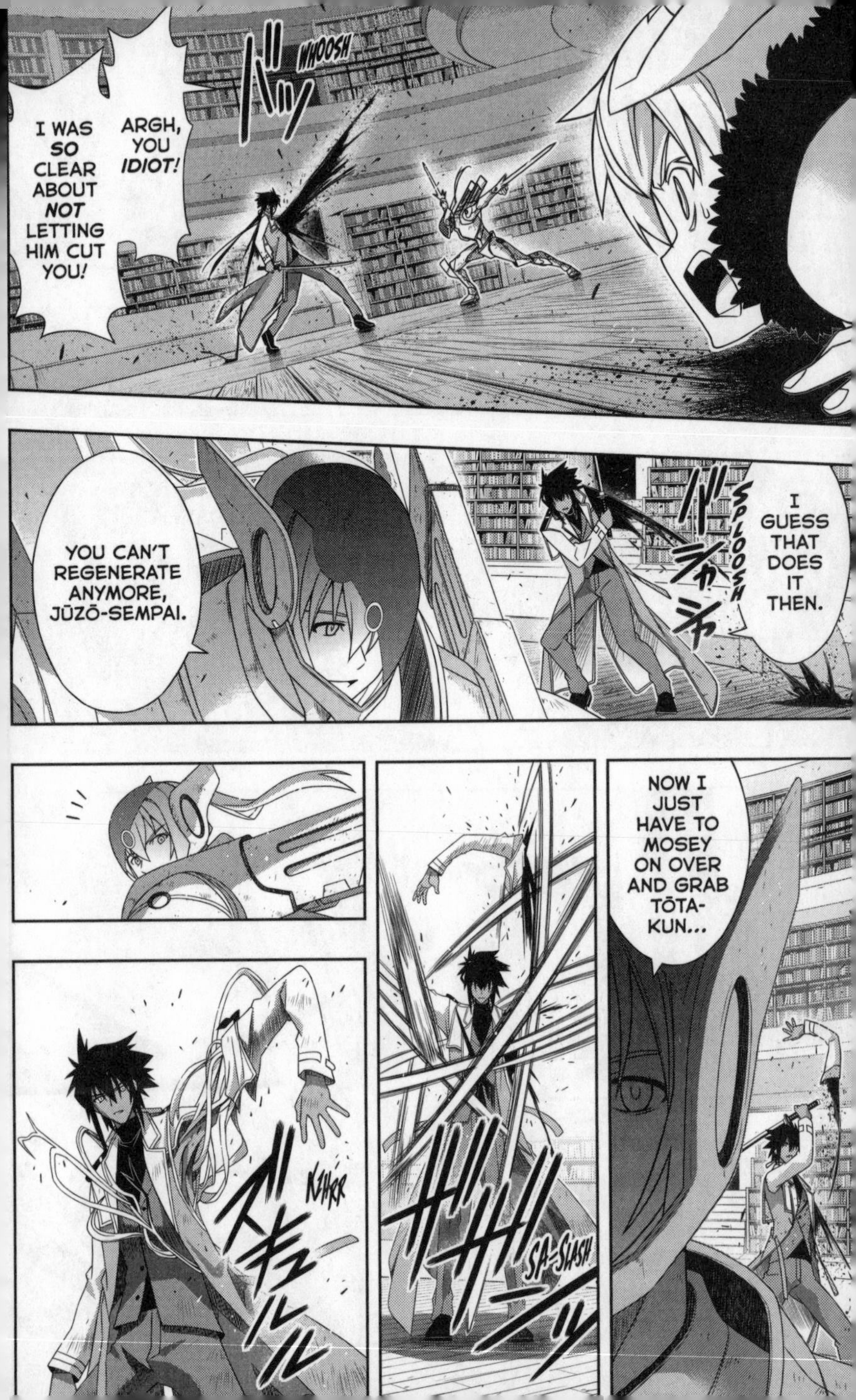
WHOOSH
ARGH, YOU IDIOT!
I WAS SO CLEAR ABOUT NOT LETTING HIM CUT YOU!
I GUESS THAT DOES IT THEN.
SPLOOSH
YOU CAN'T REGENERATE ANYMORE, JŪZŌ-SEMPAI.
NOW I JUST HAVE TO MOSEY ON OVER AND GRAB TŌTA-KUN...
SA-SLASH
KSHRR

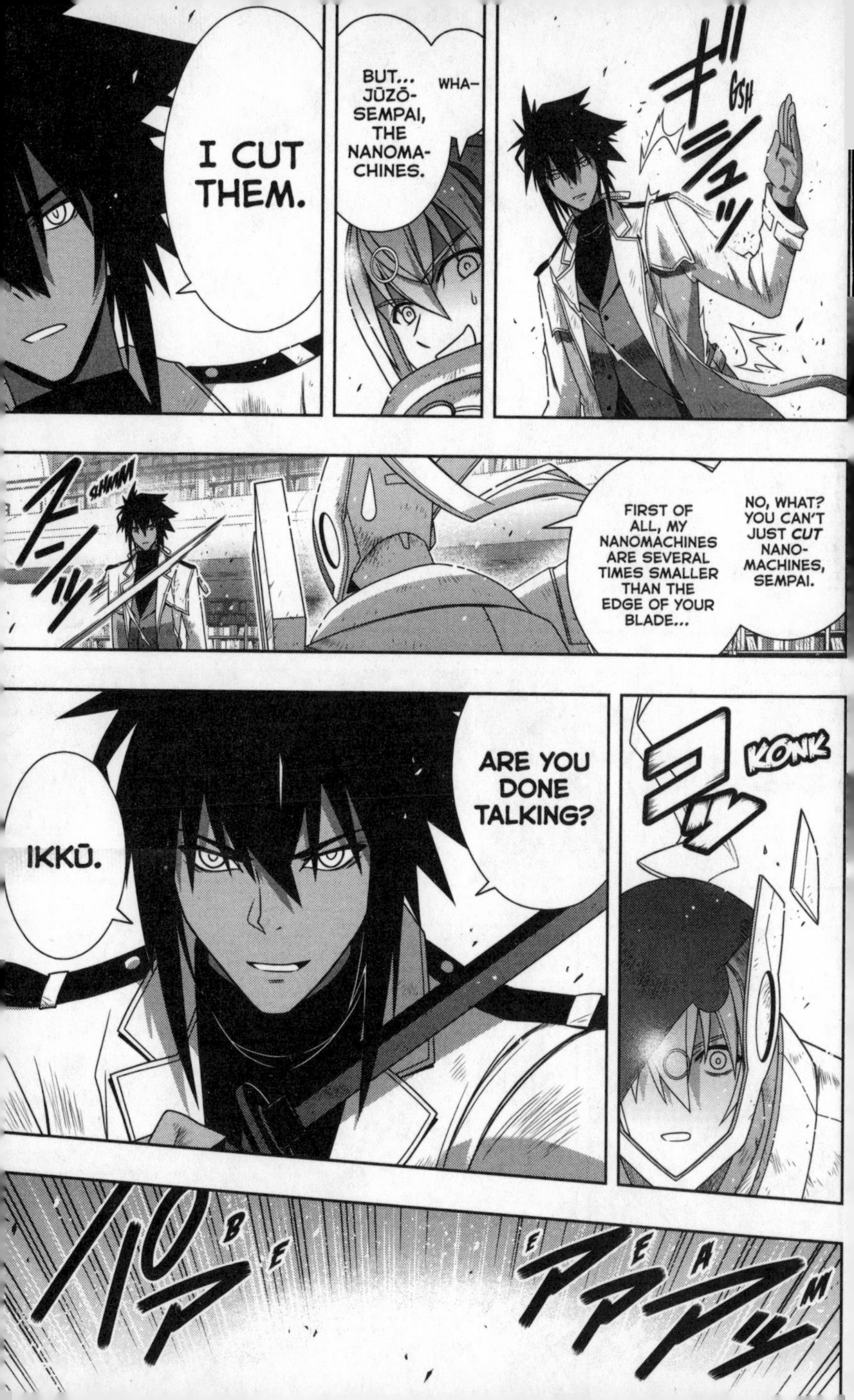
GSH
WHA—
BUT... JŪZŌ-SEMPAI, THE NANOMACHINES.
I CUT THEM.
NO, WHAT? YOU CAN'T JUST *CUT* NANOMACHINES, SEMPAI.
FIRST OF ALL, MY NANOMACHINES ARE SEVERAL TIMES SMALLER THAN THE EDGE OF YOUR BLADE...
KONK
ARE YOU DONE TALKING?
IKKŪ.
BEEAM

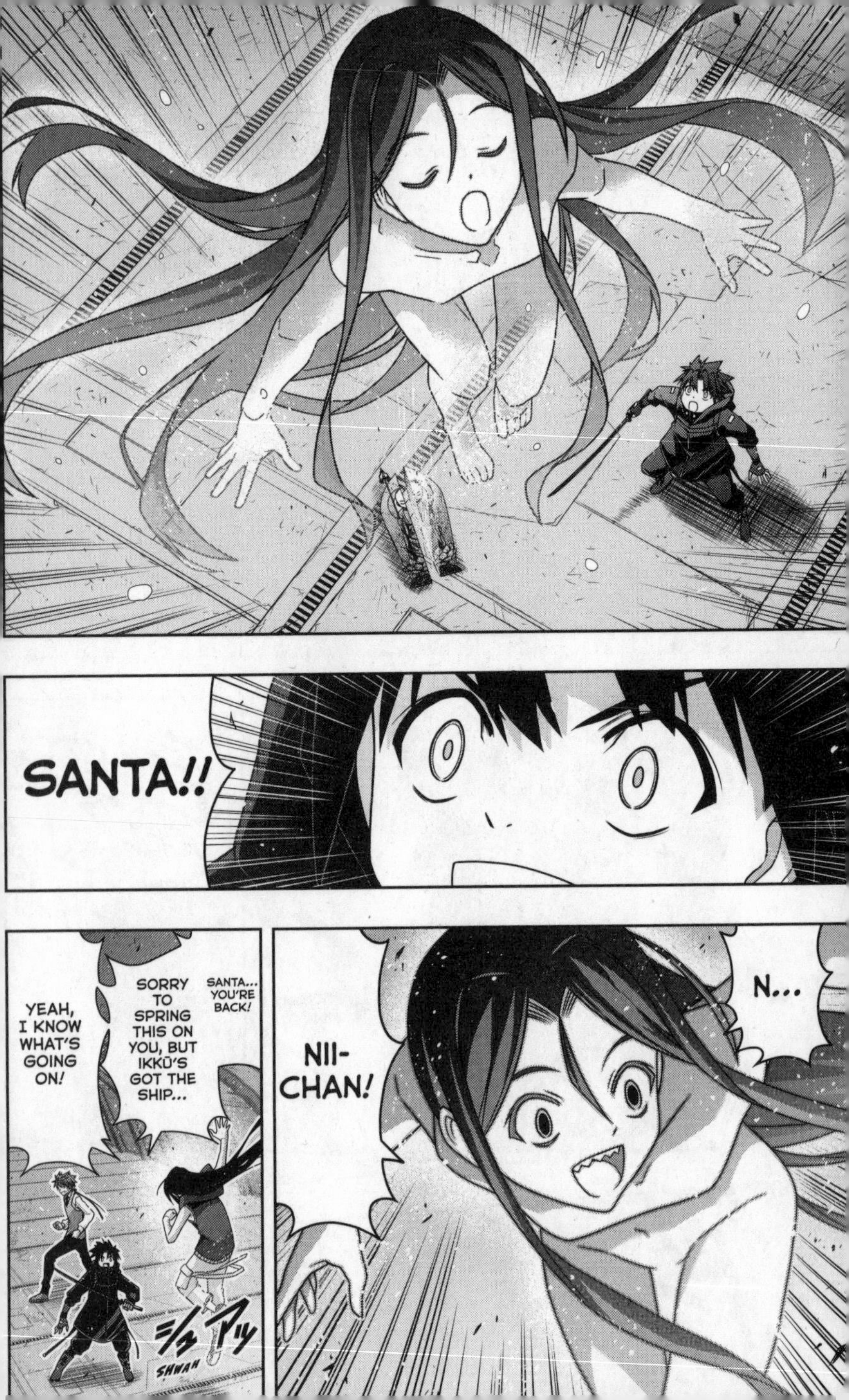
SANTA!!
N...
NII-CHAN!
SANTA... YOU'RE BACK!
SORRY TO SPRING THIS ON YOU, BUT IKKŪ'S GOT THE SHIP...
YEAH, I KNOW WHAT'S GOING ON!
シュアッ
SHWAH

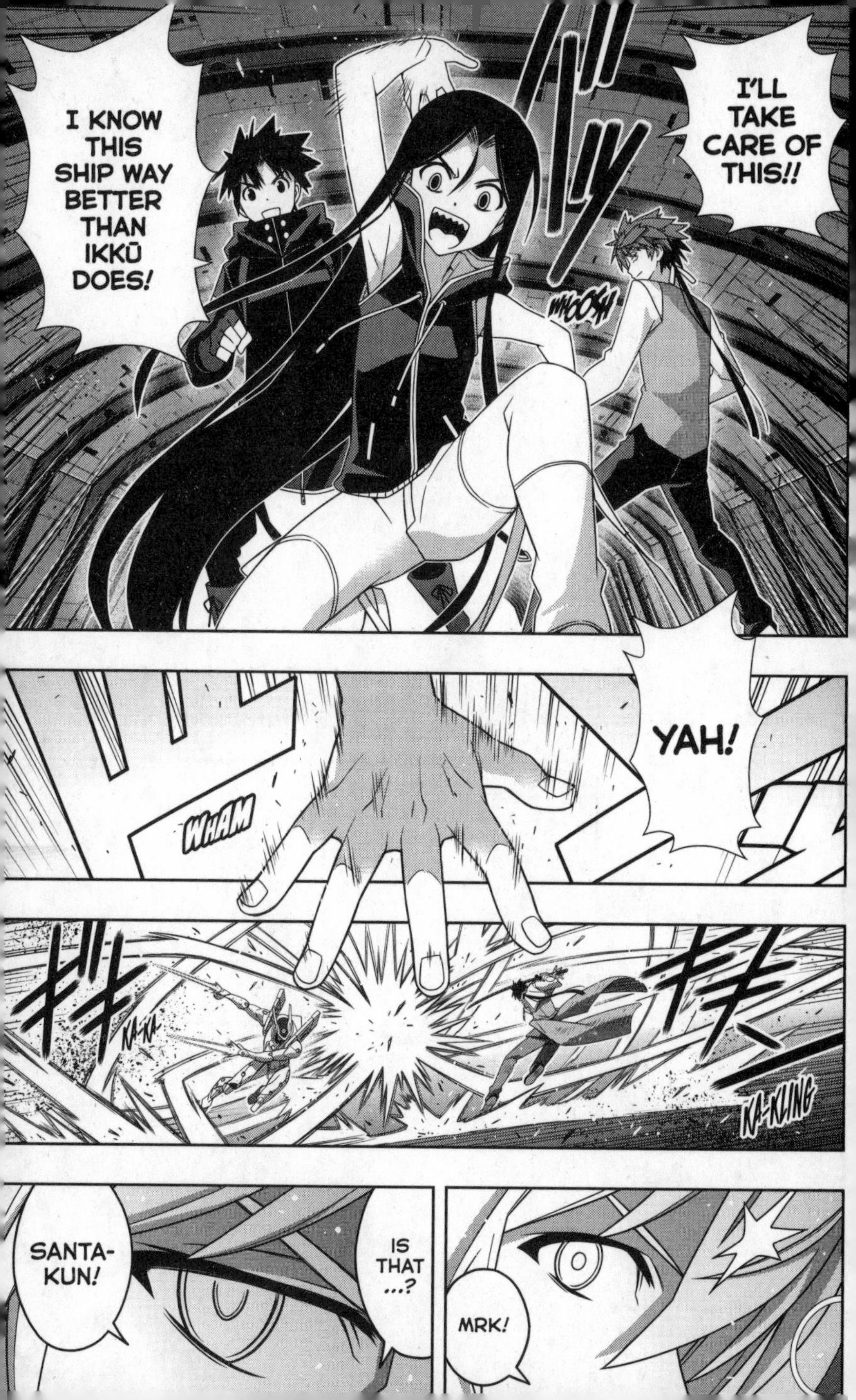
I'LL TAKE CARE OF THIS!!
I KNOW THIS SHIP WAY BETTER THAN IKKŪ DOES!
WHOOSH
YAH!
WHAM
KA-KLING
KA-KA
MRK!
IS THAT ...?
SANTA-KUN!

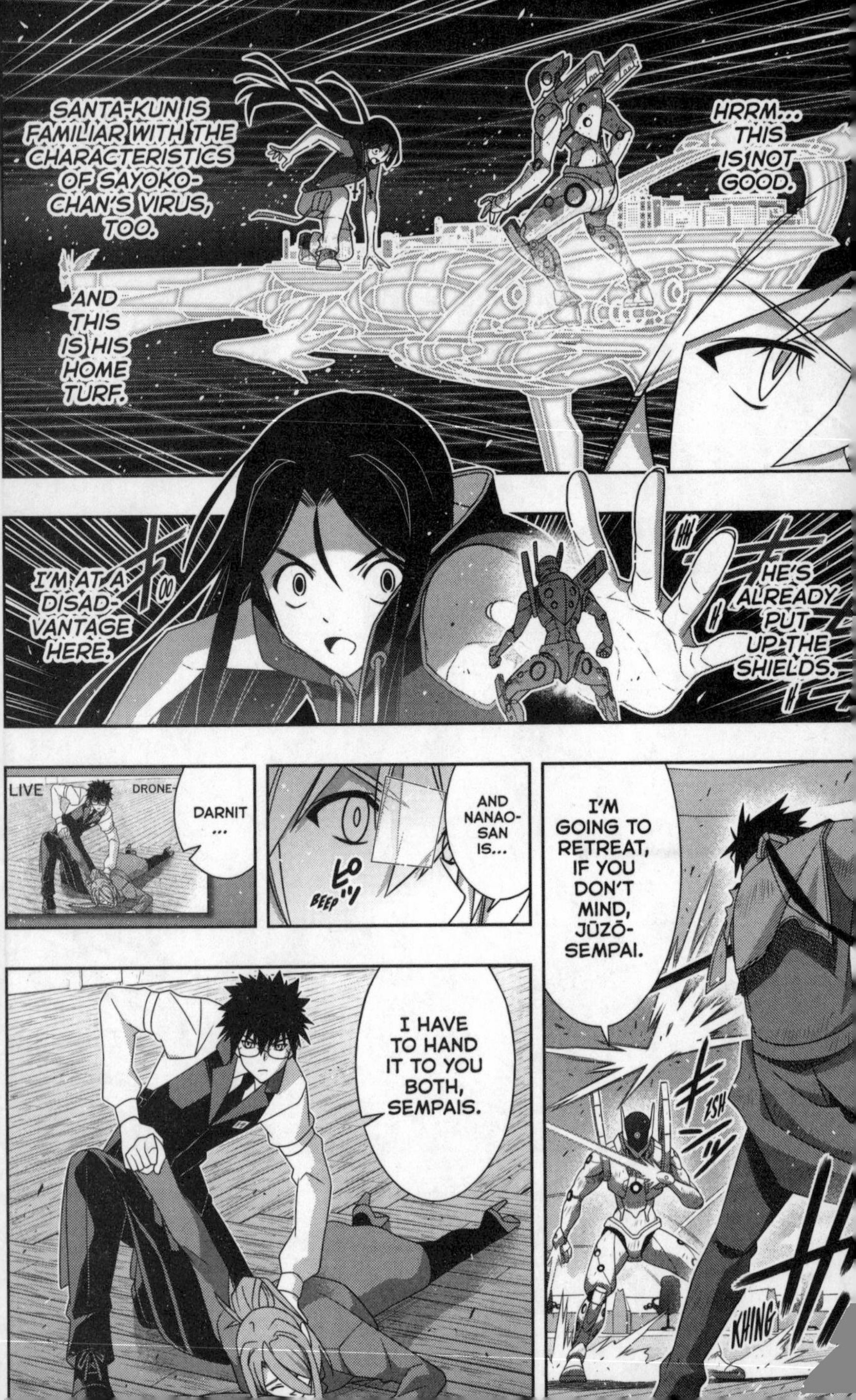
HRRM... THIS IS NOT GOOD.
SANTA-KUN IS FAMILIAR WITH THE CHARACTERISTICS OF SAYOKO-CHAN'S VIRUS, TOO.
AND THIS IS HIS HOME TURF.
HE'S ALREADY PUT UP THE SHIELDS.
I'M AT A DISAD-VANTAGE HERE.
I'M GOING TO RETREAT, IF YOU DON'T MIND, JŪZŌ-SEMPAI.
ISH
KHING
AND NANAO-SAN IS...
BEEP
LIVE
DRONE-
DARNIT...
I HAVE TO HAND IT TO YOU BOTH, SEMPAIS.

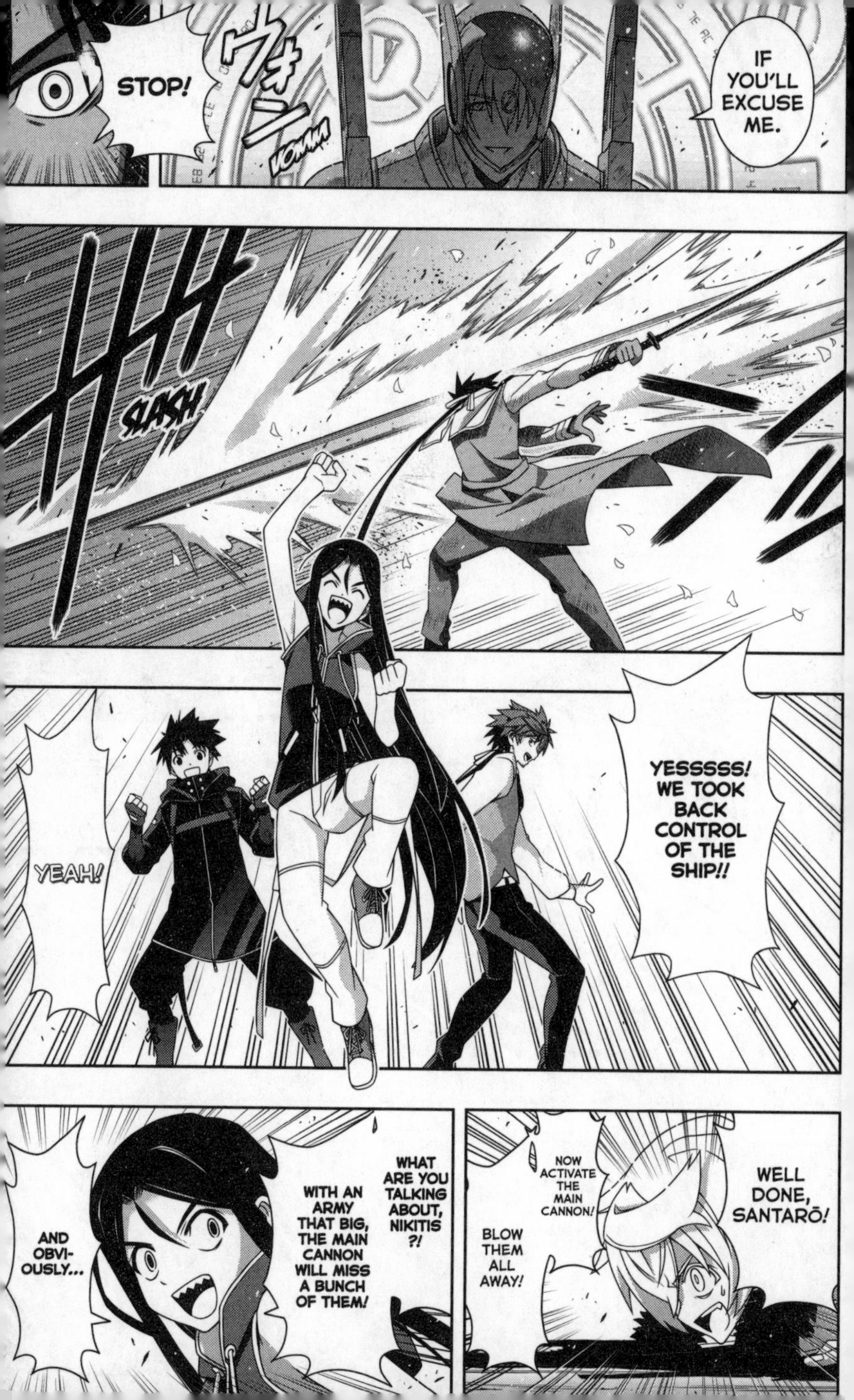
IF YOU'LL EXCUSE ME.
ヴォーン
VOMMM
STOP!
SLASH
YESSSSS! WE TOOK BACK CONTROL OF THE SHIP!!
YEAH!
WELL DONE, SANTARŌ!
NOW ACTIVATE THE MAIN CANNON!
BLOW THEM ALL AWAY!
WHAT ARE YOU TALKING ABOUT, NIKITIS?!
WITH AN ARMY THAT BIG, THE MAIN CANNON WILL MISS A BUNCH OF THEM!
AND OBVI-OUSLY...

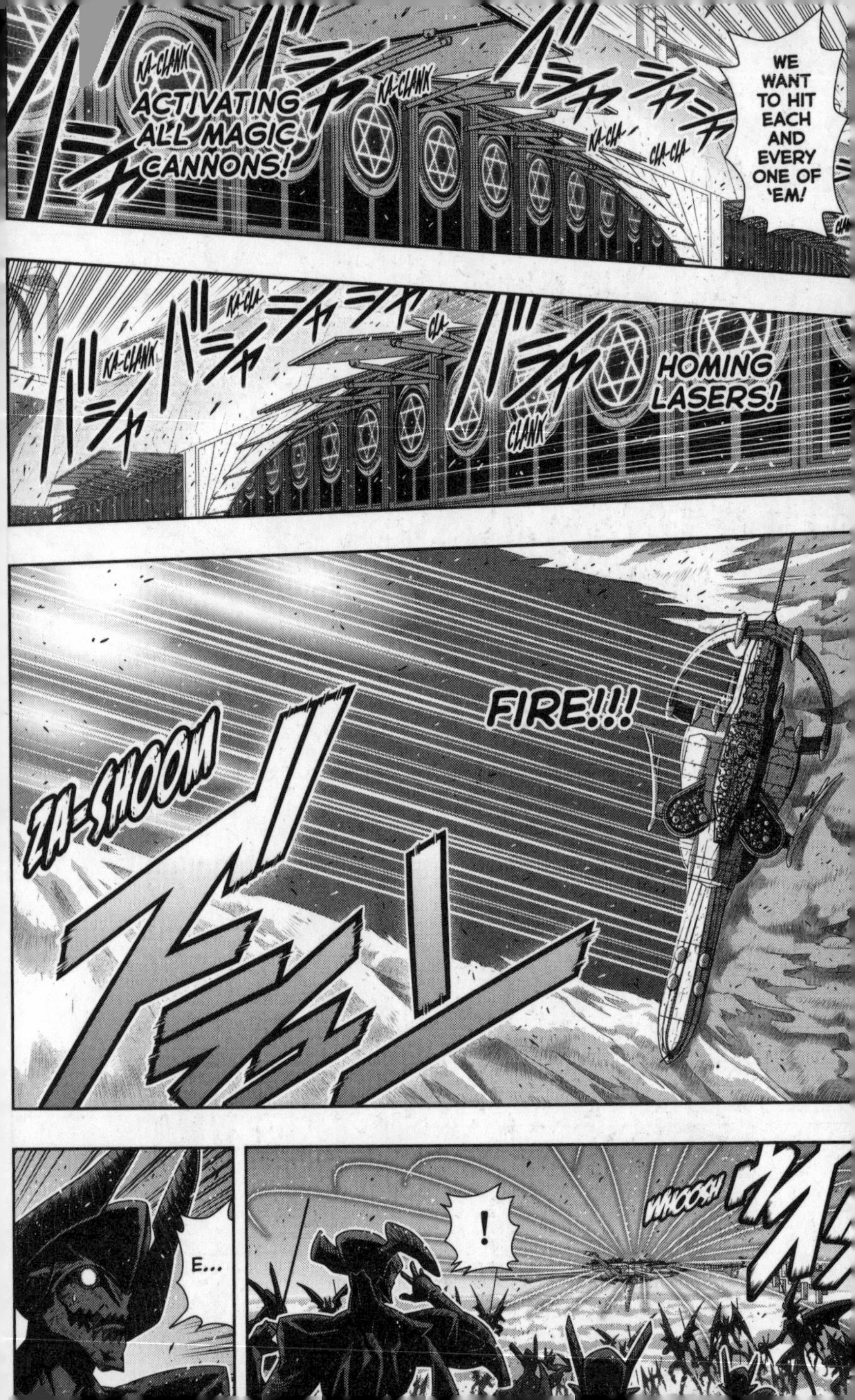
WE WANT TO HIT EACH AND EVERY ONE OF 'EM!
CLA-CLA
KA-CLA
KA-CLANK
KA-CLANK
ACTIVATING ALL MAGIC CANNONS!
HOMING LASERS!
CLANK
CLA
KA-CLA
KA-CLANK
FIRE!!!
ZA-SHOOM
WHOOSH
!
E...

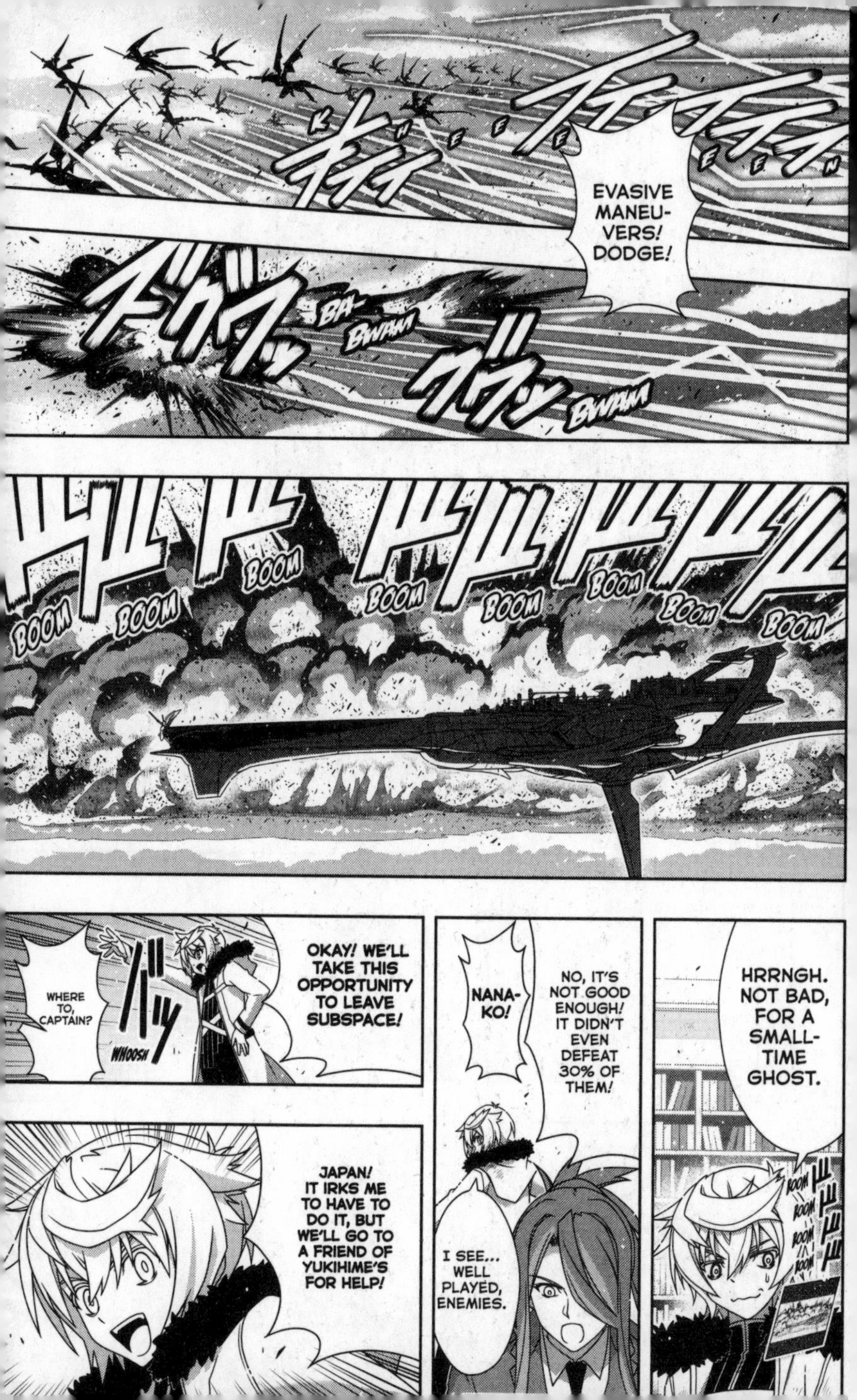
KHEEEEN
EVASIVE MANEU-VERS! DODGE!
BA-BWAAM
BWAAM
BOOM BOOM BOOM BOOM BOOM BOOM BOOM BOOM BOOM
HRRNGH. NOT BAD, FOR A SMALL-TIME GHOST.
BOOM BOOM BOOM BOOM
NANA-KO!
NO, IT'S NOT GOOD ENOUGH! IT DIDN'T EVEN DEFEAT 30% OF THEM!
I SEE... WELL PLAYED, ENEMIES.
OKAY! WE'LL TAKE THIS OPPORTUNITY TO LEAVE SUBSPACE!
WHOOSH
WHERE TO, CAPTAIN?
JAPAN! IT IRKS ME TO HAVE TO DO IT, BUT WE'LL GO TO A FRIEND OF YUKIHIME'S FOR HELP!

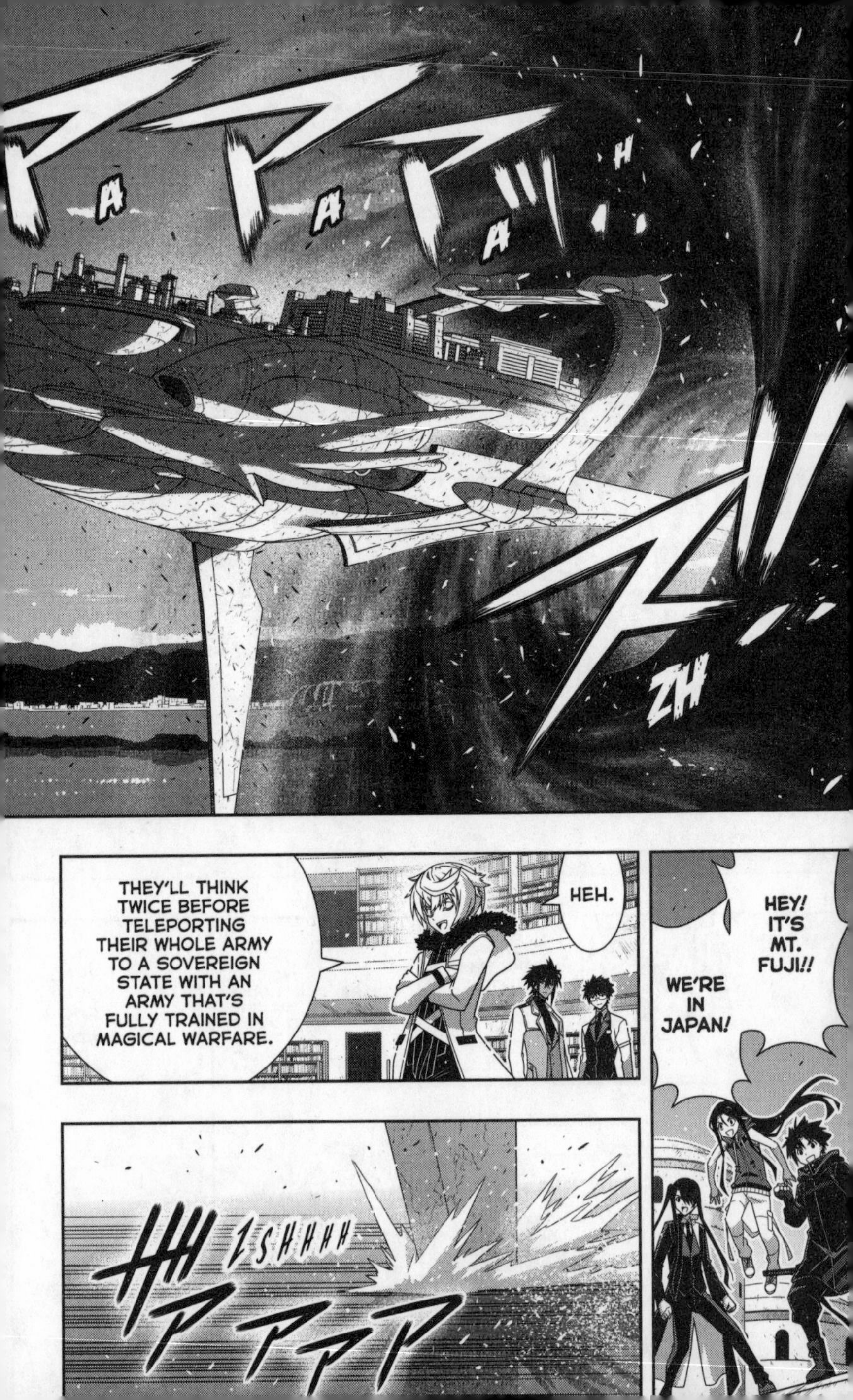
A
A
A
H
ZH
HEY! IT'S MT. FUJI!!
WE'RE IN JAPAN!
HEH.
THEY'LL THINK TWICE BEFORE TELEPORTING THEIR WHOLE ARMY TO A SOVEREIGN STATE WITH AN ARMY THAT'S FULLY TRAINED IN MAGICAL WARFARE.
ZSHHHH

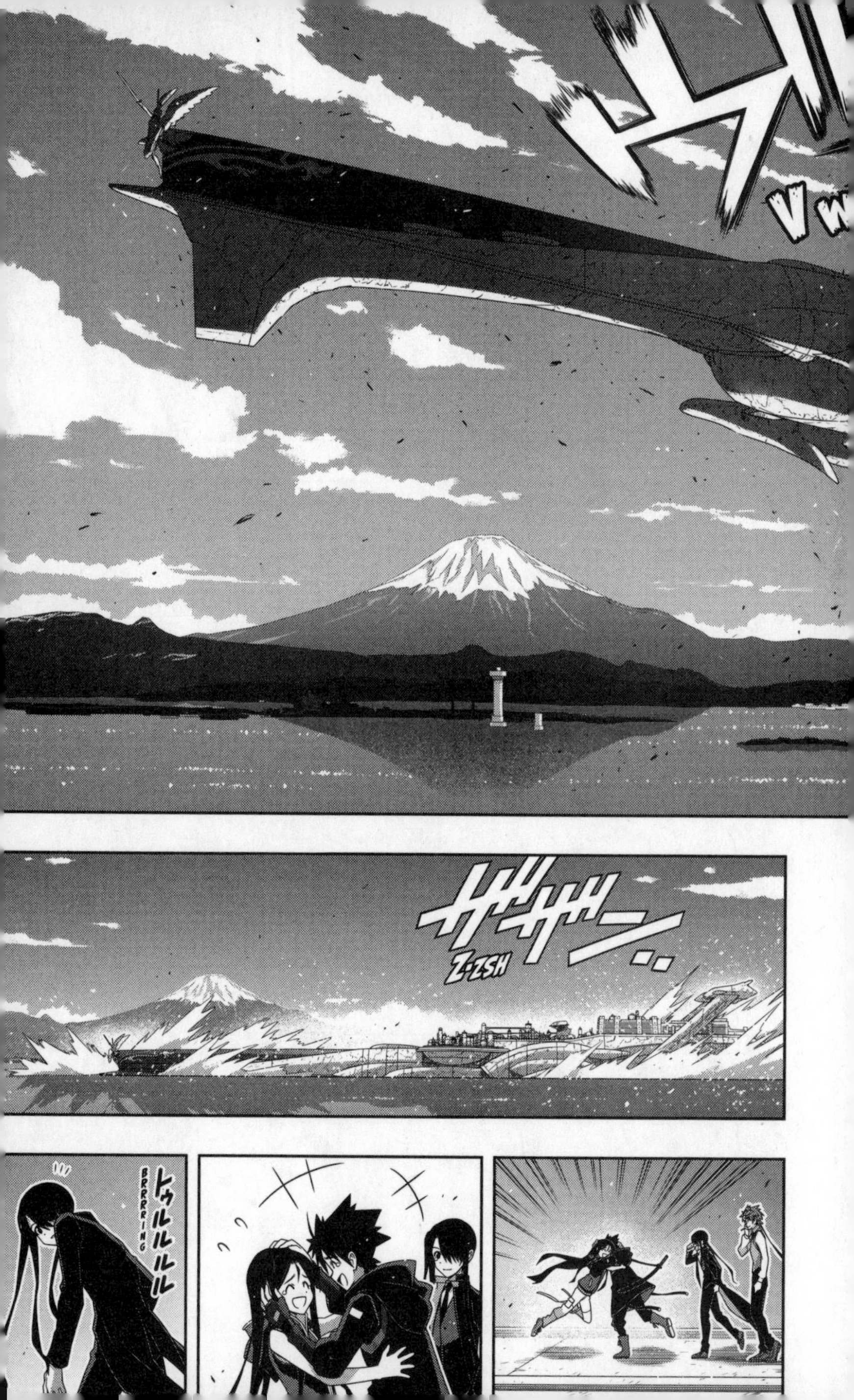
VW
ザザザー..
Z-ZSH
トゥルルルル
BRRRING

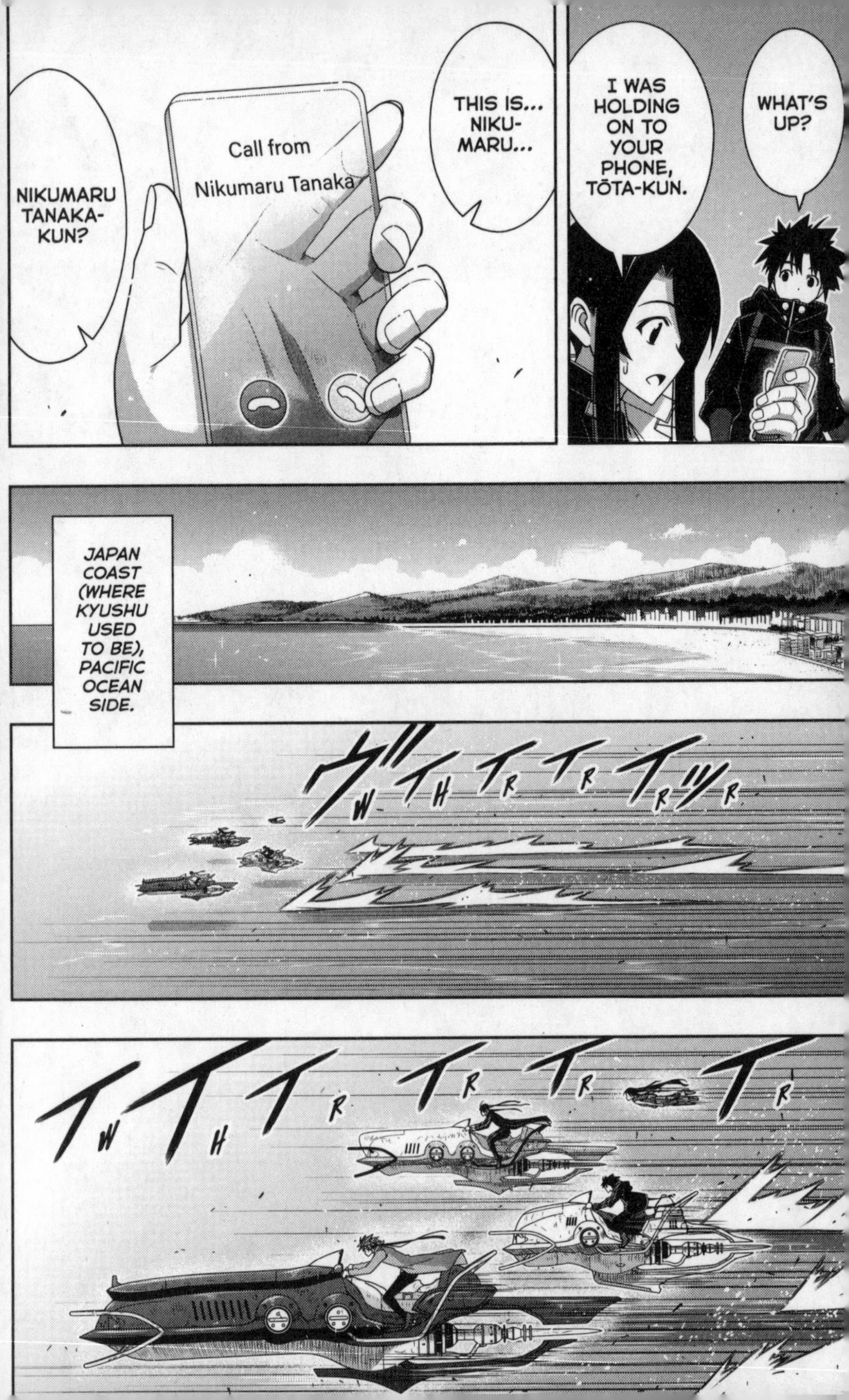
WHAT'S UP?
I WAS HOLDING ON TO YOUR PHONE, TŌTA-KUN.
THIS IS... NIKU-MARU...
Call from Nikumaru Tanaka
NIKUMARU TANAKA-KUN?
JAPAN COAST (WHERE KYUSHU USED TO BE), PACIFIC OCEAN SIDE.
WHRRRR
TWHRRRR

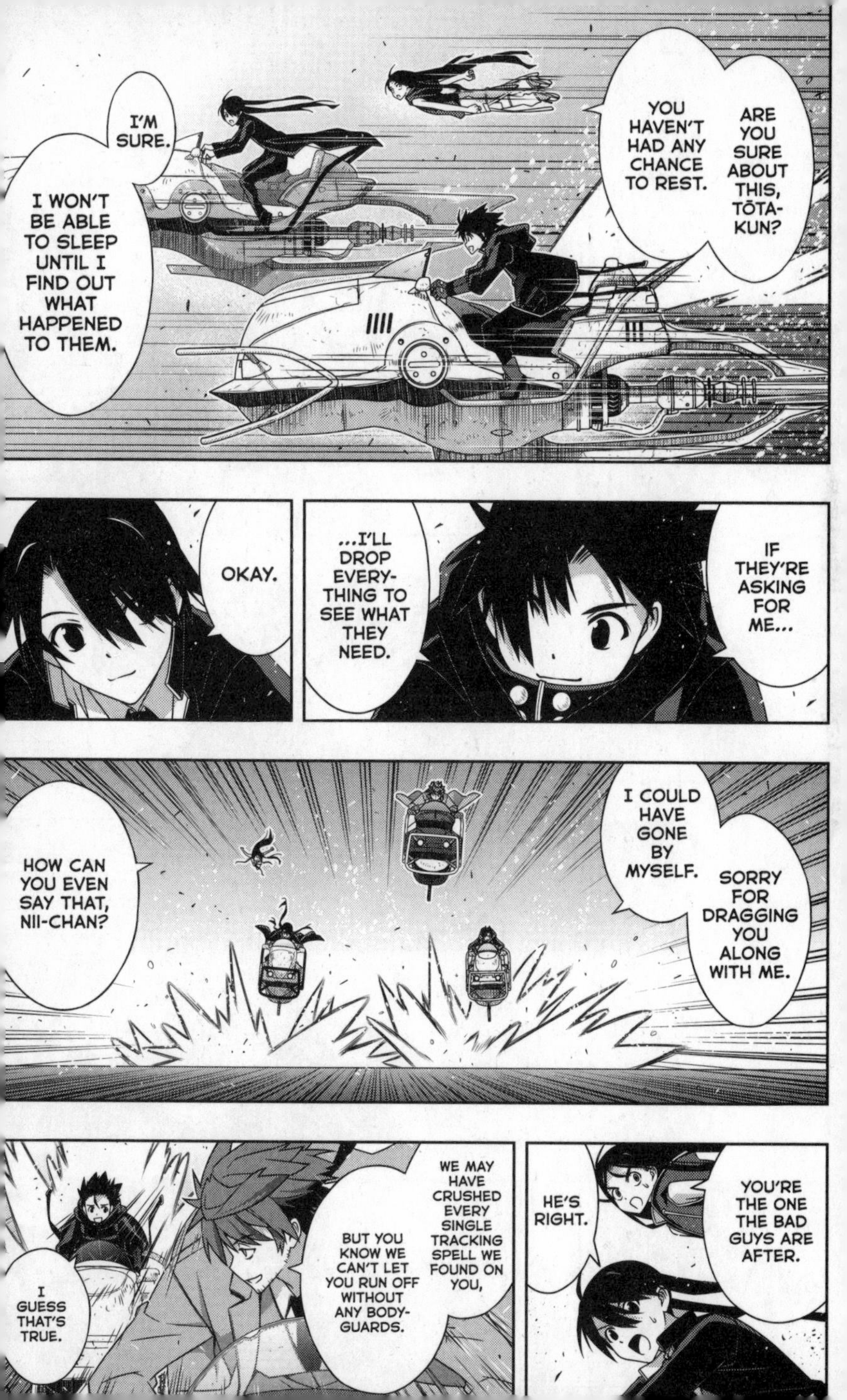
ARE YOU SURE ABOUT THIS, TŌTA-KUN?
YOU HAVEN'T HAD ANY CHANCE TO REST.
I'M SURE.
I WON'T BE ABLE TO SLEEP UNTIL I FIND OUT WHAT HAPPENED TO THEM.
IF THEY'RE ASKING FOR ME...
...I'LL DROP EVERYTHING TO SEE WHAT THEY NEED.
OKAY.
I COULD HAVE GONE BY MYSELF.
SORRY FOR DRAGGING YOU ALONG WITH ME.
HOW CAN YOU EVEN SAY THAT, NII-CHAN?
YOU'RE THE ONE THE BAD GUYS ARE AFTER.
HE'S RIGHT.
WE MAY HAVE CRUSHED EVERY SINGLE TRACKING SPELL WE FOUND ON YOU,
BUT YOU KNOW WE CAN'T LET YOU RUN OFF WITHOUT ANY BODY-GUARDS.
I GUESS THAT'S TRUE.

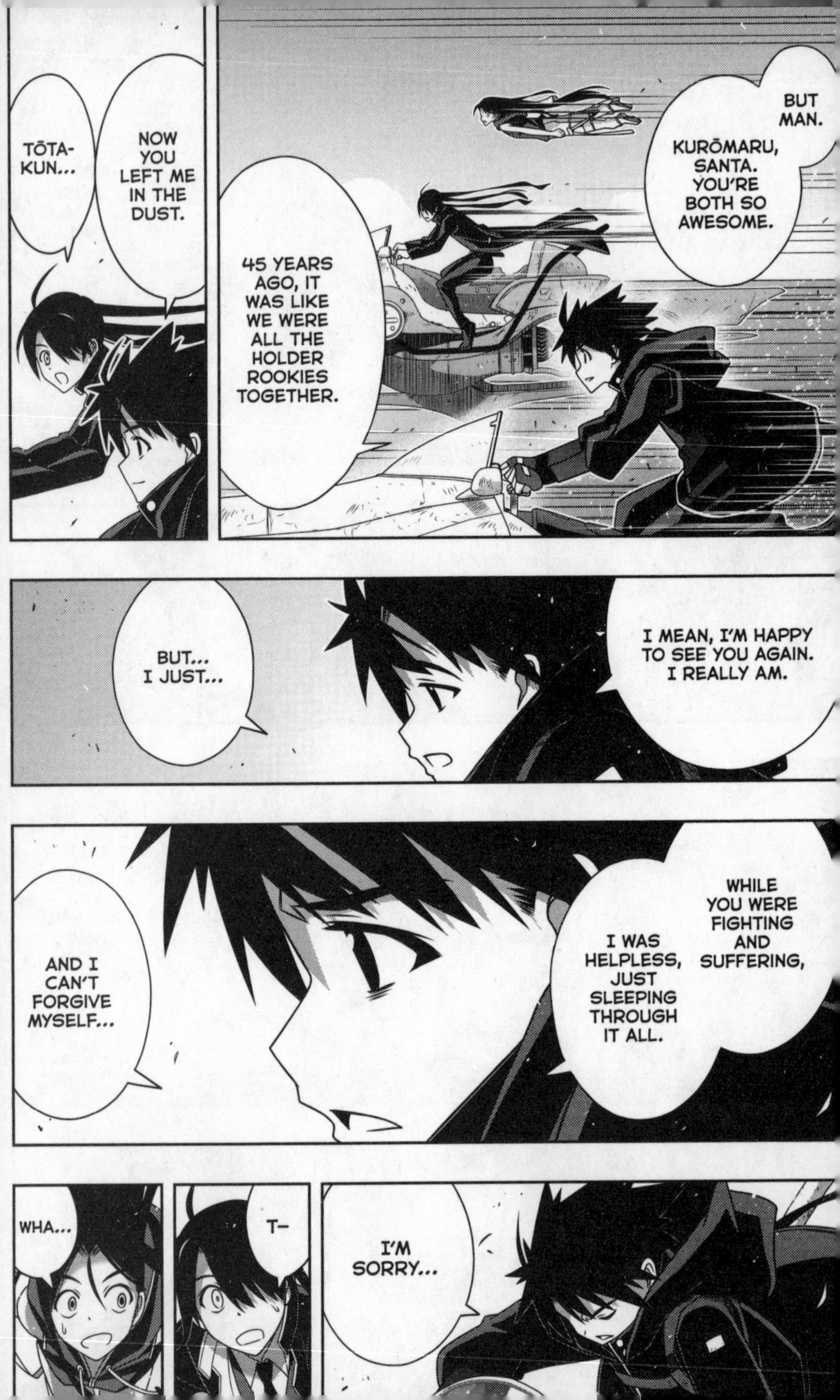
BUT MAN.
KURŌMARU, SANTA. YOU'RE BOTH SO AWESOME.
45 YEARS AGO, IT WAS LIKE WE WERE ALL THE HOLDER ROOKIES TOGETHER.
NOW YOU LEFT ME IN THE DUST.
TŌTA-KUN...
I MEAN, I'M HAPPY TO SEE YOU AGAIN. I REALLY AM.
BUT... I JUST...
WHILE YOU WERE FIGHTING AND SUFFERING,
I WAS HELPLESS, JUST SLEEPING THROUGH IT ALL.
AND I CAN'T FORGIVE MYSELF...
I'M SORRY...
T–
WHA...

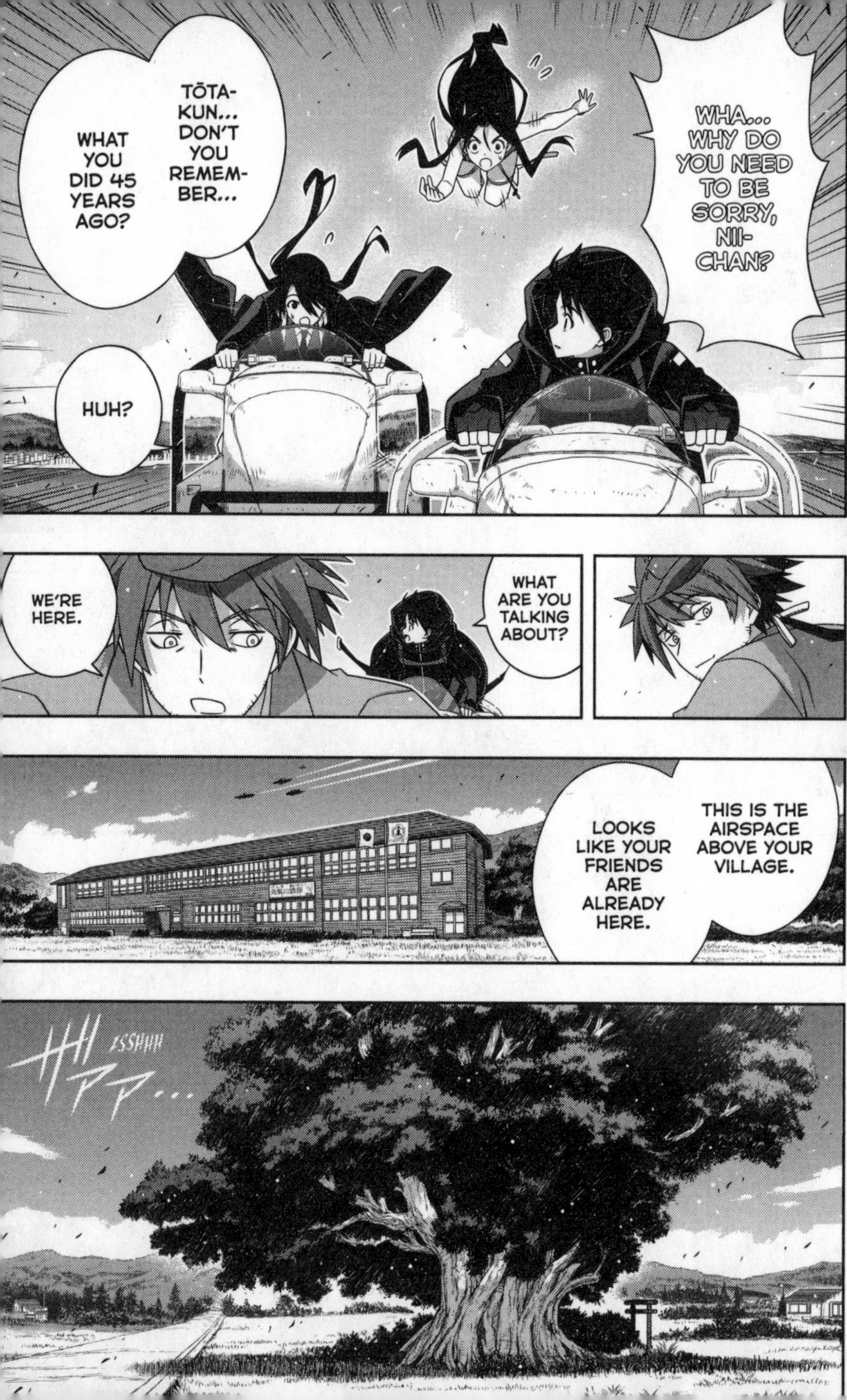
WHA... WHY DO YOU NEED TO BE SORRY, NII-CHAN?
TŌTA-KUN... DON'T YOU REMEMBER...
WHAT YOU DID 45 YEARS AGO?
HUH?
WHAT ARE YOU TALKING ABOUT?
WE'RE HERE.
THIS IS THE AIRSPACE ABOVE YOUR VILLAGE.
LOOKS LIKE YOUR FRIENDS ARE ALREADY HERE.
ISSHHH

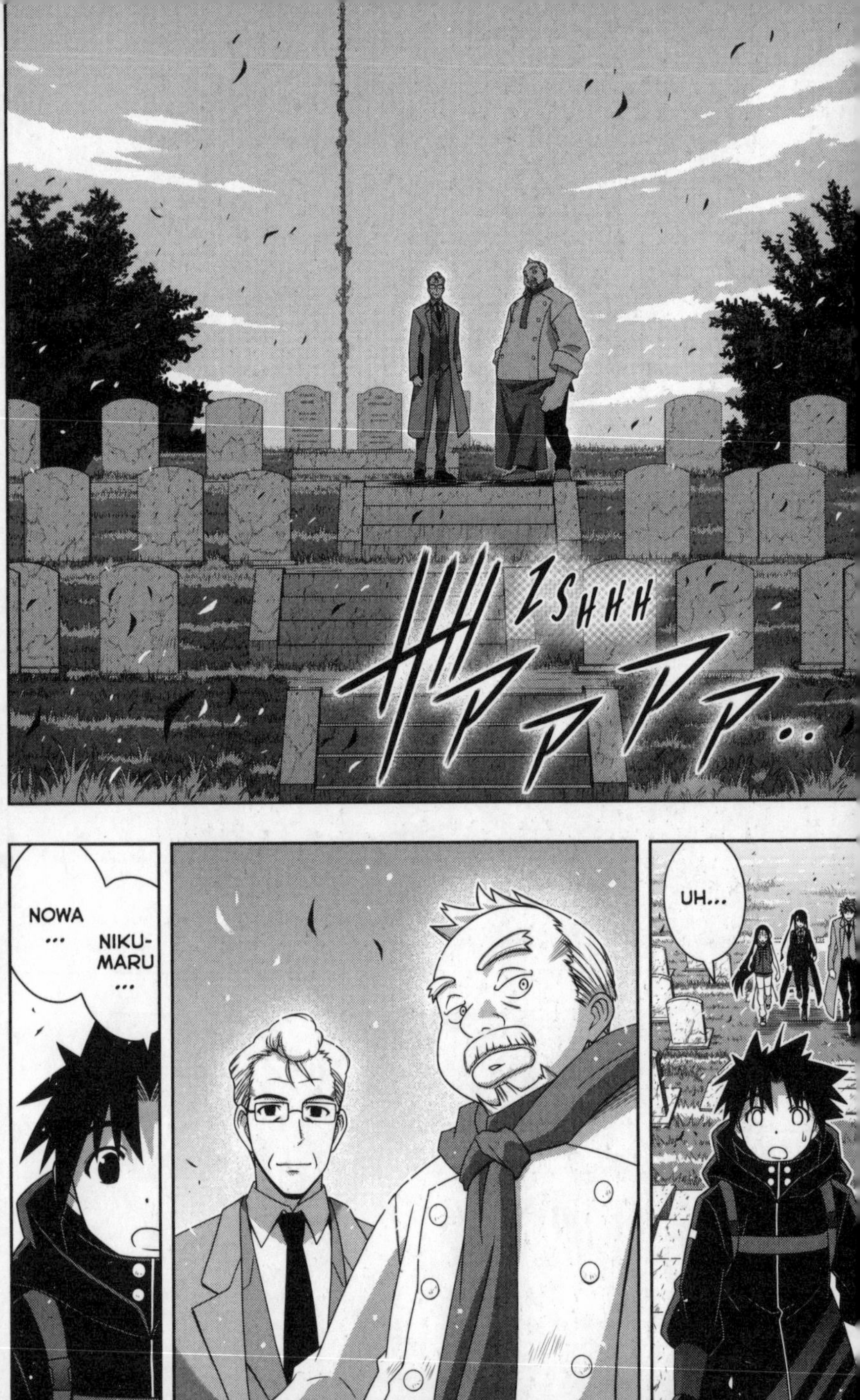
ZSHHH
UH...
NOWA ... NIKU-MARU ...

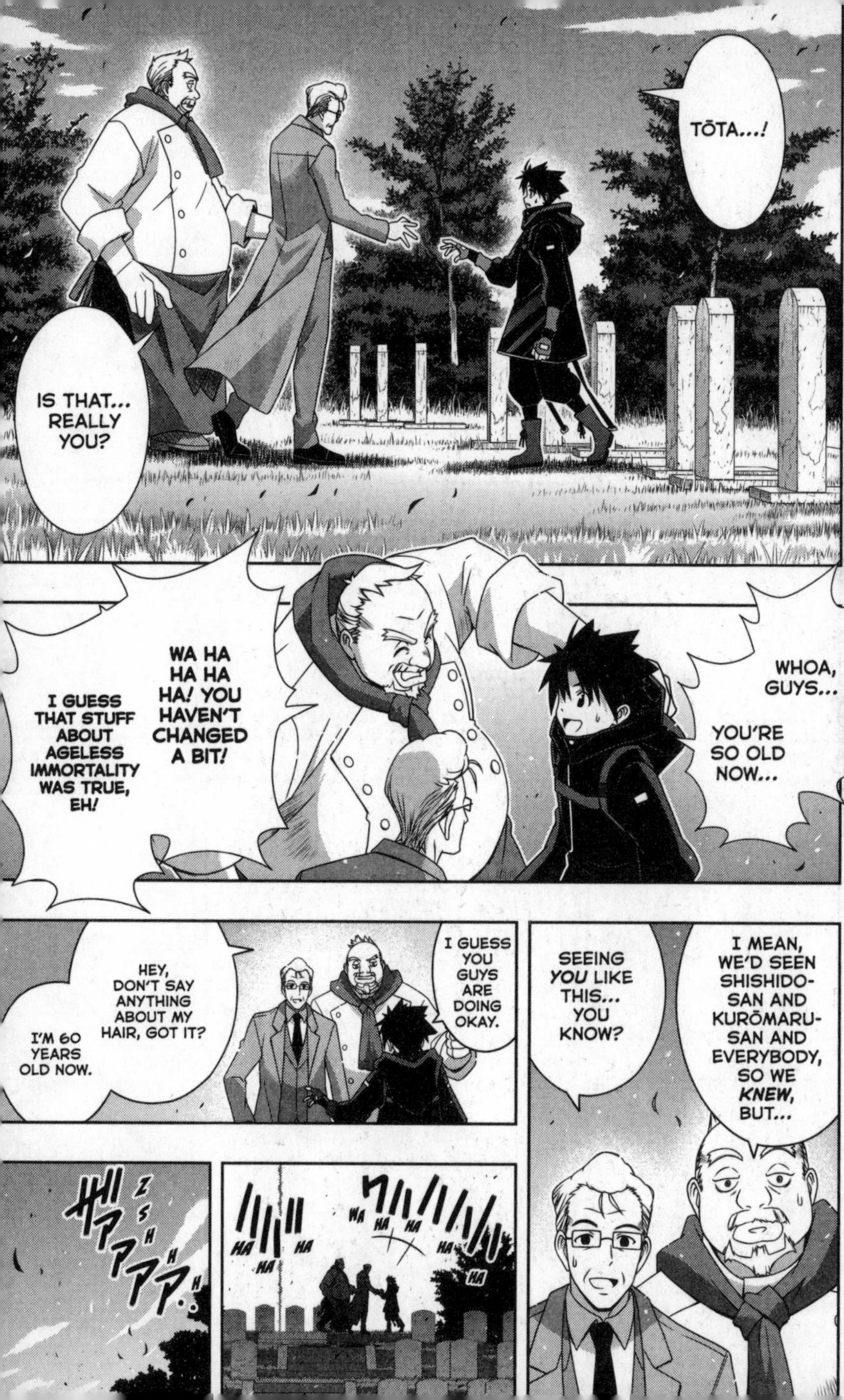
TŌTA...!
IS THAT... REALLY YOU?
WHOA, GUYS...
YOU'RE SO OLD NOW...
WA HA HA HA HA! YOU HAVEN'T CHANGED A BIT!
I GUESS THAT STUFF ABOUT AGELESS IMMORTALITY WAS TRUE, EH!
I MEAN, WE'D SEEN SHISHIDO-SAN AND KURŌMARU-SAN AND EVERYBODY, SO WE *KNEW*, BUT...
SEEING *YOU* LIKE THIS... YOU KNOW?
I GUESS YOU GUYS ARE DOING OKAY.
HEY, DON'T SAY ANYTHING ABOUT MY HAIR, GOT IT?
I'M 60 YEARS OLD NOW.
WA HA HA HA HA HA HA HA HA
ZSHHHH

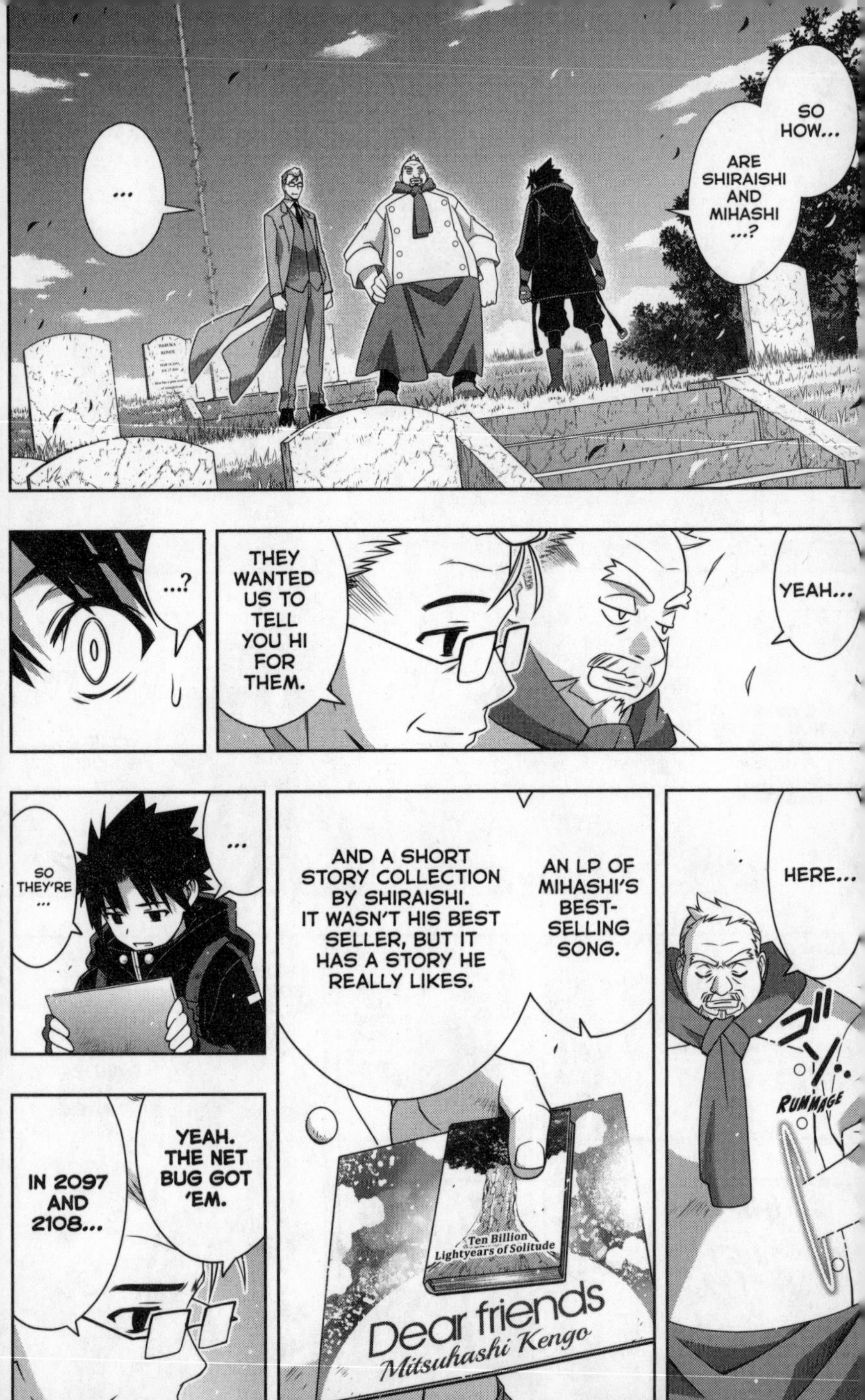
SO HOW...
ARE SHIRAISHI AND MIHASHI ...?
...
YEAH...
THEY WANTED US TO TELL YOU HI FOR THEM.
...?
HERE...
RUMMAGE
AN LP OF MIHASHI'S BEST-SELLING SONG.
AND A SHORT STORY COLLECTION BY SHIRAISHI. IT WASN'T HIS BEST SELLER, BUT IT HAS A STORY HE REALLY LIKES.
Ten Billion Lightyears of Solitude
Dear friends
Mitsuhashi Kengo
...
SO THEY'RE ...
YEAH. THE NET BUG GOT 'EM.
IN 2097 AND 2108...

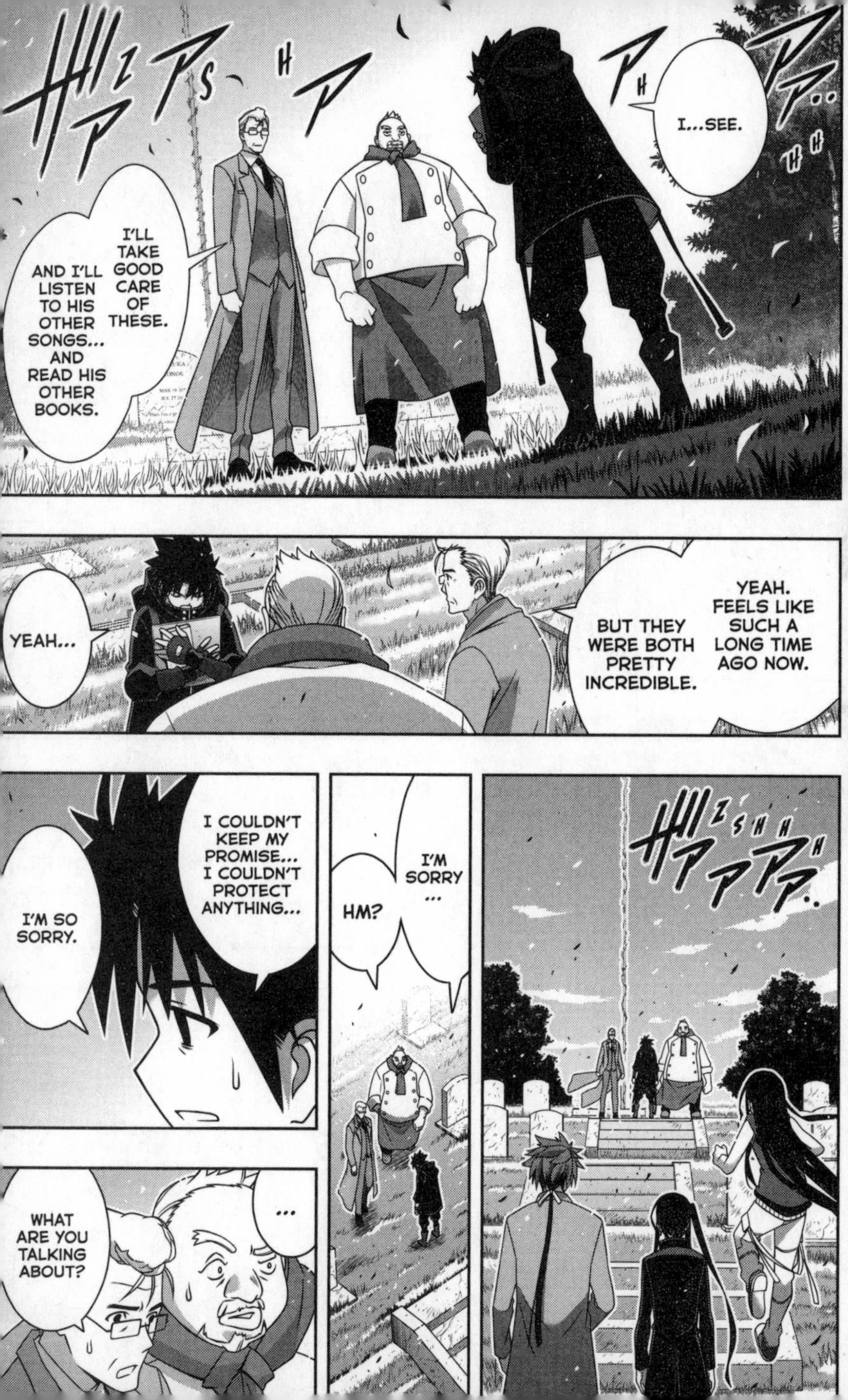
I...SEE.
I'LL TAKE GOOD CARE OF THESE.
AND I'LL LISTEN TO HIS OTHER SONGS... AND READ HIS OTHER BOOKS.
YEAH. FEELS LIKE SUCH A LONG TIME AGO NOW.
BUT THEY WERE BOTH PRETTY INCREDIBLE.
YEAH...
I'M SORRY...
HM?
I COULDN'T KEEP MY PROMISE... I COULDN'T PROTECT ANYTHING...
I'M SO SORRY.
...
WHAT ARE YOU TALKING ABOUT?

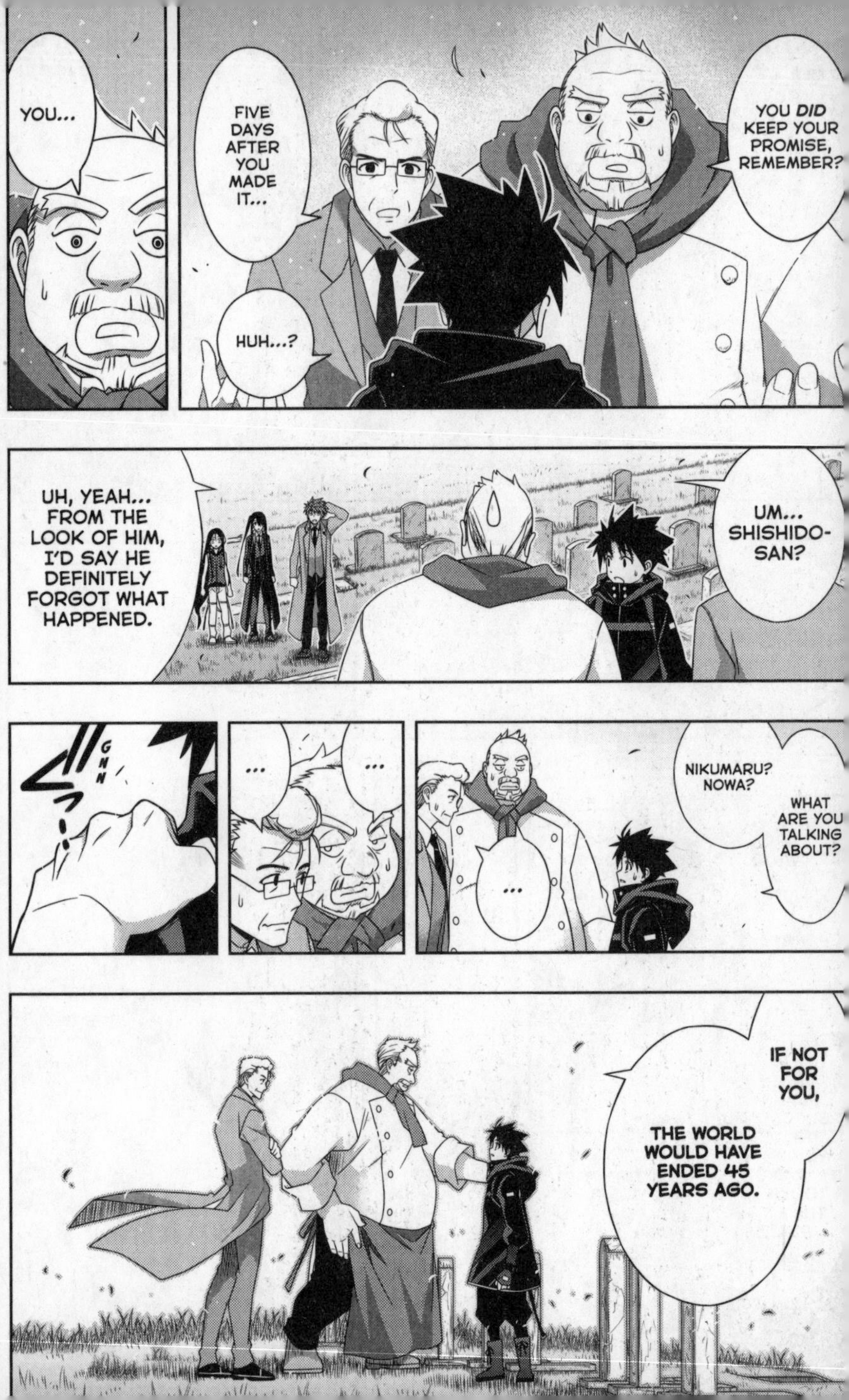
YOU *DID* KEEP YOUR PROMISE, REMEMBER?
FIVE DAYS AFTER YOU MADE IT...
HUH...?
YOU...
UM... SHISHIDO-SAN?
UH, YEAH... FROM THE LOOK OF HIM, I'D SAY HE DEFINITELY FORGOT WHAT HAPPENED.
NIKUMARU? NOWA?
WHAT ARE YOU TALKING ABOUT?
...
...
...
GNN
IF NOT FOR YOU,
THE WORLD WOULD HAVE ENDED 45 YEARS AGO.

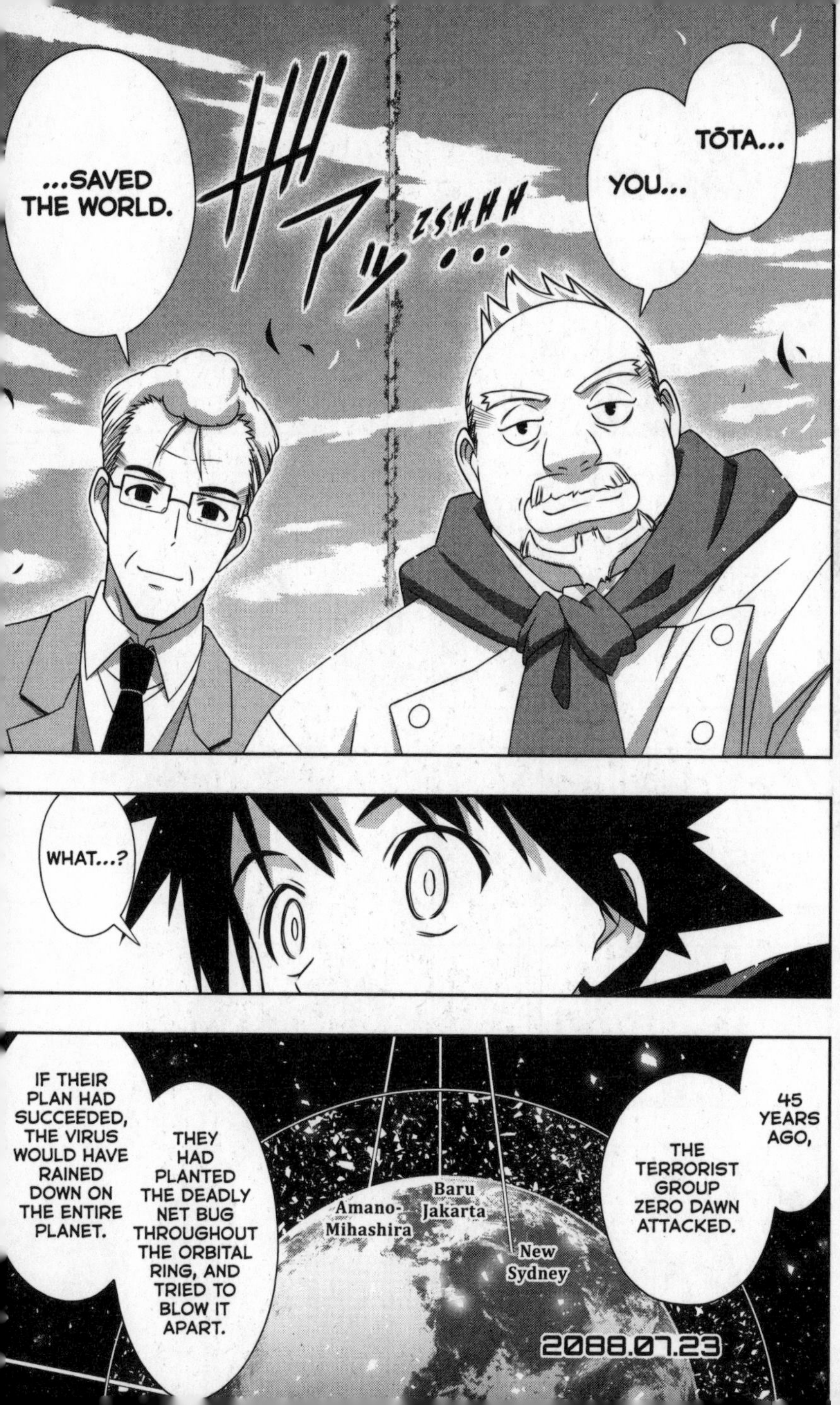
TŌTA... YOU...
ZSHHH...
ザァッ
...SAVED THE WORLD.
WHAT...?
45 YEARS AGO,
THE TERRORIST GROUP ZERO DAWN ATTACKED.
Baru Jakarta
Amano-Mihashira
New Sydney
THEY HAD PLANTED THE DEADLY NET BUG THROUGHOUT THE ORBITAL RING, AND TRIED TO BLOW IT APART.
IF THEIR PLAN HAD SUCCEEDED, THE VIRUS WOULD HAVE RAINED DOWN ON THE ENTIRE PLANET.
2088.07.23

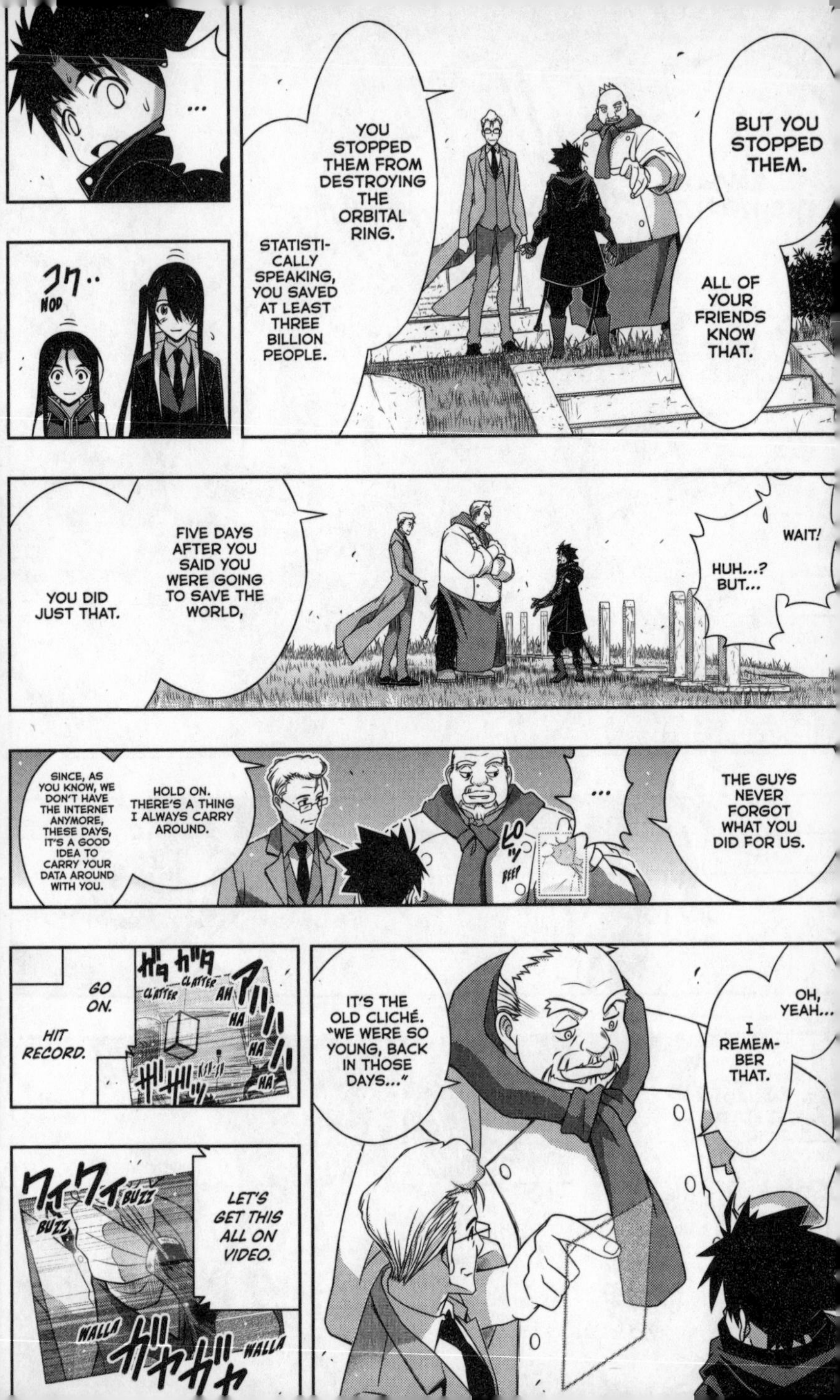
BUT YOU STOPPED THEM.
ALL OF YOUR FRIENDS KNOW THAT.
YOU STOPPED THEM FROM DESTROYING THE ORBITAL RING.
STATISTICALLY SPEAKING, YOU SAVED AT LEAST THREE BILLION PEOPLE.
...
NOD
WAIT!
HUH...? BUT...
FIVE DAYS AFTER YOU SAID YOU WERE GOING TO SAVE THE WORLD,
YOU DID JUST THAT.
THE GUYS NEVER FORGOT WHAT YOU DID FOR US.
...
BEEP
HOLD ON. THERE'S A THING I ALWAYS CARRY AROUND.
SINCE, AS YOU KNOW, WE DON'T HAVE THE INTERNET ANYMORE, THESE DAYS, IT'S A GOOD IDEA TO CARRY YOUR DATA AROUND WITH YOU.
OH, YEAH... I REMEMBER THAT.
IT'S THE OLD CLICHÉ. "WE WERE SO YOUNG, BACK IN THOSE DAYS..."
CLATTER
CLATTER
AH HA HA HA
GO ON.
HIT RECORD.
BUZZ
BUZZ
LET'S GET THIS ALL ON VIDEO.
WALLA
WALLA

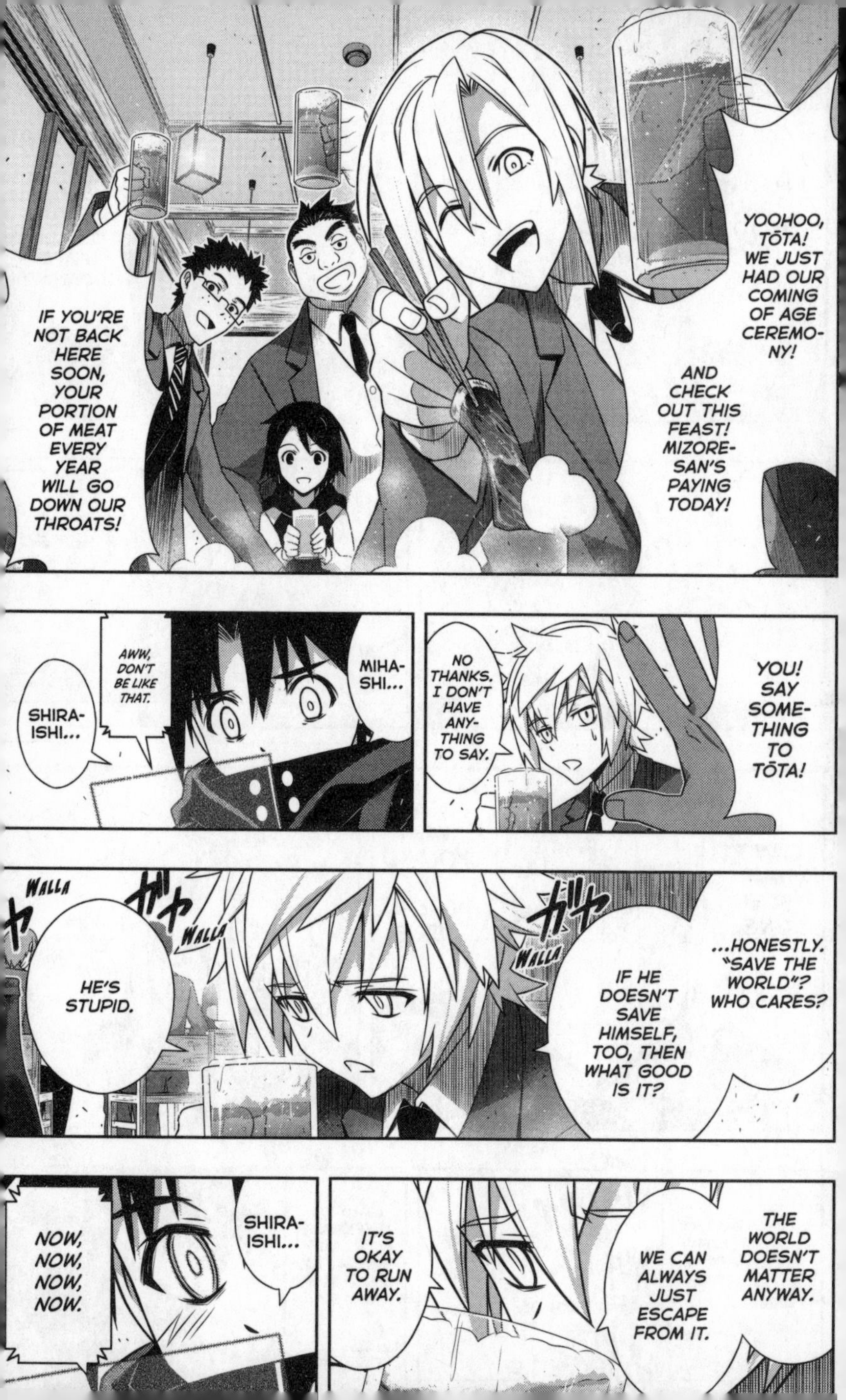
YOOHOO, TŌTA! WE JUST HAD OUR COMING OF AGE CEREMONY!
AND CHECK OUT THIS FEAST! MIZORE-SAN'S PAYING TODAY!
IF YOU'RE NOT BACK HERE SOON, YOUR PORTION OF MEAT EVERY YEAR WILL GO DOWN OUR THROATS!
YOU! SAY SOMETHING TO TŌTA!
NO THANKS. I DON'T HAVE ANYTHING TO SAY.
MIHASHI...
AWW, DON'T BE LIKE THAT.
SHIRAISHI...
...HONESTLY. "SAVE THE WORLD"? WHO CARES?
IF HE DOESN'T SAVE HIMSELF, TOO, THEN WHAT GOOD IS IT?
ガヤ
WALLA
ガヤ
WALLA
ヤ
WALLA
HE'S STUPID.
THE WORLD DOESN'T MATTER ANYWAY.
WE CAN ALWAYS JUST ESCAPE FROM IT.
IT'S OKAY TO RUN AWAY.
SHIRAISHI...
NOW, NOW, NOW, NOW.

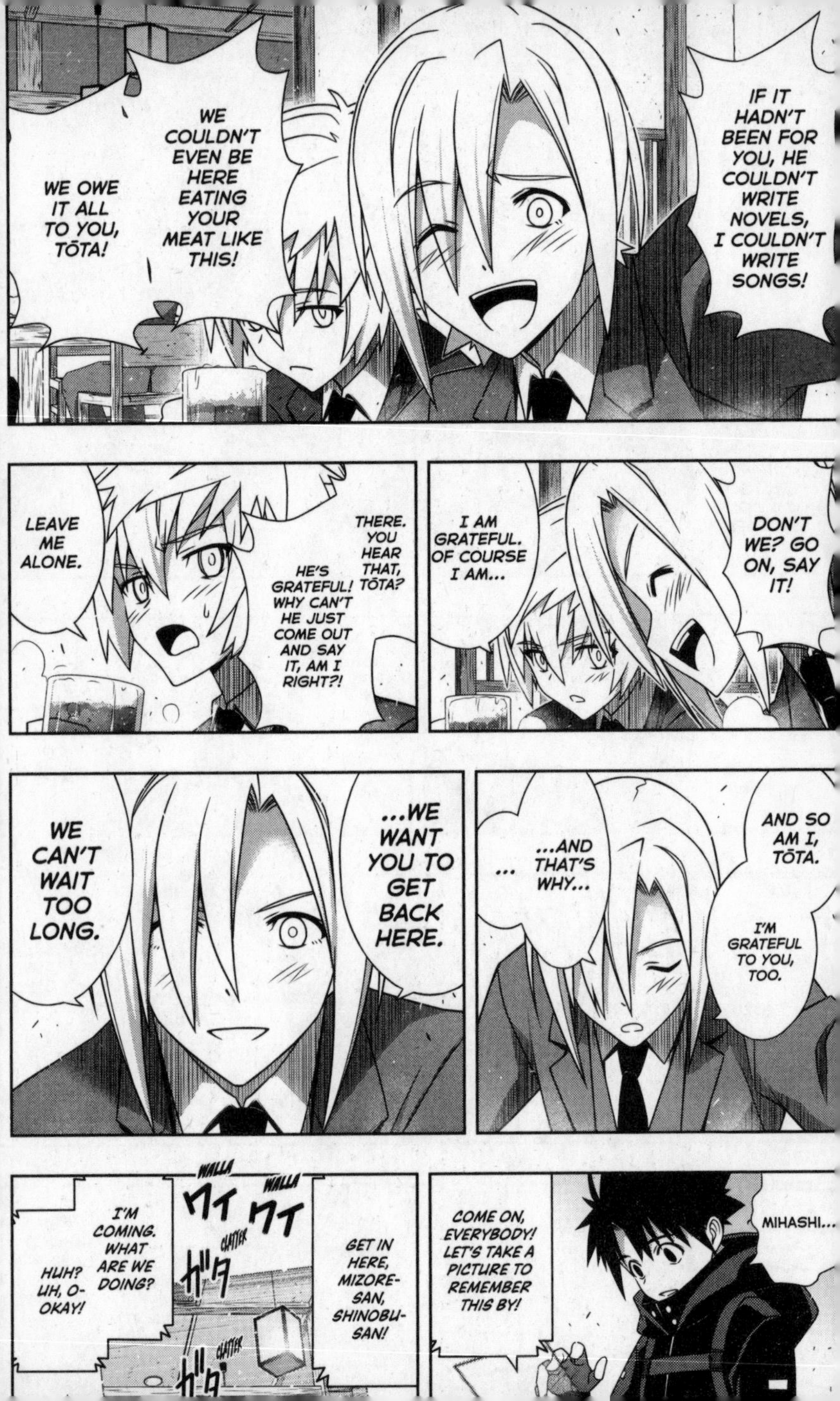
IF IT HADN'T BEEN FOR YOU, HE COULDN'T WRITE NOVELS, I COULDN'T WRITE SONGS!
WE COULDN'T EVEN BE HERE EATING YOUR MEAT LIKE THIS!
WE OWE IT ALL TO YOU, TŌTA!
DON'T WE? GO ON, SAY IT!
I AM GRATEFUL. OF COURSE I AM...
THERE. YOU HEAR THAT, TŌTA?
HE'S GRATEFUL! WHY CAN'T HE JUST COME OUT AND SAY IT, AM I RIGHT?!
LEAVE ME ALONE.
AND SO AM I, TŌTA.
I'M GRATEFUL TO YOU, TOO.
...AND THAT'S WHY...
...
...WE WANT YOU TO GET BACK HERE.
WE CAN'T WAIT TOO LONG.
MIHASHI...
COME ON, EVERYBODY! LET'S TAKE A PICTURE TO REMEMBER THIS BY!
GET IN HERE, MIZORE-SAN, SHINOBU-SAN!
WALLA ワイ
WALLA ワイ
CLATTER ガタ
I'M COMING. WHAT ARE WE DOING?
HUH? UH, O-OKAY!
CLATTER ガタ

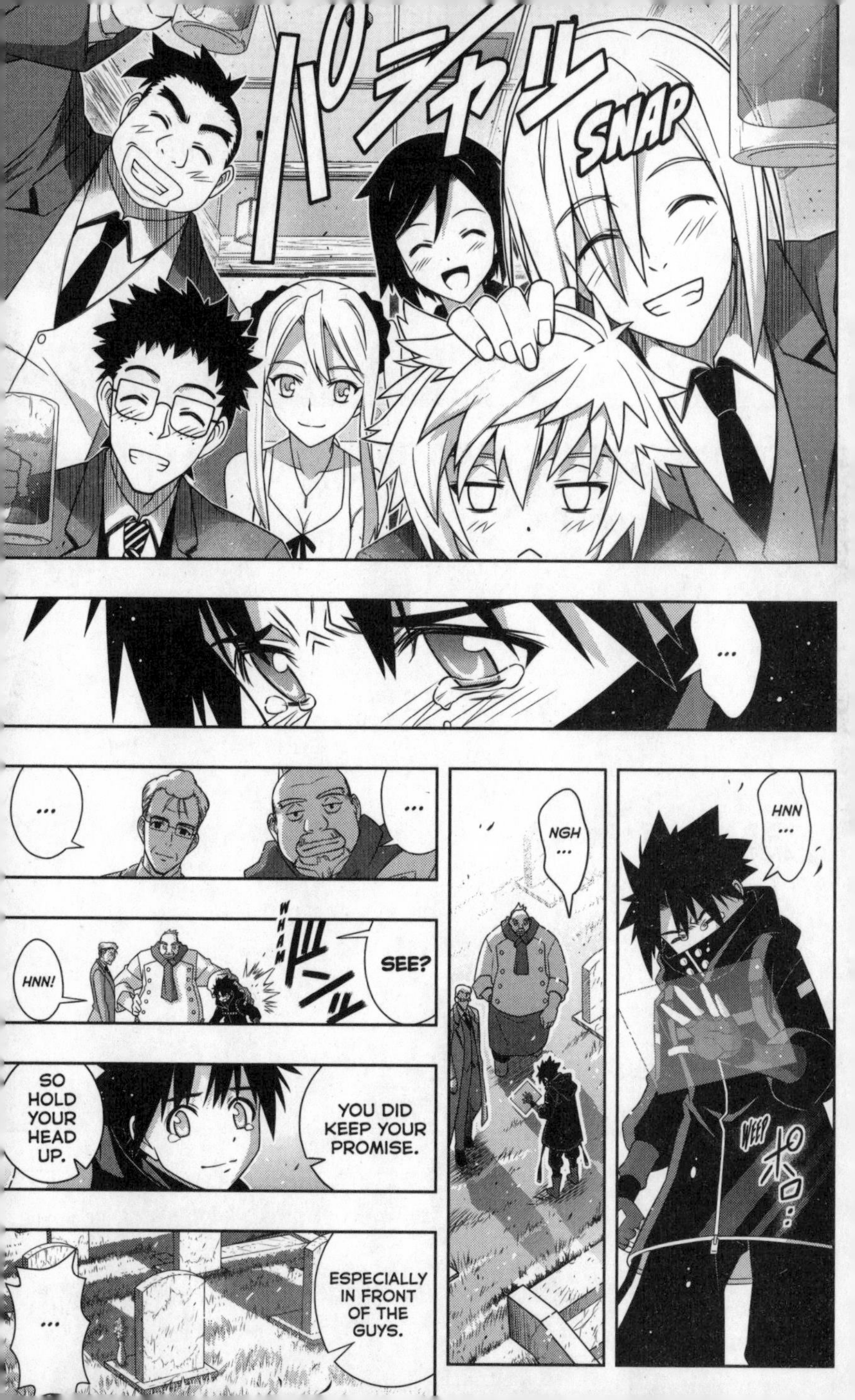

パシャッ
SNAP
...
HNN ...
WEEP
NGH ...
...
...
SEE?
WHAM
HNN!
YOU DID KEEP YOUR PROMISE.
SO HOLD YOUR HEAD UP.
ESPECIALLY IN FRONT OF THE GUYS.
...

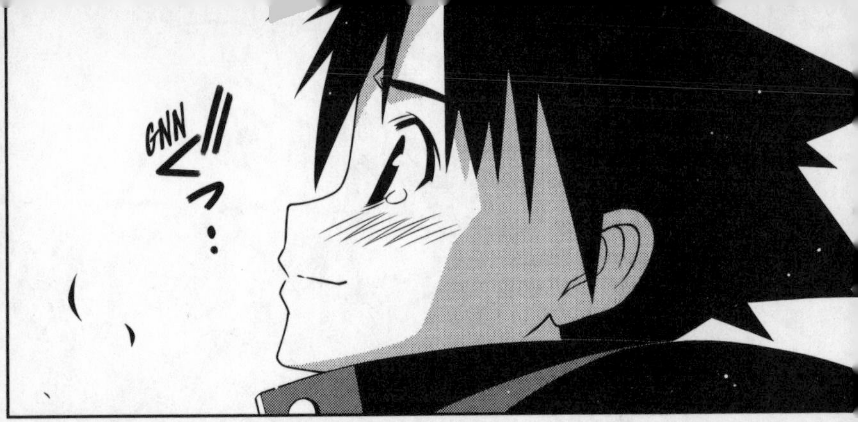
GNN
くっ‥

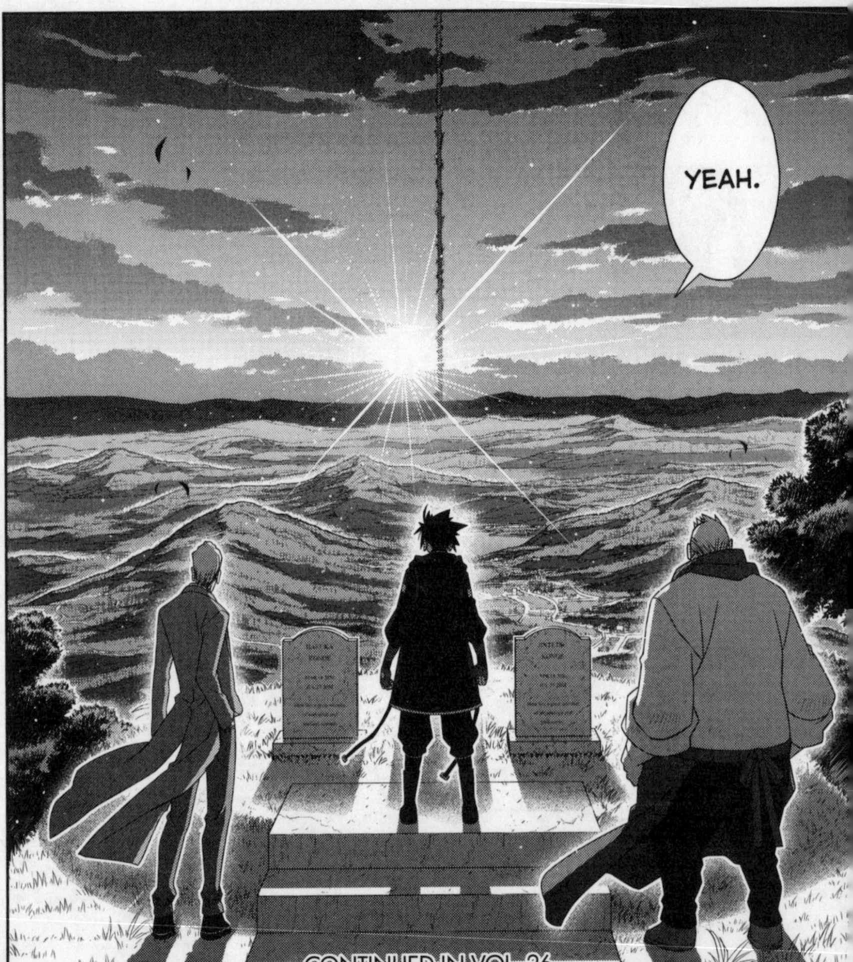
YEAH.

CONTINUED IN VOL. 26

UQ HOLDER!

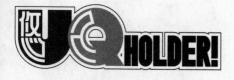

UQ HOLDER!

STAFF

Ken Akamatsu

Takashi Takemoto

Kenichi Nakamura

Keiichi Yamashita

Yuri Sasaki

Madoka Akanuma

Thanks to Ran Ayanaga

Young characters and steampunk setting, like *Howl's Moving Castle* and *Battle Angel Alita*

Beyond the Clouds © 2018 Nicke / Ki-oon

A boy with a talent for machines and a mysterious girl whose wings he's fixed will take you beyond the clouds! In the tradition of the high-flying, resonant adventure stories of Studio Ghibli comes a gorgeous tale about the longing of young hearts for adventure and friendship!

The boys are back, in 400-page hardcovers that are as pretty and badass as they are!

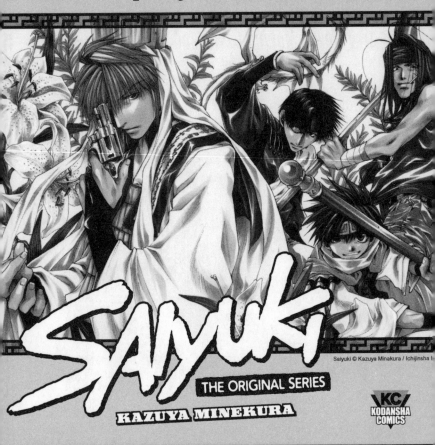

Saiyuki © Kazuya Minakura / Ichijinsha I...

SAIYUKI

THE ORIGINAL SERIES

KAZUYA MINEKURA

KC / KODANSHA COMICS

Genjo Sanzo is a Buddhist priest in the city of Togenkyo, which is being ravaged by yokai spirits that have fallen out of balance with the natural order. His superiors send him on a journey far to the west to discover why this is happening and how to stop it. His companions are three yokai with human souls. But this is no day trip — the four will encounter many discoveries and horrors on the way.

FEATURES NEW TRANSLATION, COLOR PAGES, AND BEAUTIFUL WRAPAROUND COVER ART!

THE SWEET SCENT OF LOVE IS IN THE AIR! FOR FANS OF OFFBEAT ROMANCES LIKE *WOTAKOI*

VOL. 1

Sweat and Soap © Kintetsu Yamada / Kodansha Ltd.

KINTETSU YAMADA

In an office romance, there's a fine line between sexy and awkward... and that line is where Asako — a woman who sweats copiously — meets Koutarou — a perfume developer who can't get enough of Asako's, er, scent. Don't miss a romcom manga like no other!

The adorable new odd-couple cat comedy manga from the creator of the beloved *Chi's Sweet Home*, in full color!

Sue & Tai-chan

Konami Kanata

Sue is an aging housecat who's looking forward to living out her life in peace... but her plans change when the mischievous black tomcat Tai-chan enters the picture! Hey! Sue never signed up to be a catsitter! *Sue & Tai-chan* is the latest from the reigning meow-narch of cute kitty comics, Konami Kanata.

KC KODANSHA COMICS

A Kodansha Comics Trade Paperback Original
UQ HOLDER! 25 copyright © 2021 Ken Akamatsu
English translation copyright © 2022 Ken Akamatsu

Published in the United States by Kodansha Comics, an imprint of Kodansha USA Publishing, LLC, New York.

Publication rights for this English edition arranged through Kodansha Ltd., Tokyo.

First published in Japan in 2021 by Kodansha Ltd., Tokyo.

ISBN 978-1-64651-430-4

Printed in the United States of America.

www.kodansha.us

1st Printing
Translation: Alethea Nibley & Athena Nibley
Lettering: James Dashiell
Editing: David Yoo
Kodansha Comics edition cover design by Phil Balsman

Publisher: Kiichiro Sugawara

Director of publishing services: Ben Applegate
Associate director, publishing operations: Stephen Pakula
Publishing services managing editors: Madison Salters, Alanna Ruse
Production managers: Emi Lotto, Angela Zurlo